Apart from leading to better material for your English literature folder, the right story or poem may inspire you to write something a little bit different for your English folder. There are times when an idea seems to jump out at you from a story and all you have to do is write your own piece. But often that doesn't happen. In this book you will find suggestions and ideas to start you off on English assignments.

The book has been planned so that you can work individually and independently. A lot of the time you should not need the intervention of teachers. At the same time, it's worth taking advantage of the experience they have to get an opinion about how a piece of writing is shaping up. They will also be able to give sound advice on whether a piece of writing fits more naturally into an English or English literature folder.

This is not a book that sets out to tell you how to do your work, but with luck it will help you to produce better work than you expected to. All you need is a little time, a little effort and a willingness to have a good read . . .

. . . and look out for Cal whose stepfather makes fun of his lame leg and treats him no better than dirt until one day he goes too far.

Contents

Priscilla and the Wimps

Stories and poems

selected by

John Seely
David Kitchen

Introduction

Priscilla, you ought to be warned, is not the sort of person to mess around with. Mind you, neither is Mark Klutter and look what happened to him. Actually, if you haven't looked into this book yet, you won't know what happened, but you'll find out soon enough. You'll also get some idea about why Heidi dyed her hair blue and what happened on the back seat of the bus to Skegness. Dig a little deeper and you'll come across the country (which actually exists) where they call the police if they find certain children playing on the swings and slides in the park.

With that kind of variety, there should be things you will enjoy reading in the next hundred pages. To make that even more likely, a group of young people helped us to throw away all the stories and poems that seemed worthwhile but proved to be boring. They think, and we agree, that you'll like the result. It's a good read and it shouldn't send you to sleep.

The most important reason for reading anything is because you want to and not because someone says you've got to do it to pass an exam. But if you need to pass an exam this book will help, because it allows you to get organised.

Examiners cannot know that you have understood and enjoyed a story or poem unless you show them. The problem many people face is getting more than a few lines down on paper. By directing your attention to particular areas and by asking questions that make you think, this book should help you to produce better work. By that we don't simply mean a more thorough response but a more interesting one: more interesting for your teacher to read and more interesting for you to write.

CONTENTS

It's expected of you

The Fight

There's a fight on the playground today –
  Two big boys from Mr Magee's
Are knocking the daylights out of each other
  Under the trees.

The girls are silent and staring
  And Clare whispers 'Stop it Paul'
As the fighting gets wilder, and feet jab out
  And fingers maul.

I watch, and I'm glad it's not Joe
  And me in that horrible space –
Not my stomach winded, not my nose bleeding,
  Not my burning face.

The sky is bright. Two planes fly
  Out from the base, while one
Boy holds the other down with his knee
  And breathes 'You done?'

There's a fight on the playground today –
  Paul Topple from Mr Magee's
Is crushing the daylights out of John Randall
  Under the trees.

Fred Sedgwick

Priscilla and the Wimps

RICHARD PECK

*Almost every school has a bully who roams the corridors
picking on smaller, weaker kids. Such individuals are
tough, mean, insensitive. No one is safe from their assaults.
It seems as if there is no way to stop them, no way to
get back at them. Isn't there anything that anybody can
do ? . . .*

Listen, there was a time when you couldn't even go
to the *rest room* around this school without a pass. And
I'm not talking about those little pink tickets made out
by some teacher. I'm talking about a pass that could
cost anywhere up to a buck, sold by Monk Klutter.

Not that Mighty Monk ever touched money, not in
public. The gang he ran, which ran the school for him,
was his collection agency. They were Klutter's Kobras,
a name spelled out in nailheads on six well-known
black plastic windbreakers.

Monk's threats were more . . . subtle. A pile-lined
suede battle jacket with lizard-skin flaps over tailored
Levis and a pair of ostrich-skin boots, brass-toed and
suitable for kicking people around. One of his Kobras
did nothing all day but walk a half-step behind Monk,
carrying a fitted bag with Monk's gym shoes, a roll of
rest-room passes, a cashbox and a switchblade that
Monk gave himself manicures with at lunch over the
Kobras' table.

Speaking of lunch, there were a few cases of advanced malnutrition among the newer kids. The ones who were a little slow in handing over a cut of their lunch money and were therefore barred from the cafeteria. Monk ran a tight ship.

I admit it. I'm five foot five, and when the Kobras slithered by, with or without Monk, I shrank. And I admit this, too: I paid up on a regular basis. And I might add: so would you.

This school was old Monk's Garden of Eden. Unfortunately for him, there was a serpent in it. The reason Monk didn't recognise trouble when it was staring him in the face is that the serpent in the Kobras' Eden was a girl.

Practically every guy in school could show you his scars. Fang marks from Kobras, you might say. And they were all highly visible in the shower room: lumps, lacerations, blue bruises, you name it. But girls usually got off with a warning.

Except there was this one girl named Priscilla Roseberry. Picture a girl named Priscilla Roseberry, and you'll be light years off. Priscilla was, hands down, the largest student in our particular institution of learning. I'm not talking fat. I'm talking big. Even beautiful, in a bionic way. Priscilla wasn't inclined towards organised crime. Otherwise, she could have put together a gang that would turn Klutter's Kobras into garter snakes.

Priscilla was basically a loner except she had one friend. A little guy named Melvin Detweiler. You talk about The Odd Couple. Melvin's one of the smallest guys above midget status ever seen. A really nice guy, but, you know – little. They even had lockers next to each other, in the same bank as mine. I don't know what they had going. I'm not saying this was a romance. After all, people deserve their privacy.

Priscilla was sort of above everything, if you'll pardon a pun. And very calm, as only the very big can be. If there was anybody who didn't notice Klutter's Kobras, it was Priscilla.

Until one winter day after school when we were all grabbing our coats out of our lockers. And hurrying, since Klutter's Kobras made sweeps of the corridors for afterschool shakedowns.

Anyway, up to Melvin's locker swaggers one of the Kobras. Never mind his name. Gang members don't need names. They've got group identity. He reaches down and grabs little Melvin by the neck and slams his head against his locker door. The sound of skull against steel rippled all the way down the locker row, speeding the crowds on their way.

'OK, let's see your pass,' snarls the Kobra.

'A pass for what this time?' Melvin asks, probably still dazed.

'Let's call it a pass for very short people,' says the Kobra, 'a dwarf tax.' He wheezes a little Kobra chuckle at his own wittiness. And already he's reaching for Melvin's wallet with the hand that isn't circling Melvin's windpipe. All this time, of course, Melvin and the Kobra are standing in Priscilla's big shadow.

She's taking her time shoving her books into her locker and pulling on a very large-size coat. Then, quicker than the eye, she brings the side of her enormous hand down in a chop that breaks the Kobra's hold on Melvin's throat. You could hear a pin drop in that hallway. Nobody's ever laid a finger on a Kobra, let alone a hand the size of Priscilla's.

Then Priscilla, who hardly ever says anything to

11

anybody except to Melvin, says to the Kobra, 'Who's your leader, wimp?'

This practically blows the Kobra away. First he's chopped by a girl, and now she's acting like she doesn't know Monk Klutter, the Head Honcho of the World. He's so amazed, he tells her. 'Monk Klutter.'

'Never heard of him,' Priscilla mentions. 'Send him to see me.' The Kobra just backs away from her like the whole situation is too big for him, which it is.

Pretty soon Monk himself slides up. He jerks his head once, and his Kobras slither off down the corridor. He's going to handle this interesting case personally. 'Who is it around here doesn't know Monk Klutter?'

He's standing inches from Priscilla, but since he'd have to look up at her, he doesn't. 'Never heard of him,' says Priscilla.

Monk's not happy with this answer, but by now he's spotted Melvin, who's grown smaller in spite of himself. Monk breaks his own rule by reaching for Melvin with his own hands. 'Kid,' he says, 'you're going to have to educate your girl friend.'

His hands never quite make it to Melvin. In a move of pure poetry Priscilla has Monk in a hammerlock. His neck's popping like gunfire, and his head's bowed under the immense weight of her forearm. His suede jacket's peeling back, showing pile.

Priscilla's behind him in another easy motion. And with a single mighty thrust forward, frog-marches Monk into her own locker. It's incredible. His ostrich-skin boots click once in the air. And suddenly he's gone, neatly wedged into the locker, a perfect fit. Priscilla bangs the door shut, twirls the lock, and strolls out of school. Melvin goes with her, of course, trotting along below her shoulder. The last stragglers leave quietly.

Well, this is where fate, an even bigger force than Priscilla, steps in. It snows all that night, a blizzard. The whole town ices up. And school closes for a week.

Woman is

- kicking strongly in your mother's womb, upon which she is told, 'It must be a boy, if it's so active!'
- being tagged with a pink beaded bracelet thirty seconds after you are born, and wrapped in pink blankets five minutes thereafter.
- being labelled a tomboy when all you wanted to do was to climb that tree and look out and see a distance.
- learning to sit with your legs crossed, even when your feet can't touch the floor yet.
- hating boys – because they're allowed to do things you want to do but are forbidden to – and being told hating boys is a phase.
- wondering why your father gets mad now and then, but your mother mostly sighs a lot.
- seeing grown-ups chuckle when you say you want to be an engineer or doctor when you grow up – learning to say you want to be a mommy or a nurse, instead.
- feeling basically comfortable in your own body, but gradually learning to hate it because you are: too short or tall, too fat or thin, thick-thighed or big-wristed, large-eared or stringy-haired, short-necked or long-armed, bowlegged, knock-kneed or pigeon-toed – something that might make boys not like you.
- wanting to kill yourself because of pimples, dandruff, or a natural tendency to sweat – and

discovering that commercials about miracle products just lie.
- having your first real human talk with your mother and being told about all her old hopes and lost ambitions, and how you can't fight it, and that's just the way it is: life, sex, men, the works – and loving her and hating her for having been so beaten down.
- having your first real human talk with your father and being told about all his old hopes and lost ambitions, and how women really have it easier, and 'what a man really wants in a woman,' – and loving him and hating him for having been beaten down – and for beating down your mother in turn.
- coming home from work – and starting in to work: unpack the groceries, fix supper, wash up the dishes, rinse out some laundry etc, etc.
- feeling a need to say 'thank you' when your guy actually fixes himself a meal now that you're dying with the flu.

Robin Morgan

For Heidi with Blue Hair

When you dyed your hair blue
(or, at least, ultramarine
for the clipped sides, with a crest
of jet-black spikes on top)
you were sent home from school

because, as the headmistress put it,
although dyed hair was not
specifically forbidden, yours
was, apart from anything else,
not done in the school colours.

Tears in the kitchen, telephone-calls
to school from your freedom-loving father.
'She's not a punk in her behaviour;
it's just a style.' (You wiped your eyes,
also not in a school colour.)

'She discussed it with me first –
we checked the rules.' 'And anyway, Dad,
it cost twenty-five dollars.
Tell them it won't wash out –
not even if I wanted to try.'

It would have been unfair to mention
your mother's death, but that
shimmered behind the arguments.
The school had nothing else against you;
the teachers twittered and gave in.

Next day your black friend had hers done
in grey, white and flaxen yellow –
the school colours precisely:
an act of solidarity, a witty
tease. The battle was already won.

Fleur Adcock

The Hands of the Blacks

LUIS BERNARDO HONWANA

I don't remember now how we got onto the subject, but one day Teacher said that the palms of the blacks' hands were much lighter than the rest of their bodies because only a few centuries ago they walked around on all fours, like wild animals, so their palms weren't exposed to the sun, which made the rest of their bodies darker and darker. I thought of this when Father Christiano told us after catechism that we were absolutely hopeless, and that even the blacks were better than us, and he went back to this thing about their hands being lighter, and said it was like that because they always went about with their hands folded together, praying in secret. I thought this was so funny, this thing of the black's hands being lighter, that you should just see me now – I don't let go of anyone, whoever they are, until they tell me why they think that the palms of the black's hands are lighter. Dona Dores, for instance, told me that God made their hands lighter like that so they wouldn't dirty the food they made for their masters, or anything else they were ordered to do that had to be kept quite clean.

Senhor Antunes, the Coca Cola man, who only comes to the village now and again when all the Cokes in the cantinas have been sold, said to me that everything I had been told was a lot of baloney. Of course I don't know if it was really, but he assured me it was. After I said yes, all right it was baloney, then he told me what he knew about this thing of the black's hands. It was like this: – 'Long ago, many years ago, God, Our Lord Jesus Christ, the Virgin Mary, St. Peter, many other saints, all the angels that were in Heaven then, and some of the people who had died and gone to Heaven – they all had a meeting and decided to make blacks. Do you know how? They got hold of some clay and pressed it into some second-hand moulds. And to bake the clay of the creatures they took them to the Heavenly kilns. Because they were in a hurry and there was no room next to the fire, they hung them in the chimneys. Smoke, smoke, smoke – and there you have them, black as coals. And now do you want to know why their hands stayed white? Well, didn't they have to hold on while their clay baked?'

When he had told me this Senhor Antunes and the other men who were around us were very pleased and they all burst out laughing. That very same day Senhor Frias called me after Senhor Antunes had gone away, and told me that everything I had heard from them there had been just one big pack of lies. Really and truly, what he knew about the black's hands was right – that God finished making men and told them to bathe in a lake in Heaven. After bathing the people were nice and white. The blacks, well, they were made very early in the morning, and at this hour the water in the lake was very cold, so they only wet the palms of their hands and the soles of their feet before dressing and coming into the world.

But I read in a book that happened to mention it, that the blacks have hands lighter like this because they spent their lives bent over, gathering the white cotton of Virginia and I don't know where else. Of course Dona Estefánia didn't agree when I told her this. According to her it's only because their hands became bleached with all that washing.

Well, I don't know what to think about all this, but the truth is that however calloused and cracked they may be, a black's hands are always lighter than all the rest of him. And that's that!

My mother is the only one who must be right about this question of a black's hands being lighter than the rest of his body. On the day that we were talking about it, us two, I was telling her what I already knew about the question, and she just couldn't stop laughing. What I thought was strange was that she didn't tell me at once what she thought about all this, and she only answered me when she was sure that I wouldn't get tired of bothering her about it. And even then she was crying and clutching herself around the stomach like someone who had laughed so much that it was quite unbearable. What she said was more or less this:

'God made blacks because they had to be. They had to be, my son. He thought they really had to be. . . . Afterwards he regretted having made them because the other men laughed at them and took them off to their homes and put them to serve like slaves or not much better. But because he couldn't make them all be white, for those who were used to seeing them black would complain, He made it so that the palms of their hands would be exactly like the palms of the hands of other men. And do you know why that was? Of course you don't know, and it's not surprising, because many, many people don't know. Well, listen: it was to show that what men do is only the work of men. . . . That what men do is done by hands that are the same – hands of people who, if they had any sense, would know that before everything else they are men. He must have been thinking of this when He made the hands of the blacks be the same as the hands of those men who thank God they are not black!'

After telling me all this, my mother kissed my hands. As I ran off into the yard to play ball, I thought that I had never seen a person cry so much when nobody had hit them.

Stereotype

I'm a fullblooded
West Indian stereotype
See me straw hat?
Watch it good

I'm a fullblooded
West Indian stereotype
You ask
if I got riddum
in me blood
You going ask!
Man just beat de drum
and don't forget
to pour de rum

I'm a fullblooded
West Indian stereotype
You say
I suppose you can show
us the limbo, can't you?
How you know!
How you know!
You sure
you don't want me
sing you a calypso too
How about that

I'm a fullblooded
West Indian stereotype
You call me
happy-go-lucky

Yes that's me
dressing fancy
and chasing woman
if you think ah lie
bring yuh sister

I'm a fullblooded
West Indian stereotype
You wonder
where do you people
get such riddum
could it be the sunshine
My goodness
just listen to that steelband

Isn't there one thing
you forgot to ask
go on man ask ask
This native will answer anything
How about cricket?
I suppose you're good at it?
Hear this man
good at it!
Put de willow
in me hand
and watch me stripe
de boundary

Yes I'm a fullblooded
West Indian stereotype

that's why I
graduated from Oxford University
with a degree
in anthropology

John Agard

Thinking and writing

The Fight by Fred Sedgwick

Thinking points

This poem raises a number of questions about
stereotypes.

1 It is two big boys who are fighting while 'the girls
   are silent and staring'. Is this the way it usually is?
   Why?
2 What is the difference between the girls' response
   to the fight and that of the writer?
3 For what different reasons do people fight at school?
4 What is the point of the observation that 'two
   planes fly out from the base'?
5 Is it possible to imagine a world in which there
   were never any fights?

Priscilla and the Wimps
by Richard Peck

Thinking points

1 How did Monk Klutter set up and run his protection
   racket?
2 Why did all the others give in to him?
3 'This school was old Monk's Garden of Eden.' What
   does this mean? Is it a good comparison?
4 What impression did you get of Priscilla and
   Melvin?
5 Part of the entertainment of this story is the way it
   is told. What kind of person do you think is telling
   it, and what does his/her voice sound like?
6 What did you think of the story's ending?

Writing: Literature

Write a conversation between two of Klutter's Kobras some time after Monk Klutter has been released from the locker.

Woman is by Robin Morgan

Thinking points

There are thirteen definitions of *What a woman is* in this piece of writing. For each one of them:
a) write down its number
b) say whether you agree strongly, agree, don't care, disagree or disagree strongly
c) give your reasons for your opinion.

Writing: English

Write your own piece entitled 'Woman Is' or 'Man Is' in the same style as Robin Morgan's piece.

For Heidi with Blue Hair
by Fleur Adcock

Thinking points

1 Why did Heidi get sent home?
2 What is the point of the sentence that begins 'It would have been unfair . . .'?
3 Why was she accepted back at school?
4 Why was what the black friend did 'a witty tease'?
5 What 'battle was already won'? And why?

Writing: Literature

Heidi's behaviour and that of her black friend – are discussed at a special meeting of the staff. Use the clues in the poem to help you work out what they may have said. Write a description of the discussion that takes place.

The Hands of the Blacks by Luis Bernardo Honwana

Thinking about the story

This story contains a number of explanations why 'the palms of the blacks' hands are much lighter than the rest of their bodies'. Many of these have their origins in the history of the black races in the past or in ideas and prejudices that white people have about them. Go through the story again and make a list of the reasons for as many of these stories as possible.

At the end of the story the boy's mother cries: why is she so upset?

Stereotype by John Agard

Reading Aloud

Try reading the poem aloud. How do you think it should be read in order to get the best effect?

Thinking points

1   What exactly do we mean by the word stereotype?
2   How does the writer say that people stereotype 'West Indians'?
3   Explain how the last four lines of the poem help to make fun of the stereotypes he describes.

Writing: English

There are many different stereotypes. Choose a different one and write a poem on this pattern about the stereotype you have chosen.

Welcome

Snow Horse

JOAN AIKEN

A pleasant place, the Forest Lodge Inn seemed, as you rode up the mountain track, with its big thatched barns and stables all around, the slate-paved courtyard in front, and the solidity of the stone house itself, promising comfort and good cheer. But, inside, there was a queer chill; guests could never get warm enough in bed, pile on howeversomany blankets they might; the wind whispered uneasily round the corners of the building, birds never nested in its eaves, and travellers who spent a night there somehow never cared to come back for another.

Summertime was different. People would come for the day then, for the pony-trekking; McGall, the innkeeper, kept thirty ponies, sturdy little mountain beasts, and parties would be going out every morning, all summer long, over the mountains, taking their lunch with them in knapsacks and returning at night tired and cheerful; then the Forest Lodge was lively enough. But in winter, after the first snow fell, scanty at first, barely covering the grass, then thicker and thicker till Glenmarrich Pass was blocked and for months no one could come up from the town below – ah, in winter the inn was cold, grim, and silent indeed. McGall tried many times to persuade the Tourist Board to instal a ski lift on Ben Marrich, but the Board were not interested in McGall's profits, they wanted to keep their tourists alive; they said there were too many cliffs and gullies on the mountain for safe skiing. So between November and March most of the ponies would go down to Loch Dune to graze in its watermeadows, where the sea winds kept the snow away; others drowsed and grew fat in the big thatched stables.

Who looked after them? Cal did, the boy who had been fished out of a snowdrift thirteen years before, a hungrily crying baby wrapped in a sheepskin jacket. Both his parents, poor young things, lay stiff and dead by him, and not a scrap of paper on them to show who they were. Nobody came forward to claim the baby, who, it turned out, was lame from frostbite; McGall's wife, a goodnatured woman, said she'd keep the child. But her own boy, Dirk, never took to the foundling, nor did his father. After Mrs McGall died of lung trouble, young Cal had a hard time of it. Still, by then he had proved his usefulness, did more than half the work in the stable and yard, and as he was never paid a penny, McGall found it handy to keep him on. He ate scraps, got bawled at, was cuffed about the head a dozen times a day, and took his comfort in loving the ponies, who, under his care, shone and throve like Derby winners.

Ride them? No, he was never allowed to do that.

'With your lame leg? Forget it,' said McGall. 'I'll not have my stock ruined by you fooling around on them. If I see you on the back of any of my string, I'll give you such a leathering that you won't be sitting down for a month.'

Cal had a humble nature. He accepted that he was not good enough to ride the ponies. Never mind! They all loved the boy who tended them. Each would turn to nuzzle him, blowing sweet warm air through his thatch of straw-yellow hair, as he limped down the stable lines.

On a gusty day in November, a one-eyed traveller came riding a grey horse up Glenmarrich Pass.

McGall and Dirk had gone down with the Landrover to Glen Dune to buy winter supplies, for the first snows were close ahead; by now the inn was shut up for the season, and Cal was the only soul there, apart from the beasts.

The traveller dismounted halfway up the track, and led his plodding grey the rest of the way; poor thing, you could see why, for it was dead lame and hobbled painfully, hanging its head as if in shame. A beautiful dark dapple-grey, it must have been a fine horse once but was now old, thin, sick and tired; looked as if it had been ridden a long, long way, maybe from the other side of the world. And the rider, leading it gently up the rocky path, eyed it with sorrow and regret, as if he knew only too well what its fate would soon be, and what had brought that fate about.

Arrived at the inn door the traveller knocked hard on the thick oak with the staff he carried: *rap, rap*! still holding his nag's reins looped over his elbow.

Cal opened the door: a small, thin, frightened boy.

'Mr McGall's not here, sir! He went down the mountain to buy winter stores. And he told me to let nobody in. The fires are all out. And there's no food cooked.'

'It's not food I need,' said the traveller. 'All I want is a drink. But my horse is lame and sick; he needs rest and care. And I must buy another, or hire one, for I am riding on an urgent errand to a distant place, a long way off on the other side of the mountain.'

Cal gazed at the man in doubt and fright. The stranger was tall, with a grey beard; he wore a blue riding cape and a broad-rimmed hat which was pulled down to conceal the missing eye with its shrunken eyelid; his face was rather stern.

'Sir,' Cal said, 'I would like to help you, but my master will beat me if I let anyone take a horse when he is not here.'

'I can pay well,' said the one-eyed man. 'Just lead me to the stables.'

Somehow, without at all meaning to, Cal found that he was leading the traveller round the corner to the stable yard, and the long, thick-roofed building where the ponies rested in warmth and comfort. The one-eyed man glanced swiftly along the row and picked out a grey mountain pony that was sturdy and trim, though nothing like so handsome as his own must once have been.

'This one will serve me,' said he. 'I will pay your master ten gold pieces for it.' Which he counted out, from a goatskin pouch. Cal's eyes nearly started from his head; he had never seen gold money before. Each coin must be worth hundreds of pounds.

'Now fetch a bucket of warm mash for my poor beast,' said the traveller.

Eagerly Cal lit a brazier, heated water, put bran into the mash, and some wine too, certain that his master would not grudge it to a customer who paid so well. The sick horse was too tired to take more than a few mouthfuls, though its master fed it and gentled it himself. Then Cal rubbed it down and buckled a warm blanket round its belly.

Watching with approval the stranger said, 'I can see that you will take good care of my grey. And I am glad of that, for he has been my faithful friend for more years than you have hairs on your head. Look after him well! And if, by sad fortune, he should die, I wish you to bury him out on the mountain under a rowan tree. But first take three hairs from his mane. Two of them you will give to me, when we meet again; tie the third round your wrist for luck. If Grey does not die, I will come back for him.'

'How will you know that he is alive, sir?'

The one-eyed man did not answer that question, but said, 'Here is another gold piece to pay for his board.'

'It is too much, sir,' objected Cal, trembling, for there was something about the stranger's voice that echoed through and through his head, like the boom of a waterfall.

'Too much? For my faithful companion?'

Cal flinched at his tone; but the man smiled.

'I can see that you are an honest boy. What is your name?'

'Cal, sir.'

'Look after my horse kindly, Cal. Now I must be on my way, for time presses. But first bring me a drink of mead.'

Cal ran into the house and came back with the inn's largest beaker, brimful of home-made mead which was powerful as the midsummer sun. The traveller, who had been murmuring words of parting to his horse, drank off the mead in one gulp, then kissed his steed on its soft grey nose.

'Farewell, old friend. We shall meet in another world, if not in this.'

He flung a leg over the fresh pony, shook up the reins, and galloped swiftly away into the thick of a dark cloud that hung in the head of the pass.

His own horse lifted up its drooping head and let out one piercing cry of sorrow, which echoed far beyond the inn buildings.

McGall, driving back up the valley with a load of

stores, heard the cry. 'What the deuce was that?' he said. 'I hope that lame layabout has not been up to mischief.'

'Stealing a ride when he shouldn't?' suggested Dirk, as the Landrover bounced into the stable yard.

Of course McGall was angry, very angry indeed, when he found that a useful weight-carrying grey pony was gone from his stables, in exchange for a sad, sick beast with hardly more flesh on its bones than a skeleton.

Cal made haste to give him the eleven gold coins, and he stared at them hard, bit them, tested them over a candle, and demanded a description of the stranger.

'A one-eyed fellow with a broad-brimmed hat and blue cape? Nobody from these parts. Didn't give his name? Probably an escaped convict. What sort of payment is *that*? I've never seen such coins. How dare you let that thief make off with one of my best hacks?'

Cal was rewarded by a stunning blow on each side of the head, and a shower of kicks.

'Now I have to go down into town again to show these coins to the bank, and it's all your fault, you little no-good. And I'm not giving stable-room and good fodder to that spavined cripple. It can go out in the bothy. And strip that blanket off it!'

The bothy was a miserable tumbledown shed, open on two sides to the weather. Cal dared not argue with his master – that would only have earned him another beating or a tooth knocked out – but he did his best to shelter the sick horse with bales of straw, and he strapped on it the tattered moth-eaten cover from his own bed. Forbidden to feed the beast, he took it his own meals, and he huddled beside it at night, to give it the warmth of his own body. But the grey would eat little, and drink only a few mouthfuls of water. And after three days it died, from grieving for its master, Cal thought, rather than sickness.

'Good riddance,' said the innkeeper, who by that time had taken the gold pieces to the bank and been told that they were worth an amazing amount of money. He kicked the grey horse's carcass. 'That's too skinny even to use for dogmeat. Bury it under the stable muck in the corner; it will do to fertilize the crops next summer.'

'But,' said Cal, 'its owner told me, if it died, to bury it under a rowan tree.'

'Get out of my sight! Bury it under a rowan – what next? Go and muck out the stables, before I give you a taste of my boot.'

So the body of the grey horse was laid under a great pile of straw and stable-sweepings. But before this, Cal took three hairs from its mane. One he tied round his wrist, the other two he folded in a paper and kept always in his pocket.

A year went by, and the one-eyed traveller never returned to inquire after his horse.

He must have known that it died, thought Cal.

'I knew he'd never come back,' said McGall. 'Ten to one those coins were stolen. It's lucky I changed them right away.'

When spring came, the heap of stable-sweepings was carted out and spread over the steep mountain pastures. There, at the bottom of the pile, lay the bones of the dead horse, and they had turned black and glistening as coal. Cal managed to smuggle them away, and he buried them, at night, under a rowan tree.

That autumn, snow fell early, with bitter, scouring

winds, so that from September onward, no more travellers took the steep track up to the Forest Lodge.

McGall grew surlier than ever, thinking of the beasts to feed and no money coming in; he cursed Cal for the slightest fault and kept him hard at work leading the ponies round the yard to exercise them.

'Lead them, don't ride them!' shouted McGall. 'Don't let me see you on the backs of any of those ponies, cripple! Why the deuce didn't you die in the blizzard with your wretched parents?'

Secretly, Cal did not see why his lame leg should prevent his being able to sit on a horse. Night after night he dreamed of riding the mounts that he tended with such care: the black, piebald, roan, bay, grey, chestnut; when they turned to greet him as he brought their feed, he would hug them and murmur, 'Ah, you'd carry me, wouldn't you, if I was allowed?' In his dreams he was not lame. In his dreams a splendid horse, fiery, swift, obedient to his lightest touch, would carry him over the mountain to wherever he wanted to go.

When winter set in, only six ponies were left in the stable; the rest had been taken down to the lowland pasture. But now a series of accidents reduced these remaining: the black threw McGall when he was out searching for a lost sheep, and galloped into a gully and broke its neck; the chestnut escaped from Dirk as he was tightening its shoe in the smithy, and ran out on to the mountain and was seen no more; the roan and grey fell sick, and lay with heaving sides and closed eyes, refusing to eat, until they died. Cal grieved for them sadly.

And, day after day, snow fell, until a ten-foot drift lay piled against the yard gate. The inmates of Forest

Lodge had little to do; Cal's care of the two remaining ponies took only an hour or two each day. Dirk sulked indoors by the fire; McGall, angry and silent, drank more and more mead. Quarrelsome with drink, he continually abused Cal.

'Find something useful to do! Shovel the snow out of the front yard; suppose a traveller came by, how could he find the door? Get outside, and don't let me see your face till suppertime.'

Cal knew that no traveller would come, but he was glad to get outside, and took broom and shovel to the front yard. Here the wind, raking over the mountain, had turned the snow hard as marble. It was too hard to shift with a broom; Cal had to dig it away in blocks. These he piled up on the slope outside the yard, until he had an enormous rugged mound. At least a way was cut to the front door – supposing that any fool-hardy wayfarer should brave the hills in such weather.

Knowing that if he went back indoors McGall would only find some other pointless task, Cal used the blade of his shovel to carve the pile of frozen snow into the rough shape of a horse. Who should know better than he how a horse was shaped? He gave it a broad chest, small proud head pulled back alertly on the strong neck, and a well-muscled rump. The legs were a problem, for snow legs might not be strong enough to support the massive body he had made, so he left the horse rising out of a block of snow and carved the suggestion of four legs on each side of the block. And he made a snow saddle, but no bridle or stirrups.

'There now!' He patted his creation affectionately. 'When we are all asleep, you can gallop off into the dark and find that one-eyed traveller, and tell him that I cared for his grey as well as I could, but I think his heart broke when his master left him.'

The front door opened and Dirk put his head out.

'Come in, no-good!' he yelled, 'and peel the spuds for supper!'

Then he saw the snow horse, and burst into a rude laugh.

'Mustn't ride the stock, so he makes himself a snow horsie. Bye, bye, baby boy, ride nice snow horsie then!' He walked round the statue and laughed even louder. 'Why, it has *eight legs*! Who in the world ever heard of a horse with eight legs? Dad! Dad, come out here and see what Useless has been doing!'

McGall, half-tipsy, had roamed into the stables and was looking over the tack to see what needed mending. At Dirk's shout he blundered hastily out into the yard, knocking in his heedless hurry the lighted lantern he had set on a shelf.

He stared angrily at Cal's carved horse.

'Is that how you've been wasting your time? Get inside, fool, and make the meal!'

Then smoke began to drift round the corner, and a loud sound of crackling.

'Lord above, Dad, you've gone and set fire to the stable!' cried Dirk.

Aghast, they all raced round to the stable block, which was burning fiercely.

What water they had, in tubs or barrels, was frozen hard, there was no possible way to put out the blaze. Cal did manage to rescue the bay horse, but the piebald, which was old, had breathed too much smoke, and staggered and fell back into the fire; and the bay, terrified of the flames, snapped the halter with which it had been tethered in the cowshed, and ran away over the mountain and was lost.

The whole stable block was soon reduced to a black shell; if the wind had not blown the flames in the other direction, the inn would have burned too.

McGall, in rage and despair, turned on Cal.

'This is your fault, you little rat!'

'Why, master,' said Cal, dumbfounded, 'I wasn't even there!'

'You bring nothing but bad luck! First my wife died, now I haven't a horse left, and my stable's ashes. Get out! I never want to see your face again!'

'But – master – how *can* I go? It's nearly dark – it's starting to snow again – '

'Why should I care? You can't stay here. You made yourself a snow horse,' said McGall, 'you can ride away on that – ride it over a cliff, and that'll be good riddance.'

He stamped off indoors. Dirk, pausing only to shout mockingly, 'Ride the snow horsie, baby boy!' followed him, slamming and bolting the door behind him.

Cal turned away. What could he do? The wind was rising; long ribbons of snow came flying on its wings. The stable was burned; he could not shelter there. His heart was heavy at the thought of all the horses he had cared for, gone now. With slow steps he moved across the yard to the massive snow horse, and laid an arm over its freezing shoulder.

'You are the only one I have left now,' he told it. And he took off his wrist the long hair from the mane of the traveller's grey, and tied the hair round the snow horse's neck. Then, piling himself slabs of snow for a mounting-block, since this was no pony but a full-sized horse, he clambered up on to its back.

Dusk had fallen; the inn building could no longer be seen. Indeed, he could hardly make out the white form under him. He could feel its utter cold, though, striking up all through his own body – and, with the cold, a feeling of tremendous power, like that of the wind itself. Then – after a moment – he could feel the snow horse begin to move and tingle with aliveness, with a cold wild thrilling life of its own. He could feel its eight legs begin to stamp and stretch and strike the ground.

Then they began to gallop.

When McCall rose next morning, sober and bloodshot-eyed and rather ashamed of himself, the very first thing he did was to open the front door.

More snow had fallen during the night; the path Cal had dug to the gate yesterday was filled in again, nine inches deep.

A line of footprints led through this new snow to the inn door – led right up to the door, as if somebody had walked to the doorstep and stood there without moving for a long time, thinking or listening.

'That's mighty queer,' said McGall, scratching his head. 'Someone must have come to the door – but he never knocked, or we'd have heard him. He never came in. Where the devil did he go?'

For there was only *one* line of footprints. None led off again.

'He was a big fellow, too,' said McGall. 'That print is half as long again as my foot, Where did the fellow go? Where did he come from? I don't like it.'

But how the visitor had come, how he had gone, remained a mystery. As for Cal, he was gone too, and the snow horse with him. Where it had stood there was only a rough bare patch, already covered by new snow.

Hireling

Cars pass him by; he'll never own one.
Men won't believe in him for this.
Let them come into the hills
And meet him wandering a road,
Fenced with rain, as I have now;
The wind feathering his hair;
The sky's ruins, gutted with fire
Of the late sun, smouldering still.

Nothing is his, neither the land
Nor the land's flocks. Hired to live
On hills too lonely, sharing his hearth
With cats and hens, he has lost all
Property but the grey ice
Of a face splintered by life's stone.

                                        R S Thomas

Angel Hill

A sailor came walking down Angel Hill,
He knocked on my door with a right good will,
With a right good will he knocked on my door.
He said, 'My friend, we have met before.'
   No, never, said I.

He searched my eye with a sea-blue stare
And he laughed aloud on the Cornish air,
On the Cornish air he laughed aloud
And he said, 'My friend, you have grown too proud.'
   No, never, said I.

'In war we swallowed the bitter bread
And drank of the brine,' the sailor said.
'We took of the bread and we tasted the brine
As I bound your wounds and you bound mine.'
   No, never, said I.

'By day and night on the diving sea
We whistled to sun and moon,' said he.
'Together we whistled to moon and sun
And vowed our stars should be as one.'
   No, never, said I.

'And now,' he said, 'that the war is past
I come to your hearth and home at last.
I come to your home and hearth to share
Whatever fortune waits me there.'
   No, never, said I.

'I have no wife nor son,' he said,
'Nor pillow on which to lay my head,
No pillow have I, nor wife nor son,
Till you shall give to me my own.'
          No, never, said I.

His eye it flashed like a lightning-dart
And still as a stone then stood my heart.
My heart as a granite stone was still
And he said, 'My friend, but I think you will.'
          No, never, said I.

The sailor smiled and turned in his track
And shifted the bundle on his back
And I heard him sing as he strolled away,
'You'll send and you'll fetch me one fine day.'
          No, never, said I.

Charles Causley

The Tramp

SID CHAPLIN

Running down the lane at the end of Garden Street the boy checked himself at the fence and looked first at the faint pathway trodden through the wide expanse of meadow to the stile and then at the bull, quietly ruminating amongst the deep sweet grass by the pond in the far corner. Over the stile was the head of the pit-bank up which even now his father would be toiling; in the deep grass less than a hundred yards away was the bull who considered the field his kingdom and would assuredly rush him if he attempted to set foot on it. The only other alternative was a long meandering route by the Co-op and the old air-shaft – but that might lead him to miss his father. Gulping, he decided to run the gauntlet of the bull – black as night with smooth pelt under which the muscles rippled and with square-set head and slavering mouth. The horns he didn't dare to think about. Ducking under the rusty old cable stretched tightly between one post and another, he set foot on the bull's domain, deftly snatching up a ladybird on the way. Ladybirds were for luck, weren't they?

Halfway over he was aware without actually looking that the bull had raised his head and was curiously looking at him. It was hard not to look; harder still to walk easily as they'd told him, trying to concentrate on big patches of yellow buttercups scattered like bouquets and the clump of dickory-dock that spread out beyond and lasted all the way to the stile. In the end when it became too difficult to hold he cautiously stole a glance over his shoulder. And sure enough the bull with head down was raising first one hoof then another to the accompaniment of stentorian blowing. Even above the pounding within himself he imagined he could hear it; and for a moment he was frozen. Then he heard his father's voice: 'Walk away slowly, lad,' he was shouting. 'And for God's sake don't look.' His father was a hundred miles away. Beside him was a strange man. Even at that distance he could see his father's face. It was black with the pit and shining with sweat. Now he had taken off his cap and stood inside the meadow. Wave after wave of relief surged through him. Slowly he started walking. But his father was taking a diagonal path away from him. Nonplussed he held back. 'Make straight for the stile,' shouted his father. 'Slowly now. Slowly does it.' And then he was running, waving his cap in the air. 'Hup,' he shouted. 'Come an' get me.' He was shouting at the bull. Now he was shouting, running, waving his big red hankie. With all his heart the boy wished to run after his father, only the bull was there behind him, and with a deep sense of shame he realised that he feared the bull more than anything else in the world; that his fear of it was greater than his love for his father.

Where the dickory-docks were the stranger came running to meet him. There seemed an enormous gap between them. Ever afterwards he remembered the strange eerie silence of the field. All that existed was the pounding that went on inside him, the tall, tattered man striding towards him and the feel of the tall grass whipping against his legs – and far away the shouting of his father, taunting the bull as the tall stranger swept him up in his arms. Then in a flash he saw from his new point of vantage his father running like lightning with the bull close behind. Then he felt himself being pitched bodily over the fence and in a trice the stranger had vaulted lightly over beside him.

'It's all right, he's made it kidder,' panted the stranger. The father was waving from afar down the road, while the bull safely within the fence, stamped his baulked rage and frustration.

The father came toiling up the hill, mopping his brow and face.

'Mind, that was a bit of quick thinking.' said the stranger.

'Aye,' dismissed his father shortly. 'Mind, you're a little toy. How often have I told you?'

'I'm sorry, da,' said the boy.

'Never mind, he kept his head about him,' said the stranger. 'A chip off the old block.'

'As many brains as a shallot,' said his father. 'Can't handle a spade. Doesn't know one end of a hammer from another. God knows what we'll do with him.' To the boy's relief he turned his attention to the stranger again. 'God knows what we'd have done without you.'

'I'll tell you what,' said the stranger. 'He'd have kept on walkin', just as he was told.' His eyes were fixed on the boy's tightly clenched fist. 'What've you got in there, young 'un, if you don't mind me askin'?'

'I'll be bound it's something daft,' said the father. 'He goes around like a magpie, pickin' up all sorts of rubbish.'

For the first time since ducking under the fence, the boy became conscious of his tiny captive, and opened his fist.

'Well I'll be jiggered,' said the stranger. 'It's a ladybird.'

'What did I tell you!' said his father.

'Leave him alone,' said the stranger. 'Mebbe it'll bring me luck.' He picked up the little creature and set it on the back of his hand. It crawled about, flexing its wings. 'Look at it,' said the stranger. 'What did we used to say?' After a while he opened his eyes and chanted:

> Two little dicky birds sat on a wall,
> One called Peter and one called Paul;
> Fly away Peter, fly away Paul,
> Come back Peter, come back Paul.

With a flit of his gossamer wings the ladybird was gone. Then out of nowhere he appeared again and landed where he'd been before.

'There, little 'un, I can't go wrong today,' said the stranger, carefully placing the creature on a blade of grass. Rising from the grass he looked down at them. 'I'd better be on me way.' Despite the patches in his coat and trousers he stood there like a god. The boy felt a pang.

'Where you're makin for?' asked his father.

'Barny and a decent kip for the night,' said the stranger.

'Come and have a bite to eat with us,' said the father. 'You'll feel better with a Yorkshire Pudding behind your ribs.'

The stranger shook his head. 'I wouldn't put on good nature,' he said. 'Besides, I've barely time to make it as it is.'

'You can say what you like, you're not leaving without a bite,' persisted his father. 'Now we're havin' no arguments.'

The stranger looked at his father. 'And I mean it,' repeated his father.

'I'd be glad of a bit of bread and cheese,' temporised the stranger. Then he paused. 'And a slice of onion with it, if you can spare one.'

'I reckon we can stretch as that far,' said his father. 'Maybe a bit further. Depends on what fettle the missus is in.'

The stranger looked sharply at him. 'Like that, is it?'

'No it's not,' said his father. 'Not if your thinking what I'm thinking.'

'It was only a thought,' said the stranger mildly. 'I've had a bit trouble that way myself.'

'Oh, ay,' said his father, encouragingly.

'Well, you know what it's like,' said the stranger. 'Finished my time just as war broke out. Got married and did my stint in the trenches. Came back and they set me on as an improver – then after a year and a month they sacked me.'

'A land fit for heroes,' said my father.

'There was all hell to pay,' said the stranger. 'So I lit out and she went back to her folk. I've looked high and low for a job.'

'It's a bloody mess and that's a fact,' said his father. 'What's your trade?'

'Fitter and turner,' said the stranger. 'But the truth is that I can't shake the war out of my system. Went through the Marne and the Somme.'

'Aeroplanes and tanks and observation balloons,' said the boy. 'Did you see them?'

'Mostly mud,' said the stranger, 'if you're talkin' about the Somme. You daresn't look up for watching your step on the duckboards. We lost more through drowning than bullets.'

'What about the dog fights?' said the boy. With his arms widely extended and making a humming noise he wheeled in a wing-dipping circle.

The stranger shook his head. 'We hadn't much time for looking at aeroplanes.'

'You run ahead and tell your Mam I'm coming,' said his father. He turned to the stranger. 'Head full of trash,' he apologised. 'He's always reading.'

'Nobody knows what it smelled like,' said the stranger. 'Nobody'.

They came to the club at the bottom of the street. 'Just hang on a minute,' said his father. 'You can drink a pint, I'll bet?'

He disappeared past the doorkeeper into the noisy depths on the long bar.

George William Mattimore was sitting on his haunches beside the doorway. 'Sit down, old lad, and rest your weary bones a minute,' he said. The stranger tried to emulate him by sitting down on his hunkers pitman-fashion and collapsed on his backside. 'Sit on your heels an' prop thi backside against the wall,' said Matty. He took out a cigarette from a five Woodbine packet, tapped one end against the back of his hand, reversed it and tapped again. 'Come far this mornin?' he asked.

'I'm making it from Durham Workhouse to Barny,' he said. His eyes were eating up the Woodbine. 'There's a doss-house there that's well spoken of. I'm lookin' for a job.'

'They're scarcer than pitmen's wives with backsides decked with diamonds,' said Matty. 'Fancy a smoke?'

'Man, it's your last,' protested the stranger.

'What odds?' said Matty, breaking the Woodbine in half. Lighting the stranger's half and his own he blew out the match. 'I'm expecting a tuppenny multiplier to come off tomorrow.'

'That's lovely,' said the stranger, blowing out a ring which started narrow and broadened out to mingle with the shining diamond points of a million dust particles. The father emerged with a big dimpled glass in his hand. 'Forgot to ask you,' he said. 'Will a bitter be all right?' Gently, reverently, the stranger took off some of the froth which was brimming over the side and tasted it with his eyes closed. 'God bless you and keep you,' he said; only in a different way to Mister Willis when he gave the benediction at the Sunday School: but all the same he meant it.

'What mob were you in?' asked George William.

'Fusiliers,' said the stranger.

'Remember the Bull-ring?' asked Matty.

'I should,' said the stranger, and his face went dead.

They turned the corner. 'Happy huntin',' said a voice. When they looked it was Matty's face looking round the corner.

'Got up from his backside for that,' said his father to the stranger. 'Mind you're honoured.'

'Did you have a bull there?' asked the boy. 'A real, live bull, just like ours?'

'Oh, we had a bull all right,' said the stranger.

'I thought I told you to run and tell your Mam,' said his father impatiently.

He'd only half finished explaining to his mother, when the stranger and his father arrived.

'Now what?' said his mother dangerously in the voice that the boy knew so well.

'This is Mister Forsyth,' introduced his father. 'He's looking for a job.'

'Oh, is he?' she said.

'I've invited him in for a bite,' said his father, carefully placing the pint glass on the big dinner table, which was spread all ready.

'The dinner's hardly ready yet,' she snapped, 'and what there is'll hardly suffice for us.'

Snatching his cap the stranger moved to the door. 'Now look . . .' he began.

'Now just you sit down,' said his father, his voice dangerously level. Taking the cap he hung it behind the door. 'Butter him a couple of slices of bread,' he instructed the mother.

'I cannot stay long,' said the stranger. 'I've got to make the doss-house at Barny tonight.'

'Doss-house,' snorted the woman as she spread half a sheet of newspaper on the end of the little side table which stood by the window.

'What about a tablecloth?' demanded the husband.

'You must be joking,' she said and swept out into the scullery. The father took the glass and set it firmly on the little table.

'Howay, sit down,' he ordered.

'Sure?' said the stranger.

'Never fret,' said his father. 'Just sup up. You must be thirsty.'

'Well . . .' said the stranger hesitantly, then drank deeply. He sniffed appreciatively at the smell of roast and Yorkshire Pudding mingling. 'That's lovely,' he said, wiping his mouth with the back of his hand. It was hard to tell whether or not he was praising the taste of the beer or the lovely amalgam of Sunday dinner smells.

'I'm sorry,' said the father apologetically. 'Her bark's worse than her bite y'know. She's got a good heart in her belly, at the bottom of her.'

'Anybody can see that,' said the stranger.

'She's a good lass really,' said the father stoutly.

There was something about the way he said it that made the boy sorry for his father.

'Just like our lass at home,' concurred the stranger heartily, and with that he got his eye fixed on Jenny, who had found her way over towards him by holding on first to the stool and then on to the table leg nearest the stranger. 'And who's this, like?' he asked.

'That's our little lass,' said the father. 'Bright as a button.'

'Let's see if we've got something for her,' suggested the stranger, his right hand diving into his jacket pocket. Bringing out a rattle made of interwoven green rushes he held it out to the child. 'Ta,' said the child as she grabbed it.

'She knows how to take what she wants,' said the stranger and held out his arms. 'How about a kiss, Jenny?'

The mother came briskly in and set down a plate of bread before the stranger. Then she snatched up the child. 'Our Jenny's not partial to strangers.'

'What's this?' said the father, his face darkening. 'Bread like house-ends. I shouldn't care if there was cheese to go with it.'

'It's just the way I like it,' said the stranger. 'Home-baked bread as well.' But even the boy could see that something was wrong – something about the way the stranger kept bolting every mouthful, the way he sluiced away every last particle with the beer.

'Is that all right?' said his father.

'It's grand,' said the stranger.

'Well if that's all,' said the woman, 'I'll get on with my cooking.'

'He'll need an onion,' said the husband. 'Give him a big 'un – one of our own. D'you like it with vinegar?'

'Just on its own,' said the stranger. Still grasping the child under her arm the woman departed, but not without a defiant lift of the head. They all waited. The woman brought in the onion, a knife, salt and pepper.

'I thank you,' said the stranger with an old-fashioned courtesy.

'Don't mention it,' said the woman.

The onion seemed to help down the bread and butter. In less than no time the stranger had finished. He stood up. For some reason he seemed embarrassed. 'Well, thanks, mister, thanks, mistress; you've been very kind. I'd best be going.' The man went.

'A fine carry-on,' said the woman. 'You and your tramps.'

'That man,' said his father, 'bled and died for you.'

How funny, the boy thought, the man was alive. How could he have bled and died?

'I don't care,' said the woman defiantly. 'Dirty stinkin' tramps – they're all alike. If they really wanted work they could find it.'

'That man's like me,' said his father. 'A time-served craftsman. He'd work his guts out if they'd let him.'

'It's a bonny good job I'm here to keep you straight,' said the woman, tossing her head. 'Anybody can pull the wool over your eyes – anybody. But not me; I sharp got his measure. I know the treatment to give his sort.'

The man stared at her, then went through to the scullery. Returning he threw an opened packet of margarine on the table. 'Like margarine, for instance,' he asked.

'That's right,' she said, giving him look for look. 'And I spread it on thick for him.'

'Oh, woman, woman,' said the father. 'Do you know

what you've done?' And for a moment, while the question hung in the air, the boy shut his eyes, hoping his father wouldn't tell. Vaguely, though, he sensed the answer in what he owed to the stranger, he prayed for silence. He knew what her reaction would be. Punishment would be swift and sure.

'Of course I do,' she answered. 'Do you think I haven't got my wits about me? You've just got to look at him to know what he is. Dirty shiftless lot.'

'Ah, but we know better, don't we, old lad?' the father asked the boy.

The boy's heart pounded, worse than in the bull field. His mouth was dry and his tongue clove to the top of his mouth. He was looking down into the stranger's glass, deep and sour-smelling.

'Oh look da,' he cried, 'the man's gone away and left some beer. Shall I run and tell him?'

The father stared unseeingly at him. 'No, son, I shouldn't bother. That's only the dregs. It's not worth bothering about.' Wearily he unfastened his shirt buttons. 'God, but I'm tired,' he said. He dropped heavily on to the stool. 'He didn't want to come, you know,' he said. 'He had trouble with his own missus – that's why he left home.'

'I know, I know,' she said, unfastening his shirt buttons. 'I'm sorry I went on so much. But first the bairn fratching all morning, then you coming late – '

'It's all right,' he said. When the boy came back with the bath tin she had drawn the shirt over his head. The black was all over him, deeply set in his arms and knees, the knobs of his backbone shining where they'd rubbed against the low roof top. She filled his bath. 'That man's travelled, y'know,' he was murmuring.

'Your bath's ready,' she said.

'Ay,' he said, kneeling down before the tin. 'Up dale and down dale – there's a lot to be said for it. At least you can hear the birds singin'.'

The boy sat where the stranger had been. The smell of the beer was in his nostrils, sour and pungent. His face was clouded. The mother rumpled his hair. 'Stop worrying, Silly Billy,' she reassured him. 'He's not going to run away.'

'Ay,' said his father, smiling up through the soap-suds. 'I'll not leave you. I'm not the sort to do that. Anyway, who would I have to meet me?' The boy's heart suddenly lifted. The father wasn't leaving, after all. His father would keep his secret. Yet somehow he had disappointed his father. But beyond that he sensed a deeper hurt – and a hurt he would always remember. In some way, he felt, his mother had deeply hurt his father.

His mother was standing over his father with the laving tin full of cold tap water held at the ready – she had already washed his back. 'Come on Jack, get finished with it,' she said. 'Now!' said his father. His mother immediately tipped the water over his head and shoulders and in a trice the muck was sluiced away. Eyes closed, his father groped for the towel. He rubbed vigorously. 'It's a good job we've got bairns,' he said. 'By God it is.'

'You did your share,' she said. Her voice bubbling over with laughter. Then she departed into the scullery.

'I daresay,' said the father, 'I daresay I did,' watching her through the folds of the towel. Then he turned his attention to the boy. 'Howay, lad,' he said. 'Perk up. Dry my back for me. One way and another we've worked for our dinner today – you an' me.'

'Now,' said his mother, returning, 'what do you two think you're talkin' about?'

'Secrets,' said his father. 'Man's talk, that's all.'

She held up the pint glass distantly, wrinkling up her nose. 'The sooner this is washed out, the better,' she said. 'Then he can take it back to the doorkeeper.' The glass shone like crystal when she was finished with it. Every last trace of the sour-smelling beer had gone by the time the boy took it back. But the face of the tramp stayed with the boy forever.

Thinking and writing

Snow Horse by Joan Aiken

Thinking points

1   As you read the first part of the story what impression did you get of:
    a) Forest Lodge Inn
    b) McGall
    c) Dirk
    d) Cal?

2   When the stranger first arrives Cal says that he is frightened to sell him a horse yet in the end he does. Why?

3   By the time you got to the middle of the story, what impression had you formed of the stranger? Who did you think he was?

4   McGall won't allow Cal to ride the horses, which Cal would dearly love to do. What reason does McGall give? Is this the real reason? What is the point of this in the story?

5   What happens at the end of the story? What is the point of:
    a) Cal riding off on the snow horse
    b) the set of footprints that McGall sees in the morning?

6   Suppose you had to give this story a different title. What would you call it?

Writing: Literature

1   The news of Cal's disappearance reaches the people down in the valley. The local policeman comes up to Forest Lodge to investigate. He questions McGall and Dirk at length about what has

happened. Describe the conversations they have: either as a story using direct speech, or as a play script.

2   You could say that part of this story is missing; the author doesn't tell us the significance of the footprints or how this is connected with how Cal escapes. Imagine what she might have put if she had wanted to explain everything in detail. Now write the missing part of the story.

Hireling by R S Thomas

Thinking about the poem

R S Thomas presents this character by describing him in a landscape: he paints a picture for us.

1   Read the poem carefully and let your imagination work on it. In your own words describe the picture you can see.

2   What picture or idea do you get in your mind when you read these sections of the poem?
   a) 'The sky's ruins, gutted with fire
       Of the late sun, smouldering still.'
   b) '. . . the grey ice
       Of a face splintered by life's stone.'

Writing: Literature

Write about this poem and your reactions to it. You could include any or all of the following points:
a)   the man whom R S Thomas describes
b)   the poet's thoughts and feelings about him
c)   the way in which the poem is written (especially the images which it uses)
d)   your thoughts and feelings as you read the poem.

Angel Hill by *Charles Causley*

This poem is a kind of ballad: a rhyming poem which
uses repetition and tells a story. Often – as in this
case – it does not tell the story directly but leaves it
for you, the reader, to work out. As you read the
poem, listen to the rhythm and the rhymes and the
repetition. Ask yourself: what is the story behind this
conversation?

Thinking points

Read the poem again and make some notes on what
you can work out about each of these points:
1 Who the story-teller is.
2 Who the sailor is.
3 What happened to the two of them in the past,
   according to the sailor.
4 What has happened to the sailor since.
5 Why the story-teller keeps repeating the words 'No,
   never'.

It may help you to understand the poem to pay
particular attention to these sections:
a) The third verse tells you about what happened to
   them in the war.
b) The fourth verse tells you about the relationship
   between the two of them (according to the sailor).
c) The sixth verse tells you something of what has
   happened to the sailor.
d) The seventh verse tells you something about the
   effect the sailor has on the story-teller now.

Do you think that the story-teller will 'send and fetch'
the sailor 'one fine day'?

Writing: Literature

1 Use the notes you have made on this poem as the basis for a piece of writing about it.
2 Afterwards the story-teller's wife (or his son) asks him who the stranger was who came to the door. Write the conversation between them.

The Tramp *by Sid Chaplin*

Making notes on the story

When you have finished reading the story read it through carefully again and make notes on these points:

a) the place where the boy and his family live (the countryside, the town and their house)
b) the father
c) the mother
d) the relationship between the two parents
e) the stranger
f) the way of life of the boy's family.

Thinking points

1 Why does the boy's mother take against the stranger?
2 Why did his father take to the stranger?
3 How did the boy feel about the stranger?
4 What is the importance of the food and drink mentioned in the story?
5 It's important to the boy that his father should not tell his mother about the bull. Why is it important and why does the father keep the secret?

Writing: Literature

1   As the stranger walks away from the house he thinks about what has just happened. Describe the thoughts that go through his head.

2   Use the notes you have made as the basis for a piece of writing about this story.

Love

Skegness, or Bust!

SUSAN GREGORY

'Miss, Miss, tell 'em, Miss. Tell the lads, Miss. Tell 'em the *girls* are having the back seat.'

'Oh, I can't do that, Melanie. You'll just have to see you get there first.'

'Right, you lot. Are you ready? The coach is at the traffic lights, I can see it.'

'Create a diversion, Mel, so as the boys won't notice. Do a striptease or summat.'

'You kiddin'? What do you think I am?'

'Go on, Mel. You'll think of something. You'd bedder!'

'Hey, Dave, ain't that a squirrel up on that branch? It's just run up the trunk. Look, over there. In that tree at the side of the school there. It *is* a squirrel, ain' it, Ravinder?'

'Where? I can't see one. You need specs or something, Melanie. You're seeing things. There's nothing there.'

'There *is*. There *is*. Look, it's moving now. You must be looking at the wrong branch. You can see it, can't you, Yunus? You've got good eyesight.'

'Mel, Mel, come on. We've saved you a place.'

'Hey, look, damn it. The girls have got the back seat. We've been done. There weren't no squirrel, were there, Melanie? You were having us on.'

But Melanie had gone, and was even now skipping down the bus to join the others who were rolling around on the back seat in a state of helpless laughter. Purnima Patel had been watching Melanie's performance with envy. No one would ever ask *her* to distract the boys. They all thought of her as a creep. Nice enough, but no good for a laugh. Well, today she'd show them. Today she was going to be one of the gang. With determination she squeezed herself on to the back seat along with the others.

The lads leapt cursing on to the bus and rushed to the back. They tried to drag the girls to their feet, but they shouted for Sir who had just climbed on and was talking to the driver. He yelled at the lads to lay off it. The girls settled back into their places, smiling triumphantly.

Purnima, squashed in the middle, turned round and knelt on the seat, staring at the traffic going along the main road. By doing this she seized for herself a moment of peace away from the others. That boy Yunus! Her hand still burned from where he'd caught hold of it, trying to pull her to her feet. She'd seen him around school a lot recently. Whenever she was on prefect duty in the bottom hall he always seemed to be walking through. She'd had to tell him off because he was only in the third year and the third years were supposed to be out on the yard. But the other girls had told her to lay off him. They'd taken a fancy to him, she could tell. But they were prefects, weren't they? They couldn't favour one lad above the rest. Well, she wasn't going to, anyway.

She turned round again and sat facing forwards. He was sitting just in front of them laughing with Dave Petrovic. Trust him to be sitting with the fifth years. What a cheek! Yet he didn't look cheeky. He had a nice face – and, she had to admit, was very good-looking. And he dressed trendy for an Indian boy. Today he was wearing jeans with a scarlet webbing belt, the end hanging casually down instead of being tucked in at the back, and a golden yellow shirt, big and floppy.

Purnima clicked her tongue at herself. Fancy wasting all that thought on a third year! And a cheeky one at that! She shoved him to the back of her mind and concentrated on enjoying herself. It wasn't often that you had the opportunity to go off on a pleasure trip like this. She took a quick look round the coach. There were more Indian kids than white ones. Well, it wasn't difficult to know why. It was projects week at school and Mr Tipperton's project had been social games. They'd been playing chess and bridge and scrabble and table tennis all week and the Skegness trip was the highlight of the project. Not a serious day of study – the only social game that they might be playing was football or going on the pinball machines – but it was the day that everyone had been looking forward to. To meet the cost Mr Tipperton had had to fill the coach with fifth years who'd finished their exams. This was one of the reasons why there were so many Indians. They still liked to go back into school – even though they could have been free now – to play cricket and table-tennis and chat to the teachers. So they were around to hear that Mr Tipperton needed people to make up the numbers for his Skegness day.

But the main reason for this trip being so popular with the Indian kids, thought Purnima with a thrill, was that it was a day out, away from the sneaky eyes of parents – and with members of the opposite sex in the party!

There was another delighted burst of laughter. Purnima jumped. Melanie and Sangita were bending over a huge sheet of paper. Melanie was drawing and Sangita wrote something at the bottom.

'Here, Jasmine,' said Sangita, bending across Purnima to reach Jasmine Samuel. 'You've got the Sellotape, haven't you? Stick this up for us, will you?'

Purnima caught a glimpse of the notice as it was passed to Jasmine. It said, 'Skegness, or Bust' and a huge bosom filled the sheet. Purnima couldn't help smiling. What would their mothers say if they could see what their daughters were capable of drawing? Sangita was scrawling again. With a giggle she handed the finished product to Purnima who passed it to Jasmine. It read, 'I think you're great, but then I've always had bad taste.' She gurgled and displayed it on the back window for the travelling salesman in the flashy car behind to read.

Purnima's heart swelled with the fun of it all. What the heck, she was going to enjoy herself. For five years she'd struggled and slogged and studied for school and for her parents. Now with her 'O' levels behind her – and a place at the sixth-form college for next year – she was going to live a little. After all, it would soon be 'A' levels and college and work, work, work. She was young – time to have some fun before it was too late and life became more serious than ever.

She looked around the bus at the kids she'd been working with every day for the last five years. Over the last year they'd changed little by little. Now that the pressure of exams was over, the change seemed to be complete. Even Abdul Sheikh, who'd always been such a little boy, had had his hair punked and grown up all of a sudden. And Ravinder had acquired gold-rimmed specs and a grown-up air. And as for Dinesh Dodhia, well, what a transformation! He'd even started making suggestive remarks!

She could hear him now talking about Jatinder

Singh. 'Now that one's too innocent. It's not good for him. Do you know what he said to Melanie Fish when we were waiting outside school? He asked her what book she was reading and she said it was called *Boy Meets Girl* and asked him if he wanted to borrow it after. And you know what? He shook his head until it looked as if it was coming off and said, "I only like science fiction."' Dinesh and Ravinder went off into fits of laughter and Purnima grinned to herself.

Just like Jatinder! She pictured the way he shuffled along the road, head bent with embarrassment in case he met anyone. But he was bright! There was no doubt about that. Bright, yet backward. Poor old Jatinder! It suddenly struck Purnima that the same could be said about her. Well, today they'd see a difference!

There was a sudden roar of approval from Sangita, Melanie and Jasmine. The salesman had just condescended to wave and blow a kiss as he accelerated and overtook the coach. At that moment it lurched to the side – time for a coffee break. Purnima, stirring her coffee, sighed to herself. The other girls had just ignored the way she was squashed in the middle of them. They hadn't been unfriendly. They had simply failed to notice she was there . . .

They reached Skegness not long after the coffee stop. Everyone piled out, shrieking and laughing. Sir paused long enough to say that they had to meet on the beach in front of the pleasure ground at half past two for a game of football and then charged off with Miss Muldoon towards the nearest pub. Purnima stood uncertain for a moment, but she wasn't left out for long. 'C'mon, Purnima,' yelled Sangita. 'We're going to the pleasure beach first. Coming?'

She certainly was! She looked out of the corner of

her eye to see which lads had joined them. There was Dave Petrovic, of course – and Dinesh and Ravinder and – yes, Yunus too!

They looked round the pleasure beach first, to see what they wanted to go on. Some of the younger kids tagged along. A quiet little boy called Satish came racing up to her to show her what he'd won – a razor blade on a chain. He was as thrilled as anything, but it looked all wrong on him. 'And I'm just like *him* as well,' thought Purnima. She had thought she would enjoy herself, feel part of the gang, as soon as she got to Skegness and caught the holiday spirit. But she was no different. While the others shrieked and laughed, she remained quiet and withdrawn. The kind of girl that the younger ones came up to talk to, but not the ones of her own age. Luckily nobody seemed to notice. But she knew she was out of place and hated herself for it. She longed for the waltzer to stop as soon as she'd got on it, and she shut her eyes when she was supposed to be aiming with a gun at a target. Yunus noticed what she was doing. 'Here,' he said. 'Let me help you.' And he put his arms round her, placing his cheek against hers to take aim. She hit the target and he cheered. She backed away from him as if it was she who had been shot.

It was Melanie who spotted the boating lake. 'Let's go for a row,' she shouted. 'C'mon. Bags the oars.' They raced towards it. Melanie, who had started running as soon as she'd had the idea, got there first and jumped into the boat. Dave hurriedly jumped in after her. Dinesh shouted to Sangita, 'Come in this boat with me, Sang.' Purnima slowed down. Someone was going to get landed with her. Or perhaps Yunus and Ravinder would go in a boat together – and

Jasmine and her. She didn't know which would be worse. She didn't like to think that none of the boys would be interested in going in a boat with her – but she knew that's the way it would be.

'C'mon, Purnima,' shouted Yunus. 'You're coming with me.'

He was only being kind. Yes, that's all it was. Fancy a *third* year having to take pity on a fifth year, and a prefect at that. It was pathetic. But nevertheless she was pleased. She caught herself grinning with delight – and quickly adjusted her expression to her usual rather thoughtful, rather mournful look. She remembered Jasmine. How horrible to be chosen last and it could so easily have been her. But she should have known it wouldn't get Jasmine down. 'Looks like it's you 'n' me, boy,' she said, grinning at Ravinder. Purnima decided she could relax and let the holiday begin.

But it was easier thought than done. The others were soon helpless with laughter, soaked through from splashing one another. Melanie rocked their boat so hard that they nearly capsized. 'Time for you to take over the oars, Dave,' she said. 'It's ruinin' me hands. Look at the blisters.' She displayed them, letting go of the oars. Ravinder lunged to catch them before they slid into the water. He managed to get one but the other escaped and he nearly fell in. The boatman yelled at them to stop fooling about and the others collapsed with giggles. But Purnima felt uncomfortable. *Why* couldn't she just relax and not bother, like the others? They did and said whatever came into their heads, and never mind what happened. She seemed to get lost within her head, seeing the world through the eyes of the boatman, the teachers, her parents – where were her *own* eyes? What did she really want to see? Everybody said how responsible she was – but where was the fun or the *sense* of it all?

'What you dreaming about, Purnima?' It was Yunus leaning towards her. 'Do you want to row for a bit? C'mon. You have a go.'

She smiled at him, grateful for the way he was including her, and took the oars. But she thought too much about what she was doing instead of just letting it all flow like Yunus seemed to, and the boat kept going round in circles. Yunus laughed, but not unkindly.

But they were being called in now by the boatman. The day was slipping away fast. They bought some coke and crisps and took their sandwiches down to the beach. Purnima was amazed to see that Dinesh took Sangita's hand as soon as they left the boating lake. As soon as Ravinder noticed he got hold of Jasmine's. The girls looked embarrassed but very pleased. Even when Sir and Miss arrived with the football and they were all walking towards the sea to set up a pitch, the two boys got hold of the girls' hands again, but they made sure they kept behind the adults. When Miss turned round, though, Sangita hissed to Dinesh, 'Miss Muldoon's looking,' and they dropped hands guiltily, but Purnima noticed that Miss only grinned.

The others started playing football straight away. Purnima was determined not to be left out. She took off her high-heeled sandals and played in bare feet. Most of the girls still had their tights on – they couldn't be bothered to take them off. Some of them had already dashed, screaming with laughter, into the sea. When they came out ladders trickled from their toe-nails up their feet.

For a while Purnima appeared to play quite well. She rushed up and down so that it looked as if she was doing something, but she made sure she didn't get anywhere near the ball. Sangita kept tackling the boys, screeching, and Jasmine elbowed her way through all opposition while the lads screamed their approval. Purnima's heart sank. They were good sports. But she'd watched Satish leap bravely for a header. It had been a helpful shot and they'd shouted, 'Good one, Satish,' but Purnima knew it must have hurt him. She'd watched closely as he blinked back the tears, stunned, shook his head a few times, rubbed it, and charged back in again. She shuddered.

'Purnima, here's one for you.' It was Yunus again, neatly dribbling the ball towards her, weaving in circles until he gently kicked the ball straight to Purnima's feet. Without thinking – she was so surprised – she gave the ball a hefty kick and the players cheered. She flushed with pleasure and ran forward without even realising it. Now she dared to put up just a little effort and managed to knee the ball once and then kick it once again, but then Dinesh kicked her by mistake and she lost her nerve and left the game, wandering towards the water's edge.

It had been cold all day but when they had first arrived it had been bright. Now great grey clouds had blown up and the sea was an answering grey with fierce white flecks at the edges of the waves. Purnima tried not to notice the cigarette and crisp packets and the rather sinister-looking scum that rode there too. She concentrated her eyes out at sea, throwing her head back to enjoy the way the wind tore her hair and stung her cheeks. She loved the sea in this country. Here you felt wild and free, able to do anything, most of all, just able to *be*, to let thoughts and dreams and wishes tear through your head as if blown in by the sharp north east wind. You didn't need to wonder, 'Ought I to be thinking things like this?' or 'What would my mother say if she knew what I was thinking?'

'I wish Yunus had taken hold of my hand when Ravinder and Dinesh held hands with the others.' The pier suddenly loomed in front of her like an angry parent, and she was amazed at what she had thought. Yunus was a Muslim and she was a Hindu. Her parents didn't approve of Hindu girls talking to Hindu boys in the street, never mind holding hands with them, never *mind* holding hands with a Muslim. And Yunus was a third year, and she was a prefect. She must be crazy? He would never have dared to hold her hand, even if he'd wanted to. Had he wanted to . . .?

Oh, he was nice-looking? Such a great grin. She imagined his long slender fingers stroking the back of her hand and she shivered.

'Purnima!' Purnima jumped guiltily and turned round. Out at sea, wading up to his waist, was fat Mark. Also a third year! How different he was from Yunus! Mark would never think of Purnima as a girl-friend. He was the sort who saw girls only as mothers – and always would. He had chatted away to her on the coach, kneeling on the seat in front – about his puppy, his fishing, and how he was going to buy a snorkel and goggles when he got to Skeggy. He ate all the time, as if in need of a constant sweetened dummy.

He looked a lonely figure out at sea, wading now towards her, skin pale beneath the greying, racing afternoon sky. A blob among the waves, stomach oozing over his boxer shorts, snorkelled and goggled like some unlikely sea creature, shivering, quivering towards her. 'Purnima,' he shouted again. 'Will you get me a towel?'

Purnima nodded and looked round the beach for it. Then she saw that the others were using it to wipe their sandy feet. She was running over to them when Yunus came charging towards her. Her stomach lurched in the direction of her ears. But he was only chasing the ball. It flew into the sea and he tore in after it, up to his knees in the water. That shirt and those jeans were new on today! He'd said so on the coach. 'Yunus, you fool,' she couldn't help shouting, but he only turned and grinned. 'It's a great game of football,' he said in self-defence.

Purnima felt nothing but scorn for him. What would his parents say when he got home that night with a salt mark on his new jeans? But then, what would her parents say if they knew that she still wanted to hold hands with him, for all he was an idiot? Wanted to, more than anything else in the world. More than good 'O' levels or going to sixth-form college or doing 'A' levels or any of that.

'Purnima!' wailed Mark through chattering teeth. Purnima ran towards the little crowd of girls who were snatching Mark's towel from one another and slapping each other with it. The ends kept trailing in the sand. As Purnima ran up there was a diversion and the towel was forgotten. Further down the beach a streaker (male) was charging into the sea urged on by his cheering mates. The girls were all of a twitter. 'Oh, Purnima, did you see that?' Agitation, agitation. Giggle, giggle.

Purnima tried to keep her eyes on shaking the towel but they seemed to swivel of their own accord. She caught sight of the man's bottom leaping above the waves, white below his narrow brown back, rising out of the water like two pale melons. Smaller melons than she'd imagined. Neat at the bottom of the long curve of his back. Guiltily she looked away. How stupid the men were, shouting and jeering like that! And the girls, screaming and giggling and drawing attention to themselves! Her mind switched back to Yunus running into the sea with all his clothes on. She flung the towel over her arm and made back towards Mark before her mind could travel further and make more guilty pictures.

The towel was soaking! And sandy. Mark pulled a face and went 'Yuk!' when he took it. She couldn't exactly blame him! They started across the sand together. The others had gathered up their parkas and sweatshirts and shoes and were making for the promenade. Purnima watched anxiously as Sangita and Jasmine ran squealing away from Ravinder and Dinesh and Yunus. Yunus caught hold of Sangita before Dinesh did. Purnima could have sworn that his arm went round her shoulders for a moment or two. Tears rushed to her eyes and she mumbled to Mark, 'Got sand in them.' But he hadn't noticed. He was too busy trying to squeeze himself into his shirt, his spherical body still wet. At last he had his shirt on. There were far fewer dry patches than wet ones. The sight of him irritated Purnima. She snapped at him for kicking sand up at her. 'I never!' he said indignantly.

'Ooh, Purnima,' he said when they reached the edge of the beach. (By now Dinesh was holding Sangita's hand again and Yunus was teasing her, flicking at her hair while she and Dinesh batted him away, laughing.) 'Ooh, Purnima, I've forgotten summat. Wait on. Wait there.'

'What've you forgotten, Mark?' asked Purnima, thoroughly fed up with him. (Yunus looked over his shoulder but seeing her walking with Mark he turned away and was now flicking Sangita's hair more than ever.)

'Me pants!' exclaimed Mark in tones of deep grief. 'I'm going back for 'em. Wait for us.' And he waddled off across the sand, a white globule against the grey of the sky. At last he returned, clutching a pair of sodden lilac pants. Purnima couldn't help staring. Luckily he seemed to have no thoughts of actually *changing* into his pants at the moment. He seemed quite happy just waving them round his head like a flag.

At last she managed to get away. But then she caught up with four smaller kids who were intent on tearing one another to pieces by the shirt ends. 'Sati chapatti!' they kept chanting at Satish. He only grinned and charged at them like a miniature bull. He charged so hard that one boy crumpled, winded. Satish rubbed his head.

'There,' said Purnima, exasperated, leaning over the winded boy. 'Will that teach you?' She heard a laugh and turned round to see Yunus watching her. 'You're good with them,' he said. 'The others don't bother. C'mon. It's time we got on the coach.'

She felt herself blushing. They walked across the car park. Her hand seemed to ache from wanting him to take hold of it. He walked rather close to her but he made no move towards her hand. They didn't say anything, and now they were climbing on the coach, still in silence. Purnima felt bitterly disappointed.

But to her surprise there were changes! The girls

were no longer on the back seat. They were sitting in the double seats at the back of the coach. And they weren't sitting girls together. Sangita was with Dinesh, and Jasmine with Ravinder, and Melanie with Dave, of course. 'Hurry up, then,' said Yunus, sounding pleased, giving Purnima a push. 'Go opposite Dinesh and Sangita.' Purnima took her seat by the window and he swung himself round, fingers on the rack, and lowered himself beside her. How tall he was for a third year!

The couples didn't have much to say to each other. Sangita and Jasmine kept making faces at each other and jumping up to mouth messages, giggling and embarrassed. Purnima just sat there, beside herself with happiness. But what if their dads were waiting to meet the bus? They were kidding themselves. They couldn't go out together after today, not like the white kids did, as if it was the most natural thing in the world. It wasn't like that, for them.

There was a party spirit, now that the coach had started up. Miss Muldoon gave out song-sheets and soon they were all singing – 'I'm for ever blowing bubbles' and 'Daisy Daisy'. Purnima didn't know the songs but she soon got the hang of the tunes. Yunus bawled away beside her as they swung round the country lanes. She noticed that Satish was wearing a badge with a dazed-looking little man on it. 'Avoid hangovers. Shtay drunk.' 'How long have you been sitting on these, Jeanie?' somebody asked, waving a squashed looking packet of biscuits. Everybody laughed.

When Miss Muldoon came to the back to collect the song-sheets, the kids broke into 'Build a Bonfire'.

> 'Build a bonfire, build a bonfire
> Put the tea-chers on the top.
> Put Mr Tipperton in the mi-ddle
> And set fire to the flaming lot!'

Mr Tipperton stood up and shook his fist at them and they all laughed. Then he and Miss Muldoon stood up and sang very loud:

> 'Build a bonfire, build a bonfire,
> Put the pu-pils on the top.
> Put the fifth year in the mi-ddle,
> And set fire to the flaming lot.'

Purnima felt she couldn't bear to leave it all. She didn't want to go to sixth-form college any more. There'd be no Yunus walking through the bottom hall grinning at all the prefects every morning. Or rather, he'd still be there and she wouldn't – and he'd be grinning at another girl and forgetting about her.

The coach was quietening down now. Some of the kids were playing cards. Purnima saw Dinesh bend towards Sangita and give her a quick kiss. She looked away hurriedly. When she looked back, Dinesh had his arm round her. She shut her eyes in desperation. In the end nothing had really happened. And it could've, if only she'd been different. If she'd been cheeky like Sangita. But because she was the way she was, Yunus'd never dare. Not a Muslim. Not a third year. And they'd soon be home. It would soon all be over.

It didn't matter that he was only a third year. No, it didn't. She knew that the other girls didn't think it did. They'd been giggling about him and commenting on him for weeks now. Purnima kept her eyes shut as her brain raced. She could hear what the boys in front were talking about and it kept getting in the way of her own thoughts. 'And she said if you breathed up a horse's nostrils it'd be your friend for life,' she heard Mark say. 'I tried it on our cat, but it scratched me.'

Always other people's conversations, other people's lives. And today was going to have been so special. And Yunus liked her, she was sure of that. Yes, but unless she showed him she liked him, he'd never know – and it would be too late. It was probably the only chance she'd ever have to show she cared about a boy whom she'd chosen. But it was no good. It couldn't come to anything. She might get into bad trouble at home. It wasn't worth it. And, in any case, she just wouldn't *dare!*

Then an idea formed in Purnima's mind. It made her feel hot just to think about it. But, yes, she was going to do it. Nothing open. Nothing that would make him know definitely that she liked him. But just so that she'd done *something*. So that she wouldn't feel all her life that she'd thrown away a chance.

She still had her eyes closed. And now she sighed lightly, and shifted on her seat as if she was fast asleep. Then slowly, very slowly, she let her head slip down the back of the seat until it came to rest on Yunus's shoulder.

She nearly stopped breathing as it landed. He was talking across the gangway to Ravinder. She felt him jerk slightly as if in surprise. She waited. Then he moved a little as if to make her head more comfortable, and shifted up closer to her.

It wasn't easy, pretending to be asleep all the way back to Roylston. The coach grew noisy again as they were nearing home, and there were loud shrieks that surely would've woken anybody? But Purnima refused to be woken. She lay relaxed, snuggled against Yunus's yellow shirt, smelling the sea and the sweetness of his warm body all the way back home.

But at last there was a great stirring and shuffling that she couldn't block out. A hefty jerk, and the coach came to a stop. What if the dads were already waiting there? But she kept her head firmly down on Yunus's shoulder.

'Purnima,' she heard Yunus say gently. 'Purnima, wake up. We're back.'

She opened her eyes to find herself looking straight into his. She didn't feel shy. He was smiling at her. 'You did have a long sleep,' he whispered to her. 'I hope you enjoyed it as much as I did.' She lifted her head and shook herself, smiling back. 'Oh, I did.'

The dads hadn't arrived. The coach had returned quicker than the teachers had thought. They weren't supposed to be back for another ten minutes. The kids flung themselves off the coach, some shouting their thanks to the driver, others punching one another and bounding about after being cooped up so long.

But Sangita and Dinesh weren't bounding. They were kissing on the pavement while Sir and Miss had their heads down, picking up the last bits of litter into polythene bags. They were taking an awful risk. Sangita's dad could be here any minute.

Yunus turned to Purnima. 'I shall miss you next year. Don't forget us when you're at the sixth form and there are all those new lads around.' He took hold of her hand and lifted it to his cheek and she felt his fingers stroke it, gently, gently . . .

He let it fall just as her father's car was the first to swing round the corner . . .

You Liberate Me

Never has anyone
given me the freedom
which you give me
– and therefore I love you.

Never was I allowed to be myself
among others
as much as with you
– and therefore I love you.

Never did I discover myself as much
as in the freedom
which you leave me
– and therefore I love you.

Ulrich Schaffer

Manwatching

From across the party I watch you,
Watching her.
Do my possessive eyes
Imagine your silent messages?
I think not.
She looks across at you
And telegraphs her flirtatious reply.
I have come to recognise this code,
You are on intimate terms with this
   pretty stranger,
And there is nothing I can do.
My face is calm, expressionless,
But my eyes burn into your back.
While my insides shout with rage.
She weaves her way towards you,
Turning on a bewitching smile.
I can't see your face, but you are
   mesmerised I expect.
I can predict you: I know this scene so well.
Some acquaintance grabs your arm,
You turn and meet my accusing stare
   head on,
Her eyes follow yours, meet mine,
And then slide away, she understands,
She's not interested enough to compete.
It's over now.
She fades away, you drift towards me,
'I'm bored' you say, without a trace of
   guilt,

So we go.
Passing the girl in the hall.
'Bye' I say frostily,
I suppose
You winked.

Georgia Garrett

The Cleaner

I've seen it all, you know. Men.
Well, I've been married for thirty-two years,
I can do without them.
I know what they're after.

And these students. They're young, you know.
They don't know what it's all about,
The first years. And these post-grads;
I know what they're after.

They're older, you know. And by Christmas
They've finished here, they've gone. A girl
Can get hurt. I've been here eight years.
I've seen it happen.

Sometimes I say to her friend
You ought to talk to her. Does she know
What she's doing? And the friend'll say
Yes, she does know. Well, I hope I did right.

No need for any of 'em to have a baby,
But do they know? I feel a mother, like.
Once I did ask. I said *Do you know*
And she said *O yes, we know how far we're going.*

But these post-grads are older,
They take advantage. These girls, mind,
They're not all as innocent as you'd think.
Twenty stubs in the ashtray.

I can tell a lot from that.

U A Fanthorpe

Thinking and writing

Skegness, or Bust! by Susan Gregory

Immediate reactions

As soon as you've finished reading the story write down quickly:
a) your immediate reactions to the story
b) your first impressions of Purnima
c) any impressions you have of any of the other people on the trip.

Thinking points

1   There are a lot of different characters in this story and if you read it quickly it is quite easy to get confused between them. As you read the story again make a list of the main characters and against each one write a sentence summing up what you think he or she is like.

2   Now focus your attention on Purnima. As you read through the story, pay particular attention to how she thinks and feels about what is going on: what she is doing and how the others behave and talk. Each time you notice something new, make a brief note.

3   Here are some comments on what Purnima is like. For each of them say:
   (i) who you think might have said it
   (ii) whether you would agree with them
   (iii) your reasons.

   a) She's frightened of her own shadow she wouldn't even say boo to a goose. She's a bit of a drip – rather boring really.

b) Rather a shy child. She seems very aware of what other people think about her. It's a pity she hasn't got more self-confidence.

c) She is a good Hindu girl and she knows how she ought to behave. She has been brought up in the traditional Hindu way and that is how she will run her life.

d) She's really good she's very kind to the younger kids.

e) Well I think she's a bit mixed up really, she's very nice underneath but she's so quiet it's difficult to know what her thoughts and feelings are.

Writing: Literature

Look at all the notes and comments you have made about Purnima so far. Use them to write a description of her character. You can write about any or all of these points:

a) the facts about her life, her home background, and how she has been brought up

b) what she is like at school

c) how she feels about her home life and her school life

d) the way in which she wants to rebel against these things

e) her feelings about other people at the school

f) her feelings about Yunus.

You Liberate Me by *Ulrich Schaffer*

Thinking about the poem

This poem has two patterns. The first one is repeated
in each verse. There is also a development from the
beginning of the poem through to the end. Read the
poem through carefully and work out what these two
patterns are.

Writing: English

You can write a poem of your own using the verse
pattern of *You Liberate Me*: begin each verse with
'Never . . .' and start the last line of each verse with
'And therefore I . . .'

Manwatching by *Georgia Garrett*

Thinking points

Reading this poem is a bit like watching part of a film
or TV play. We get some clues about what has been
going on and what will happen next, but we are not
told everything: we have to work it out for ourselves.
Read the poem again and think about these points:
a) How many people are involved and who are they?
b) What is the relationship between 'I' and 'you'?
c) What is the relationship between 'you' and 'her'?
d) What is the background to this party: what has
    happened before? (Does the man know the woman
    he has been watching? Is it a secret? What about
    the speaker and the man, are they married? Are
    they close friends? Have they ever discussed this
    other woman?)

e) From the way the poem is written what impression do you get of the speaker? Why?

Writing

When you have thought about the poem and imagined your way into the story which it hints at, write one of the following:

1 A conversation between 'I' and 'you' immediately after they have left the party. You can write it as a story, or as a script for a short play.
2 The other girl in the story ('her') describes the party to a friend. Give her opinion of what happened, of the man, and of the speaker ('I').
3 Expand the poem so that it becomes a short story entitled 'The Party'.

The Cleaner by U A Fanthorpe

Reading aloud

You can't really get full value from this poem unless you read it aloud. Try to imagine what kind of voice the speaker has and how she speaks. Notice that where the poem is printed in italics she is quoting from conversations she has had. When you read the poem try to make this clear by the way you say those lines.

Thinking points

1 What exactly is she talking about?
2 Does she think clearly or is she confused? What are your reasons for saying this?

3 What does she mean by the last two lines:
> 'Twenty stubs in the ashtray.
> I can tell a lot from that'?

What do you think she can tell and how likely is it to be true?

4 What do we learn about the cleaner from the poem?

Writing: Literature

In this poem there are short extracts from two different conversations. Choose one of them and write the whole conversation.

Fighting for freedom

The Park

JAMES MATTHEWS

He looked longingly at the children on the other side of the railings; the children sliding down the chute, landing with feet astride on the bouncy lawn; screaming as they almost touched the sky with each upward curve of their swings; their joyful demented shrieks at each dip of the merry-go-round. He looked at them and his body trembled and ached to share their joy; buttocks to fit board, and hands and feet to touch steel. Next to him, on the ground, was a bundle of clothing, washed and ironed, wrapped in a sheet.

Five small boys pursued by two bigger ones, ran past, ignoring him. One of the bigger boys stopped. 'What are you looking at, you brown ape?' the boy said, stooping to pick up a lump of clay. He recognised him. The boy had been present the day he was put out of the park. The boy pitched the lump, shattering it on the rail above his head, and the fragments fell on his face.

He spat out the particles of clay clinging to the lining of his lips, eyes searching for an object to throw at the boys separated from him by the railing. More boys joined the one in front of him and he was frightened by their number.

Without a word he shook his bundle free of clay, raised it to his head and walked away.

As he walked he recalled his last visit to the park. Without hesitation he had gone through the gates and got onto the nearest swing. Even now he could feel that pleasurable thrill that travelled the length of his body as he rocketed himself higher, higher, until he felt that the swing would upend him when it reached its peak. Almost leisurely he had allowed it to come to a halt like a pendulum shortening its stroke and then ran towards the seesaw. A white boy, about his own age, was seated opposite him. Accordion-like their legs folded to send the seesaw jerking from the indentation it pounded in the grass. A hand pressed on his shoulder stopping a jerk. He turned around to look into the face of the attendant.

'Get off!'

The skin tightened between his eyes. Why must I get off? What have I done? He held on, hands clamped onto the iron attached to the wooden seesaw. The white boy jumped off from the other end and stood a detached spectator.

'You must get off!' The attendant spoke in a low voice so that it would not carry to the people who were gathering. 'The council say,' he continued, 'that us Blacks don't use the same swings as the whites. You must use the swings where you stay,' his voice apologising for the uniform he wore that gave him the right to watch that little white boys and girls were not hurt while playing.

'There no park where I stay.' He waved a hand in the direction of a block of flats. 'Park on the other side of town but I don't know where.' He walked past them. The mothers with their babies, pink and belching, cradled in their arms, the children lolling on the grass, his companion from the seesaw, the nurse girls – their uniforms their badge of indemnity – pushing prams. Beside him walked the attendant.

The attendant pointed an accusing finger at a notice board at the entrance. 'There. You can read for yourself.' Absolving him of all blame.

He struggled with the red letters on the white background. 'Blankes Alleen. Whites Only.' He walked through the gates and behind him the swings screeched, the seesaw rattled, and the merry-go-round rumbled.

He walked past the park each occasion he delivered the washing, eyes wistfully taking in the scene.

He shifted the bundle to a more comfortable position, easing the pain biting into his shoulder muscles. What harm would I be doing if I were to use the swings? Would it stop the swings from swinging? Would the chute collapse? The bundle pressed deeper and the pain became an even line across his shoulders and he had no answer to his reasoning.

The park itself, with its wide lawns and flower beds and rockeries and dwarf trees, meant nothing to him. It was the gaily painted red-and-green tubing, the silver chains and brown boards, transport to never-never land, which gripped him.

Only once, long ago, and then almost as if by mistake, had he been on something to beat it. He had been taken by his father, one of the rare times he was taken anywhere, to a fairground. He had stood captivated by the wooden horses with their gilded reins and scarlet saddles dipping in time to the music as they whirled by.

For a brief moment he was astride one, and he prayed it would last forever, but the moment lasted only the time it took him to whisper the prayer. Then he was standing clutching his father's trousers, watching the others astride the dipping horses.

Another shifting of the bundle and he was at the house where he delivered the clothing his mother had washed in a round tub filled with boiling water, the steam covered her face with a film of sweat. Her voice, when she spoke, was as soft and clinging as the steam enveloping her.

He pushed the gate open and walked around the back watching for the aged lap dog, which at his entry would rush out to wheeze asthmatically around his feet and nip with blunt teeth at his ankles.

A round-faced African girl, her blackness heightened by the white starched uniform she wore, opened the kitchen door to let him in. She cleared the table and he placed the bundle on it.

'I call madam,' she said, the words spaced and highly-pitched as if she had some difficulty in uttering the syllables in English. Her buttocks bounced beneath the tight uniform and the backs of her calves shone with fat.

'Are you sure you've brought everything?' was the greeting he received each time he brought the bundle, and each time she checked every item and as usual nothing was missing. He looked at her and lowered his voice as he said; 'Everything there, merrum.'

What followed had become a routine between the three of them.

'Have you had anything to eat?' she asked him.

He shook his head.

'Well, we can't let you go off like that.' Turning to the African woman in the white, starched uniform. 'What have we got?'

The maid swung open the refrigerator door and took out a place of food. She placed it on the table and set a glass of milk next to it.

The white woman left the kitchen when he was seated and he was alone with the maid.

His nervousness left him and he could concentrate on what was on the plate.

A handful of peas, a dab of mashed potatoes, a tomato sliced into bleeding circles, a sprinkling of grated carrot, and no rice.

White people are funny, he told himself. How can anyone fill himself with this? It doesn't form a lump like the food my mama makes.

He washed it down with milk.

'Thank you, Annie,' he said as he pushed the glass aside.

Her teeth gleamed porcelain white as she smiled.

He sat fidgeting, impatient to be outside away from the kitchen with its glossy, tiled floor and steel cupboards ducoued[1] a clinical white to match the food-stacked refrigerator.

'I see you've finished.' The voice startled him. She held out an envelope containing the rand note – payment for his mother's weekly struggle over the wash tub. 'This is for you.' A five cent piece was dropped into his hand, a long fingernail raking his palm.

'Thank you, merrum.' His voice hardly audible.

'Tell your mother I'm going away on holiday for about a month and I'll let her know when I'm back.'

Then he was dismissed and her high heels tapped out of the kitchen.

He nodded his head at the African maid who took an apple from a bowl bursting with fruit and handed it to him.

He grinned his thanks and her responding smile bathed her face in light.

He walked down the path finishing the apple with big bites.

[1] painted

The dog was after him before he reached the gate, its hot breath warming his heels. He turned and poked his toes on its face. It barked hoarsely in protest, a look of outrage on its face.

He laughed delightedly at the expression which changed the dog's features into those of an old man.

'See you do that again.' He waved his feet in front of the pug's nose. The nose retreated and made an about-turn, waddling away with its dignity deflated by his affront.

As he walked, he mentally spent his money.

I'll buy a penny drops, the sour ones that taste like limes, a penny bull's eyes, a packet of sherbet with the licorice tube at the end of the packet, and a penny star toffees, red ones that turn your spit into blood.

His glands were titillated and his mouth filled with saliva. He stopped at the first shop and walked in.

Trays were filled with expensive chocolates and sweets of a type never seen in the jars on the shelves of the Indian shop on the corner where he stayed. He walked out not buying a thing.

His footsteps lagged as he reached the park.

The nurse girls with their babies and prams were gone, their places occupied by old men, who, with their hands holding up their stomachs, were casting disapproving eyes over the confusion and clatter confronting them.

A ball was kicked perilously close to an old man, and the boy who ran after it stopped short as the old man raised his stick, daring him to come closer.

The rest of them called to the boy to get the ball. He edged closer and made a grab at it as the old man swung his cane. The cane missed the boy by more than a foot and he swaggered back, the ball held under his arm. The game was resumed.

He watched them from the other side of the railings – the boys kicking the ball, the children cavorting on the grass, even the old men, senile on the seats; but most of all, the children enjoying themselves with what was denied him, and his whole body yearned to be part of them.

'Shit it!' He looked over his shoulder to see if anyone had heard him. 'Shit it!' he said louder. 'Shit on them! Their park, the grass, the swings, the seesaw, everything! Shit it! Shit it!'

His small hands impotently shook the tall railings towering above his head.

It struck him that he would not be seeing the park for a whole month, that there would be no reason for him to pass it.

Despair filled him. He had to do something to ease his anger.

A bag filled with fruit peelings was on top of the rubbish stacked in a waste basket fitted to a pole. He reached for it and frantically threw it over the railings. He ran without waiting to see the result.

Out of breath three streets further, he slowed down pain stabbing beneath his heart. The act had brought no relief, only intensified the longing.

He was oblivious of the people passing, the hoots of the vehicles whose paths he crossed without thinking. And once, when he was roughly pushed aside, he did not even bother to look and see who had done it.

The familiar shrieks and smells told him that he was home.

The Indian shop could not draw him out of melancholy mood and he walked past it, his five cent piece unspent in his pocket.

A group of boys were playing with tyres on the pavement.

Some of them called him but he ignored them and turned into a short side street.

He mounted the flat step of a two-storey house with a facade that must once have been painted but had now turned a nondescript grey with the red brick underneath showing.

Beyond the threshold the room was dim. He walked past the scattered furniture with a familiarity that did not need guidance.

His mother was in the kitchen hovering over a pot perched on a pressure stove.

He placed the envelope on the table. She put aside the spoon and stuck a finger under the flap of the envelope, tearing it into half. She placed the rand note in a spoutless teapot on the shelf.

'You hungry?'

He nodded his head.

She poured him a cup of soup and added a thick slice of brown bread.

Between bites of bread and sips of soup which scalded his throat, he told his mother that there would not be any washing coming during the week.

'Why?' What the matter? What I do?'

'Nothing. Merrum say she go away for month. She let mama know she back.'

'What I do now?' Her voice took on a whine and her eyes strayed to the teapot containing the money. The whine hardened to reproach as she continued. 'Why don't she let me know she going away then I look for another merrum?' she paused. 'I slave away and the pain never leave my back but it too much for her to let me know she go away. The money I get from her keep us nice and steady. How I go cover the hole?'

He wondered how the rand notes he had brought helped to keep them nicely steady. There was no change in their meals. It was, as usual, not enough, and the only time they received new clothes was at Christmas.

'I must pay the burial, and I was going to tell Mr Lemonsky to bring lino for the front room. I'm sick looking at the lino full of holes but I can forget now. With no money you got as much hope as getting wine on Sunday.'

He hurried his eating to get away from the words wafted towards him, before it could soak into him, trapping him in the chair to witness his mother's miseries.

Outside, they were still playing with their tyres. He joined them half-heartedly. As he rolled the tyre his spirit was still in the park on the swings. There was no barrier to his coming and he could do as he pleased. He was away from the narrow streets and squawking children and speeding cars. He was in a place of green grass and red tubing and silver steel. The tyre rolled past him. He made no effort to grab it.

'Get the tyre.' 'You sleep?' 'Don't you want to play anymore?'

He walked away ignoring their cries.

Rage boiled up inside him. Rage against the house with its streaked walls and smashed panes filled by too many people; against the overflowing garbage pails outside doors; the alleys and streets; and against a law he could not understand – a law that shut him out of the park.

He burst into tears. He swept his arms across his cheeks to check his weeping.

He lowered his hands to peer at the boy confronting him.

'I think you cry!'

'Who say I cry? Something in my eye and I rub it.'

He pushed past and continued towards the shop; 'Cry baby!' the boy's taunt rang after him.

The shop's sole iron-barred window was crowded. Oranges were mixed with writing paper and dried figs were strewn on school slates. Clothing and crockery gathered dust. Across the window a cockroach made its leisurely way, antennae on the alert.

Inside the shop was as crowded as the window. Bags covered the floor leaving a narrow path to the counter.

The shopkeeper, an ancient Indian with a face tanned like cracked leather leaned across the counter. 'Yes, boy?' He showed teeth scarlet with betel. 'Come'n, boy. What you want? No stand here all day.' His jaws worked at the betel nut held captive by his stained teeth.

He ordered penny portions of his selection.

He transferred the sweets to his pockets and threw the torn containers on the floor and walked out. Behind him the Indian murmured grimly, jaws working faster.

One side of the street was in shadow. He sat with his back against the wall, savouring the last of the sun.

Bull's eye, peppermint, a piece of licorice – all lumped together in his cheek. For a moment the park was forgotten.

He watched without interest the girl advancing.

'Mama say you must come'n eat.' She stared at his bulging cheek. One hand rubbing the side of her nose. 'Gimme.' He gave her a bull's eye which she dropped into her mouth between dabs at her nose.

'Wipe your snot!' he ordered her, showing his superiority. He walked past. She followed sucking and sniffing.

Their father was already seated at the table when they entered the kitchen.

'Must I always send somebody after you?' his mother asked.

He slipped into his seat and then hurriedly got up to wash his hands before his mother could find fault with yet another point.

Supper was a silent affair except for the scraping of spoon across a plate and an occasional sniff from his sister.

A thought came into his mind almost at the end of the meal. He sat spoon poised in the air shaken by its magnitude. Why not go to the park after dark? After it had closed its gates on the old men, the children, and nurses with their prams! There would be no one to stop him.

He could think no further. He was lightheaded with the thought of it. His mother's voice, as she related her day to his father, was not the steam that stung, but a soft breeze wafting past him, leaving him undisturbed. Then qualms troubled him. He had never been in that part of town at night. A band of fear tightened across his chest, contracting his insides, making it hard for him to swallow his food. He gripped his spoon tightly, stretching his skin across his knuckles.

I'll do it! I'll go to the park as soon as we're finished eating. He controlled himself with difficulty. He swallowed what was left on his place and furtively watched to see how the others were faring. Hurry up! Hurry up!

He hastily cleared the table when his father pushed the last plate aside and began washing up.

Each piece of crockery washed was passed to his sister whose sniffing kept pace with their combined operation.

The dishes done, he swept the kitchen and carried out the garbage bin.

'Can I go play, mama?'

'Don't let me have to send for you again.'

His father remained silent buried behind the newspaper.

'Before you go,' his mother stopped him – 'light the lamp and hang it in the passage.'

He filled the lamp with paraffin, turned up the wick and lit it. The light glimmered weakly through the streaked glass.

The moon, to him, was a fluorescent ball; light without warmth – and the stars, fragments chipped off it. Beneath street lights card games were in session. He sniffed the nostril-prickling smell of dagga as he walked past. Dim doorways could not conceal couples clutching each other.

Once clear of the district, he broke into a trot. He did not slacken his pace as he passed through the down-town area with its wonderland shop windows. His elation seeped out as he neared the park and his foot-steps dragged.

In front of him was the park with its gate and iron railings. Behind the railings, impaled, the notice board, he could see the swings beyond. The sight strength-ened him.

He walked over, his breath coming faster. There was no one in sight. A car turned a corner and came towards him and he started at the sound of its engine. The car swept past, the tyres softly licking the asphalt.

The railings were icy-cold to his touch and the shock

sent him into action. He extended his arms and with monkey-like movements pulled himself up to perch on top of the railings then dropped onto the newly-turned earth.

The grass was damp with dew and he swept his feet across it. Then he ran and the wet grass bowed beneath his bare feet.

He ran towards the swings, the merry-go-round, seesaw to chute, hands covering the metal.

Up the steps to the top of the chute. He stood outlined against the sky. He was a bird, an eagle. He flung himself down on his stomach, sliding swiftly. Wheeeeeee! He rolled over when he slammed onto the grass. He looked at the moon for an instant then propelled himself to his feet and ran for the steps of the chute to recapture that feeling of flight. Each time he swept down the chute, he wanted the trip never to end, to go on sliding, sliding, sliding.

He walked reluctantly past the seesaw, consoling himself with pushing at one end to send it whacking on the grass.

'Shit it!' he grunted as he strained to set the merry-go-round into action. Thigh tensed, leg stretched, he pushed. The merry-go-round moved. He increased his exertions and jumped on, one leg trailing at the ready to shove if it should slow down. The merry-go-round dipped and swayed. To keep it moving, he had to push more than he rode. Not wanting to spoil his pleasure, he jumped off and raced for the swings.

Feet astride, hands clutching silver chains, he jerked his body to gain momentum. He crouched like a runner then violently straightened. The swing widened its arc. It swept higher, higher, higher. It reached the sky. He could touch the moon. He plucked a star to pin to his breast. The earth was far below. No bird could fly as high as he. Upwards and onwards he went.

A light switched on in the hut at the far side of the park. It was a small patch of yellow on a dark square. The door opened and he saw a figure in the doorway. Then the door was shut and the figure strode towards him. He knew it was the attendant. A torch glinted brightly as it swung at his side.

He continued swinging.

The attendant came to a halt in front of him, out of reach of the swing's arc, and flashed his torch. The light caught him in mid-air.

God dammit!' the attendant swore. 'I told you before you can't get on the swings.'

The rattle of the chains when the boy shifted his feet was the only answer he received.

'Why you come back?'

'The swings, I come back for the swings.'

The attendant catalogued the things denied them because of their colour. Even his job depended on their goodwill.

'Blerry whites! They get everything!'

All his feelings urged him to leave the boy alone, to let him continue to enjoy himself but the fear that someone might see them hardened him.

'Get off! Go home!' he screamed, his voice harsh, his anger directed at the system that drove him against his own. 'If you don't get off, I go for the police. You know what they do to you.'

The swing raced back and forth.

The attendant turned and hurried towards the gate.

'Mama, Mama.' His lips trembled, wishing himself safe in his mother's kitchen, sitting next to the still-burning stove with a comic spread across his knees. 'Mama, Mama.' His voice mounted, wrenched from his throat, keeping pace with the soaring swing as it climbed the sky. Voice and swing. Swing and voice. Higher. Higher. Higher. Until they were one.

At the entrance of the park the notice board stood tall, its shadow elongated, pointing towards him.

When . . .

When will I stop hearing Violins
and hear only Drums,
When will I stop seeing Grey
and see only Colours,
When will I stop hearing Scratches
and hear only Music,
When will I stop being two
and be only one,
When will I stop feeling half
and start feeling whole,
When will I stop saying tomorrow
and start saying NOW
When will I stop trying
and start doing,
When will I stop crying
and start laughing,
When will I stop humming
and start singing,
When will I stop thinking
and start loving.
When will I be free, when, when?

Mustapha Matura

Touch

When I get out
I'm going to ask someone
   to touch me
   very gently please
   and slowly
   touch me
   I want
   to learn again
   how life feels.

I've not been touched
for seven years
   for seven years
   I've been untouched
   out of touch
   and I've learnt
   to know now
   the meaning of
   untouchable.

Untouched – not quite
I can count the things
that have touched me

One: fists
At the beginning
   fierce mad fists
beating, beating
   till I remember
   screaming
   don't touch me
   please don't touch me.

Two: paws
The first four years of paws
   every day
   patting paws, searching
   – arms up, shoes off
   legs apart –
   prodding paws, systematic
   heavy, indifferent
   probing away
   all privacy.

I don't want fists and paws
I want
   to want to be touched
   again
   and to touch.
   I want to feel alive
   again
   I want to say
   when I get out
Here I am
please touch me.

Hugh Lewin

Dube's First Day

RALPH GOLDSWAIN

Dube lay under the bed, still holding his breath, even though the noise had stopped a long time ago. He didn't know how long, but it was all silent now. He couldn't make himself move and was afraid of what he would see when he did. So he lay there, his eyes screwed tightly shut, every muscle in his body rigid.

Where was Tombi? The last thing she'd said was, 'Under the bed Dube! Quick!' He'd thought she was going to follow him but she hadn't. Nor had she spoken again. Thousands of bullets had come through the window and then there'd been soldiers in the room, but no sign of Tombi. He was afraid to think about it.

And Wilson? He hadn't come home last night. They'd waited and waited and then gone to bed. He had said he was coming.

Dube tried to relax his muscles; to breathe, deeply at first, then more regularly, until he was lying quite calmly, looking up at the bed springs although he couldn't see them in the dark.

He remembered just such an early morning in Soweto when he'd got up to go to the meeting. Wilson Gampu was a prefect at school so when he'd come and asked, Dube had been flattered.

'Come Dube,' he'd said, 'We need you.'

Only those chosen by Wilson were at the meeting and Dube was proud to be there because everybody respected Wilson. Even the teachers were careful when they spoke to him.

'This is nineteen eighty-five,' began Wilson, 'the year of the Cadre. It is a turning point.'

As Dube sat listening, his mind was more on Wilson's clothes than on what he was saying. Wilson always dressed smartly and was wearing a navy blue blazer with its prefect's badge, and clean neat grey trousers. The younger boys hero-worshipped him but Dube was, of course, too old for that. He was sixteen – only two years younger than Wilson. But he admired Wilson and envied his smooth confident manner.

Afterwards, when Wilson asked Dube to join the Umkonto we Sizwe he took his arm and spoke intensely.

'Listen Dube,' he said. 'I know that you are one of us. How would you like to be a freedom fighter?'

Just like that! He was one of the chosen!

'Yes,' he said. 'I want it. 'There was something about Wilson that made him want it.

All around him, particularly during the last year, people seemed to be interested only in politics. His mother discouraged political discussions in the house and begged him not to go to any meetings. He had tried to please her but since the riots all gatherings seemed to turn into political meetings.

'You will have to leave school,' said Wilson. His hand was still on Dube's arm.

Dube thought about it. He wasn't doing very well at school anyway. Since they'd burnt the school down last year they'd been having lessons in the beer hall; all the classes crammed together. Their books had been burnt and some of the teachers had left. School seemed a waste of time.

'You will have to leave your mother,' said Wilson.

'But I will see her again?' He looked up at Wilson's

serious face.

'In a new South Africa,' said Wilson. 'Only in a new South Africa.'

'My mother . . .' began Dube, but Wilson interrupted him.

'She will be proud or you. Like she was proud of your father.'

Dube wasn't so sure about that any more. Now that he was almost grown up she was worried about him. She didn't want him to end up like his father.

'You stay out of politics,' she always said. 'You get your matrick and get a good job. You're a clever boy. You can get your matrick. They need educated boys in Jo'burg. There are good jobs for educated boys.'

'She will be proud of me,' said Dube, looking into Wilson's eyes. Then he looked down again, puzzled, confused. 'But what . . .?'

'You have to fight for your country.'

Wilson spoke sharply, confidently. It was the voice of authority. Dube knew he was right. He knew that was what he had to do. If Wilson said so it was true.

'I will do it,' he said.

'Your father would be happy if he could see you,' said Wilson.

Dube had never known his father – he had died just three months before Dube was born. But he couldn't go anywhere without people telling him stories about the famous Jackson Sela. He was one of the most famous men in South Africa. He'd died in custody and there'd been a big courtcase. His mother had always spoken bitterly about the way the man who'd murdered her husband had turned and grinned at her as they'd left the court.

Dube had been born six days later and the one thing

his mother had always said was that she wasn't going to have them take her son as well. So all the day, sitting in the beer hall, instead of listening to the teachers, he thought about how he was going to tell her.

When the time came he spoke plainly. It was just after her favourite programme and she was still laughing.

'I'm going to Botswana,' he said.

She didn't reply. She just threw herself onto the floor and began to wail like a funeral mourner.

'Mama,' he began, and tried to approach her as she lay prostrate on the new carpet she'd saved for two years to buy.

But she just wailed more loudly so he went and sat out in the front, looking at the children playing on the hard red clay street, until the golden clouds turned to an inky blue and the chilly darkness closed in, then he went back. His mother was sitting on the floor, her legs crossed.

'You are your father,' she said, and wouldn't talk about it any more.

It was in nineteen sixty-eight, in the great decade of resistance, that they had taken his father. Then soon after, his family had been visited in the middle of the night and told to collect his body. He had hanged himself in a police cell, they said.

'Never!' his Uncle Harrison had said when Dube had first spoken to him about it a few years ago. 'Your father would never hang himself. They murdered him.'

That was enough for Dube. His mother had always said so too. He had asked Uncle Harrison when a boy at school had taunted him. 'Your father was a coward,' the boy had said, 'He hanged himself.'

But Jackson Sela was a hero and everybody knew about his bravery. Others had been found hanged in their cells in the same month and everybody knew that they hadn't killed themselves either.

The man who'd murdered his father was called de Lange and in his family that was a very bad word. As he grew up the name de Lange came to mean the same as the Devil. In his imagination he used to think of de Lange standing at the courthouse door grinning diabolically, swishing his sharp tail and pointing his horns at him. Then one day he saw a book with pictures of his father's body – a book all about his father and other heroes of the sixties – and there was a picture of de Lange. He remembered being surprised to see that de Lange looked like any other Afrikaner.

His father's reputation brought Dube right into politics in spite of his mother. Phrases like 'your father would be happy,' 'you must do it for your father,' 'your father was a great man,' followed him everywhere he went.

But he was sad about his mother. He wanted to talk to her about it but she knew it would be no good. He knew her well. She was proud of her husband but she was afraid of losing her son too. She had worked hard for the party and that's how she had met Jackson but his death had frightened her. She would never talk politics and he knew that trying to explain to her would do no good. He would just have to go.

So he went.

It was hard to go. Wilson had told him to take nothing and to wear only dark clothes. It was hard to leave his things behind. His mother watched him. Her eyes were dry and all she said was, 'You are your father.' He tried to embrace her but she just stood there making no response.

And then he left. He had to meet Wilson and the others five kilometres out of Soweto on the Krugersdorp road in a big barn piled all round with hay bales. As he walked in the moonlight he wondered why he'd never been out there before. He'd never been in the country. Except the road to Jo'burg. He'd been to Jo'burg about five or six times.

Three other boys were walking along the road too, but Wilson had told him not to talk to anybody, so he looked down and ignored them. They ignored him too – and each other.

He found the barn, looked for a gap in the hay bales and went in. There were lots of others and he recognised some of them. There were also many he didn't know and he was surprised to see that there were some girls too.

Tombi was there. It had not occurred to him that she could be involved – she was so pretty – and looked as though she would be more interested in being an actress or a model. He had liked her for a long time although he had only spoken to her once.

She smiled when she saw him.

'Dube!' she whispered. 'I knew you were coming.'

'How did you know?' He hadn't even thought she'd noticed him at school.

'Wilson told me.'

It occurred to Dube that she must be a trusted member because Wilson had stressed the need for secrecy.

Wilson was standing in the middle of the barn shining a tiny pocket torch onto a list clipped to the board he was holding, and ticking the names off. There was a strange man with him. Dube couldn't make out his features but he could see that the man was big and bearded. He wore a uniform and his trousers were gathered round at the bottom, beneath puttees. It was almost too exciting for Dube. It was like being in a film.

'I'll see you later,' Tombi whispered and brushed his hand with her fingers. It sent a tingle through him. He watched her go up to the bearded man and touch his shoulder. The man turned to look at her. They were no more than shadows in the moonlight filtering through the gaps in the roof.

Ten minutes had passed since his arrival and it seemed that they were all there now because Wilson suddenly looked up from the clipboard and nodded to the bearded man. Tombi was still standing beside him. Wilson pointed to each one in turn, counting, and Dube counted with him. There were eighteen.

Wilson came towards the door and stood there. All eyes were on him.

'Alright, my brothers and sisters,' he said. 'Follow me. And don't talk.'

He stepped out and they followed him round the side to where, parked in a cave of bales, was a truck. The bearded man got into the driver's seat while Wilson opened the flap at the back. They started to get in. Tombi was beside him again and they sat down together. Wilson closed the flap and they heard the passenger door slam with a tinny sound. The truck started up, vibrating violently, and moved forward, knocking some bales over.

'It is a long journey, my brother,' said Tombi.

'It is Botswana,' he said. 'Only two hundred kilometres.'

She laughed. 'But we are not going directly. We have to go through Bophuthatswana. And not on the main roads.'

He was suddenly annoyed with himself. He felt stupid. Of course they wouldn't be able to go on the big roads.

'If we get caught,' she said, 'they will kill us.'

Dube hadn't thought about getting killed and for the first time he felt the seriousness of it. But he still couldn't think about it.

'Who is that man?' he said.

'That is my father.'

A great relief came over him and he felt like laughing for joy. He couldn't help it and he did laugh.

'Why are you laughing?' she said.

'Because that man is your father.'

She was silent. He was very aware of her presence in the dark beside him. He wanted to take her hand but didn't dare.

'Is he coming with us?' he said at last.

'Who?'

'Your father.'

'He has come to fetch us. He is an Umkonto captain.'

'What will we do in Botswana?' he said.

'They will take us to Gaberone. Then we'll be sent to army camps for training.'

'The girls too?'

She shrugged. 'I don't know. My father says maybe.'

They were leaving the tarred road now and Dube could smell the dust which came through into the vehicle. They were bouncing and it was uncomfortable.

'When we get to Bophuthatswana they will help us,' Tombi said. 'But it's a long way and you should sleep.'

He didn't feel like sleeping – he was too excited, both by the adventure and by the beautiful girl beside him.

She put her head on his shoulder and closed her eyes. He sat, not daring to move for fear of disturbing her. Her body was relaxed and moved naturally with the truck's bouncing. He remained stiff and his back began to hurt. He wanted to shift his position but sat as still as he could.

The others were talking softly. They spoke of the chance they were getting to stand up to their enemy and to liberate their people. Dube was filled more with feelings about this girl leaning against him than about his country. She was breathing softly and he could smell her hair. He closed his eyes and took a deep breath.

The night dragged on and it seemed that they would never get anywhere. Sometimes they came up off the corrugated dirt roads onto tar. Then it would be like heaven, but it never lasted for long. Most of the time they were either grinding over the corrugations or groaning slowly along rutted tracks. And always the dust.

He hadn't thought it would happen but he fell asleep and woke up in the blue light of morning when the truck stopped. The blessed silence jerked him out of his uneasy sleep. Tombi sat up too.

It was very quiet. The two doors of the cab slammed and they heard Wilson and Tombi's father padding away. Then a dog barked.

'We are there, my sister,' said Dube.

'No, no.' she shook her head. 'Bophuthatswana, I think.'

Then the flap opened and Tombi's father stood there smiling. He leant forward and put his head in. Everybody was awake now.

'We are going over the border soon,' he said. 'But

first we will have some breakfast. Come.'

They got up slowly. Dube was stiff, sore and his leg went numb as he stood up. He limped painfully to the back and jumped down onto the yellow earth. Tombi followed, landing gracefully, like a ballet dancer.

They followed her father to a corrugated iron building. The sun was coming up; huge, red, washing the thorn trees with pink. It was very cold.

There was a long trestle table inside the building with thick slices of white bread and jam and mugs of steaming tea. Wilson was spreading jam on the bread.

When they had each taken some food and drink Tombi's father spoke.

'My brothers and sisters,' he said, 'When I look around I see the children of brave parents, children of South Africa, strong and brave. You will not be sorry that you have chosen this path.'

Dube felt proud to be there – to be addressed by this man, Tombi's father.

'We are going into Botswana in a short while,' he continued. 'And once there you will have left your country. But you are only leaving so that you may return in glory to claim for your people that which is theirs.'

The young people cheered. Everybody was happy. Dube looked at Tombi. How proud she must be of her father.

'Now, my brothers and sisters,' he said. 'When we get there we will be going to different houses in the city where you will prepare for your journey into the desert – for it is there – far out of the reach of the Afrikaner – that you are going.'

There were more cheers and the young people put their bread and tea on the floor so that they could clap.

When they had all eaten enough they were taken back to the truck and he helped Tombi up. She left her hand in his for longer than she needed to and he again felt that tingle. Her hand was soft and slightly sweaty.

And then they drove fast for two hours on a straight desert road, then swerved back into the thorny, shrubby veld and finally entered the outskirts of Gaberone with its scattered buildings and dry vacant lots.

Dube and Wilson and Tombi were put in a room with three others. There were six beds in a row, all made up with the same grey blankets. Wilson was now one of them – just another trainee freedom fighter – but Dube knew he would soon be a leader. He knew that Wilson was going to be a great leader.

There were only the six of them in this house. The rest were taken to houses in other parts of the city.

'That's to evade attacks by the Afrikaners,' said Wilson. 'It's very difficult. Gaberone is only fifteen kilometres from the South African border.'

'How long will we stay here?' Dube asked him. They were all exhausted but too excited to sleep.

'Two days,' said Wilson. 'Something like that.'
'So long?'

'There is much to do,' said Wilson. 'This is a proper army. In six months you will be a fully trained guerilla.'

It seemed like a century ago that they were sitting in the beer hall listening to the teacher.

'I wonder what our teachers will think has happened to us,' said Dube.

Tombi laughed. 'They know,' she said. 'What do you think happened to Mr Mkize? He is also an Umkonto officer.'

They finally slept. Dube woke up as the sun was going down. He was cold, and he needed to relieve himself.

In the evening after the meal – dry porridge and oxtail stew – the officers started processing them. They were called in one at a time and the officers filled in forms. Then they went to a doctor where they were examined. The doctor looked at their teeth, their eyes and Dube even had his penis squeezed.

'You are very healthy,' the doctor told him.

While they were waiting their turn they talked. They spoke about the freedom they would bring to their people, about the life they would lead as freedom fighters, and about the future of South Africa as a new African country. Dube knew that he'd done the right thing.

Then they talked about weapons – guns and hand-grenades – and the conversation turned into a babble of excitement as each one shouted his knowledge of weapons. The two girls sat listening. Dube glanced at Tombi. He could see that weapons did not interest her so much. But he couldn't help himself. It was as though this was what he'd been born for.

The next day they were given games to play. They were placed in situations – with problems which they had to solve together. Wilson always took the lead and Tombi usually seemed to find the answers just when they thought they were completely stuck. It was good fun.

In the evening Wilson went off with somebody in a jeep. The others talked a bit – more subdued than on the previous evening – they knew they were leaving for the desert camp the next day – then went to bed. It looked like Wilson wasn't going to return.

Tombi came to him when the others were asleep.

'I am here,' she said simply and slid into bed beside him.

It was as though something he had dreamt about was real. They lay for a long time, close against each other. He kissed her on her cheeks and forehead and felt a deep stirring within himself. They fell asleep in each others' arms.

When the attack came the sky was as bright as day and Afrikaner voices came, metallic, through loudspeakers.

'Stay in your house and you won't get hurt,' they said. 'Do not come out into the street.'

Then there was a noise like the end of the world and Dube knew they were shooting bullets into the room.

'Quickly. Under the bed,' Tombi said, and he rolled down and under the bed and waited for her but she didn't come.

The noise went on for a long time, then stopped. Two Afrikaner soldiers came into the room. He saw their boots, then they left. He heard vehicles starting up and driving off. Then silence.

And now the sharp morning sunlight was in the room. He could see a piece of the wall where that sharpness was blindingly reflected. He edged himself slowly out from under the bed. He couldn't believe what he saw. There was no roof and hardly any walls. The floor and all the beds were piled with rubble. He stood up and looked quickly at his own bed. Tombi lay there, as though asleep, but the blanket which covered her was stiff with dried blood.

He turned blindly away, unable to look at her, and then he remembered Wilson. Thank God he hadn't come home.

He stepped over some bricks and made his way to Wilson's bed on the other side of the room. Thank God, thank God, he kept repeating, mumbling the words with numb lips.

But then he saw that there was somebody on the bed, buried beneath large beams and sections of the roof. He pushed some of it aside to look at the face. It was Wilson. He must have come in after they'd gone to sleep.

Dube looked desperately at the other beds. Everything was twisted and broken – swimming – even more distorted through his tears. But he could see that they were all occupied.

All dead.

There were sounds coming from the street now. Police and soldiers shouted to each other and then Tombi's father was standing in front of him.

'Tombi,' he said and Dube's eyes moved in the direction of the bed.

Tombi's father went over and stood looking at his daughter for a while. Then he turned back to Dube.

'They have attacked all the houses,' he said, 'and others. Innocent people too.'

'How many of us are left?' said Dube.

'You are the third.' He turned back to where his daughter lay silent and unmoving on the narrow bed.

'Are we still going today?' said Dube.

Tombi's father unbowed his head slowly and regarded him. Then he nodded.

'We will go, my brother,' he said.

Dube remembered the deep stirring he had felt when Tombi lay in his arms and realised, as he looked at the bearded guerilla leader before him, that the stirring was there again, but stronger, different, and growing into something overpowering.

He searched the sad but unwavering eyes of the captain.

'I am ready, Father,' he said.

The Park by *James Matthews*

Thinking points

1 Where and when does this story take place?
2 Apart from the boy, who are the other main characters and what race does each belong to?
3 How does each of them react to apartheid?
4 Why is it so important to the boy to play in the park?
5 Look at the way the park attendant behaves at the beginning of the story and at the end of the story. Bearing in mind that, like the boy, he is black, why do you think he behaves like that?
6 The white woman and the boy's mother react in very different ways to the importance of stopping the laundry for a month. How and why?
7 At the end of the story why doesn't the boy just get off the swing and go home?
8 Look at the last two paragraphs. What do you think they add to the meaning of the story?

The story as a whole

The problem of apartheid affects all aspects of the lives of blacks, coloureds and Indians in South Africa. Many people have died in the conflict between white and black. This story seems to be about a very unimportant thing: whether a black boy is allowed to play in a park reserved for white children. Why do you think James Matthews chose to focus on this very small aspect of apartheid? Was he successful? What are your reasons?

Writing: Literature

Look at the ways in which the system of apartheid affects every aspect of the lives of the black African characters in this story. Then use this as the basis for a piece of writing about the story as a whole.

When . . . by Mustapha Matura

Thinking points

1 This poem consists of a series of definitions of freedom each of which starts with the words 'When will I . . .' Look at each one carefully. Ask yourself:
   a) Do I understand?
   b) Do I agree?
   c) Do I disagree?
   d) Am I undecided?
2 Can you think of other definitions of freedom that you would add to this list?
3 Choose one of Mustapha Matura's definitions and explain in full what you think it means.

Writing: English

Use this poem as a pattern and write your own poem about freedom or some other subject that is important to you that uses the pattern:

When will I stop . . . . . . and . . . .

Touch by Hugh Lewin

Thinking points

1 Where has he been for seven years?
2 The word touch is used in many different ways in

the poem. Why has he been 'out of touch' for seven years? Why has he been 'untouchable'?

3 What does he mean by 'untouched – not quite'?
4 Why does he talk about 'paws' Is this a good word to use and if so why?
5 So why does he want 'to be touched' now?

The poem as a whole

Has this poem brought home to you the experience which the writer is trying to describe? If it has, are there any particular parts of the poem which have done this?

Writing: Literature

Write about the poem: your thoughts and feelings while you read it and immediately afterwards; and how it made you feel about imprisonment.

Dube's First Day by *Ralph Goldswain*

Thinking points

1 Why did Dube agree to leave school and join the freedom fighters when Wilson asked him?
2 Why was he worried about what his mother would think?
3 How did she feel about his leaving home?
4 Why didn't they go straight to Botswana?
5 Why was Dube one of the few volunteers to survive?
6 At the end of the story why does he call Tombi's father 'Father': what is the significance of this?
7 What reasons can you find for the story's title: *Dube's First Day?*

Writing: Literature

Use your responses to the thinking points as the basis for a piece of writing about the story as a whole. You could write about any or all of these points:

a) the way in which everything in the story is seen through the eyes of a young boy.

b) the way in which the writer gives information about the background of the story.

c) how the writer conveys his own sympathy for Dube and people like him.

Writing about both stories

In this unit there are two stories about young people growing up in South Africa. In each case the story is seen through the eyes of a young person. Use this fact as the basis for a comparison between the two stories.

Themes and variations

FTP   Feed the Plants
SU   Stations Underground
FO   Frogs and Oranges
(s)   story
(p)   poem

Other themes in this book

Childhood

The Park (s)
The Fight (p)
This theme is also represented in other books in this series:
The Lion (s) – FTP
The Choosing (p) – FTP
Tich Miller (p) – FTP
The Dare (p) – SU
Fear of the Dark (p) – SU
Arctic Blues (s) – SU
Who (p) – FO

School

For Heidi with Blue Hair (p)
Skegness, or Bust! (s)
The Fight (p)
Priscilla and the Wimps (s)
This theme is also represented in other books in this series:
Tich Miller (p) – FTP
After English Class (p) – FO

Adolescence

For Heidi with Blue Hair (p)
Dube's First Day (s)
When . . . (p)
This theme is also represented in other books in this series:
The Moustache (s) – FTP
The Seduction (p) – FTP
Guess What? I Almost Kissed My Father Goodnight (s) – SU

Loneliness

Snow Horse (s)
Hireling (p)
This theme is also represented in other books in this series:
Andrina (s) – FTP

Place

The Fight (p)
This theme is also represented in other books in this series:
Granny in de Market Place (p) – FTP
Clearing (p) – FTP
The Seduction (p) – FTP
The Tower (s) – FO
Stopping by Woods on a Snowy Evening (p) – FO
Great Grandfather's Bridge (p) – SU

Humour

Priscilla and the Wimps (s)
Stereotype (p)

This theme is also represented in other books in this series:

Granny in de Market Place (p) – FTP
The Telephone Call (p) – FTP
Feed The Plants (p) – FTP
You Will Be Hearing from Us Shortly (p) – FTP
Engineers' Corner (p) – FO

Animals

Snow Horse (s)
The Tramp (s)
This theme is also represented in other books in this series:

Parrot (p) – FTP
The Star Beast (s) – FTP
The Lion (s) – FTP
The Fish (p) – FTP
A Small Death (s) – SU
A White Birthday (s) – SU
Kittens (p) – SU
The Early Purges (p) – SU

Past/memories

Angel Hill (p)
This theme is also represented in other books in this series:

Clearing (p) – FTP
Stupid (s) – FTP
The Drawer (p) – FTP
The Choosing (p) – FTP
Tich Miller (p) – FTP
Stopping by Woods on a Snowy Evening (p) – FO
Who? (p) – FO

Stations Underground: Fanfare (p) – SU
Great Grandfather's Bridge (p) – SU
Welcome (s) – SU
In Memory of My Grandfather (p) – SU

Individuality/character

The Cleaner (p)
The Tramp (s)
When . . . (p)
Touch (p)
Stereotype (p)
This theme is also represented in other books in this series:
Clearing (p) – FTP
Tich Miller (p) – FTP
Note for the Future (p) – FTP
Parrot (p) – FTP
Let Me Die a Youngman's Death (p) – FTP
The Choosing (p) – FTP
Stations Underground: Fanfare (p) – SU
Great Grandfather's Bridge (p) – SU
You Liberate Me (p) – PW

Voices

Stereotype (p)
The Cleaner (p)
You Liberate Me (p)
This theme is also represented in other books in this series:
The Telephone Call (p) – FTP
You Will Be Hearing from Us Shortly (p) – FTP
The Cleaner (p) – FTP
Granny in de Market Place (p) – FTP

Love

You Liberate Me (p)
This theme is also represented in other books in this series:
Anancy's Thoughts on Love (p) – FTP
Andrina (s) – FTP
The Seduction (p) – FTP

Parrot by Alan Brownjohn
The Telephone Call by Fleur Adcock
You Will Be Hearing from Us Shortly by U A Fanthorpe

Stations Underground

Family feelings

Guess What? I Almost Kissed My Father Goodnight by
   Robert Cormier
Welcome by Ouida Sebestyen
Stations Underground: Fanfare by U A Fanthorpe
In Memory of My Grandfather by Edward Storey
Great Grandfather's Bridge by Kaleem Omar

Only animals . . .

A Small Death by Henry Livings
The Early Purges by Seamus Heaney
Kittens by Maki Kureishi
A White Birthday by Gwyn Jones

Dare you?

The Dare by Judith Nicholls
Fear of the Dark by Vernon Scannell
Arctic Blues by Caroline Scott

You can't beat the system . . .

In the Hereafter Hilton by Bob Shaw
In a Ship Called Darkness 3 by Christopher Leach

Telling of a tragedy

The Ballad of Charlotte Dymond by Charles Causley
Death of an Aircraft by Charles Causley

Frogs and Oranges

Hauntings

Crossing Over by Catherine Storr
Miller's End by Charles Causley
Who? by Charles Causley
The Tower by Aidan Chambers

Writing

Stopping by Woods on a Snowy Evening by Robert Frost
After English Class by Jean Little
Frogs and Oranges by Heather Massie
Engineers' Corner by Wendy Cope
The Great Automatic Grammatizator by Roald Dahl

Please look after this universe

A Piece of Wood by Ray Bradbury
Harvest Hymn by John Betjeman
Who Can Replace a Man? by Brian Aldiss
Professor Tuholsky's Facts by Christopher Logue
Protected Species by H B Fyte
Mushrooms by Mike Evans

Acknowledgements

We are grateful to the following for permission to reproduce copyright material:

Authors' Agents for poem 'Stereotype' by John Agard from *Mangos and Bullets* (Pluto Press); Authors' Agents for poem 'Angel Hill' by Charles Causley from *Collected Poems* (Macmillan 1975); Chatto & Windus Ltd for poem 'When . . .' by Mustapha Matura from *News from Babylon* edited by James Berry; Delacorte Press, A Division of Bantam Doubleday Dell Pubg Group Inc for the title story 'Priscilla and the Wimps' by Richard Peck from *SIXTEEN Short Stories by Outstanding Writers for Young Adults* edited by Donald R Gallo. Copyright © 1984 by Richard Peck; the Author; Georgia Garrett & Thames Television Plc for her poem 'Manwatching' from *I See a Voice* edited by Michael Rosen. Copyright © Georgia Garrett 1981; Authors' Agents for story 'Dube's First Day' by Ralph Goldswain from *Winters Tales 2* edited by R Baird-Smith (Constable); Victor Gollancz Ltd for story Snow Horse' by Joan Aiken from *A Goose on Your Grave* © Joan Aiken 1987; Grafton Books for poem 'Hireling' by R S Thomas from *Selected Poems 1946–1968*; Heinemann Educational Books Ltd for poem 'Touch' by Hugh Lewin from *Poets to the People: South African Freedom Poems* edited by Barry Feinberg and story 'The Hands of the Blacks' by Louis Bernardo Honwana from *We Killed Mangy Dog*; Michael Joseph Ltd for story 'The Tramp' by Sid Chaplin from *Dandelion Clocks* (1968) edited by A Bradley & K Jamieson. Lion Publishing Plc for poem 'You Liberate Me' by Ulrich Schaffer from *Love Reaches Out*; the Author, James Matthews for his story 'The Park' from *The Park and Other Stories* (BLAC). © James Matthews; Oxford University Press for poem 'For Heidi with Blue Hair' by Fleur Adcock from *The Incident Book* (1986); Penguin Books Ltd for story 'Skegness, or Bust!' by Susan Gregory from *Kill-A-Louse Week* (Kestral Books 1986). Copyright © Susan Gregory 1986; Peterloo Poets for poem 'The Cleaner' by U A Fanthorpe from *Voices Off*, Peterloo Poets 1984, reprinted in *Selected Poems*, Peterloo Poets, 1986; the Author, Fred Sedgwick for his poem 'The Fight'.

We have unfortunately been unable to trace the copyright holder of the poem 'Woman is' by Robin Morgan, and would appreciate any information which would enable us to do so.

Longman Group UK Limited
Longman House, Burnt Mill, Harlow, Essex, CM20 2JE,
England and Associated Companies throughout the World.

First published 1990
ISBN 0 582 03929 0

Set in 10/12.5pt Palatino (Linotron 202)
Produced by Longman Singapore Publishers (Pte) Ltd,
Printed in Singapore.

PENGUIN BOOKS

A Confederacy of Dunces

John Kennedy Toole was born in New Orleans in 1937 and died in 1969. He received a master's degree in English from Columbia University and taught at Hunter College and at the University of Southwestern Louisiana. He wrote *A Confederacy of Dunces* in the early sixties and tried unsuccessfully to get his novel published; depressed by his failure to do so he committed suicide. It is only through the tenacity of his mother, whose faith in her son's work never wavered, that his book has found its deserved audience. Penguin also publish his long suppressed novel *The Neon Bible* written when John Kennedy Toole was only sixteen.

A Confederacy of Dunces won the 1981 Pulitzer Prize for Fiction.

When a true genius appears in the world,
you may know him by this sign, that the dunces
are all in confederacy against him.

Jonathan Swift –
"THOUGHTS ON VARIOUS SUBJECTS,
MORAL AND DIVERTING"

JOHN KENNEDY TOOLE

A Confederacy of Dunces

Foreword by Walker Percy

PENGUIN BOOKS

PENGUIN BOOKS

Published by the Penguin Group
Penguin Books Ltd, 80 Strand, London WC2R ORL, England
Penguin Group (USA) Inc., 375 Hudson Street, New York, New York 10014, USA
Penguin Group (Canada), 90 Eglinton Avenue East, Suite 700,
Toronto, Ontario, Canada M4P 2Y3 (a division of Pearson Penguin Canada Inc.)
Penguin Ireland, 25 St Stephen's Green, Dublin 2, Ireland
(a division of Penguin Books Ltd)
Penguin Group (Australia), 250 Camberwell Road, Camberwell, Victoria 3124,
Australia (a division of Pearson Australia Group Pty Ltd)
Penguin Books India Pvt Ltd, 11 Community Centre,
Panchsheel Park, New Delhi – 110 017, India
Penguin Group (NZ), cnr Airborne and Rosedale Roads, Albany,
Auckland 1310, New Zealand (a division of Pearson New Zealand Ltd)
Penguin Books (South Africa) (Pty) Ltd, 24 Sturdee Avenue,
Rosebank, Johannesburg 2196, South Africa

Penguin Books Ltd, Registered Offices: 80 Strand, London WC2R ORL, England

www.penguin.com

First published in the USA by Louisiana State University Press 1980
Published in Great Britain simultaneously by Allen Lane and Penguin Books 1981
Reprinted in Penguin Classics 2000
Published as a Penguin Red Classic 2006

1

Excerpts from *A Confederacy of Dunces*
appeared in *New Orleans Review*, V (1978)

Set in MT Dante
Typeset by Palimpsest Book Production Limited, Polmont, Stirlingshire
Printed in England by Clays Ltd, St Ives plc

ISBN 13: 978-0-14102-346-5
ISBN 10: 0-14102-346-5

Foreword

Perhaps the best way to introduce this novel—which on my third reading of it astounds me even more than the first—is to tell of my first encounter with it. While I was teaching at Loyola in 1976 I began to get telephone calls from a lady unknown to me. What she proposed was preposterous. It was not that she had written a couple of chapters of a novel and wanted to get into my class. It was that her son, who was dead, had written an entire novel during the early sixties, a big novel, and she wanted me to read it. Why would I want to do that? I asked her. Because it is a great novel, she said.

Over the years I have become very good at getting out of things I don't want to do. And if ever there was something I didn't want to do, this was surely it: to deal with the mother of a dead novelist and, worst of all, to have to read a manuscript that she said was *great*, and that, as it turned out, was a badly smeared, scarcely readable carbon.

But the lady was persistent, and it somehow came to pass that she stood in my office handing me the hefty manuscript. There was no getting out of it; only one hope remained—that I could read a few pages and that they would be bad enough for me, in good conscience, to read no farther. Usually I can do just that. Indeed the first paragraph often suffices. My only fear was that this one might not be bad enough, or might be just good enough, so that I would have to keep reading.

In this case I read on. And on. First with the sinking feeling that it was not bad enough to quit, then with a prickle of interest, then a growing excitement, and finally an incredulity:

surely it was not possible that it was so good. I shall resist the temptation to say what first made me gape, grin, laugh out loud, shake my head in wonderment. Better let the reader make the discovery on his own.

Here at any rate is Ignatius Reilly, without progenitor in any literature I know of—slob extraordinary, a mad Oliver Hardy, a fat Don Quixote, a perverse Thomas Aquinas rolled into one—who is in violent revolt against the entire modern age, lying in his flannel nightshirt, in a back bedroom on Constantinople Street in New Orleans, who between gigantic seizures of flatulence and eructations is filling dozens of Big Chief tablets with invective.

His mother thinks he needs to go to work. He does, in a succession of jobs. Each job rapidly escalates into a lunatic adventure, a full-blown disaster; yet each has, like Don Quixote's, its own eerie logic.

His girlfriend, Myrna Minkoff of the Bronx, thinks he needs sex. What happens between Myrna and Ignatius is like no other boy-meets-girl story in my experience.

By no means a lesser virtue of Toole's novel is his rendering of the particularities of New Orleans, its back streets, its out-of-the-way neighborhoods, its odd speech, its ethnic whites—and one black in whom Toole has achieved the near-impossible, a superb comic character of immense wit and resourcefulness without the least trace of Rastus minstrelsy.

But Toole's greatest achievement is Ignatius Reilly himself, intellectual, ideologue, deadbeat, goof-off, glutton, who should repel the reader with his gargantuan bloats, his thunderous contempt and one-man war against everybody— Freud, homosexuals, heterosexuals, Protestants, and the assorted excesses of modern times. Imagine an Aquinas gone to pot, transported to New Orleans from whence he makes a wild foray through the swamps to LSU at Baton Rouge, where his lumber jacket is stolen in the faculty men's room where he is seated, overcome by mammoth gastro-intestinal problems. His pyloric valve periodically closes in response to the lack of a "proper geometry and theology" in the modern world.

I hesitate to use the word *comedy*—though comedy it is—because that implies simply a funny book, and this novel is a great deal more than that. A great rumbling farce of Falstaffian dimensions would better describe it; *commedia* would be closer to it.

It is also sad. One never quite knows where the sadness comes from—from the tragedy at the heart of Ignatius's great gaseous rages and lunatic adventures or the tragedy attending the book itself.

The tragedy of the book is the tragedy of the author—his suicide in 1969 at the age of thirty-two. Another tragedy is the body of work we have been denied.

It is a great pity that John Kennedy Toole is not alive and well and writing. But he is not, and there is nothing we can do about it but make sure that this gargantuan tumultuous human tragicomedy is at least made available to a world of readers.

Walker Percy

There is a New Orleans city accent . . . associated with downtown New Orleans, particularly with the German and Irish Third Ward, that is hard to distinguish from the accent of Hoboken, Jersey City, and Astoria, Long Island, where the Al Smith inflection, extinct in Manhattan, has taken refuge. The reason, as you might expect, is that the same stocks that brought the accent to Manhattan imposed it on New Orleans.

"You're right on that. We're Mediterranean. I've never been to Greece or Italy, but I'm sure I'd be at home there as soon as I landed."

He would, too, I thought. New Orleans resembles Genoa or Marseilles, or Beirut or the Egyptian Alexandria more than it does New York, although all seaports resemble one another more than they can resemble any place in the interior. Like Havana and Port-au-Prince, New Orleans is within the orbit of a Hellenistic world that never touched the North Atlantic. The Mediterranean, Caribbean and Gulf of Mexico form a homogeneous, though interrupted, sea.

A. J. Liebling,
THE EARL OF LOUISIANA

A Confederacy of Dunces

One

A green hunting cap squeezed the top of the fleshy balloon of a head. The green earflaps, full of large ears and uncut hair and the fine bristles that grew in the ears themselves, stuck out on either side like turn signals indicating two directions at once. Full, pursed lips protruded beneath the bushy black moustache and, at their corners, sank into little folds filled with disapproval and potato chip crumbs. In the shadow under the green visor of the cap Ignatius J. Reilly's supercilious blue and yellow eyes looked down upon the other people waiting under the clock at the D. H. Holmes department store, studying the crowd of people for signs of bad taste in dress. Several of the outfits, Ignatius noticed, were new enough and expensive enough to be properly considered offenses against taste and decency. Possession of anything new or expensive only reflected a person's lack of theology and geometry; it could even cast doubts upon one's soul.

Ignatius himself was dressed comfortably and sensibly. The hunting cap prevented head colds. The voluminous tweed trousers were durable and permitted unusually free loco-motion. Their pleats and nooks contained pockets of warm, stale air that soothed Ignatius. The plaid flannel shirt made a jacket unnecessary while the muffler guarded exposed Reilly skin between earflap and collar. The outfit was acceptable by any theological and geometrical standards, however abstruse, and suggested a rich inner life.

Shifting from one hip to the other in his lumbering, elephantine fashion, Ignatius sent waves of flesh rippling beneath the tweed and flannel, waves that broke upon buttons and seams. Thus rearranged, he contemplated the long while that he had been waiting for his mother. Principally he considered the discomfort he was beginning to feel. It seemed as if his whole being was ready to burst from his swollen suede desert boots, and, as if to verify this, Ignatius turned his singular eyes toward his feet. The feet did indeed look swollen. He was prepared to offer the sight of those bulging boots to his mother as evidence of her thoughtlessness. Looking up, he saw the sun beginning to descend over the Mississippi at the foot of Canal Street. The Holmes clock said almost five. Already he was polishing a few carefully worded accusations designed to reduce his mother to repentance or, at least, confusion. He often had to keep her in her place.

She had driven him downtown in the old Plymouth, and while she was at the doctor's seeing about her arthritis, Ignatius had bought some sheet music at Werlein's for his trumpet and a new string for his lute. Then he had wandered into the Penny Arcade on Royal Street to see whether any new games had been installed. He had been disappointed to find the miniature mechanical baseball game gone. Perhaps it was only being repaired. The last time that he had played it the batter would not work and, after some argument, the management had returned his nickel, even though the Penny Arcade people had been base enough to suggest that Ignatius had himself broken the baseball machine by kicking it.

Concentrating upon the fate of the miniature baseball machine, Ignatius detached his being from the physical reality of Canal Street and the people around him and therefore did not notice the two eyes that were hungrily watching him from behind one of D. H. Holmes' pillars, two sad eyes shining with hope and desire.

Was it possible to repair the machine in New Orleans? Probably so. However, it might have to be sent to some place

2

like Milwaukee or Chicago or some other city whose name Ignatius associated with efficient repair shops and permanently smoking factories. Ignatius hoped that the baseball game was being carefully handled in shipment, that none of its little players was being chipped or maimed by brutal railroad employees determined to ruin the railroad forever with damage claims from shippers, railroad employees who would subsequently go on strike and destroy the Illinois Central.

As Ignatius was considering the delight which the little baseball game afforded humanity, the two sad and covetous eyes moved toward him through the crowd like torpedoes zeroing in on a great woolly tanker. The policeman plucked at Ignatius' bag of sheet music.

"You got any identification, mister?" the policeman asked in a voice that hoped that Ignatius was officially unidentified.

"What?" Ignatius looked down upon the badge on the blue cap. "Who are you?"

"Let me see your driver's license."

"I don't drive. Will you kindly go away? I am waiting for my mother."

"What's this hanging out your bag?"

"What do you think it is, stupid? It's a string for my lute."

"What's that?" The policeman drew back a little. "Are you local?"

"Is it the part of the police department to harass me when this city is a flagrant vice capital of the civilized world?" Ignatius bellowed over the crowd in front of the store. "This city is famous for its gamblers, prostitutes, exhibitionists, anti-Christs, alcoholics, sodomites, drug addicts, fetishists, onanists, pornographers, frauds, jades, litterbugs, and lesbians, all of whom are only too well protected by graft. If you have a moment, I shall endeavor to discuss the crime problem with you, but don't make the mistake of bothering *me*."

The policeman grabbed Ignatius by the arm and was struck

on his cap with the sheet music. The dangling lute string whipped him on the ear.

"Hey," the policeman said.

"Take that!" Ignatius cried, noticing that a circle of interested shoppers was beginning to form.

Inside D. H. Holmes, Mrs. Reilly was in the bakery department pressing her maternal breast against a glass case of macaroons. With one of her fingers, chafed from many years of scrubbing her son's mammoth, yellowed drawers, she tapped on the glass case to attract the saleslady.

"Oh, Miss Inez," Mrs. Reilly called in that accent that occurs south of New Jersey only in New Orleans, that Hoboken near the Gulf of Mexico. "Over here, babe."

"Hey, how you making?" Miss Inez asked. "How you feeling, darling?"

"Not so hot," Mrs. Reilly answered truthfully.

"Ain't that a shame." Miss Inez leaned over the glass case and forgot about her cakes. "I don't feel so hot myself. It's my feet."

"Lord, I wisht I was that lucky. I got arthuritis in my elbow."

"Aw, no!" Miss Inez said with genuine sympathy. "My poor old poppa's got that. We make him go set himself in a hot tub fulla berling water."

"My boy's floating around in our tub all day long. I can't hardly get in my own bathroom no more."

"I thought he was married, precious."

"Ignatius? Eh, la la," Mrs. Reilly said sadly. "Sweetheart, you wanna gimme two dozen of them fancy mix?"

"But I thought you told me he was married," Miss Inez said while she was putting the cakes in a box.

"He ain't even got him a prospect. The little girl friend he had flew the coop."

"Well, he's got time."

"I guess so," Mrs. Reilly said disinterestedly. "Look, you

4

wanna gimme half a dozen wine cakes, too? Ignatius gets nasty if we run outta cake."

"Your boy likes his cake, huh?"

"Oh, Lord, my elbow's killing me," Mrs. Reilly answered.

In the center of the crowd that had formed before the department store the hunting cap, the green radius of the circle of people, was bobbing about violently.

"I shall contact the mayor," Ignatius was shouting.

"Let the boy alone," a voice said from the crowd.

"Go get the strippers on Bourbon Street," an old man added. "He's a good boy. He's waiting for his momma."

"Thank you," Ignatius said haughtily. "I hope that all of you will bear witness to this outrage."

"You come with me," the policeman said to Ignatius with waning self-confidence. The crowd was turning into something of a mob, and there was no traffic patrolman in sight. "We're going to the precinct."

"A good boy can't even wait for his momma by D. H. Holmes." It was the old man again. "I'm telling you, the city was never like this. It's the communiss."

"Are you calling me a communiss?" the policeman asked the old man while he tried to avoid the lashing of the lute string. "I'll take you in, too. You better watch out who you calling a communiss."

"You can't arress me," the old man cried. "I'm a member of the Golden Age Club sponsored by the New Orleans Recreation Department."

"Let that old man alone, you dirty cop," a woman screamed. "He's prolly somebody's grampaw."

"I am," the old man said. "I got six granchirren all studying with the sisters. Smart, too."

Over the heads of the people Ignatius saw his mother walking slowly out of the lobby of the department store carrying the bakery products as if they were boxes of cement.

"Mother!" he called. "Not a moment too soon. I've been seized."

Pushing through the people, Mrs. Reilly said, "Ignatius! What's going on here? What you done now? Hey, take your hands off my boy."

"I'm not touching him, lady," the policeman said. "Is this here your son?"

Mrs. Reilly snatched the whizzing lute string from Ignatius.

"Of course I'm her child," Ignatius said. "Can't you see her affection for me?"

"She loves her boy," the old man said.

"What you trying to do my poor child?" Mrs. Reilly asked the policeman. Ignatius patted his mother's hennaed hair with one of his huge paws. "You got plenty business picking on poor chirren with all the kind of people they got running in this town. Waiting for his momma and they try to arrest him."

"This is clearly a case for the Civil Liberties Union," Ignatius observed, squeezing his mother's drooping shoulder with the paw. "We must contact Myrna Minkoff, my lost love. She knows about those things."

"It's the communiss," the old man interrupted.

"How old is he?" the policeman asked Mrs. Reilly.

"I am thirty," Ignatius said condescendingly.

"You got a job?"

"Ignatius hasta help me at home," Mrs. Reilly said. Her initial courage was failing a little, and she began to twist the lute string with the cord on the cake boxes. "I got terrible arthuritis."

"I dust a bit," Ignatius told the policeman. "In addition, I am at the moment writing a lengthy indictment against our century. When my brain begins to reel from my literary labors, I make an occasional cheese dip."

"Ignatius makes delicious cheese dips," Mrs. Reilly said.

"That's very nice of him," the old man said. "Most boys are out running around all the time."

"Why don't you shut up?" the policeman said to the old man.

"Ignatius," Mrs. Reilly asked in a trembling voice, "what you done, boy?"

"Actually, Mother, I believe that it was he who started everything." Ignatius pointed to the old man with his bag of sheet music. "I was simply standing about, waiting for you, praying that the news from the doctor would be encouraging."

"Get that old man outta here," Mrs. Reilly said to the policeman. "He's making trouble. It's a shame they got people like him walking the streets."

"The police are all communiss," the old man said.

"Didn't I say for you to shut up?" the policeman said angrily.

"I fall on my knees every night to thank my God we got protection," Mrs. Reilly told the crowd. "We'd all be dead without the police. We'd all be laying in our beds with our throats cut open from ear to ear."

"That's the truth, girl," some woman answered from the crowd.

"Say a rosary for the police force." Mrs. Reilly was now addressing her remarks to the crowd. Ignatius caressed her shoulder wildly, whispering encouragement. "Would you say a rosary for a communiss?"

"No!" several voices answered fervently. Someone pushed the old man.

"It's true, lady," the old man cried. "He tried to arrest your boy. Just like in Russia. They're all communiss."

"Come on," the policeman said to the old man. He grabbed him roughly by the back of the coat.

"Oh, my God!" Ignatius said, watching the wan little policeman try to control the old man. "Now my nerves are totally frayed."

"Help!" the old man appealed to the crowd. "It's a takeover. It's a violation of the Constitution!"

7

"He's crazy, Ignatius," Mrs. Reilly said. "We better get outta here, baby." She turned to the crowd. "Run, folks. He might kill us all. Personally, I think maybe *he's* the communiss."

"You don't have to overdo it, Mother," Ignatius said as they pushed through the dispersing crowd and started walking rapidly down Canal Street. He looked back and saw the old man and the bantam policeman grappling beneath the department store clock. "Will you please slow down a bit? I think I'm having a heart murmur."

"Oh, shut up. How you think I feel? I shouldn't haveta be running like this at my age."

"The heart is important at any age, I'm afraid."

"They's nothing wrong with your heart."

"There will be if we don't go a little slower." The tweed trousers billowed around Ignatius' gargantuan rump as he rolled forward. "Do you have my lute string?"

Mrs. Reilly pulled him around the corner onto Bourbon Street, and they started walking down into the French Quarter.

"How come that policeman was after you, boy?"

"I shall never know. But he will probably be coming after us in a few moments, as soon as he has subdued that aged fascist."

"You think so?" Mrs. Reilly asked nervously.

"I would imagine so. He seemed determined to arrest me. He must have some sort of quota or something. I seriously doubt that he will permit me to elude him so easily."

"Wouldn't that be awful! You'd be all over the papers, Ignatius. The disgrace! You musta done something while you was waiting for me, Ignatius. I know you, boy."

"If anyone was ever minding his business, it was I," Ignatius breathed. "Please. We must stop. I think I'm going to have a hemorrhage."

"Okay." Mrs. Reilly looked at her son's reddening face and realized that he would very happily collapse at her feet just to prove his point. He had done it before. The last time that

8

she had forced him to accompany her to mass on Sunday he had collapsed twice on the way to the church and had collapsed once again during the sermon about sloth, reeling out of the pew and creating an embarrassing disturbance. "Let's go in here and sit down."

She pushed him through the door of the Night of Joy bar with one of the cake boxes. In the darkness that smelled of bourbon and cigarette butts they climbed onto two stools. While Mrs. Reilly arranged her cake boxes on the bar, Ignatius spread his expansive nostrils and said, "My God, Mother, it smells awful. My stomach is beginning to churn."

"You wanna go back on the street? You want that policeman to take you in?"

Ignatius did not answer; he was sniffing loudly and making faces. A bartender, who had been observing the two, asked quizzically from the shadows, "Yes?"

"I shall have a coffee," Ignatius said grandly. "Chicory coffee with boiled milk."

"Only instant," the bartender said.

"I can't possibly drink that," Ignatius told his mother. "It's an abomination."

"Well, get a beer, Ignatius. It won't kill you."

"I may bloat."

"I'll take a Dixie 45," Mrs. Reilly said to the bartender.

"And the gentleman?" the bartender asked in a rich, assumed voice. "What is his pleasure?"

"Give him a Dixie, too."

"I may not drink it," Ignatius said as the bartender went off to open the beers.

"We can't sit in here for free, Ignatius."

"I don't see why not. We're the only customers. They should be glad to have us."

"They got strippers in here at night, huh?" Mrs. Reilly nudged her son.

9

"I would imagine so," Ignatius said coldly. He looked quite pained. "We might have stopped somewhere else. I suspect that the police will raid this place momentarily anyway." He snorted loudly and cleared his throat. "Thank God my moustache filters out some of the stench. My olfactories are already beginning to send out distress signals."

After what seemed a long time during which there was much tinkling of glass and closing of coolers somewhere in the shadows, the bartender appeared again and set the beers before them, pretending to knock Ignatius' beer into his lap. The Reillys were getting the Night of Joy's worst service, the treatment given unwanted customers.

"You don't by any chance have a cold Dr. Nut, do you?" Ignatius asked.

"No."

"My son loves Dr. Nut," Mrs. Reilly explained. "I gotta buy it by the case. Sometimes he sits himself down and drinks two, three Dr. Nuts at one time."

"I am sure that this man is not particularly interested," Ignatius said.

"Like to take that cap off?" the bartender asked.

"No, I wouldn't!" Ignatius thundered. "There's a chill in here."

"Suit yourself," the bartender said and drifted off into the shadows at the other end of the bar.

"Really!"

"Calm down," his mother said.

Ignatius raised the earflap on the side next to his mother.

"Well, I will lift this so that you won't have to strain your voice. What did the doctor tell you about your elbow or whatever it is?"

"It's gotta be massaged."

"I hope you don't want me to do that. You know how I feel about touching other people."

"He told me to stay out the cold as much as possible."

"If I could drive, I would be able to help you more, I imagine."

"Aw, that's okay, honey."

"Actually, even riding in a car affects me enough. Of course, the worst thing is riding on top in one of those Greyhound Scenicruisers. So high up. Do you remember the time that I went to Baton Rouge in one of those? I vomited several times. The driver had to stop the bus somewhere in the swamps to let me get off and walk around for a while. The other passengers were rather angry. They must have had stomachs of iron to ride in that awful machine. Leaving New Orleans also frightened me considerably. Outside of the city limits the heart of darkness, the true wasteland begins."

"I remember that, Ignatius," Mrs. Reilly said absently, drinking her beer in gulps. "You was really sick when you got back home."

"I felt better *then*. The worst moment was my arrival in Baton Rouge. I realized that I had a round-trip ticket and would have to return on the bus."

"You told me that, babe."

"The taxi back to New Orleans cost me forty dollars, but at least I wasn't violently ill during the taxi ride, although I felt myself beginning to gag several times. I made the driver go very slowly, which was unfortunate for him. The state police stopped him twice for being below the minimum highway speed limit. On the third time that they stopped him they took away his chauffeur's license. You see, they had been watching us on the radar all along."

Mrs. Reilly's attention wavered between her son and the beer. She had been listening to the story for three years.

"Of course," Ignatius continued, mistaking his mother's rapt look for interest, "that was the only time that I had ever been out of New Orleans in my life. I think that perhaps it was the lack of a center of orientation that might have upset me. Speeding along in that bus was like hurtling into the abyss. By the time we had left the swamps and reached those rolling hills near Baton Rouge, I was getting afraid that some rural rednecks might toss bombs at the bus. They love to attack vehicles, which are a symbol of progress, I guess."

"Well, I'm glad you didn't take the job," Mrs. Reilly said automatically, taking *guess* as her cue.

"I couldn't possibly take the job. When I saw the chairman of the Medieval Culture Department, my hands began breaking out in small white bumps. He was a totally soulless man. Then he made a comment about my not wearing a tie and made some smirky remark about the lumber jacket. I was appalled that so meaningless a person would dare such effrontery. That lumber jacket was one of the few creature comforts to which I've ever been really attached, and if I ever find the lunatic who stole it, I shall report him to the proper authorities."

Mrs. Reilly saw again the horrible, coffee-stained lumber jacket that she had always secretly wanted to give to the Volunteers of America along with several other pieces of Ignatius' favorite clothing.

"You see, I was so overwhelmed by the complete grossness of that spurious 'chairman' that I ran from his office in the middle of one of his cretinous ramblings and rushed to the nearest bathroom, which turned out to be the one for 'Faculty Men.' At any rate, I was seated in one of the booths, having rested the lumber jacket on top of the door of the booth. Suddenly I saw the jacket being whisked over the door. I heard footsteps. Then the door of the restroom closed. At the moment, I was unable to pursue the shameless thief, so I began to scream. Someone entered the bathroom and knocked at the door of the booth. It turned out to be a member of the campus security force, or so he said. Through the door I explained what had just happened. He promised to find the jacket and went away. Actually, as I have mentioned to you before, I have always suspected that he and the 'chairman' were the same person. Their voices sounded somewhat similar."

"You sure can't trust nobody nowadays, honey."

"As soon as I could, I fled from the bathroom, eager only to get away from that horrible place. Of course, I was almost frozen standing on that desolate campus trying to hail a taxi. I finally got one that agreed to take me to New Orleans for forty dollars, and the driver was selfless enough to lend me his jacket. By the time we arrived here, however, he was quite depressed about losing his license and had grown rather surly. He also appeared to be developing a bad cold, judging by the frequency of his sneezes. After all, we were on the highway for almost two hours."

"I think I could drink me another beer, Ignatius."

"Mother! In this forsaken place?"

"Just one, baby. Come on, I want another."

"We're probably catching something from these glasses. However, if you're quite determined about the thing, get me a brandy, will you?"

Mrs. Reilly signaled to the bartender, who came out of the shadows and asked, "Now what happened to you on that bus, bud? I didn't get the end of the story."

"Will you kindly tend the bar properly?" Ignatius asked furiously. "It is your duty to silently serve when we call upon you. If we had wished to include you in our conversation, we would have indicated it by now. As a matter of fact, we are discussing rather urgent personal matters."

"The man's just trying to be nice, Ignatius. Shame on you."

"That in itself is a contradiction in terms. No one could possibly be nice in a den like this."

"We want two more beers."

"One beer and one brandy," Ignatius corrected.

"No more clean glasses," the bartender said.

"Ain't that a shame," Mrs. Reilly said. "Well, we can use the ones we got."

The bartender shrugged and went off into the shadows.

II

In the precinct the old man sat on a bench with the others, mostly shoplifters, who composed the late afternoon haul. He had neatly arranged along his thigh his Social Security card, his membership card in the St. Odo of Cluny Holy Name Society, a Golden Age Club badge, and a slip of paper identifying him as a member of the American Legion. A young black man, eyeless behind spaceage sunglasses, studied the little dossier on the thigh next to his.

"Whoa!" he said, grinning. "Say, you mus belong to everthin."

The old man rearranged his cards meticulously and said nothing.

"How come they draggin in somebody like you?" The sunglasses blew smoke all over the old man's cards. "Them po-lice mus be gettin desperate."

"I'm here in violation of my constitutional rights," the old man said with sudden anger.

"Well, they not gonna believe that. You better think up somethin else." A dark hand reached for one of the cards. "Hey, wha this mean, 'Colder Age'?"

The old man snatched the card and put it back on his thigh.

"Them little card not gonna do you no good. They throw you in jail anyway. They throw everbody in jail."

"You think so?" the old man asked the cloud of smoke.

"Sure." A new cloud floated up. "How come you here, man?"

"I don't know."

"You don know? Whoa! That crazy. You gotta be here for somethin. Plenty time they pickin up color peoples for nothin, but, mister, you gotta be here for somethin."

"I really don't know," the old man said glumly. "I was just standing in a crowd in front of D. H. Holmes."

"And you lif somebody wallet."

"No, I called a policeman a name."

"Like wha you callin him?"

"'Communiss.'"

"Cawmniss! Ooo-woo. If I call a po-lice a cawmniss, my ass be in Angola right now for sure. I like to call one of them mother a cawmniss, though. Like this afternoon I standin aroun in Woolsworth and some cat steal a bag of cashew nuts out the 'Nut House' star screamin like she been stab. Hey! The nex thing, a flo'walk grabbin me, and then a police mother draggin me off. A man ain got a chance. Whoa!" His lips sucked at the cigarette. "Nobody findin them cashews on me, but that po-lice still draggin me off. I think that flo'walk a cawmniss. Mean motherfucker."

The old man cleared his throat and played with his cards.

"They probly let you go," the sunglasses said. "Me, they probly gimma a little talk think it scare me, even though they know I ain got them cashews. They probly try to prove I got them nuts. They probly buy a bag, slip it in my pocket. Woolsworth probly try to send me up for life."

The Negro seemed quite resigned and blew out a new cloud of blue smoke that enveloped him and the old man and the little cards. Then he said to himself, "I wonder who lif them nuts. Probly that flo'walk hisself."

A policeman summoned the old man up to the desk in the center of the room where a sergeant was seated. The patrolman who had arrested him was standing there.

"What's your name?" the sergeant asked the old man.

"Claude Robichaux," he answered and put his little cards on the desk before the sergeant.

The sergeant looked over the cards and said, "Patrolman Mancuso here says you resisted arrest and called him a communiss."

"I didn't mean it," the old man said sadly, noticing how fiercely the sergeant was handling the little cards.

"Mancuso says you says all policemen are communiss."

"Oo-wee," the Negro said across the room.

"Will you shut up, Jones?" the sergeant called out.

"Okay," Jones answered.

"I'll get to you next."

"Say, I didn call nobody no cawmniss," Jones said. "I been frame by that flo'walk in Woolsworth. I don even like cashews."

"Shut your mouth up."

"Okay," Jones said brightly and blew a great thundercloud of smoke.

"I didn't mean anything I said," Mr. Robichaux told the sergeant. "I just got nervous. I got carried away. This policeman was trying to arress a poor boy waiting for his momma by Holmes."

"What?" the sergeant turned to the wan little policeman. "What were you trying to do?"

"He wasn't a boy," Mancuso said. "He was a big fat man dressed funny. He looked like a suspicious character. I was just trying to make a routine check and he started to resist. To tell you the truth, he looked like a big prevert."

"A pervert, huh?" the sergeant asked greedily.

"Yes," Mancuso said with new confidence. "A great big prevert."

"How big?"

"The biggest I ever saw in my whole life," Mancuso said, stretching his arms as if he were describing a fishing catch.

The sergeant's eyes shone. "The first thing I spotted was this green hunting cap he was wearing."

Jones listened in attentive detachment somewhere within his cloud.

"Well, what happened, Mancuso? How come he's not standing here before me?"

"He got away. This woman came out the store and got everything mixed up, and she and him run around the corner into the Quarter."

"Oh, two Quarter characters," the sergeant said, suddenly enlightened.

"No, sir," the old man interrupted. "She was really his momma. A nice, pretty lady. I seen them downtown before. This policeman frightened her."

"Oh, listen, Mancuso," the sergeant screamed. "You're the only guy on the force who'd try to arrest somebody away from his mother. And why did you bring in grampaw here? Ring up his family and tell them to come get him."

"Please," Mr. Robichaux pleaded. "Don't do that. My daughter's busy with her kids. I never been arrested in my whole life. She can't come get me. What are my granchirren gonna think? They're all studying with the sisters."

"Get his daughter's number, Mancuso. That'll teach him to call us communiss!"

"Please!" Mr. Robichaux was in tears. "My granchirren respect me."

"Jesus Christ!" the sergeant said. "Trying to arrest a kid with his momma, bringing in somebody's grampaw. Get the hell outta here, Mancuso, and take grampaw with you. You wanna arrest suspicious characters? We'll fix you up."

"Yes, sir," Mancuso said weakly, leading the weeping old man away.

"Ooo-wee!" Jones said from the secrecy of his cloud.

III

Twilight was settling around the Night of Joy bar. Outside, Bourbon Street was beginning to light up. Neon signs flashed off and on, reflecting in the streets dampened by the light mist that had been falling steadily for some time. The taxis bringing the evening's first customers, midwestern tourists and conventioneers, made slight splashing sounds in the cold dusk.

A few other customers were in the Night of Joy, a man who ran his finger along a racing form, a depressed blonde who seemed connected with the bar in some capacity, and an elegantly dressed young man who chainsmoked Salems and drank frozen daiquiris in gulps.

"Ignatius, we better go," Mrs. Reilly said and belched.

"What?" Ignatius bellowed. "We must stay to watch the corruption. It's already beginning to set in."

The elegant young man spilled his daiquiri on his bottle-green velvet jacket.

"Hey, bartender," Mrs. Reilly called. "Get a rag. One of the customers just spilled they drink."

"That's *quite* all right, darling," the young man said angrily. He arched an eyebrow at Ignatius and his mother. "I think I'm in the wrong bar anyway."

"Don't get upset, honey," Mrs. Reilly counseled. "What's that you drinking? It looks like a pineapple snowball."

"Even if I described it to you, I doubt whether you'd understand what it is."

"How dare you talk to my dear, beloved mother like that!"

"Oh, hush, you big thing," the young man snapped. "Just look at my jacket."

"It's totally grotesque."

"Okay, now. Let's be friends," Mrs. Reilly said through

foamy lips. "We got enough bombs and things already."

"And your son seems to delight in dropping them, I must say."

"Okay, you two. This is the kinda place where everybody oughta have themselves some fun." Mrs. Reilly smiled at the young man. "Let me buy you another drink, babe, for the one you spilled. And I think I'll take me another Dixie."

"I really must run," the young man sighed. "Thanks anyway."

"On a night like this?" Mrs. Reilly asked. "Aw, don't pay no mind to what Ignatius says. Why don't you stay and see the show?"

The young man rolled his eyes heavenward.

"Yeah." The blonde broke her silence. "See some ass and tits."

"Mother," Ignatius said coldly. "I do believe that you are encouraging these preposterous people."

"Well, you're the one wanted to stay, Ignatius."

"Yes, I did want to stay as an observer. I am not especially anxious to mingle."

"Honey, to tell you the truth, I can't listen to that story about that bus no more tonight. You already told it four times since we got here."

Ignatius looked hurt.

"I hardly suspected that I was boring you. After all, that bus ride was one of the more formative experiences of my life. As a mother, you should be interested in the traumas that have created my worldview."

"What's with the bus?" the blonde asked, moving to the stool next to Ignatius. "My name's Darlene. I like good stories. You got a spicy one?"

The bartender slammed the beer and the daiquiri down just as the bus was starting off on its journey in the vortex.

"Here, have a clean glass," the bartender snarled at Mrs. Reilly.

"Ain't that nice. Hey, Ignatius, I just got a clean glass."

But her son was too preoccupied with his arrival in Baton Rouge to hear her.

"You know, sweetheart," Mrs. Reilly said to the young man, "me and my boy was in trouble today. The police tried to arress him."

"Oh, my dear. Policemen are always so adamant, aren't they?"

"Yeah, and Ignatius got him a master's degree and all."

"What in the world was he doing?"

"Nothing. Just standing waiting for his poor, dear momma."

"His outfit is a little bizarre. I thought he was a performer of some sort when I first came in, although I tried not to imagine the nature of his act."

"I keep on telling him about his clothes, but he won't listen." Mrs. Reilly looked at the back of her son's flannel shirt and at the hair curling down the back of his neck. "That's sure pretty, that jacket you got."

"Oh, this?" the young man asked, feeling the velvet on the sleeve. "I don't mind telling you it cost a fortune. I found it in a dear little shop in the Village."

"You don't look like you from the country."

"Oh, my," the young man sighed and lit a Salem with a great click of his lighter. "I meant Greenwich Village in New York, sweetie. By the way, where did you ever get that hat? It's truly fantastic."

"Aw, Lord, I had this since Ignatius made his First Communion."

"Would you consider selling it?"

"How come?"

"I'm a dealer in used clothing. I'll give you ten dollars for it."

"Aw, come on. For this?"

"Fifteen?"

"Really?" Mrs. Reilly removed the hat. "Sure, honey."

The young man opened his wallet and gave Mrs. Reilly three five dollar bills. Draining his daiquiri glass, he stood up and said, "Now I really must run."

"So soon?"

"It's been perfectly delightful meeting you."

"Take care out in the cold and wet."

The young man smiled, placed the hat carefully beneath his trench coat, and left the bar.

"The radar patrol," Ignatius was telling Darlene, "is obviously rather foolproof. It seems that the cab driver and I were making small dots on their screen all the way from Baton Rouge."

"You was on radar," Darlene yawned. "Just think of that."

"Ignatius, we gotta go now," Mrs. Reilly said. "I'm hungry."

She turned toward him and knocked her beer bottle to the floor where it broke into a spray of brown, jagged glass.

"Mother, are you making a scene?" Ignatius asked irritably. "Can't you see that Miss Darlene and I are speaking? You have some cakes with you. Eat those. You're always complaining that you never go anywhere. I would have imagined that you would be enjoying your night on the town."

Ignatius was back on radar, so Mrs. Reilly reached in her boxes and ate a brownie.

"Like one?" she asked the bartender. "They nice. I got some nice wine cakes, too."

The bartender pretended to be looking for something on his shelves.

"I smell wine cakes," Darlene cried, looking past Ignatius.

"Have one, honey," Mrs. Reilly said.

"I think that I shall have one, too," Ignatius said. "I imagine that they taste rather good with brandy."

Mrs. Reilly spread the box out on the bar. Even the man

with the racing form agreed to take a macaroon.

"Where you bought these nice wine cakes, lady?" Darlene asked Mrs. Reilly. "They're nice and juicy."

"Over by Holmes, sugar. They got a good selection. Plenty variety."

"They are rather tasty," Ignatius conceded, sending out his flabby pink tongue over his moustache to hunt for crumbs. "I think that I shall have a macaroon or two. I have always found coconut to be good roughage."

He picked around in the box purposefully.

"Me, I always like some good cake after I finish eating," Mrs. Reilly told the bartender, who turned his back on her.

"I bet you cook good, huh?" Darlene asked.

"Mother doesn't cook," Ignatius said dogmatically. "She burns."

"I use to cook too when I was married," Darlene told them. "I sort of used a lot of that canned stuff, though. I like that Spanish rice they got and that spaghetti with the tomato gravy."

"Canned food is a perversion," Ignatius said. "I suspect that it is ultimately very damaging to the soul."

"Lord, my elbow's starting up again," Mrs. Reilly sighed.

"Please. I am speaking," her son told her. "I never eat canned food. I did once, and I could feel my intestines starting to atrophy."

"You got a good education," Darlene said.

"Ignatius graduated from college. Then he stuck around there for four more years to get him a master's degree. Ignatius graduated smart."

"'Graduated smart,'" Ignatius repeated with some pique. "Please define your terms. Exactly what do you mean by 'graduated smart.'"

"Don't talk to your momma like that," Darlene said.

"Oh, he treats me bad sometimes," Mrs. Reilly said loudly

and began to cry. "You just don't know. When I think of all I done for that boy . . ."

"Mother, what are you saying?"

"You don't appreciate me."

"Stop that right now. I'm afraid that you've had too much beer."

"You treat me like garbage. I been good," Mrs. Reilly sobbed. She turned to Darlene. "I spent all his poor Grammaw Reilly's insurance money to keep him in college for eight years, and since then all he's done is lay around the house watching television."

"You oughta be ashamed," Darlene said to Ignatius. "A big man like you. Look at your poor momma."

Mrs. Reilly had collapsed, sobbing, on the bar, one hand clenched around her beer glass.

"This is ridiculous. Mother, stop that."

"If I knew you was so crool, mister, I wouldna listened to your crazy story about that Greyhound bus."

"Get up, Mother."

"You look like a big crazyman anyway," Darlene said. "I shoulda known. Just look how that poor woman's crying."

Darlene tried to push Ignatius from his stool but sent him crashing into his mother, who suddenly stopped crying and gasped, "My elbow!"

"What's going on here?" a woman asked from the padded chartreuse leatherette door of the bar. She was a statuesque woman nearing middle age, her fine body covered with a black leather overcoat that glistened with mist. "I leave this place for a few hours to go shopping and look what happens. I gotta be here every minute, I guess, to watch out you people don't ruin my investment."

"Just two drunks," the bartender said. "I've been giving them the cold shoulder since they come in, but they've been sticking like flies."

"But you, Darlene," the woman said. "You're big friends with them, huh? Playing games on the stools with these two characters?"

"This guy's been mistreating his momma," Darlene explained.

"Mothers? We got mothers in here now? Business already stinks."

"I beg your pardon," Ignatius said.

The woman ignored him and looked at the broken and empty cake box on the bar, saying, "Somebody's been having a picnic in here. Goddamit. I already told you people about ants and rats."

"I beg your pardon," Ignatius said again. "My mother is present."

"It's just my luck to have this crap broken all over here just when I'm looking for a janitor." The woman looked at the bartender. "Get these two out."

"Yes, Miss Lee."

"Don't you worry," Mrs. Reilly said. "We're leaving."

"We certainly are," Ignatius added, lumbering toward the door, leaving his mother behind to climb off her stool. "Hurry along, Mother. This woman looks like a Nazi commandant. She may strike us."

"Wait!" Miss Lee screamed, grabbing Ignatius' sleeve. "How much these characters owe?"

"Eight dollars," the bartender said.

"This is highway robbery!" Ignatius thundered. "You will hear from our attorneys."

Mrs. Reilly paid with two of the bills the young man had given her and, as she swayed past Miss Lee, she said, "We know when we not wanted. We can take our trade elsewheres."

"Good," Miss Lee answered. "Beat it. Trade from people like you is the kiss of death."

After the padded door had closed behind the Reillys, Miss

Lee said, "I never liked mothers. Not even my own."

"My mother was a whore," the man with the racing form said, not looking up from his paper.

"Mothers are full of shit," Miss Lee observed and took off her leather coat. "Now let's you and me have a little talk, Darlene."

Outside, Mrs. Reilly took her son's arm for support, but, as much as they tried, they moved forward very slowly, although they seemed to move sideward more easily. Their walking had developed a pattern: three quick steps to the left, pause, three quick steps to the right, pause.

"That was a terrible woman," Mrs. Reilly said.

"A negation of all human qualities," Ignatius added. "By the way, how far is the car? I'm very tired."

"On St. Ann, honey. Just a few blocks."

"You left your hat in the bar."

"Oh, I sold it to that young man."

"You sold it? Why? Did you ask me whether I wanted it to be sold ? I was very attached to that hat."

"I'm sorry, Ignatius. I didn't know you liked it so much. You never said nothing about it."

"I had an unspoken attachment to it. It was a contact with my childhood, a link with the past."

"But he gave me fifteen dollars, Ignatius."

"Please. Don't talk about it anymore. The whole business is sacrilegious. Goodness knows what degenerate uses he will find for that hat. Do you have the fifteen dollars on you?"

"I still got seven left."

"Then why don't we stop and eat something?" Ignatius pointed to the cart at the corner. It was shaped like a hot dog on wheels. "I believe that they vend foot-long hot dogs."

"Hot dogs? Honey, in all this rain and cold we gonna stand outside and eat weenies?"

"It's a thought."

"No," Mrs. Reilly said with somewhat beery courage. "Let's get home. I wouldn't eat nothing outta one of them dirty wagons anyway. They all operated by a bunch of bums."

"If you insist," Ignatius said, pouting. "Although I am rather hungry, and you have, after all, just sold a memento of my childhood for thirty pieces of silver, so to speak."

They continued their little pattern of steps along the wet flagstones of Bourbon Street. On St. Ann they found the old Plymouth easily. Its high roof stood above all the other cars, its best feature. The Plymouth was always easy to find in supermarket parking lots. Mrs. Reilly climbed the curb twice trying to force the car out of the parking place and left the impression of a 1946 Plymouth bumper in the hood of the Volkswagon in the rear.

"My nerves!" Ignatius said. He was slumped down in the seat so that just the top of his green hunting cap appeared in the window, looking like the tip of a promising watermelon. From the rear, where he always sat, having read somewhere that the seat next to the driver was the most dangerous, he watched his mother's wild and inexpert shifting with disapproval. "I suspect that you have effectively demolished the small car that someone innocently parked behind this bus. You had better succeed in getting out of this spot before its owner happens along."

"Shut up, Ignatius. You making me nervous," Mrs. Reilly said, looking at the hunting cap in the rear view mirror.

Ignatius got up on the seat and looked out of the rear window.

"That car is a total wreck. Your driver's license, if you do indeed have one, will doubtlessly be revoked. I certainly wouldn't blame them."

"Lay down there and take a nap," his mother said as the car jerked back again.

"Do you think that I could sleep now? I'm afraid for my

26

life. Are you sure that you're turning the wheel the right way?"

Suddenly the car leaped out of the parking spot and skidded across the wet street into a post supporting a wrought-iron balcony. The post fell away to one side, and the Plymouth crunched against the building.

"Oh, my God!" Ignatius screamed from the rear. "What have you done now?"

"Call a priest!"

"I don't think that we're injured, Mother. However, you have just ruined my stomach for the next few days." Ignatius rolled down one of the rear windows and studied the fender that was pressed against the wall. "We shall need a new head-light on this side, I imagine."

"What we gonna do?"

"If I were driving, I would put the auto in reverse and back gracefully away from the scene. Someone will certainly press charges. The people who own this wreck of a building have been waiting for an opportunity like this for years. They probably spread grease on the street after nightfall hoping that motorists like you will spin toward their hovel." He belched. "My digestion has been destroyed. I think that I am beginning to bloat!"

Mrs. Reilly shifted the worn gears and inched slowly backward. As the car moved, the splintering of wood sounded over their heads, a splintering that changed into splitting of boards and scraping of metal. Then the balcony was falling in large sections, thundering on the roof of the car with the dull, heavy thud of grenades. The car, like a stoned human, stopped moving, and a piece of wrought-iron decoration shattered a rear window.

"Honey, are you okay?" Mrs. Reilly asked wildly after what seemed to be the final bombardment.

Ignatius made a gagging sound. The blue and yellow eyes were watering.

27

"Say something, Ignatius," his mother pleaded, turning around just in time to see Ignatius stick his head out of a window and vomit down the side of the dented car.

Patrolman Mancuso was walking slowly down Chartres Street dressed in ballet tights and a yellow sweater, a costume which the sergeant said would enable him to bring in genuine, bona fide suspicious characters instead of grandfathers and boys waiting for their mothers. The costume was the sergeant's punishment. He had told Mancuso that from now on he would be strictly responsible for bringing in suspicious characters, that police headquarters had a costume wardrobe that would permit Mancuso to be a new character every day. Forlornly, Patrolman Mancuso had put on the tights before the sergeant, who had pushed him out of the precinct and told him to shape up or get off the force.

In the two hours that he had been cruising the French Quarter, he had captured no one. Twice things had looked hopeful. He had stopped a man wearing a beret and asked for a cigarette, but the man had threatened to have him arrested. Then he accosted a young man in a trench coast who was wearing a lady's hat, but the young man had slapped him across the face and dashed away.

As Patrolman Mancuso walked down Chartres rubbing his cheek, which still smarted from the slap, he heard what seemed to be an explosion. Hoping that a suspicious character had just thrown a bomb or shot himself, he ran around the corner onto St. Ann and saw the green hunting cap emitting vomit among the ruins.

Two

"With the breakdown of the Medieval system, the gods of Chaos, Lunacy, and Bad Taste gained ascendancy." Ignatius was writing in one of his Big Chief tablets.

After a period in which the western world had enjoyed order, tranquility, unity, and oneness with its True God and Trinity, there appeared winds of change which spelled evil days ahead. An ill wind blows no one good. The luminous years of Abélard, Thomas à Beckett, and Everyman dimmed into dross; Fortuna's wheel had turned on humanity, crushing its collarbone, smashing its skull, twisting its torso, puncturing its pelvis, sorrowing its soul. Having once been so high, humanity fell so low. What had once been dedicated to the soul was now dedicated to the sale.

"That is rather fine," Ignatius said to himself and continued his hurried writing.

Merchants and charlatans gained control of Europe, calling their insidious gospel "The Enlightenment." The day of the locust was at hand, but from the ashes of humanity there arose no Phoenix. The humble and pious peasant, Piers Plowman, went to town to sell his children to the lords of the New Order for purposes that we may call questionable at best. (See Reilly, Ignatius J., *Blood on Their Hands: The Crime of It All, A study of some selected abuses in sixteenth century Europe*, a

Monograph, 2 pages, 1950, Rare Book Room, Left Corridor, Third Floor, Howard-Tilton Memorial Library, Tulane University, New Orleans 18, Louisiana. Note: I mailed this singular monograph to the library as a gift; however, I am not really certain that it was ever accepted. It may well have been thrown out because it was only written in pencil on tablet paper.) The gyro had widened; The Great Chain of Being had snapped like so many paper clips strung together by some drooling idiot; death, destruction, anarchy, progress, ambition, and self-improvement were to be Piers' new fate. And a vicious fate it was to be: now he was faced with the perversion of having to GO TO WORK.

His vision of history temporarily fading, Ignatius sketched a noose at the bottom of the page. Then he drew a revolver and a little box on which he neatly printed GAS CHAMBER. He scratched the side of the pencil back and forth across the paper and labeled this APOCALYPSE. When he had finished decorating the page, he threw the tablet to the floor among many others that were scattered about. This had been a very productive morning, he thought. He had not accomplished so much in weeks. Looking at the dozens of Big Chief tablets that made a rug of Indian headdresses around the bed, Ignatius thought smugly that on their yellowed pages and wide-ruled lines were the seeds of a magnificent study in comparative history. Very disordered, of course. But one day he would assume the task of editing these fragments of his mentality into a jigsaw puzzle of a very grand design; the completed puzzle would show literate men the disaster course that history had been taking for the past four centuries. In the five years that he had dedicated to this work, he had produced an average of only six paragraphs monthly. He could not even remember what he had written in some of the tablets, and he realized that several were filled principally with doodling. However, Ignatius thought calmly, Rome was not built in a day.

Ignatius pulled his flannel nightshirt up and looked at his bloated stomach. He often bloated while lying in bed in the morning contemplating the unfortunate turn that events had taken since the Reformation. Doris Day and Greyhound Scenicruisers, whenever they came to mind, created an even more rapid expansion of his central region. But since the attempted arrest and the accident, he had been bloating for almost no reason at all, his pyloric valve snapping shut indiscriminately and filling his stomach with trapped gas, gas which had character and being and resented its confinement. He wondered whether his pyloric valve might be trying, Cassandralike, to tell him something. As a medievalist Ignatius believed in the *rota Fortunae*, or wheel of fortune, a central concept in *De Consolatione Philosophiae*, the philosophical work which had laid the foundation for medieval thought. Boethius, the late Roman who had written the *Consolatione* while unjustly imprisoned by the emperor, had said that a blind goddess spins us on a wheel, that our luck comes in cycles. Was the ludicrous attempt to arrest him the beginning of a bad cycle? Was his wheel rapidly spinning downward? The accident was also a bad sign. Ignatius was worried. For all his philosophy, Boethius had still been tortured and killed. Then Ignatius' valve closed again, and he rolled over on his left side to press the valve open.

"Oh, Fortuna, blind, heedless goddess, I am strapped to your wheel," Ignatius belched. "Do not crush me beneath your spokes. Raise me on high, divinity."

"What you mumbling about in there, boy?" his mother asked through the closed door.

"I am praying," Ignatius answered angrily.

"Patrolman Mancuso's coming today to see me about the accident. You better say a little Hail Mary for me, honey."

"Oh, my God," Ignatius muttered.

"I think it's wonderful you praying, babe. I been wondering what you do locked up in there all the time."

"Please go away!" Ignatius screamed. "You're shattering my religious ecstasy."

Bouncing up and down on his side vigorously, Ignatius sensed a belch rising in his throat, but when he expectantly opened his mouth he emitted only a small burp. Still, the bouncing had some physiological effect. Ignatius touched the small erection that was pointing downward into the sheet, held it, and lay still trying to decide what to do. In this position, with the red flannel nightshirt around his chest and his massive stomach sagging into the mattress, he thought somewhat sadly that after eighteen years with his hobby it had become merely a mechanical physical act stripped of the flights of fancy and invention that he had once been able to bring to it. At one time he had almost developed it into an art form, practicing the hobby with the skill and fervor of an artist and philosopher, a scholar and gentleman. There were still hidden in his room several accessories which he had once used, a rubber glove, a piece of fabric from a silk umbrella, a jar of Noxema. Putting them away again after it was all over had eventually grown too depressing.

Ignatius manipulated and concentrated. At last a vision appeared, the familiar figure of the large and devoted collie that had been his pet when he was in high school. "Woof!" Ignatius almost heard Rex say once again. "Woof! Woof! Arf!" Rex looked so lifelike. One ear dropped. He panted. The apparition jumped over a fence and chased a stick that somehow landed in the middle of Ignatius' quilt. As the tan and white fur grew closer, Ignatius' eyes dilated, crossed, and closed, and he lay wanly back among his four pillows, hoping that he had some Kleenex in his room.

II

"I come about that porter job you got advertise in the paper."

"Yeah?" Lana Lee looked at the sunglasses. "You got any references?"

"A po-lice gimme a reference. He tell me I better get my ass gainfully employ," Jones said and shot a jet of smoke out into the empty bar.

"Sorry. No police characters. Not in a business like this. I got an investment to watch."

"I ain exactly a character yet, but I can tell they gonna star that vagran no visible mean of support stuff on me. They told me." Jones withdrew into a forming cloud. "I thought maybe the Night of Joy like to help somebody become a member of the community, help keep a poor color boy outta jail. I keep the picket off, give the Night of Joy a good civil right ratin."

"Cut out the crap."

"Hey! Whoa!"

"You got any experience as a porter?"

"Wha? Sweepin and moppin and all that nigger shit?"

"Watch your mouth, boy. I got a clean business."

"Hell, anybody do that, especially color peoples."

"I've been looking," Lana Lee said, becoming a grave personnel manager, "for the right boy for this job for several days." She put her hands in the pockets of her leather overcoat and looked into the sunglasses. This was really a deal, like a present left on her doorstep. A colored guy who would get arrested for vagrancy if he didn't work. She would have a captive porter whom she could work for almost nothing. It was beautiful. Lana felt good for the first time since she had come upon those two characters messing up her bar. "The pay is twenty dollars a week."

"Hey! No wonder the right man ain show up. Ooo-wee. Say, whatever happen to the minimal wage?"

"You need a job, right? I need a porter. Business stinks. Take it from there!"

"The las person workin in here musta starve to death."

"You work six days a week from ten to three. If you come in regular, who knows? You might get a little raise."

"Don worry. I come in regular, anything keep my ass away from a po-lice for a few hour," Jones said, blowing some smoke on Lana Lee. "Where you keep them motherfuckin broom?"

"One thing we gotta understand is keeping our mouth clean around here."

"Yes, *ma'm*. I sure don wanna make a bad impressia in a fine place like the Night of Joy. Whoa!"

The door opened and Darlene came in wearing a satin cocktail dress and a flowered hat, flouncing her skirt gracefully as she walked.

"How come you're so late?" Lana screamed at her. "I told you to be here at one today."

"My cockatoo come down with a cold last night, Lana. It was awful. The whole night he was up coughing right in my ear."

"Where do you think up excuses like that?"

"Well, it's true," Darlene answered in an injured voice. She put her huge hat on the bar and climbed on a stool up into a cloud that Jones had blown. "I hadda take him to the vet's this morning to get a vitamin shot. I don't want that poor bird coughing all over my furniture."

"What got into your head that made you encourage those two characters last night? Every day, every day, Darlene, I try to explain to you the kind of clientele we want in here. Then

34

I walk in and find you eating crap off my bar with some old lady and a fat turd. You trying to close down my business? People look in the door, see a combination like that, they walk off to another bar. What I have to do to make you *understand*, Darlene? How does a human being get through to a mind like yours?"

"I already told you I felt sorry for that poor woman, Lana. You oughta seen how her son treated her. You oughta heard the story he told me about a Greyhound bus. And all the time that sweet old lady sitting there paying for his drinks. I *had* to take one of her cakes to make her feel good."

"Well, the next time I find you encouraging people like that and ruining my investment, I'm gonna kick you out on your behind. Is that clear?"

"Yes, ma'm."

"You sure you got what I said?"

"Yes, ma'm."

"Okay. Now show this boy where we keep our brooms and crap and get that bottle that old lady broke cleaned up. You're in charge of getting this whole goddam place as clean as a pin for what you did me last night. I'm going shopping." Lana got to the door and turned around. "I don't want nobody fooling with that cabinet under the bar."

"I swear," Darlene said to Jones after Lana had swung through the door, "this place is worse than the army. She just hire you today?"

"Yeah," Jones answered. "She ain exactly *hire* me. She kinda buyin me off a auction block."

"At least you gonna get a salary. I only work on commission for how much I get people to drink. You think that's easy? Try to get some guy to buy more than one of the kinda drinks they serve in here. All water. They gotta spend ten, fifteen dollars to get any effect at all. I swear, it's a tough job. Lana even pumps water in the champagne. You oughta taste that. Then she's all the time complaining about how business stinks. She oughta buy a drink at this bar and find out. Even when she's got only about five people drinking in here she's making a fortune. Water don't cost nothing."

"Wha she go shoppin for? A whip?"

"Don't ask me. Lana never tells me nothing. That Lana's a funny one." Darlene blew her nose daintily. "What I really wanna be is an exotic. I been practicing in my apartment on a routine. If I can get Lana to let me dance in here at night, I can get me a regular salary and quit hustling water on commission. Now that I think of it, I oughta get me some commission for what them people drank up in here last night. That old lady sure drank up a lotta beer. I don't see what Lana's got to complain about. Business is business. That fat man and his momma wasn't much worse than plenty we get in here. I think the thing got Lana was that funny green cap he had stuck up on his head. When he was talking, he'd pull the earflap down, and when he was listening, he'd stick it up again. By the time Lana got here, everybody was hollering at him, so he had both flaps stuck out like wings. You know, it looked sorta funny."

"And you say this fat cat travlin around with his momma?" Jones asked, making a mental association.

"Uh huh." Darlene folded her handkerchief and slipped it into her bosom. "I sure hope they don't ever decide to hang around here again. I'll really be in trouble. Jesus." Darlene sounded worried. "Look, we better do something about this place before Lana comes back. But listen. Don't knock yourself out cleaning up this dump. I never seen it really clean since I been here. And it's so dark in here all the time, nobody can tell the difference. To hear Lana talk, you'd think this hole was the Ritz."

Jones shot out a fresh cloud. Through his glasses he could hardly see anything at all.

III

Patrolman Mancuso enjoyed riding the motorcycle up St. Charles Avenue. At the precinct he had borrowed a large and loud one that was all chromium and baby blue, and at the touch of a switch it could become a pinball machine of flashing, winking, blinking red and white lights. The siren, a cacophany of twelve crazed bobcats, was enough to make suspicious characters within a half-mile radius defecate in panic and rush for cover. Patrolman Mancuso's love for the motorcycle was platonically intense.

The forces of evil generated by the hideous—and apparently impossible to uncover—underground of suspicious characters seemed remote to him this afternoon, though. The ancient oaks of St. Charles Avenue arched over the avenue like a canopy shielding him from the mild winter sun that splashed and sparkled on the chrome of the motorcycle. Although the days had lately been cold and damp, the afternoon had that sudden, surprising warmth that makes New Orleans winters gentle. Patrolman Mancuso appreciated the mildness, for he was wearing only a T-shirt and Bermuda shorts, the sergeant's costume selection for the day. The long red beard that hooked over his ears by means of wires did manage to warm his chest a little; he had snatched the beard from the locker while the sergeant wasn't looking.

Patrolman Mancuso inhaled the moldy scent of the oaks and thought, in a romantic aside, that St. Charles Avenue must be the loveliest place in the world. From time to time he passed the slowly rocking streetcars that seemed to be leisurely moving toward no special destination, following their route through the old mansions on either side of the avenue. Everything looked so calm, so prosperous, so unsuspicious. On his own time he was going up to see that poor Widow

Reilly. She had looked so pitiful crying in the middle of that wreck. The least he could do was try to help her.

At Constantinople Street he turned toward the river, sputtering and growling through a declining neighborhood until he reached a block of houses built in the 1880s and 90s, wooden Gothic and Gilded Age relics that dripped carving and scrollwork, Boss Tweed suburban stereotypes separated by alleys so narrow that a yardstick could almost bridge them and fenced in by iron pikes and low walls of crumbling brick. The larger houses had become impromptu apartment buildings, their porches converted into additional rooms. In some of the frontyards there were aluminum carports, and bright aluminum awnings had been installed on one or two of the buildings. It was a neighborhood that had degenerated from Victorian to nothing in particular, a block that had moved into the twentieth century carelessly and uncaringly—and with very limited funds.

The address that Patrolman Mancuso was looking for was the tiniest structure on the block, aside from the carports, a Lilliput of the eighties. A frozen banana tree, brown and stricken, languished against the front of the porch, the tree preparing to collapse as the iron fence had done long ago. Near the dead tree there was a slight mound of earth and a leaning Celtic cross cut from plywood. The 1946 Plymouth was parked in the frontyard, its bumper pressed against the porch, its tail-lights blocking the brick sidewalk. But, except for the Plymouth and the weathered cross and the mummified banana tree, the tiny yard was completely bare. There were no shrubs. There was no grass. And no birds sang.

Patrolman Mancuso looked at the Plymouth and saw the deep crease in its roof and the fender, filled with concave circles, that was separated from the body by three or four inches of space. VAN CAMP'S PORK AND BEANS was printed on the piece of cardboard taped across the hole that had been

38

the rear window. Stopping by the grave, he read REX in faded letters on the cross. Then he climbed the worn brick steps and heard through the closed shutters a booming chant.

> Big girls don't cry.
> Big girls don't cry.
> Big girls, they don't cry-yi-yi.
> They don't cry.
> Big girls, they don't cry . . . yi.

While he was waiting for someone to answer the bell, he read the faded sticker on the crystal of the door, "A slip of the lip can sink a ship." Below a WAVE held her finger to lips that had turned tan.

Along the block some people were out on their porches looking at him and the motorcycle. The shutters across the street that slowly flipped up and down to get the proper focus indicated that he also had a considerable unseen audience, for a police motorcycle in the block was an event, especially if its driver wore shorts and a red beard. The block was poor, certainly, but honest. Suddenly self-conscious, Patrolman Mancuso rang the bell again and assumed what he considered his erect, official posture. He gave his audience his Mediterranean profile, but the audience saw only a small and sallow figure whose shorts hung clumsily in the crotch, whose spindly legs looked too naked in comparison to the formal garters and nylon socks that hung near the ankles. The audience remained curious, but unimpressed; a few were not even especially curious, the few who had expected some such vision to visit that miniature house eventually.

> Big girls don't cry.
> Big girls don't cry.

Patrolman Mancuso knocked savagely at the shutters.

Big girls don't cry.
Big girls don't cry.

"They home," a woman screamed through the shutters of the house next door, an architect's vision of Jay Gould domestic. "Miss Reilly's prolly in the kitchen. Go around the back. What are you, mister? A cop?"

"Patrolman Mancuso. Undercover," he answered sternly.

"Yeah?" There was a moment of silence. "Which one you want, the boy or the mother?"

"The mother."

"Well, that's good. You'd never get a hold of him. He's watching the TV. You hear that? It's driving me nuts. My nerves is shot."

Patrolman Mancuso thanked the woman's voice and walked into the dank alley. In the back yard he found Mrs. Reilly hanging a spotted and yellowed sheet on a line that ran through the bare fig trees.

"Oh, it's you," Mrs. Reilly said after a moment. She had almost started to scream when she saw the man with the red beard appear in her yard. "How you doing, Mr. Mancuso? What them people said?" She stepped cautiously over the broken brick paving in her brown felt moccasins. "Come on in the house and we'll have us a nice cup of coffee."

The kitchen was a large, high-ceilinged room, the largest in the house, and it smelled of coffee and old newspapers. Like every room in the house, it was dark; the greasy wallpaper and brown wooden moldings would have transformed any light into gloom, and from the alley very little light filtered in anyway. Although the interiors of homes did not interest Patrolman Mancuso, still he did notice, as anyone would have, the antique stove with the high oven and the refrigerator with the cylindrical motor on top. Thinking of the electric fryers, gas driers, mechanical mixers and beaters, waffle plates, and motorized rotisseries that seemed to be always whirring, grinding, beating, cooling, hissing, and broiling in the lunar kitchen of his wife, Rita, he wondered what Mrs. Reilly did in this sparse room. Whenever a new appliance was advertised on television, Mrs. Mancuso bought it no matter how obscure its uses were.

"Now tell me what the man said." Mrs. Reilly began boiling a pot of milk on her Edwardian gas stove. "How much I gotta pay? You told him I was a poor widow with a child to support, huh?"

"Yeah, I told him that," Patrolman Mancuso said, sitting erectly in his chair and looking hopefully at the kitchen table covered with oilcloth. "Do you mind if I put my beard on the table? It's kinda hot in here and it's sticking my face."

"Sure, go ahead, babe. Here. Have a nice jelly doughnut. I just bought them fresh this morning over by Magazine Street. Ignatius says to me this morning, 'Momma, I sure feel like a jelly doughnut.' You know? So I went over by the German and bought him two dozen. Look, they got a few left."

She offered Patrolman Mancuso a torn and oily cake box that looked as if it had been subjected to unusual abuse during someone's attempt to take all of the doughnuts at once. At the bottom of the box Patrolman Mancuso found two withered pieces of doughnut out of which, judging by their moist edges, the jelly had been sucked.

"Thank you anyway, Miss Reilly. I had me a big lunch."

"Aw, ain't that a shame." She filled two cups half full with thick cold coffee and poured the boiling milk in up to the rim. "Ignatius loves his doughnuts. He says to me, 'Momma, I love my doughnuts.'" Mrs. Reilly slurped a bit at the rim of her cup. "He's out in the parlor right now looking at TV.

Every afternoon, as right as rain, he looks at that show where them kids dance." In the kitchen the music was somewhat fainter than it had been on the porch. Patrolman Mancuso pictured the green hunting cap bathed in the blue-white glow of the television screen. "He don't like the show at all, but he won't miss it. You oughta hear what he says about them poor kids."

"I spoke with the man this morning," Patrolman Mancuso said, hoping that Mrs. Reilly had exhausted the subject of her son.

"Yeah?" She put three spoons of sugar in her coffee and, holding the spoon in the cup with her thumb so that the handle threatened to puncture her eyeball, she slurped a bit more. "What he said, honey?"

"I told him I investigated the accident and that you just skidded on a wet street."

"That sounds good. So what he said then, babe?"

"He said he don't want to go to court. He wants a settlement now."

"Oh, my God!" Ignatius bellowed from the front of the house. "What an egregious insult to good taste."

"Don't pay him no mind," Mrs. Reilly advised the startled policeman. "He does that all the time he looks at the TV. A 'settlement.' That means he wants some money, huh?"

"He even got a contractor to appraise the damage. Here, this is the estimate."

Mrs. Reilly took the sheet of paper and read the typed column of itemized figures beneath the contractor's letterhead.

"Lord! A thousand and twenty dollars. This is terrible. How I'm gonna pay that?" She dropped the estimate on the oilcloth. "You sure that is right?"

"Yes, ma'm. He's got a lawyer working on it, too. It's all on the up and up."

"Where I'm gonna get a thousand dollars, though? All me

and Ignatius got is my poor husband's Social Security and a little two-bit pension, and that don't come to much."

"Do I believe the total perversion that I am witnessing?" Ignatius screamed from the parlor. The music had a frantic, tribal rhythm; a chorus of falsettos sang insinuatingly about loving all night long.

"I'm sorry," Patrolman Mancuso said, almost heartbroken over Mrs. Reilly's financial quandary.

"Aw, it's not your fault, darling," she said glumly. "Maybe I can get a mortgage on the house. We can't do nothing about it, huh?"

"No, ma'm," Patrolman Mancuso answered, listening to some sort of approaching stampede.

"The children on that program should all be gassed," Ignatius said as he strode into the kitchen in his nightshirt. Then he noticed the guest and said coldly, "Oh."

"Ignatius, you know Mr. Mancuso. Say 'Hello.'"

"I do believe that I've seen him about," Ignatius said and looked out the back door.

Patrolman Mancuso was too startled by the monstrous flannel nightshirt to reply to Ignatius' pleasantry.

"Ignatius, honey, the man wants over a thousand dollars for what I did to his building."

"A thousand dollars? He will not get a cent. We shall have him prosecuted immediately. Contact our attorneys, Mother."

"Our attorneys? He's got a estimate from a contractor. Mr. Mancuso here says they's nothing I can do."

"Oh. Well, you shall have to pay him then."

"I could take it to court if you think it's best."

"Drunken driving," Ignatius said calmly. "You haven't a chance."

Mrs. Reilly looked depressed.

"But Ignatius, a thousand twenty dollars."

"I am certain that you can procure some funds," he told

43

her. "Is there any more coffee, or have you given the last to this carnival masker?"

"We can mortgage the house."

"Mortgage the house? Of course we won't."

"What else we gonna do, Ignatius?"

"There are means," Ignatius said absently. "I wish that you wouldn't bother me with this. That program always increases my anxiety anyway." He smelled the milk before putting it into the pot. "I would suggest that you telephone that dairy immediately. This milk is quite aged."

"I can get a thousand dollars over by the Homestead," Mrs. Reilly told the silent patrolman quietly. "The house is good security. I had me a real estate agent offered me seven thousand last year."

"The ironic thing about that program," Ignatius was saying over the stove, keeping one eye peeled so that he could seize the pot as soon as the milk began to boil, "is that it is supposed to be an *exemplum* to the youth of our nation. I would like very much to know what the Founding Fathers would say if they could see these children being debauched to further the cause of Clearasil. However, I always suspected that democracy would come to this." He painstakingly poured the milk into his Shirley Temple mug. "A firm rule must be imposed upon our nation before it destroys itself. The United States needs some theology and geometry, some taste and decency. I suspect that we are teetering on the edge of the abyss."

"Ignatius, I'm gonna have to go by the Homestead tomorrow."

"We shall not deal with those usurers, Mother." Ignatius was feeling around in the cookie jar. "Something will turn up."

"Ignatius, honey, they can put me in jail."

"Ho hum. If you are going to stage one of your hysterical scenes, I shall have to return to the living room. As a matter of fact, I think I will."

He billowed out again in the direction of the music, the shower shoes flapping loudly against the soles of his huge feet.

"What I'm gonna do with a boy like that?" Mrs. Reilly sadly asked Patrolman Mancuso. "He don't care about his poor dear mother. Sometimes I think Ignatius wouldn't mind if they did throw me in jail. He's got a heart of ice, that boy."

"You spoiled him," Patrolman Mancuso said. "A woman's gotta watch she don't spoil her kids."

"How many chirren you got, Mr. Mancuso?"

"Three. Rosalie, Antoinette, and Angelo, Jr."

"Aw, ain't that nice. I bet they sweet, huh? Not like Ignatius." Mrs. Reilly shook her head. "Ignatius was such a precious child. I don't know what made him change. He used to say to me, 'Momma, I love you.' He don't say that no more."

"Aw, don't cry," Patrolman Mancuso said, deeply moved. "I'll make you some more coffee."

"He don't care if they lock me up," Mrs. Reilly sniffed. She opened the oven and took out a bottle of muscatel. "You want some nice wine, Mr. Mancuso?"

"No thanks. Being on the force, I gotta make a impression. I gotta always be on the lookout for people, too."

"You don't mind?" Mrs. Reilly asked rhetorically and took a long drink from the bottle. Patrolman Mancuso began boiling the milk, hovering over the stove in a very domestic manner. "Sometimes I sure get the blues. Life's hard. I worked hard, too. I been good."

"You oughta look on the bright side," Patrolman Mancuso said.

"I guess so," Mrs. Reilly said. "Some people got it harder than me, I guess. Like my poor cousin, wonderful woman. Went to mass every day of her life. She got knocked down by a streetcar over on Magazine Street early one morning

45

while she was on her way to Fisherman's Mass. It was still dark out."

"Personally, I never let myself get low," Patrolman Mancuso lied. "You gotta look up. You know what I mean? I got a dangerous line of work."

"You could get yourself killed."

"Sometimes I don't apprehend nobody all day. Sometimes I apprehend the wrong person."

"Like that old man in front of D. H. Holmes. That's my fault, Mr. Mancuso. I shoulda guessed Ignatius was wrong all along. It's just like him. All the time I'm telling him, 'Ignatius, here, put on this nice shirt. Put on this nice sweater I bought you.' But he don't listen. Not that boy. He's got a head like a rock."

"Then sometimes I get problems at home. With three kids, my wife's very nervous."

"Nerves is a terrible thing. Poor Miss Annie, the next-door lady, she's got nerves. Always screaming about Ignatius making noise."

"That's my wife. Sometimes I gotta get outta the house. If I was another kind of man, sometimes I could really go get myself good and drunk. Just between us."

"I gotta have my little drink. It relieves the pressure. You know?"

"What I do is go bowl."

Mrs. Reilly tried to imagine little Patrolman Mancuso with a big bowling ball and said, "You like that, huh?"

"Bowling's wonderful, Miss Reilly. It takes your mind off things."

"Oh, my heavens!" a voice shouted from the parlor. "These girls are doubtless prostitutes already. How can they present horrors like this to the public?"

"I wish I had me a hobby like that."

"You oughta try bowling."

46

"Ay-yi-yi. I already got arthuritis in my elbow. I'm too old to play around with them balls. I'd wrench my back."

"I got a aunt, sixty-five, a grammaw, and she goes bowling all the time. She's even on a team."

"Some women are like that. Me, I never was much for sports."

"Bowling's more than a sport," Patrolman Mancuso said defensively. "You meet plenty people over by the alley. Nice people. You could make you some friends."

"Yeah, but it's just my luck to drop one of them balls on my toe. I got bum feet already."

"Next time I go by the alley, I'll let you know. I'll bring my aunt. You and me and my aunt, we'll go down by the alley. Okay?"

"Mother, when was this coffee dripped?" Ignatius demanded, flapping into the kitchen again.

"Just about a hour ago. Why?"

"It certainly tastes brackish."

"I thought it was very good," Patrolman Mancuso said. "Just as good as they serve at the French Market. I'm making some more now. You want a cup?"

"Pardon me," Ignatius said. "Mother, are you going to entertain this gentleman all afternoon? I would like to remind you that I am going to the movies tonight and that I am due at the theater promptly at seven so that I can see the cartoon. I would suggest that you begin preparing something to eat."

"I better go," Patrolman Mancuso said.

"Ignatius, you oughta be ashamed," Mrs. Reilly said in an angry voice. "Me and Mr. Mancuso here just having some coffee. You been nasty all afternoon. You don't care where I raise that money. You don't care if they lock me up. You don't care about nothing."

"Am I going to be attacked in my own home before a stranger with a false beard?"

47

"My heart's broke."

"Oh, really." Ignatius turned on Patrolman Mancuso. "Will you kindly leave? You are inciting my mother."

"Mr. Mancuso's not doing nothing but being nice."

"I better go," Patrolman Mancuso said apologetically.

"I'll get that money," Mrs. Reilly screamed. "I'll sell this house. I'll sell it out from under you, boy. I'll go stay by a old folks' home."

She grabbed an end of the oilcloth and wiped her eyes.

"If you do not leave," Ignatius said to Patrolman Mancuso, who was hooking on his beard, "I shall call the police."

"He *is* the police, stupid."

"This is totally absurd," Ignatius said and flapped away. "I am going to my room."

He slammed his door and snatched a Big Chief tablet from the floor. Throwing himself back among the pillows on the bed, he began doodling on a yellowed page. After almost thirty minutes of pulling at his hair and chewing on the pencil, he began to compose a paragraph.

Were Hroswitha with us today, we would all look to her for counsel and guidance. From the austerity and tranquility of her medieval world, the penetrating gaze of this legendary Sybil of a holy nun would exorcise the horrors which materialize before our eyes in the name of television. If we could only juxtapose one eyeball of this sanctified woman and a television tube, both being roughly of the same shape and design, what a phantasmagoria of exploding electrodes would occur. The images of those lasciviously gyrating children would disintegrate into so many ions and molecules, thereby effecting the catharsis which the tragedy of the debauching of the innocent necessarily demands.

Mrs. Reilly stood in the hall looking at the DO NOT DISTURB sign printed on a sheet of Big Chief paper and stuck to the door by an old flesh-colored Band-aid.

"Ignatius, let me in there, boy," she screamed.

"Let you in here?" Ignatius said through the door. "Of course I won't. I am occupied at the moment with an especially succinct passage."

"You let me in."

"You know that you are never allowed in here."

Mrs. Reilly pounded at the door.

"I don't know what is happening to you, Mother, but I suspect that you are momentarily deranged. Now that I think of it, I am too frightened to open the door. You may have a knife or a broken wine bottle."

"Open up this door, Ignatius."

"Oh, my valve! It's closing!" Ignatius groaned loudly. "Are you satisfied now that you have ruined me for the rest of the evening?"

Mrs. Reilly threw herself against the unpainted wood.

"Well, don't break the door," he said finally and, after a few moments, the bolt slid open.

"Ignatius, what's all this trash on the floor?"

"That is my worldview that you see. It still must be incorporated into a whole, so be careful where you step."

"And all the shutters closed. Ignatius! It's still light outside."

"My being is not without its Proustian elements," Ignatius said from the bed, to which he had quickly returned. "Oh, my stomach."

"It smells terrible in here."

"Well, what do you expect? The human body, when confined, produces certain odors which we tend to forget in this age of deodorants and other perversions. Actually, I find the atmosphere of this room rather comforting. Schiller needed the scent of apples rotting in his desk in order to

49

write. I, too, have my needs. You may remember that Mark Twain preferred to lie supinely in bed while composing those rather dated and boring efforts which contemporary scholars try to prove meaningful. Veneration of Mark Twain is one of the roots of our current intellectual stalemate."

"If I know it was like this, I'd been in here long ago."

"I do not know why you are in here *now*, as a matter of fact, or why you have this sudden compulsion to invade my sanctuary. I doubt whether it will ever be the same after the trauma of this intrusion by an alien spirit."

"I came to talk to you, boy. Get your face out them pillows."

"This must be the influence of that ludicrous representative of the law. He seems to have turned you against your own child. By the way, he has left, hasn't he?"

"Yes, and I apologized to him over the way you acted."

"Mother, you are standing on my tablets. Will you please move a little? Isn't it enough that you have destroyed my digestion without destroying the fruits of my brain also?"

"Well, where I'm gonna stand, Ignatius? You want me to get in bed with you?" Mrs. Reilly asked angrily.

"Watch out where you're stepping, please!" Ignatius thundered. "My God, never has anyone been so totally and so literally stormed and besieged. What is it anyway that has driven you in here in this state of complete mania? Could it be the stench of cheap muscatel that is assaulting my nostrils?"

"I made up my mind. You gonna go out and get you a job."

Oh, what low joke was Fortuna playing on him now? Arrest, accident, job. Where would this dreadful cycle ever end?

"I see," Ignatius said calmly. "Knowing that you are congenitally incapable of arriving at a decision of this importance,

I imagine that that mongoloid law officer put this idea into your head."

"Me and Mr. Mancuso talked like I used to talk to your poppa. You poppa used to tell me what to do. I wish he was alive today."

"Mancuso and my father are alike only in that they both give the impression of being rather inconsequential humans. However, your current mentor is apparently the type of person who thinks that everything will be all right if everyone works continually."

"Mr. Mancuso works hard. He's got a hard road at the precinct."

"I am certain that he supports several unwanted children who all hope to grow up to be policemen, the girls included."

"He's got three sweet chirren."

"I can imagine." Ignatius began to bounce slowly. "Oh!"

"What are you doing? Are you fooling with that valve again? Nobody else got him a valve but you. *I* ain't got no valve."

"*Everyone* has a valve!" Ignatius screamed. "Mine is simply more developed. I am trying to open a passage which you have succeeded in blocking. It may be permanently closed now for all I know."

"Mr. Mancuso says if you work you can help me pay off the man. He says he thinks the man might take the money in installments."

"Your friend the patrolman says a great deal. You certainly bring people out, as they say. I never suspected that he could be so loquacious or that he was capable of such perceptive comment. Do you realize that he is trying to destroy our home? It began the moment that he attempted that brutal arrest in front of D. H. Holmes. Although you are too limited to comprehend it all, Mother, this man is our nemesis. He's spun our wheel downward."

"Whee! Mr. Mancuso is a good man. You oughta be glad he didn't take you in!"

"In my private apocalypse he will be impaled upon his own night-stick. Anyway, it is inconceivable that I should get a job. I am very busy with my work at the moment, and I feel that I am entering a very fecund stage. Perhaps the accident jarred and loosened my thought. At any rate, I accomplished a great deal today."

"We gotta pay that man, Ignatius. You wanna see me in jail? Wouldn't you be ashamed with your poor momma behind bars?"

"Will you please stop talking about imprisonment? You seem to be preoccupied with the thought. Actually, you seem to enjoy thinking about it. Martyrdom is meaningless in our age." He belched quietly. "I would suggest certain economies around the house. Somehow you will soon see that you have the required amount."

"I spend all the money on you for food and whatnots."

"I have found several empty wine bottles about lately, the contents of which I certainly did not consume."

"Ignatius!"

"I made the mistake of heating the oven the other day before inspecting it properly. When I opened it to put in my frozen pizza, I was almost blinded by a bottle of broiled wine that was preparing to explode. I suggest that you divert some of the monies that you are pouring into the liquor industry."

"For shame, Ignatius. A few bottles of Gallo muscatel, and you with all them trinkets."

"Will you please define the meaning of *trinkets?*" Ignatius snapped.

"All them books. That gramaphone. That trumpet I bought you last month."

"I consider the trumpet a good investment, although our

neighbor, Miss Annie, does not. If she beats on my shutters again, I'll pour water on her."

"Tomorrow we looking at the want ads in the paper. You gonna dress up and go find you a job."

"I am afraid to ask what your idea of 'dressing up' is. I will probably be turned into an utter mockery."

"I'm gonna iron you a nice white shirt and you gonna put on one of your poppa's nice ties."

"Do I believe what I am hearing?" Ignatius asked his pillow.

"It's either that, Ignatius, or I gotta take out a mortgage. You wanna lose the roof over your head?"

"No! You will not mortgage this house." He pounded a great paw into the mattress. "The whole sense of security which I have been trying to develop would crumble. I will not have any disinterested party controlling my domicile. I couldn't stand it. Just the thought of it makes my hands break out."

He extended a paw so that his mother could examine the rash.

"That is out of the question," he continued. "It would bring all of my latent anxieties to a head, and the result, I fear, would be very ugly indeed. I would not want you to have to spend the remainder of your life caring for a lunatic locked away somewhere in the attic. We shall not mortgage the house. You must have some funds somewhere."

"I got a hundred fifty in the Hibernia Bank."

"My God, is that all? I hardly thought that we were existing so precariously. However, it is fortunate that you have kept this from me. Had I known how close we were to total penury, my nerves would have given out long ago." Ignatius scratched his paws. "I must admit, though, that the alternative for me is rather grim. I doubt very seriously whether anyone will hire me."

"What do you mean, babe? You a fine boy with a good education."

"Employers sense in me a denial of their values." He rolled over onto his back. "They fear me. I suspect that they can see that I am forced to function in a century which I loathe. That was true even when I worked for the New Orleans Public Library."

"But, Ignatius, that was the only time you worked since you got out of college, and you was only there for two weeks."

"That is exactly what I mean," Ignatius replied, aiming a paper ball at the bowl of the milk glass chandelier.

"All you did was paste them little slips in the books."

"Yes, but I had my own esthetic about pasting those slips. On some days I could only paste in three or four slips and at the same time feel satisfied with the quality of my work. The library authorities resented my integrity about the whole thing. They only wanted another animal who could slop glue on their best sellers."

"You think maybe you could get a job there again?"

"I seriously doubt it. At the time I said some rather cutting things to the woman in charge of the processing department. They even revoked my borrower's card. You must realize the fear and hatred which my *Weltanschauung* instills in people." Ignatius belched. "I won't mention that misguided trip to Baton Rouge. That incident, I believe, caused me to form a mental block against working."

"They was nice to you at college, Ignatius. Now tell the truth. They let you hang around there a long time. They even let you teach a class."

"Oh, it was basically the same. Some poor white from Mississippi told the dean that I was a propagandist for the Pope, which was patently untrue. I do not support the current Pope. He does not at all fit my concept of a good, authoritarian Pope. Actually, I am opposed to the relativism of modern Catholicism quite violently. However, the boldness of this ignorant lily-white redneck fundamentalist led my

54

other students to form a committee to demand that I grade and return their accumulated essays and examinations. There was even a small demonstration outside the window of my office. It was rather dramatic. For being such simple, ignorant children, they managed it quite well. At the height of the demonstration I dumped all of the old papers—ungraded, of course—out of the window and right onto the students' heads. The college was too small to accept this act of defiance against the abyss of contemporary academia."

"Ignatius! You never told me that."

"I did not want to excite you at the time. I also told the students that, for the sake of humanity's future, I hoped that they were all sterile." Ignatius arranged the pillows about his head. "I could never have possibly read over the illiteracies and misconceptions burbling from the dark minds of these students. It will be the same wherever I work."

"You can get you a good job. Wait till they see a boy with a master's degree."

Ignatius sighed heavily and said, "I see no alternative." He twisted his face into a mask of suffering. There was no use fighting Fortuna until the cycle was over. "You realize, of course, that this is all your fault. The progress of my work will be greatly delayed. I suggest that you go to your confessor and make some penance, Mother. Promise him that you will avoid the path of sin and drinking in the future. Tell him what the consequence of your moral failure has been. Let him know that you have delayed the completion of a monumental indictment against our society. Perhaps he will comprehend the magnitude of your failing. If he is my type of priest, the penance will no doubt be rather strict. However, I have learned to expect little from today's clergyman."

"I'm gonna be good, Ignatius. You'll see."

"There, there, I shall find some employment, although it will not necessarily be what you would call a *good* job. I may have some valuable insights which may benefit my employer. Perhaps the experience can give my writing a new dimension. Being actively engaged in the system which I criticize will be an interesting irony in itself." Ignatius belched loudly. "If only Myrna Minkoff could see how low I've fallen."

"What that girl's doing now?" Mrs. Reilly asked suspiciously. "I put out good money for you to go to college, and you have to pick up with somebody like that."

"Myrna is still in New York, her native habitat. No doubt she is trying to taunt the police into arresting her in some demonstration at this very moment."

"She sure used to get me nervous playing on that guitar of hers all over this house. If she's got money like you said, maybe you shoulda married her. You two might of settled down and had a nice baby or something."

"Do I believe that such obscenity and filth is coming from the lips of my own mother?" Ignatius bellowed. "Now run along and fix me some dinner. I must be at the theater on time. It's a circus musical, a heralded excess which I have been waiting to see for some time. We study the want ads tomorrow."

"I'm so proud you gonna work at last," Mrs. Reilly said emotionally and kissed her son somewhere in his damp moustache.

IV

"Look at that old gal," Jones mused to his psyche as the bus bounced and threw him against the woman sitting beside him. "She think cause I color I gonna rape her. She about to throw her grammaw ass out the window. Whoa! I ain gonna rape nobody."

He moved discreetly away from her, crossing his legs and

wishing that he could smoke on the bus. He wondered who the fat cat in the green cap was who was suddenly all over town. Where would that fat mother show up next? There was something ghostly about that green-cap freak.

"Well, I gonna tell that po-lice I gainfully employ, keep him off my back, tell him I met up with a humanitaria payin me twenty dollar a week. He say, 'That fine, boy. I'm glad to see you straighten out.' And I say, 'Hey!' And he say, 'Now maybe you be becomin a member of the community.' And I say, 'Yeah, I got me a nigger job and nigger pay. Now I really a member of the community. Now I a real nigger. No vagran. Just nigger.' Whoa! What kinda change you got?"

The old woman pulled the bell cord and got out of the seat, trying self-consciously to avoid any contact with the anatomy of Jones, who watched her writhing through the detachment of his green lenses.

"Look at that. She think I got siphlus and TB and a hard on and I gonna cut her up with a razor and lif her purse. Ooo-wee."

The sunglasses watched the woman climb off the bus into a crowd standing at the bus stop. Somewhere in the rear of the crowd an altercation was going on. A man with a rolled up newspaper in his hand was striking another man who had a long red beard and was wearing bermuda shorts. The man in the beard looked familiar. Jones felt uneasy. First there was the green-cap phantom and now this person he couldn't identify.

Jones turned from the window when the man in the red beard ran off and opened the *Life* magazine that Darlene had given him. At least Darlene had been pleasant to him at the Night of Joy. Darlene subscribed to *Life* for purposes of self-improvement and, in giving it to Jones, had suggested that he might find it helpful, too. Jones tried to plow through an editorial about American involvement in the Far East but stopped midway, wondering how something like that could help Darlene to become an exotic, the goal that she had referred to again and again. He turned back to the advertisements, for they were the things that interested him in magazines. The selection in this magazine was excellent. He liked the Aetna Life Insurance ad with the picture of the lovely home that a couple had just bought. The Yardley Shaving Lotion men looked cool and rich. That's how the magazine could help him. He wanted to look just like those men.

V

When Fortuna spins you downward, go out to a movie and get more out of life. Ignatius was about to say this to himself; then he remembered that he went to the movies almost every night, no matter which way Fortuna was spinning.

He sat at attention in the darkness of the Prytania only a few rows from the screen, his body filling the seat and protruding into the two adjoining ones. On the seat to his right he had stationed his overcoat, three Milky Ways, and two auxiliary bags of popcorn, the bags neatly rolled at the top to keep the popcorn warm and crisp. Ignatius ate his current popcorn and stared raptly at the previews of coming attractions. One of the films looked bad enough, he thought, to bring him back to the Prytania in a few days. Then the screen glowed in bright, wide technicolor, the lion roared, and the title of the excess flashed on the screen before his miraculous blue and yellow eyes. His face froze and his popcorn bag began to shake. Upon entering the theater, he had carefully buttoned the two earflaps to the top of his cap, and now the strident score of the musical assaulted his naked ears from a variety of speakers. He listened to the music, detecting two popular songs which he particularly disliked, and scrutinized the credits closely to find any names of performers who normally nauseated him.

When the credits had ended and Ignatius had noted that several of the actors, the composer, the director, the hair designer, and the assistant producer were all people whose efforts had offended him at various times in the past, there appeared in the technicolor a scene of many extras milling about a circus tent. He greedily studied the crowd and found the heroine standing near a sideshow.

"Oh, my God!" he screamed. "There she is."

The children in the rows in front of him turned and stared, but Ignatius did not notice them. The blue and yellow eyes were following the heroine, who was gaily carrying a pail of water to what turned out to be her elephant.

"This is going to be even worse than I thought," Ignatius said when he saw the elephant.

He put the empty popcorn bag to his full lips, inflated it, and waited, his eyes gleaming with reflected technicolor. A tympany beat and the soundtrack filled with violins. The heroine and Ignatius opened their mouths simultaneously, hers in song, his in a groan. In the darkness two trembling hands met violently. The popcorn bag exploded with a bang. The children shrieked.

"What's all that noise?" the woman at the candy counter asked the manager.

"He's here tonight," the manager told her, pointing across the theater to the hulking silhouette at the bottom of the screen. The manager walked down the aisle to the front rows, where the shrieking was growing wilder. Their fear having dissipated itself, the children were holding a competition of shrieking. Ignatius listened to the bloodcurdling little trebles and giggles and gloated in his dark lair. With a few mild threats, the manager quieted the front rows and then glanced down the row in which the isolated figure of Ignatius rose like some great monster among the little heads. But he was treated only to a puffy profile. The eyes that shone under the green visor were following the heroine and her elephant across the wide screen and into the circus tent.

For a while Ignatius was relatively still, reacting to the unfolding plot with only an occasional subdued snort. Then what seemed to be the film's entire cast was up on the wires. In the foreground, on a trapeze, was the heroine. She swung back and forth to a waltz. She smiled in a huge close-up. Ignatius inspected her teeth for cavities and fillings. She extended one leg. Ignatius rapidly surveyed its contours for structural defects. She began to sing about trying over and over again until you succeeded. Ignatius quivered as the philosophy of the lyrics became clear. He studied her grip on the trapeze in the hope that the camera would record her fatal plunge to the sawdust far below.

On the second chorus the entire ensemble joined in the song, smiling and singing lustily about ultimate success while they swung, dangled, flipped, and soared.

"Oh, good heavens!" Ignatius shouted, unable to contain himself any longer. Popcorn spilled down his shirt and gathered in the folds of his trousers. "What degenerate produced this abortion?"

"Shut up," someone said behind him.

"Just look at those smiling morons! If only all of those wires would snap!" Ignatius rattled the few kernels of popcorn in his last bag. "Thank God that scene is over."

When a love scene appeared to be developing, he bounded up out of his seat and stomped up the aisle to the candy counter for more popcorn, but as he returned to his seat, the two big pink figures were just preparing to kiss.

"They probably have halitosis," Ignatius announced over the heads of the children. "I hate to think of the obscene places that those mouths have doubtlessly been before!"

"You'll have to do something," the candy woman told the manager laconically. "He's worse than ever tonight."

The manager sighed and started down the aisle to where Ignatius was mumbling, "Oh, my God, their tongues are probably all over each other's capped and rotting teeth."

Three

Ignatius staggered up the brick path to the house, climbed the steps painfully, and rang the bell. One stalk of the dead banana tree had expired and collapsed stiffly onto the hood of the Plymouth.

"Ignatius, baby," Mrs. Reilly cried when she opened the door. "What's wrong? you look like you dying."

"My valve closed on the streetcar."

"Lord, come in quick out the cold."

Ignatius shuffled miserably back to the kitchen and fell into a chair.

"The personnel manager at that insurance company treated me very insultingly."

"You didn't get the job?"

"Of course I didn't get the job."

"What happened?"

"I would rather not discuss it."

"Did you go to the other places?"

"Obviously not. Do I appear to be in a condition that would attract prospective employers? I had the good judgment to come home as soon as possible."

"Don't feel blue, precious."

"'Blue'? I am afraid that I never feel 'blue.'"

"Now don't be nasty. You'll get a nice job. You only been on the streets a few days," his mother said and looked at him. "Ignatius, was you wearing that cap when you spoke to the insurance man?"

"Of course I was. That office was improperly heated. I don't know how the employees of that company manage to stay alive exposing themselves to that chill day after day. And then there are those florescent tubes baking their brains out and blinding them. I did not like the office at all. I tried to explain the inadequacies of the place to the personnel manager, but he seemed rather uninterested. He was ultimately very hostile." Ignatius let out a monstrous belch. "However, I told you that it would be like this. I am an anachronism. People realize this and resent it."

"Lord, babe, you gotta look up."

"Look up?" Ignatius repeated savagely. "Who has been sowing that unnatural garbage into your mind?"

"Mr. Mancuso."

"Oh, my God! I should have known. Is he an example of 'looking up'?"

"You oughta hear the whole story of that poor man's life. You oughta hear what this sergeant at the precinct's trying . . ."

"Stop!" Ignatius covered one ear and beat a fist on the table. "I will not listen to another word about that man. Throughout the centuries it has been the Mancusos of the world who have caused wars and spread diseases. Suddenly the spirit of that evil man is haunting this house. He has become your Svengali!"

"Ignatius, get a holt of yourself."

"I refuse to 'look up.' Optimism nauseates me. It is perverse. Since man's fall, his proper position in the universe has been one of misery."

"I ain't miserable."

"You *are*."

"No, I ain't."

"Yes, you are."

"Ignatius, I *ain't* miserable. If I was, I'd tell you."

"If I had demolished private property while intoxicated and had thereby thrown my child to the wolves, I would be beating my breast and wailing. I would kneel in penance until my knees bled. By the way, what penance has the priest given you for your sin?"

"Three Hail Mary's and a Our Father."

"Is that all?" Ignatius screamed. "Did you tell him what you did, that you halted a critical work of great brilliance?"

"I went to confession, Ignatius. I told Father everything. He says, 'It don't sound like your fault, honey. It sounds to me like you just took a little skid on a wet street.' So I told him about you. I says 'My boy says I'm the one stopping him from writing in his copybooks. He's been writing on this story for almost five years.' And Father says, 'Yeah? Well, don't sound too important to me. You tell him to get out the house and go to work.'"

"No wonder I cannot support the Church," Ignatius bellowed. "You should have been lashed right there in the confessional."

"Now tomorrow, Ignatius, you go try some other place. They got plenty jobs in the city. I was talking to Miss Marie-Louise, the old lady works in the German's. She's got a crippled brother with a car phone. He's kinda deaf, you know? He got himself a good job over by the Goodwill Industries."

"Perhaps I should try there."

"Ignatius! They only hire blind people and dummies to make brooms and things."

"I am certain that those people are pleasant co-workers."

"Let's us look in the afternoon's paper. Maybe they got a nice job in there!"

"If I must go out tomorrow, I am not leaving the house so early. I felt very disoriented all the while I was downtown."

"You didn't leave here until after lunch."

"Still, I was not functioning properly. I suffered several bad dreams last night. I awoke bruised and muttering."

"Here, listen to this. I been seeing this ad in the paper

every day," Mrs. Reilly said, holding the newspaper very close to her eyes. "'Clean, hard-worker man . . .'"

"That's 'hard-work*ing*.'"

"'Clean, hard-working man, dependable, quite type . . . .'"

"'*Quiet* type.' Give that to me," Ignatius said, snatching the paper from his mother. "It's unfortunate that you couldn't complete your education."

"Poppa was very poor."

"Please! I couldn't bear to hear that grim story again at the moment. 'Clean, hard-working, dependable, quiet type.' Good God! What kind of monster is this that they want. I am afraid that I could never work for a concern with a world-view like that."

"Read the rest, babe."

"'Clerical work. 25–35 years old. Apply Levy Pants, Industrial Canal and River, between 8 and 9 daily.' Well, that's out. I could never get all the way down there before nine o'clock."

"Honey, if you gonna work, you gotta get up early."

"No, Mother." Ignatius threw the paper on top of the oven. "I have been setting my sights too high. I cannot survive this type of work. I suspect that something like a newspaper route would be rather agreeable."

"Ignatius, a big man like you can't peddle around on no bike delivering newspapers."

"Perhaps you could drive me about in the car and I could toss the papers from the rear window."

"Listen, boy," Mrs. Reilly said angrily. "You gonna go try somewheres tomorrow. I mean it. The first thing you gonna do is answer this ad. You playing around, Ignatius. I know you."

"Ho hum," Ignatius yawned, exhibiting the flabby pink of his tongue. "Levy Pants sounds just as bad if not worse than the titles of the other organizations I have contacted. I can

65

see that I am obviously beginning to scrape the bottom of the job market already."

"Just you wait, babe. You'll make good."

"Oh, my God!"

II

Patrolman Mancuso had a good idea that had been given to him by, of all people, Ignatius Reilly. He had telephoned the Reillys' house to ask Mrs. Reilly when she could go bowling with him and his aunt. But Ignatius had answered the telephone and screamed, "Stop molesting us, you mongoloid. If you had any sense, you would be investigating dens like that Night of Joy in which my beloved mother and I were mistreated and robbed. I, unfortunately, was the prey of a vicious, depraved B-girl. In addition, the proprietress is a Nazi. We barely escaped with our lives. Go investigate that gang and let us alone, you home-wrecker."

Then Mrs. Reilly had wrestled the phone away from her son.

The sergeant would be glad to know about the place. He might even compliment Patrolman Mancuso for getting the tip. Clearing his throat, Patrolman Mancuso stood before the sergeant and said, "I got a lead on a place where they got B-girls."

"You got a lead?" the sergeant asked. "Who gave you the lead?"

Patrolman Mancuso decided against dragging Ignatius into the matter for several reasons. He settled on Mrs. Reilly.

"A lady I know," he answered.

"How come this lady knows about the place?" the sergeant asked. "Who took her to this place?"

Patrolman Mancuso couldn't say "her son." It might

66

reopen some wounds. Why couldn't conversations with the sergeant ever go smoothly?

"She was there alone," Patrolman Mancuso said finally, trying to save the interview from becoming a shambles.

"A lady was in a place like that alone?" the sergeant screamed. "What kinda lady was this? She's probly a B-girl herself. Get outta here, Mancuso, and bring me in a suspicious character. You ain't brought in one person yet. Don't gimme no tips from B-girls. Go look in your locker. You're a soldier today. Beat it."

Patrolman Mancuso drifted sadly off to the lockers, wondering why he could never do anything right for the sergeant. When he was gone, the sergeant turned to a detective and said, "Send a couple men over to that Night of Joy some night. Someone there might've been just dumb enough to talk to Mancuso. But don't tell him. I don't want that goon taking any credit. He stays in costume until he brings me in a character."

"You know, we got another complaint on Mancuso today from somebody who says a small man wearing a sombrero pressed up against her in a bus last night," the detective said.

"No kidding," the sergeant said thoughtfully. "Well, any more complaints like that, and we *arrest* Mancuso."

III

Mr. Gonzalez turned the lights on in the small office and lit the gas heater beside his desk. In the twenty years that he had been working for Levy Pants, he had always been the first person to arrive each morning.

"It was still dark when I got here this morning," Mr. Gonzalez would say to Mr. Levy on those rare occasions when Mr. Levy was forced to visit Levy Pants.

"You must be leaving home too early," Mr. Levy would say.

"I was standing out on the steps of the office this morning talking to the milkman."

"Oh, shut up, Gonzalez. Did you get my plane ticket to Chicago for the Bears' game with the Packers?"

"I had the office all warm by the time everybody else came in for work."

"You're burning up my gas. Sit in the cold. It's good for you."

"I did two pages in the ledger this morning when I was in here all by myself. Look, I caught a rat near the water cooler. He didn't think anybody was around yet, and I hit him with a paper weight."

"Get that damned rat away from me. This place depresses me enough. Get on the phone and make my hotel reservations for the Derby."

But the criteria at Levy Pants were very low. Promptness was sufficient excuse for promotion. Mr. Gonzalez became the office manager and took control of the few dispirited clerks under him. He could never really remember the names of his clerks and typists. They seemed, at times, to come and go almost daily, with the exception of Miss Trixie, the octogenarian assistant accountant, who had been copying figures inaccurately into the Levy ledgers for almost half a century. She even wore her green celluloid visor on her way to and from work, a gesture that Mr. Gonzalez interpreted as a symbol of loyalty to Levy Pants. On Sundays she sometimes wore the visor to church, mistaking it for a hat. She had even worn it to her brother's funeral, where it was ripped from her head by her more alert and slightly younger sister-in-law. Mrs. Levy, though, had issued orders that Miss Trixie was to be retained, no matter what.

Mr. Gonzalez rubbed a rag over his desk and thought, as

68

he did every morning at this time when the office was still chilly and deserted and the wharf rats played frenetic games among themselves within the walls, about the happiness that his association with Levy Pants had brought him. On the river the freighters gliding through the lifting mist bellowed at one another, the sound of their deep foghorns echoing among the rusting file cabinets in the office. Beside him the little heater popped and cracked as its parts grew warmer and expanded. He listened unconsciously to all the sounds that had begun his day for twenty years and lit the first of the ten cigarettes that he smoked every day. When he had smoked the cigarette down to its filter, he put it out and emptied the ashtray into the wastebasket. He always liked to impress Mr. Levy with the cleanliness of his desk.

Next to his desk was Miss Trixie's rolltop desk. Old newspapers filled every half-opened drawer. Among the little spherical formations of lint under the desk a piece of cardboard had been wedged under one corner to make the desk level. In place of Miss Trixie, a brown paper bag filled with old pieces of material, and a ball of twine occupied the chair. Cigarette butts spilled out of the ashtray on the desk. This was a mystery which Mr. Gonzalez had never been able to solve, for Miss Trixie did not smoke. He had questioned her about this several times, but had never received a coherent answer. There was something magnetic about Miss Trixie's area. It attracted whatever refuse there was in the office, and whenever pens, eyeglasses, purses, or cigarette lighters were missing they could usually be found somewhere in her desk. Miss Trixie also hoarded all of the telephone books, which were stored in some cluttered drawer in her desk.

Mr. Gonzalez was about to search Miss Trixie's area for his missing stamp pad when the door of the office opened and she shuffled in, scuffing her sneakers across the wooden floor. She had with her another paper bag that seemed to contain the same assortment of material and twine, aside from the stamp pad which was sticking out of the top of the bag. For two or three years Miss Trixie had been carrying these bags with her, sometimes accumulating three or four by the side of her desk, never disclosing their purpose or destination to anyone.

"Good morning, Miss Trixie," Mr. Gonzalez called in his effervescent tenor. "And how are we this morning?"

"Who? Oh, hello, Gomez," Miss Trixie said feebly and drifted off toward the ladies' room as if she were tacking into a gale. Miss Trixie was never perfectly vertical; she and the floor always met at an angle of less than ninety degrees.

Mr. Gonzalez took the opportunity of her disappearance to retrieve his stamp pad from the bag and discovered that it was covered with what felt and smelled like bacon grease. While he was wiping his stamp pad, he wondered how many of the other workers would appear. One day a year ago only he and Miss Trixie had shown up for work, but that was before the company had granted a five-dollar monthly increase. Still, the office help at Levy Pants often quit without even telephoning Mr. Gonzalez. This was a constant worry, and always after Miss Trixie's arrival he watched the door hopefully, especially now that the factory was supposed to begin shipment of its spring and summer line. The truth of the matter was that he needed office help desperately.

Mr. Gonzalez saw a green visor outside the door. Had Miss Trixie gone out through the factory and decided to reenter through the front door? It was like her. She had once gone to the ladies' room in the morning and been found by Mr. Gonzalez late that afternoon asleep on a pile of piece goods in the factory loft. Then the door opened, and one of the largest men that Mr. Gonzalez had ever seen entered the office. He removed the green cap and revealed thick black hair plastered to his skull with Vaseline in the style of the

1920s. When the overcoat came off, Mr. Gonzalez saw rings of fat squeezed into a tight white shirt that was vertically divided by a wide flowered tie. It appeared that Vaseline had also been applied to the moustache for it gleamed very brightly. And then there were the unbelievable blue and yellow eyes laced with the finest tracing of pinkish veins. Mr. Gonzalez prayed almost audibly that this bohemoth was an applicant for a job. He was impressed and overwhelmed.

Ignatius found himself in perhaps the most disreputable office that he had ever entered. The naked light bulbs that hung irregularly from the stained ceiling cast a weak yellow light upon the warped floorboards. Old filing cabinets divided the room into several small cubicles, in each of which was a desk painted with a peculiar orange varnish. Through the dusty windows of the office there was a gray view of the Poland Avenue wharf, the Army Terminal, the Mississippi, and, far in the distance, the drydocks and the roofs of Algiers across the river. A very old woman hobbled into the room and bumped into a row of filing cabinets. The atmosphere of the place reminded Ignatius of his own room, and his valve agreed by opening joyfully. Ignatius prayed almost audibly that he would be accepted for the job. He was impressed and overwhelmed.

"Yes?" the dapper man at the clean desk asked brightly.

"Oh. I thought that the lady was in charge," Ignatius said in his most stentorian voice, finding the man the only blight in the office. "I have come in response to your advertisement."

"Oh, wonderful. Which one?" the man cried enthusiastically. "We're running two in the paper, one for a woman and one for a man."

"Which one do you think I'm answering?" Ignatius hollered.

"Oh," Mr. Gonzalez said in great confusion. "I'm very sorry. I wasn't thinking. I mean, the sex doesn't matter. You could handle either job. I mean, I'm not concerned with sex."

"Please forget it," Ignatius said. He noticed with interest

71

that the old woman was beginning to nod at her desk. Working conditions looked wonderful.

"Come sit down, please. Miss Trixie will take your coat and hat and put them in the employees' locker. We want you to feel at home at Levy Pants."

"But I haven't even spoken with you yet."

"That's all right. I'm sure that we'll see eye to eye. Miss Trixie. Miss Trixie."

"Who?" Miss Trixie cried, knocking her loaded ashtray to the floor.

"Here, I'll take your things." Mr. Gonzalez was slapped on the hand when he reached for the cap, but he was permitted to have the coat. "Isn't that a fine tie. You see very few like that anymore."

"It belonged to my departed father."

"I'm sorry to hear that," Mr. Gonzalez said and put the coat into an old metal locker in which Ignatius saw a bag like the two beside the old woman's desk. "By the way, this is Miss Trixie, one of our oldest employees. You'll enjoy knowing her."

Miss Trixie had fallen asleep, her white head among the old newspapers on her desk.

"Yes," Miss Trixie finally sighed. "Oh, it's you, Gomez. Is it quitting time already?"

"Miss Trixie, this is one of our new workers."

"Fine big boy," Miss Trixie said, turning her rheumy eyes up toward Ignatius. "Well fed."

"Miss Trixie has been with us for over fifty years. That will give you some idea of the satisfaction that our workers get from their association with Levy Pants. Miss Trixie worked for Mr. Levy's late father, a fine old gentleman."

"Yes, a fine old gentleman," Miss Trixie said, unable to remember the elder Mr. Levy at all anymore. "He treated me well. Always had a kind word, that man."

"Thank you, Miss Trixie," Mr. Gonzalez said quickly, like a master of ceremonies trying to end a variety act that had failed horribly.

"The company says it's going to give me a nice boiled ham for Easter," Miss Trixie told Ignatius. "I certainly hope so. They forgot all about my Thanksgiving turkey."

"Miss Trixie has stood by Levy Pants through the years," the office manager explained while the ancient assistant accountant babbled something else about the turkey.

"I've been waiting for years to retire, but every year they say I have one more to go. They work you till you drop," Miss Trixie wheezed. Then losing interest in retirement, she added, "I could have used that turkey."

She began sorting through one of her bags.

"Can you begin work today?" Mr. Gonzalez asked Ignatius.

"I don't believe that we have discussed anything concerning salary and so forth. Isn't that the normal procedure at this time?" Ignatius asked condescendingly.

"Well, the filing job, which is the one you'll have because we really need someone on the files, pays sixty dollars a week. Any days that you are absent due to sickness, et cetera, are deducted from your weekly wage."

"That is certainly far below the wage that I had expected." Ignatius sounded abnormally important. "I have a valve which is subject to vicissitudes which may force me to lie abed on certain days. Several more attractive organizations are currently vying for my services. I must consider them first."

"But listen," the office manager said confidentially. "Miss Trixie here earns only forty dollars a week, and she does have some seniority."

"She does look rather worn," Ignatius said, watching Miss Trixie spread the contents of her bag on her desk and sort through the scraps. "Isn't she past retirement?"

"Sshh," Mr. Gonzalez hissed. "Mrs. Levy won't let us retire her. She thinks it's better for Miss Trixie to keep active. Mrs. Levy is a brilliant, educated woman. She's taken a correspondence course in psychology." Mr. Gonzalez let this sink in. "Now, to return to your prospects, you are very fortunate to start with the salary I quoted. This is all part of the Levy Pants Plan to attract new blood into the company. Miss Trixie, unfortunately, was hired before the plan went into effect. It was not retroactive, and therefore doesn't cover her."

"I hate to disappoint you, sir, but I am afraid that the salary is not adequate. An oil magnate is currently dangling thousands before me trying to tempt me to be his personal secretary. At the moment, I am trying to decide whether I can accept the man's materialistic worldview. I suspect that I am going to finally tell him, 'Yes.'"

"We'll include twenty cents a day for carfare," Mr. Gonzalez pleaded.

"Well. That does change things," Ignatius conceded. "I shall take the job temporarily. I must admit that the 'Levy Pants Plan' rather attracts me."

"Oh, that's wonderful," Mr. Gonzalez blurted. "He'll love it here, won't he, Miss Trixie?"

Miss Trixie was too preoccupied with her scraps to reply.

"I find it strange that you have not even asked for my name," Ignatius snorted.

"Oh, my goodness. I completely forgot about that. Who are you?"

That day one other office worker, the stenographer, appeared. One woman telephoned to say that she had decided to quit and go on relief instead. The others did not contact Levy Pants at all.

IV

"Take those glasses off. How the hell can you see all that crap on the floor?"

"Who wanna look at all that crap?"

"I told you to take the glasses off, Jones."

"The glasses stayin *on*." Jones bumped the push broom into a bar stool. "For twenty dollar a week, you ain running a plantation in here."

Lana Lee started snapping a rubber band around the pile of bills and making little piles of nickels that she was taking out of the cash register.

"Stop knocking that broom against the bar," she screamed. "Goddamit to hell, you making me nervous."

"You want quiet sweeping, you get you a old lady. I sweep *yawng*."

The broom bumped against the bar several more times. Then the cloud of smoke and the broom moved off across the floor.

"You oughta tell your customer use they ashtray, tell them peoples you workin a man in here below the minimal wage. Maybe they be a little considerate."

"You better be glad I'm giving you a chance, boy," Lana Lee said. "There's plenty colored boys looking for work these days."

"Yeah, and they's plenty color boy turnin vagran, too, when they see what kinda wage peoples offerin. Sometime I think if you color, it better to be a vagran."

"You better be glad you're working."

"Ever night I'm fallin on my knee."

The broom bumped against a table.

"Let me know when you finish with that sweeping," Lana Lee said. "I got a little errand I want you to run for me."

"Erran? Hey! I thought this a sweepin and moppin job."
Jones blew out a cumulus formation. "What this erran shit?"

"Listen here, Jones," Lana Lee dumped a pile of nickels
into the cash register and wrote down a figure on a sheet of
paper. "All I gotta do is phone the police and report you're
out of work. You understand me?"

"And I tell the po-lice the Night of Joy a glorify cathouse.
I fall in a trap when I come to work in this place. Whoa! Now
I jus waitin to get some kinda evidence. When I do, I really
gonna flap my mouth at the precinct."

"Watch your tongue."

"Times changin," Jones said, adjusting his sunglasses. "You
cain scare color peoples no more. I got me some peoples form
a human chain in front your door, drive away your business,
get you on the TV news. Color peoples took enough horse-
shit already, and for twenty dollar a week you ain piling no
more on. I getting pretty tire of bein vagran or workin below
the minimal wage. Get somebody else run your erran."

"Aw, knock it off and finish my floor. I'll get Darlene to
go."

"That po gal." Jones explored a booth with the broom.
"Hustlin water, runnin erran. Whoa!"

"Ring up the precinct about her. She's a B-drinker."

"I waitin till I can ring up the precinct about *you*. Darlene
don *wanna* be a B-drinker. She *force* to be a B-drinker. She say
she wanna go in show biz."

"Yeah? Well, with the brains that girl's got she's lucky they
haven't shipped her off to the funny farm."

"She be better off there."

"She'd be better off if she just put that mind of hers to
selling my liquor and quit with the dancing crap. I can just
imagine what somebody like her would do on my stage.
Darlene's the kinda person ruin your investment if you don't
watch her."

The padded door banged open and a young boy clicked into the bar, scraping the metal taps on his flamenco boots across the floor.

"Well, it's about time," Lana said to him.

"You got a new jig, huh?" The boy looked out at Jones through his swirls of oiled hair. "What happened to the last one? He die or something?"

"Honey," said Lana blandly.

The boy opened a flashy hand-tooled wallet and gave Lana a number of bills.

"Everything went okay, George?" she asked him. "The orphans liked them?"

"They liked the one on the desk with the glasses on. They thought it was some kinda teacher or something. I want only that one this time."

"You think they want another like that?" Lana asked with interest.

"Yeah. Why not? Maybe one with a blackboard and a book. You know. Doing something with a piece of chalk."

The boy and Lana smiled at each other.

"I get the picture," Lana said and winked.

"Hey, you a junkie?" the boy called to Jones. "You look like a junkie to me."

"You be lookin pretty junky with a Night of Joy broom stickin out your ass," Jones said very slowly. "Night of Joy broom old, they good and splintery."

"Okay, okay," Lana screamed. "I don't want a race riot in here. I got an investment to protect."

"You better tell your little ofay kid friend move along." Jones blew some smoke on the two. "I ain takin no insult with this kinda job."

"Come on, George," Lana said. She opened the cabinet under the bar and gave George a package wrapped in brown paper. "This is the one you want. Now go on. Beat it."

George winked at her and banged out the door.

"That suppose to be a messenger for the orphans?" Jones asked. "I like to see the orphans he operatin for. I bet the United Fun don know about them orphans."

"What the hell are you talking about?" Lana asked angrily. She studied Jones's face, but the glasses prevented her reading anything there. "There's nothing wrong with a little charity. Now get back on my floor."

Lana started to make sounds, like the imprecations of a priestess, over the bills that the boy had given her. Whispered numerals and words floated upward from her coral lips, and, closing her eyes, she copied some figures onto a pad of paper. Her fine body, itself a profitable investment through the years, bent reverently over the formica top altar. Smoke, like incense, rose from the cigarette in the ashtray at her elbow, curling upward with her prayers, up above the host which she was elevating in order to study the date of its minting, the single silver dollar that lay among the offerings. Her bracelet tinkled, calling communicants to the altar, but the only one in the temple had been excommunicated from the Faith because of his parentage and continued mopping. An offering fell to the floor, the host, and Lana knelt to venerate and retrieve it.

"Hey, watch out," Jones called, violating the sanctity of the rite. "You droppin your profit from the orphans, butterfinger."

"Did you see where it went to, Jones?" she asked. "See if you can find it."

Jones rested his mop against the bar and scouted for the coin, squinting through his sunglasses and smoke.

"Ain this the shit," he mumbled to himself while the two searched the floor. "Ooo-wee!"

"I found it," Lana said emotionally. "I got it."

"Whoa! I'm sure glad you did. Hey! You better not be droppin silver dollars on the floor like that, Night of Joy be

78

going bankrup. You be havin trouble meetin that big payroll."

"And why don't you try keeping your mouth shut, boy?"

"Say, who you callin 'boy'?" Jones took the handle of the broom and pushed vigorously toward the altar. "You ain Scarla O'Horror."

V

Ignatius eased himself into the taxi and gave the driver the Constantinople Street address. From the pocket of his overcoat he took a sheet of Levy Pants stationery, and borrowing the driver's clipboard for a desk, he began to write as the taxi joined the dense traffic on St. Claude Avenue.

I am really quite fatigued as my first working day draws to a close. I do not wish to suggest, however, that I am disheartened or depressed or defeated. For the first time in my life I have met the system face to face, fully determined to function within its context as an observer and critic in disguise, so to speak. Were there more firms like Levy Pants, I do believe that America's working forces would be better adjusted to their tasks. The obviously reliable worker is completely unmolested. Mr. Gonzalez, my "boss," is rather a cretin, but is nonetheless quite pleasant. He seems eternally apprehensive, certainly too apprehensive to criticize any worker's performance of duty. Actually, he will accept anything, almost, and is therefore appealingly democratic in his retarded way. As an example of this, Miss Trixie, our Earth Mother of the world of commerce, inadvertently set flame to some important orders in the process of lighting a heater. Mr. Gonzalez was quite tolerant of this *gaffe* when one considers that the company of late has been receiving fewer and fewer orders and that the orders were a demand from Kansas City for some five hundred dollars ($500!) worth of our product. We must remember, though, that Mr. Gonzalez is under orders from that mysterious tycooness, the reputedly brilliant and learned Mrs. Levy, to treat Miss Trixie well and to make her feel active and wanted. But he has also been most courteous to me, permitting me to have my will among the files.

I intend to draw Miss Trixie out rather shortly; I suspect that this Medusa of capitalism has many valuable insights and more than one pithy observation to offer.

The only sour note—and here I degenerate into slang to more properly set the mood for the creature whom I am about to discuss—was Gloria, the stenographer, a young and brazen tart. Her mind was reeling with misconceptions and abysmal value judgments. After she had made one or two bold and unsolicited comments about my person and bearing, I drew Mr. Gonzalez aside to tell him that Gloria was planning to quit without notice at the end of the day. Mr. Gonzalez, thereupon, grew quite manic, and fired Gloria immediately, affording himself an opportunity at authority which, I could see, he rarely enjoyed. Actually, it was the awful sound of Gloria's stake-like heels that led me to do what I did. Another day of that clatter would have sealed my valve for good. Then, too, there was all of that mascara and lipstick and other vulgarities which I would rather not catalogue.

I have many plans for my filing department and have taken—from among the many empty ones—a desk near a window. There I sat with my little gas heater at full force throughout the afternoon, watching the ships from many an exotic port steaming through the cold, dark waters of the harbor. Miss Trixie's light snore and the furious typing of Mr. Gonzalez provided a pleasant counterpoint to my reflections.

Mr. Levy did not appear today; I am given to understand that he visits the business rarely, that he is actually, as Mr. Gonzalez puts it, "trying to sell out as soon as possible." Perhaps the three of us (for I shall endeavor to make Mr. Gonzalez dismiss the other workers if they arrive tomorrow; too many people in that office will probably prove distracting) in the office can revitalize the business and restore the faith of Mr. Levy The Younger. I have several excellent ideas already, and I know that I, for one, will eventually make Mr. Levy decide to put his heart and soul in the firm.

I have, incidentally, made a very shrewd bargain with Mr. Gonzalez: I convinced him that because I had helped him save the expense of Gloria's salary, he could respond by transporting me to and fro by taxi. The haggling that ensued was a blot upon an otherwise pleasant day, but I finally won my point by explaining to the man the dangers of my valve and of my health in general.

So we see that even when Fortuna spins us downward, the wheel sometimes halts for a moment and we find ourselves in a good, small cycle within the larger bad cycle. The universe, of course, is based upon the principle of the circle within the circle. At the moment, I am in an inner circle. Of course, smaller circles within this circle are also possible.

Ignatius gave the driver the clipboard and a variety of instructions upon speed, direction, and shifting. By the time they had reached Constantinople Street there was a hostile silence in the taxi, which was only broken by the driver's request for the fare.

As Ignatius pulled himself angrily up and out of the taxi,

he saw his mother coming down the street. She was wearing her short pink topper and the small red hat that tilted over one eye so that she looked like a refugee starlet from the *Golddiggers* film series. Ignatius noticed hopelessly that she had added a dash of color by pinning a wilted poinsettia to the lapel of her topper. Her brown wedgies squeaked with discount price defiance, as she walked redly and pinkly along the broken brick sidewalk. Even though he had been seeing her outfits for years, the sight of his mother in full regalia always slightly appalled his valve.

"Oh, honey," Mrs. Reilly said breathlessly when they met by the rear bumper of the Plymouth, which blocked all sidewalk traffic. "A terrible thing's happened."

"Oh, my God. What is it now?"

Ignatius imagined it was something in his mother's family, a group of people who tended to suffer violence and pain. There was the old aunt who had been robbed of fifty cents by some hoodlums, the cousin who had been struck by the Magazine streetcar, the uncle who had eaten a bad cream puff, the godfather who had touched a live wire knocked loose in a hurricane.

"It's poor Miss Annie next door. This morning she took a little fainting spell in the alley. Nerves, babe. She says you woke her up this morning playing on your banjo."

"That is a lute, not a banjo," Ignatius thundered. "Does she think that I'm one of these perverse Mark Twain characters?"

"I just come from seeing her. She's staying over by her son's house on St. Mary Street."

"Oh, that offensive boy." Ignatius climbed the steps ahead of his mother. "Well, thank God Miss Annie has left for a while. Now perhaps I can play my lute without her rasping denunciations assailing me from across the alley."

"I stopped off at Lenny's and bought her a nice little pair of beads filled with Lourdes water."

"Good grief. Lenny's. Never in my life have I seen a shop filled with so much religious hexerei. I suspect that that jewelry shop is going to be the scene of a miracle before long. Lenny himself may ascend."

"Miss Annie loved them beads, boy. Right away she started saying a rosary."

"No doubt that was better than conversing with you."

"Have a chair, babe, and I'll fix you something to eat."

"In the confusion of Miss Annie's collapse, you seem to have forgotten that you shipped me off to Levy Pants this morning."

"Oh, Ignatius, what happened?" Mrs. Reilly asked, putting a match to a burner that she had turned on several seconds before. There was a localized explosion on the top of the stove. "Lord, I almost got myself burnt."

"I am now an employee of Levy Pants."

"Ignatius!" his mother cried, circling his oily head in a clumsy pink woolen embrace that crushed his nose. Tears welled in her eyes. "I'm so proud of my boy."

"I'm quite exhausted. The atmosphere in that office is hypertense."

"I knew you'd make good."

"Thank you for your confidence."

"How much Levy Pants is gonna pay you, darling?"

"Sixty American dollars a week."

"Aw, that's all? Maybe you should of looked around some more."

"There are wonderful opportunities for advancement, wonderful plans for the alert young man. The salary may soon change."

"You think so? Well, I'm still proud, babe. Take off your overcoat." Mrs. Reilly opened a can of Libby's stew and tossed it in the pot. "They got any cute girls working there?"

Ignatius thought of Miss Trixie and said, "Yes, there is one."

"Single?"

"She appears to be."

Mrs. Reilly winked at Ignatius and threw his overcoat on top of the cupboard.

"Look, honey, I put a fire under this stew. Open you a can of peas, and they's bread in the icebox. I got a cake from the German's, too, but I can't remember right off where I put it. Take a look around the kitchen. I gotta go."

"Where are you going now?"

"Mr. Mancuso and his aunt, they gonna pick me up in a few minutes. We going down by Fazzio's to bowl."

"What?" Ignatius screamed. "Is that true?"

"I'll be in early. I told Mr. Mancuso I can't stay out late. And his aunt's a grammaw, so I guess she needs her sleep."

"This is certainly a fine reception that I am given after my first day of work," Ignatius said furiously. "You can't bowl. You have arthritis or something. This is ridiculous. Where are you going to eat?"

"I can get me some chili down by the bowling alley." Mrs. Reilly was already going to her room to change clothes. "Oh, honey, a letter come for you today from New York. I put it behind the coffee can. It looks like it came from that Myrna girl because the envelope's all dirty and smudged up. How come that Myrna's gotta send out mail looking like that? I thought you said her poppa's got money."

"You can't go bowling," Ignatius bellowed. "This is the most absurd thing that you have ever done."

Mrs. Reilly's door slammed. Ignatius found the envelope and tore it to shreds in opening it. He pulled out some art theater's year-old schedule for a summer film festival. On the reverse side of the rumpled schedule there was a letter written in the uneven and angular hand that constituted Minkoffian penmanship. Myrna's habit of writing to editors rather than friends was always reflected in her salutation:

Sirs:

What is this strange, frightening letter that you have written me, Ignatius? How can I contact the Civil Liberties Union with the little evidence that you have given me? I can't imagine why a policeman would try to arrest you. You stay in your room all the time. I might have believed the arrest if you hadn't written about that "automobile accident." If both of your wrists were broken, how could you write me a letter?

Let us be honest with each other, Ignatius. I do not believe a word of what I read. But I am frightened—for you. The fantasy about the arrest has all the classic paranoid qualities. You are aware, of course, that Freud linked paranoia with homosexual tendencies.

"Filth!" Ignatius shouted.

However, we won't go into that aspect of the fantasy because I know how dedicated you are in your opposition to sex of any sort. Still your emotional problem is very apparent. Since you flunked that interview for the teaching job in Baton Rouge (meanwhile blaming it on the bus and things—a transferral of guilt), you have probably suffered feelings of failure. This "automobile accident" is a new crutch to help you make excuses for your meaningless, impotent existence. Ignatius, you must identify with something. As I've told you time and again, you must commit yourself to the crucial problems of the times.

"Ho hum," Ignatius yawned.

Subconsciously you feel that you must attempt to explain away your failure, as an intellectual and soldier of ideas, to actively participate in critical social movements. Also, a *satisfying sexual encounter would purify your mind and body. You need the therapy of sex desperately. I'm afraid— from what I know about clinical cases like yours—that you may end up a psychosomatic invalid like Elizabeth B. Browning.*

"How unspeakably offensive," Ignatius spluttered.

I don't feel much sympathy for you. You have closed your mind to both love and society. At the moment my every waking hour is spent in helping some dedicated friends raise money for a bold and shattering movie that they are planning to film about an interracial marriage. Although it will be a low-budget number, the script itself is chock full of disturbing truths and has the most fascinating tonalities and ironies. It was written by Shmuel, a boy I've known since Taft High days. Shmuel will also play the husband in the movie. We have found a girl from the streets of Harlem to play the wife. She is such a real, vital person that I have made her my very closest friend. I discuss her racial problems with her constantly, drawing her out even when she doesn't feel like discussing them—and I can tell how fervently she appreciates these dialogues with me.

There is a sick, reactionary villain in the script, an Irish landlord who refuses to rent to the couple, who by this time have been married in this subdued Ethical Culture ceremony. The landlord lives in this little womb-room whose walls are covered with pictures of the Pope and stuff like that. In other words, the audience will have no trouble reading him as soon as they get one glimpse at that room. We have not cast the landlord yet. You, of course, would be fantastic for the part. You see, Ignatius, if you would just decide to cut the umbilical cord that binds you to that stagnant city, that mother of yours, and that bed, you could be up here having opportunities like this. Are you interested in the part? We can't pay much, but you can stay with me.

I may play a little mood music or protest music on my guitar for the sound-track. I hope that we can finally get this magnificent project on film soon because Leola, the unbelievable girl from Harlem, is beginning to bug us about salary. Already I've bled about $1,000 from my father, who is suspicious (as usual) of the whole enterprise.

Ignatius, I've humored you long enough in our correspondence. Don't write to me again until you've taken part. I hate cowards.

M. Minkoff

P.S. Also write if you'd like to play the landlord.

"I'll show this offensive trollop," Ignatius mumbled, throwing the art theater schedule into the fire beneath the stew.

Four

Levy Pants was two structures fused into one macabre unit. The front of the plant was a brick commercial building of the nineteenth century with a mansard roof that bulged out into several rococo dormer windows, the panes of which were mostly cracked. Within this section the office occupied the third floor, a storage area the second, and refuse the first. Attached to this building, which Mr. Gonzalez referred to as "the brain center," was the factory, a barnlike prototype of an airplane hangar. The two smokestacks that rose from the factory's tin roof leaned apart at an angle that formed an outsized rabbit-eared television antenna, an antenna that received no hopeful electronic signal from the outside world but instead discharged occasional smoke of a very sickly shade. Alongside the neat gray wharf sheds that lined the river and canal across the railroad tracks, Levy Pants huddled, a silent and smoky plea for urban renewal.

Within the brain center there was more than the usual amount of activity. Ignatius was tacking to a post near his files a wide cardboard sign that said in bold blue Gothic lettering:

DEPARTMENT OF RESEARCH AND REFERENCE
I.J. REILLY, CUSTODIAN

He had neglected the morning filing to make the sign, spreading himself upon the floor with the cardboard and blue poster paint and painting meticulously for more than an hour. Miss Trixie had stepped on the sign during one of her occasional pointless tours of the office, but the damage was limited to only a small sneaker print on one corner of the cardboard. Still, Ignatius found the tiny imprint offensive, and over it he painted a dramatic and stylized version of a fleur-de-lis.

"Isn't that nice," Mr. Gonzalez said when Ignatius had stopped hammering. "It gives the office a certain tone."

"What does it mean?" Miss Trixie demanded, standing directly beneath the sign and examining it frantically.

"It is simply a guidepost," Ignatius said proudly.

"I don't understand all this," Miss Trixie said. "What's going on around here?" She turned to Ignatius. "Gomez, who is this person?"

"Miss Trixie, you know Mr. Reilly. He's been working with us for a week now."

"Reilly? I thought it was Gloria."

"Go back and work on your figures," Mr. Gonzalez told her. "We have to send that statement to the bank before noon."

"Oh, yes, we must send that statement," Miss Trixie agreed and shuffled off to the ladies' room.

"Mr. Reilly, I don't want to pressure you," Mr. Gonzalez said cautiously, "but I do notice that you have quite a pile of material on your desk that hasn't been filed yet."

"Oh, that. Yes. Well, when I opened the first drawer this morning, I was greeted by a rather large rat which seemed to be devouring the Abelman's Dry Goods folder. I thought it politic to wait until he was sated. I would hate to contract the bubonic plague and lay the blame upon Levy Pants."

"Quite right," Mr. Gonzalez said anxiously, his dapper person quivering at the prospect of an on-the-job accident.

"In addition, my valve has been misbehaving and has prevented me from bending over to reach the lower drawers."

"I have just the thing for that," Mr. Gonzalez said and went into the little office storeroom to get, Ignatius imagined, some type of medicine. But he returned with one of the smallest metal stools that Ignatius had ever seen. "Here. The person who used to work on the files used to wheel back and forth on this along the lower drawers. Try it."

"I don't believe that my particular body structure is easily adaptable to that type of device," Ignatius observed, a gimlet eye fixed upon the rusting stool. Ignatius had always had a poor sense of balance, and ever since his obese childhood, he had suffered a tendency to fall, trip, and stumble. Until he was five years old and had finally managed to walk in an almost normal manner, he had been a mass of bruises and hickeys. "However, for the sake of Levy Pants, I shall try."

Ignatius squatted lower and lower until his great buttocks touched the stool, his knees reaching almost to his shoulders. When he was at last nestled upon his perch, he looked like an eggplant balanced atop a thumb tack.

"This will never do. I feel quite uncomfortable."

"Give it a try," Mr. Gonzalez said brightly.

Propelling himself with his feet, Ignatius traveled anxiously along the side of the files until one of the miniature wheels lodged in a crack. The stool tipped slightly and then turned over, dumping Ignatius heavily to the floor.

"Oh, my God!" he bellowed. "I think I've broken my back."

"Here," Mr. Gonzalez cried in his terrorized tenor. "I'll help you up."

"No! You must never move a person with a broken back unless you have a stretcher. I won't be paralyzed through your incompetence."

"Please try to get up, Mr. Reilly." Mr. Gonzalez looked at the mound at his feet. His heart sank. "I'll help you. I don't think you're badly injured."

"Let me alone," Ignatius screamed. "You fool. I refuse to spend the remainder of my life in a wheel chair."

Mr. Gonzalez felt his feet turn cold and numb.

The thud of Ignatius' fall had attracted Miss Trixie from the ladies' room; she came around the files and tripped on the mountain of supine flesh.

"Oh, dear," she said feebly. "Is Gloria dying, Gomez?"

"No," Mr. Gonzalez said sharply.

"Well, I'm certainly glad of that," Miss Trixie said, stepping onto one of Ignatius' outstretched hands.

"Good grief!" Ignatius thundered and sprang into a sitting position. "The bones in my hand are crushed. I'll never be able to use it again."

"Miss Trixie is very light," the office manager told Ignatius. "I don't think she could have hurt you much."

"Has she ever stepped on you, you idiot? How would you know?"

Ignatius sat at the feet of his co-workers and studied his hand.

"I suspect that I won't be able to use this hand again today. I had better go home immediately and bathe it."

"But the filing has to be done. Look how behind you are already."

"Are you talking about filing at a time like this? I am prepared to contact my attorneys and have them sue you for making me get on that obscene stool."

"We'll help you up, Gloria." Miss Trixie assumed what was apparently a hoisting position. She spread her sneakers far apart, toes pointing outward, and squatted like a Balinese dancer.

"Get up," Mr. Gonzalez snapped at her. "You're going to fall over."

"No," she answered through tight, withered lips. "I'm going to help Gloria. Get down on that side, Gomez. We'll just grab Gloria by the elbows."

Ignatius watched passively while Mr. Gonzalez squatted on his other side.

"You are distributing your weight incorrectly," he told them didactically. "If you are going to attempt to raise me, that position offers you no leverage. I suspect that the three of us will be injured. I suggest that you try a standing position. In that way you can easily bend over and hoist me."

"Don't be nervous, Gloria," Miss Trixie said, rocking back and forth on her haunches. Then she fell forward onto Ignatius, throwing him on his back once again. The edge of her celluloid visor hit him in the throat.

"Oof," gurgled from somewhere in the depths of Ignatius' throat. "Braah."

"Gloria!" Miss Trixie wheezed. She looked into the full face directly beneath hers. "Gomez, call a doctor."

"Miss Trixie, get off Mr. Reilly," the office manager hissed from where he squatted beside his two underlings.

"Braah."

"What are you people doing down there on the floor?" a man asked from the door. Mr. Gonzalez' chipper face hardened into a mask of horror, and he squeaked, "Good morning, Mr. Levy. We're so glad to see you."

"I just came in to see if I have any personal mail. I'm driving back to the coast right away. What's this big sign over here for? Somebody's going to get his eye knocked out on that thing."

"Is that Mr. Levy?" Ignatius called from the floor. He could not see the man over the row of filing cabinets. "Braah. I have been wanting to meet him."

Shedding Miss Trixie, who slumped to the floor, Ignatius struggled to his feet and saw a sportily dressed middle-aged man holding the handle of the office door so that he could flee as rapidly as he had entered.

"Hello there," Mr. Levy said casually. "New worker, Gonzalez?"

"Oh, yes sir. Mr. Levy, this is Mr. Reilly. He's very efficient.

A whiz. As a matter of fact, he's made it possible for us to do away with several other workers."

"Braah."

"Oh, yeah, the name on this sign." Mr. Levy gave Ignatius a strange look.

"I have taken an unusual interest in your firm," Ignatius said to Mr. Levy. "The sign which you noticed upon entering is only the first of several innovations which I plan. Braah. I will change your mind about this firm, sir. Mark my word."

"You don't say?" Mr. Levy studied Ignatius with certain curiosity. "What about the mail, Gonzalez?"

"There's not much. You received your new credit cards. Trans-global Airlines sent you a certificate making you an honorary pilot for flying one hundred hours with them." Mr. Gonzalez opened his desk and gave Mr. Levy the mail. "There's also a brochure from a hotel in Miami."

"You'd better start making my spring practice reservations. I gave you my itinerary of practice camps, didn't I?"

"Yes, sir. By the way, I have some letters for you to sign. I had to write a letter to Abelman's Dry Goods. We always have trouble with them."

"I know. What do those crooks want now?"

"Abelman claims that the last lot of trousers we shipped him were only two feet long in the leg. I'm trying to straighten out the matter."

"Yeah? Well, stranger things have happened around this place," Mr. Levy said quickly. The office was already beginning to depress him. He had to get out. "Better check with that foreman in the factory. What's his name? Look, suppose you sign those letters like always. I have to go." Mr. Levy pulled the door open. "Don't work these kids too hard, Gonzalez. So long, Miss Trixie. My wife asked about you."

Miss Trixie was sitting on the floor relacing one of her sneakers.

"Miss Trixie," Mr. Gonzalez screamed. "Mr. Levy is talking to you."

"Who?" Miss Trixie snarled. "I thought you said he was dead."

"I hope that you will see some vast changes the next time that you drop in on us," Ignatius said. "We are going to re-vitalize, as it were, your business."

"Okay. Take it easy," Mr. Levy said and slammed the door.

"He's a wonderful man," Mr. Gonzalez told Ignatius fervently. From a window the two watched Mr. Levy get into his sports car. The motor roared, and Mr. Levy sped away within a few seconds, leaving a settling cloud of blue exhaust.

"Perhaps I shall get to the filing," Ignatius said when he found himself staring out the window at only an empty street. "Will you please sign that correspondence so that I can file the carbon copies. It should now be safe to approach what that rodent has left of the Abelman folder."

Ignatius spied while Mr. Gonzalez, painstaking, forged *Gus Levy* to the letters.

"Mr. Reilly," Mr. Gonzalez said, carefully screwing the top onto his two-dollar pen, "I am going into the factory to speak with the foreman. Please keep an eye on things."

By *things*, Ignatius imagined that Mr. Gonzalez meant Miss Trixie, who was snoring loudly on the floor in front of the file cabinet.

"*Seguro,*" Ignatius said and smiled. "A little Spanish in honor of your noble heritage."

As soon as the office manager went through the door, Ignatius rolled a sheet of Levy stationery into Mr. Gonzalez' high black typewriter. If Levy Pants was to succeed, the first step would be imposing a heavy hand upon its detractors. Levy Pants must become more militant and authoritarian in order to survive in the jungle of modern commercialism. Ignatius began to type the first step:

Abelman's Dry Goods
Kansas City, Missouri
U. S. A.

Mr. I. Abelman, Mongoloid, Esq.:

   We have received via post your absurd comments about our trousers, the comments revealing, as they did, your total lack of contact with reality. Were you more aware, you would know or realize by now that the offending trousers were dispatched to you with our full knowledge that they were inadequate so far as length was concerned.

   "Why? Why?" you are in your incomprehensible babble, unable to assimilate stimulating concepts of commerce into your retarded and blighted worldview.

   The trousers were sent to you (1) as a means of testing your initiative (A clever, wide-awake business concern should be able to make three-quarter length trousers a by-word of masculine fashion. Your advertising and merchandising programs are obviously faulty.) and (2) as a means of testing your ability to meet the standards requisite in a distributor of our quality product. (Our loyal and dependable outlets can vend any trouser bearing the Levy label no matter how abominable their design and construction. You are apparently a faithless people.)

   We do not wish to be bothered in the future by such tedious complaints. Please confine your correspondence to orders only. We are a busy and dynamic organization whose mission needless effrontery and harassment can only hinder. If you molest us again, sir, you may feel the sting of the lash across your pitiful shoulders.

Yours in anger,
Gus Levy, Pres.

Happily pondering the thought that the world understood only strength and force, Ignatius copied the Levy signature onto the letter with the office manager's pen, tore up Mr. Gonzalez' letter to Abelman, and slipped his own into the correspondence Outgoing box. Then he tiptoed carefully around the little inert figure of Miss Trixie, returned to the filing department, picked up the stack of still unfiled material, and threw it into the wastebasket.

II

"Hey, Miss Lee, that fat mother got him the green cap, he comin in here anymore?"

"No, thank God. It's characters like that ruin your investment."

"When your little orphan frien comin here again? Whoa! I like to fin out what goin on with them orphan. I bet they be the firs orphan the po-lice be interes in ever."

"I told you I send the orphans things. A little charity never hurt nobody. It makes you feel good."

"That really soun like Night of Joy chariddy when them orphan payin in a lotta money for whatever they gettin."

"Stop worrying about the orphans and start worrying about my floor. I got enough problems already. Darlene wants to dance. You want a raise. And I got worse problems on top of that." Lana thought of the plainclothesmen who had suddenly started to appear in the club late at night. "Business stinks."

"Yeah. I can tell that. I starvin to death in this cathouse."

"Say, Jones, you been over to the precinct lately?" Lana asked cautiously, wondering whether there was an outside chance that Jones might be leading the cops to the place. This Jones was turning out to be a headache, in spite of the low salary.

"No, I ain been visitin all my po-lice frien. I waitin till I get some good evidence." Jones shot out a nimbus formation. "I waitin for a break in the orphan case. Ooo-wee!"

Lana twisted up her coral lips and tried to imagine who had tipped off the police.

III

Mrs. Reilly could not believe that it had really happened to her. There was no television. There were no complaints. The bathroom was empty. Even the roaches seemed to have pulled up stakes. She sat at the kitchen table sipping a little muscatel and blew away the one baby roach that was starting to cross the table. The tiny body flew off the table and disappeared, and Mrs. Reilly said, "So long, darling." She poured another inch of wine, realizing for the first time that the house smelled different, too. It smelled as close as it ever did, but her son's curious personal odor, which always reminded her of the scent of old tea bags, seemed to have lifted. She lifted her glass and wondered whether Levy Pants was beginning to reek a little of used pekoe.

Suddenly Mrs. Reilly remembered the horrible night that she and Mr. Reilly had gone to the Prytania to see Clark Gable and Jean Harlow in *Red Dust*. In the heat and confusion that had followed their return home, nice Mr. Reilly had tried one of his indirect approaches, and Ignatius was conceived. Poor Mr. Reilly. He had never gone to another movie as long as he lived.

Mrs. Reilly sighed and looked at the floor to see whether the baby roach was still around and functioning. She was in too pleasant a mood to harm anything. While she was studying the linoleum, the telephone rang in the narrow hall. Mrs. Reilly corked her bottle and put it in the cold oven.

"Hello," she said into the telephone.

"Hey, Irene?" a woman's hoarse voice asked. "What you doing, babe? It's Santa Battaglia."

"How you making, honey?"

"I'm beat. I just finished opening four dozen ersters out in the backyard," Santa said in her rocky baritone. "That's hard work, believe me, banging that erster knife on them bricks."

"I wouldn't try nothing like that," Mrs. Reilly said honestly.

"I don't mind. When I was a little girl I use to open ersters up for my momma. She had her a little seafood stand outside the Lautenschlaeger Market. Poor momma. Right off the boat. Couldn't speak a word of English hardly. There I was just a little thing breaking them ersters open. I didn't go to no school. Not me, babe. I was right there with them ersters banging away on the banquette. Every now and then momma start banging away on me for something. We always had a lotta commotion around our stand, us."

"Your momma was very excitable, huh?"

"Poor girl. Standing there in the rain and cold with her old sunbonnet on not knowing what nobody was saying half the time. It was hard in them days, Irene. Things was tough, kid."

"You can say that again," Mrs. Reilly agreed. "We sure had us some hard times down on Dauphine Street. Poppa was very poor. He had him a job by a wagon works, but then the automobiles come in, and he gets his hand caught in a fanbelt. Many's the week we lived on red beans and rice."

"Red beans gives me gas."

"Me, too. Listen, Santa, why you called, sugar?"

"Oh, yeah, I almost forgot. You remember when we was out bowling the other night?"

"Tuesday?"

"No, it was Wednesday, I think. Anyway, it was the night Angelo got arrested and couldn't come."

"Wasn't that awful. The police arresting one of they very own."

"Yeah. Poor Angelo. He's so sweet. He sure got trouble at that precinct." Santa coughed hoarsely into the telephone. "Anyway, it was the night you come for me in that car of yours and we went to the alley alone. This morning I was over by the fish market buying them ersters, and this old man comes up to me and says, 'Wasn't you by the bowling alley the other night?' So I says, 'Yeah, mister, I go there a lot.' And he says, 'Well, I was there with my daughter and her husband and I seen you with a lady got sorta red hair.' I says, 'You mean the lady got the henna hair? That's my friend Miss Reilly. I'm learning her how to bowl.' That's all, Irene. He just tips his hat and walks out the market."

"I wonder who that could be," Mrs. Reilly said with great interest. "That's sure funny. What he looks like, babe?"

"Nice man, kinda old. I seen him around the neighborhood before taking some little kids to Mass. I think they his granchirren."

"Ain't that strange? Who'd be asking about me?"

"I don't know, kid, but you better watch out. Somebody's got they eye on you."

"Aw, Santa! I'm too old, girl."

"Listen to you. You still cute, Irene. I seen plenty men giving you the eye in the bowling alley."

"Aw, go on."

"That's the truth, kid. I ain't lying. You been stuck away with that son of yours too long."

"Ignatius says he's making good at Levy Pants," Mrs. Reilly said defensively. "I don't wanna get mixed up with no old man."

"He ain't *that* old," Santa said, sounding a little hurt. "Listen, Irene, me and Angelo coming by for you about seven tonight."

"I don't know, darling. Ignatius been telling me I oughta stay home more."

"Why you gotta stay home, girl? Angelo says he's a big man."

"Ignatius says he's afraid when I leave him alone here at night. He says he's scared of burgulars."

"Bring him along, and Angelo can learn him how to bowl, too."

"Whoo! Ignatius ain't what you'd call the sporting type," Mrs. Reilly said quickly.

"You come along anyways, huh?"

"Okay," Mrs. Reilly said finally. "I think the exercise is helping my elbow out. I'll tell Ignatius he can lock himself up in his room."

"Sure," Santa said. "Nobody's gonna hurt him."

"We ain't got nothing worth stealing anyways. I don't know where Ignatius gets them ideas of his."

"Me and Angelo be by at seven."

"Fine, and listen, precious, try and ask by the fish market who that old man is."

IV

The Levy home stood among the pines on a small rise overlooking the gray waters of Bay St. Louis. The exterior was an example of elegant rusticity; the interior was a successful attempt at keeping the rustic out entirely, a permanently seventy-five-degree womb connected to the year-round air-conditioning unit by an umbilicus of vents and pipes that silently filled the rooms with filtered and reconstituted Gulf of Mexico breezes and exhaled the Levys' carbon dioxide and cigarette smoke and ennui. The central machinery of the great life-giving unit throbbed somewhere in the acoustically tiled bowels of the home, like a Red Cross instructor giving cadence in an artificial respiration class,

"*In* comes the good air, *out* goes the bad air, *in* comes the good air."

The home was as sensually comfortable as the human womb supposedly is. Every chair sank several inches at the lightest touch, foam and down surrendering abjectly to any pressure. The tufts of the acrylic nylon carpets tickled the ankles of anyone kind enough to walk on them. Beside the bar what looked like a radio dial would, upon being turned, make the lighting throughout the house as mellow or as bright as the mood demanded. Located throughout the house within easy walking distance of one another were contour chairs, a massage table, and a motorized exercising board whose many sections prodded the body with a motion that was at once gentle yet suggestive. Levy's Lodge—that was what the sign at the coast road said—was a Xanadu of the senses; within its insulated walls there was something that could gratify anything.

Mr. and Mrs. Levy, who considered each other the only ungratifying objects in the home, sat before their television set watching the colors merge together on the screen.

"Perry Como's face is all green," Mrs. Levy said with great hostility. "He looks like a corpse. You'd better take this set back to the shop."

"I just brought it back from New Orleans this week," Mr. Levy said, blowing on the black hairs of his chest that he could see through the V of his terry cloth robe. He had just taken a steam bath and wanted to dry himself completely. Even with year-round air conditioning and central heating one could never be sure.

"Well, take it back again. I'm not going to go blind looking at a broken TV."

"Oh, shut up. He looks all right."

"He does not look all right. Look how green his lips are."

"It's the makeup those people use."

"You mean to tell me they put green makeup on Como's lips?"

"I don't know what they do."

"Of course you don't," Mrs. Levy said, turning her aquamarine-lidded eyes toward her husband, who was submerged somewhere among the pillows of a yellow nylon couch. She saw some terry cloth and a rubber shower clog at the end of a hairy leg.

"Don't bother me," he said. "Go play with your exercising board."

"I can't get on that thing tonight. My hair was done today."

She touched the high plasticized curls of her platinum hair.

"The hairdresser told me that I should get a wig, too," she said.

"What do you want with a wig? Look at all the hair you've got already."

"I want a brunette wig. That way I can change my personality."

"Look, you're already a brunette anyway, right? So why don't you let your hair grow out naturally and buy a blonde wig?"

"I hadn't thought of that."

"Well, think about it for a while and keep quiet. I'm tired. When I went into town today I stopped at the company. That always makes me depressed."

"What's happening there?"

"Nothing. Absolutely nothing."

"That's what I thought," Mrs. Levy sighed. "You've thrown your father's business down the drain. That's the tragedy of your life."

"Christ, who wants that old factory? Nobody's buying the kind of pants they make anymore. That's all my father's fault. When pleats came in in the thirties, he wouldn't change over from plain-front trousers. He was the Henry

Ford of the garment industry. Then when the plain front came back in the fifties, he started making trousers with pleats. Now you should see what Gonzalez calls 'the new summer line.' They look like those balloon pants the clowns wear in circuses. And the fabric. I wouldn't use it for a dishrag myself."

"When we were married, I idolized you, Gus. I thought you had drive. You could have made Levy Pants really big. Maybe even an office in New York. It was handed all to you and you threw it away."

"Oh, stop all that crap. You're comfortable."

"Your father had character. I respected him."

"My father was a very mean and cheap man, a little tyrant. I had some interest in that company when I was young. I had plenty interest. Well, he destroyed all that with his tyranny. So far as I'm concerned, Levy Pants is *his* company. Let it go down the drain. He blocked every good idea I had for that firm just to prove that he was the father and I was the son. If I said, 'Pleats,' he said, 'No pleats! Never!' If I said, 'Let's try some of the new synthetics,' he said, 'Synthetics over my dead body.'"

"He started peddling pants in a wagon. Look what he built that into. With your start you could have made Levy Pants nationwide."

"The nation is lucky, believe me. I spent my childhood in those pants. Anyway, I'm tired of listening to you talk. Period."

"Good. Let's keep quiet. Look, Como's lips are turning pink."

"You've never been a father figure to Susan and Sandra."

"The last time Sandra was home, she opened her purse to get cigarettes and a pack of rubbers falls on the floor right at my feet."

"That's what I'm trying to say to you. You never gave your

daughters an image. No wonder they're so mixed up. *I* tried with them."

"Listen, let's not discuss Susan and Sandra. They're away at college. We're lucky we don't know what's going on. When they get tired, they'll marry some poor guy and everything will be all right."

"Then what kind of a grandfather are you going to be?"

"I don't know. Let me alone. Go get on your exercising board, get in the whirlpool bath. I'm enjoying this show."

"How can you enjoy it when the faces are all discolored."

"Let's not start that again."

"Are we going to Miami next month?"

"Maybe. Maybe we could settle there."

"And give up everything we have?"

"Give up what? They can fit your exercising board in a moving van."

"But the company."

"The company has made all the money it's ever going to make. Now is the time to sell."

"It's a good thing your father's dead. He should have lived to see this." Mrs. Levy gave the shower shoe a tragic glance. "Now I guess you'll spend all your time at the World Series or the Derby or Daytona. It's a real tragedy, Gus. A real tragedy."

"Don't try to make a big Arthur Miller play out of Levy Pants."

"Thank goodness I'm around to watch over you. Thank goodness *I* have an interest in that company. How's Miss Trixie? I hope she's still relating and functioning pretty well."

"She's still alive, and that's saying a lot for her."

"At least I have an interest in her. You would have thrown her out in the snow long ago."

"The woman should have been retired long ago."

"I told you retirement will kill her. She must be made to feel wanted and loved. That woman's a real prospect for psychic rejuvenation. I want you to bring her out here someday. I'd like to really get to work on her."

"Bring that old bag here? Are you nuts? I don't want a reminder of Levy Pants snoring in my den. She'll wet all over your couch. You can play with her by long distance."

"How typical," Mrs. Levy sighed. "How I've stood this heartlessness through the years I'll never know."

"I've already let you keep Trixie at the office, where I know she must drive that Gonzalez nuts all day long. When I went there this morning everybody was on the floor. Don't ask me what they were doing. It could have been anything." Mr. Levy whistled through his teeth. "Gonzalez is on the moon, as usual, but you should see this other character working in there. I don't know where they got him from. You wouldn't believe your eyes, believe me. I'm afraid to guess what those three clowns do in that office all day long. It's a wonder nothing's happened already."

V

Ignatius had decided against going to the Prytania. The movie being shown was a widely praised Swedish drama about a man who was losing his soul, and Ignatius was not particularly interested in seeing it. He would have to speak with the manager of the theater about booking such dull fare.

He checked the bolt on his door and wondered when his mother would be coming home. Suddenly she was going out almost every night. But Ignatius had other considerations at the moment. Opening his desk, he looked at a pile of articles he had once written with an eye on the magazine market. For the journals of opinion there were "Boethius Observed" and "In Defense of Hroswitha: To Those Who Say She Did Not Exist." For the family magazines he had written "The Death of Rex" and "Children, the Hope of the World." In an attempt to crack the Sunday supplement market he had done "The Challenge of Water Safety," "The Danger of Eight-Cylinder Automobiles," "Abstinence, the Safest Method of Birth Control," and "New Orleans, City of Romance and Culture." As he looked through the old manuscripts, he wondered why he had failed to send any of them off, for each was excellent in its own way.

There was a new, extremely commercial project at hand, though. Ignatius quickly cleared the desk by brushing the magazine articles and Big Chief tablets smartly to the floor with one sweep of his paws. He placed a new looseleaf folder before him and printed slowly on its rough cover with a red crayon THE JOURNAL OF A WORKING BOY, OR, UP FROM SLOTH. When he had finished that, he tore the Blue Horse bands from the stacks of new lined paper and placed them in the folder. With a pencil he punched holes in the sheets of Levy stationery which already held some notes and inserted them in the front section of the folder. Taking up his Levy Pants ballpoint pen, he began writing on the first sheet of new Blue Horse paper:

Dear Reader,
Books are immortal sons defying their sires.

—Plato

I find, dear reader, that I have grown accustomed to the hectic pace of office life, an adjustment which I doubted I could make. Of course, it is true that in my brief career at Levy Pants, Limited, I have succeeded in initiating several work-saving methods. Those of you who are fellow office workers and find yourselves reading this incisive journal during a coffee break or such might take note of one or two of my innovations. I direct these observations to officers and tycoons, also.

I have taken to arriving at the office one hour later than I am expected. Therefore, I am far more rested and refreshed when I do arrive, and I avoid that bleak first hour of the working day during which my still sluggish senses and body make every chore a penance. I find that in arriving later, the work which I do perform is of a much higher quality.

My innovation in connection with the filing system must remain secret for the moment, for it is rather revolutionary, and I shall have to see how it works out. In theory the innovation is magnificent. However, I will say that the brittle and yellowing papers in the files constitute a fire hazard. A more special aspect that may not apply in all cases is that my files apparently are a tenement for assorted vermin. The bubonic plague is a valid Medieval fate; I do believe, though, that contracting the plague in this dreadful century would be only ludicrous.

Today our office was at last graced by the presence of our lord and master, Mr. G. Levy. To be quite honest, I found him rather casual and unconcerned. I brought to his attention the sign (Yes, reader, it has finally been painted and posted; a rather imperial fleur-de-lis now gives it added significance.), but that, too, elicited little interest on his part. His stay was brief and not at all businesslike, but who are we to question the motives of these giants of commerce whose whims rule the course of our nation. In time he will learn of my devotion to his firm, of my dedication. My example, in turn, may lead him to once again believe in Levy Pants.

La Trixie still keeps her own counsel, thereby proving

herself even wiser than I had thought. I suspect that this woman knows a great deal, that her apathy is a façade for her seeming resentment against Levy Pants. She grows more coherent when she speaks of retirement. I have noticed that she needs a new pair of white socks, her current pair having grown rather gray. Perhaps I shall gift her with a pair of absorbent white athletic socks in the near future; this gesture may affect her and lead her to conversation. She seems to have grown fond of my cap, for she has taken to wearing it rather than her celluloid visor on occasion.

As I have told you in earlier installments, I was emulating the poet Milton by spending my youth in seclusion, meditation, and study in order to perfect my craft of writing as he did; my mother's cataclysmic intemperance has thrust me into the world in the most cavalier manner; my system is still in a state of flux. Therefore, I am still in the process of adapting myself to the tension of the working world. As soon as my system becomes used to the office, I shall take the giant step of visiting the factory, the bustling heart of Levy Pants. I have heard more than a little hissing and roaring through the factory door, but my presently somewhat enervated condition precludes a descent into that particular inferno at the moment. Now and then some factory worker straggles into the office to illiterately plead some cause (usually the drunkenness of the foreman, a chronic tosspa). When I am once again whole, I shall visit those factory people; I have deep and abiding convictions concerning social action. I am certain that I can perhaps do something to aid these factory folk. I cannot abide those who would act cowardly in the face of a social injustice. I believe in bold and shattering commitment to the problems of our times.

Social note: I have sought escape in the Prytania on more than one occasion, pulled by the attractions of some technicolored horrors, filmed abortions that were offenses against any criteria of taste and decency, reels and reels of perversion and blasphemy that stunned my disbelieving eyes, that shocked my virginal mind, and sealed my valve.

My mother is currently associating with some undesirables who are attempting to transform her into an athlete of sorts, depraved specimens of mankind who regularly bowl their way to oblivion. At times I find carrying on my blossoming business career rather painful, suffering as I do from these distractions at home.

Health note: My valve did close quite violently this afternoon when Mr. Gonzalez asked me to add a column of figures for him. When he saw the state into which I was thrown by the request, he thoughtfully added the figures himself. I tried not to make a scene, but my valve got the better of me. That office manager could, incidentally, develop into something of a nuisance.

Until later,
Darryl, Your Working Boy

Ignatius read what he had just written with pleasure. The *Journal* had all sorts of possibilities. It could be a contemporary, vital, real document of a young man's problems. At last he closed the looseleaf folder and contemplated a reply to Myrna, a slashing, vicious attack upon her being and worldview. It would be better to wait until he had visited the factory and seen what possibilities for social action there were there. Such boldness had to be handled properly; he might be able to do something with the factory workers which would make Myrna look like a reactionary in the field of social action. He had to prove his superiority to the offensive minx.

Picking up his lute, he decided to relax in song for a moment. His massive tongue rolled up over his moustache in preparation and, strumming, he began to sing, "Tarye no longer; toward thyn heritage/ Hast on thy weye, and be of ryght good chere."

"Shut up!" Miss Annie hollered through her closed shutters.

"How dare you!" Ignatius replied, ripping open his own shutters and looking out into the dark, cold alley. "Open up there. How dare you hide behind those shutters."

He ran furiously to the kitchen, filled a pot with water, and rushed back to his room. Just as he was about to throw the water on Miss Annie's still unopened shutters, he heard a car door slam out on the street. Some people were coming down the alley. Ignatius closed his shutters and turned off the light, listening to his mother speaking to someone. Patrolman Mancuso said something as they passed under his window, and a woman's hoarse voice said, "It looks safe to me, Irene. There ain't no lights on. He must of gone to the show."

Ignatius slipped his overcoat on and ran down the hall to the front door as they were opening the kitchen door. He went down the front steps and saw Patrolman Mancuso's white Rambler parked before the house. Bending over with great effort, Ignatius stuck a finger into the valve of one of the tires until the hissing stopped and the tire's bottom pancaked across the brick gutter. Then he walked down the alley, which was just wide enough for his bulk, to the rear of the house.

Bright lights were burning in the kitchen, and he could hear his mother's cheap radio through the closed window. Ignatius climbed the back steps silently and looked in through the greasy glass of the back door. His mother and Patrolman Mancuso were sitting at the table around an almost full fifth of Early Times. Patrolman Mancuso looked more downtrodden than ever, but Mrs. Reilly was tapping one foot on the linoleum and laughing shyly at what she was watching in the center of the room. A stocky woman with kinky gray hair was dancing alone on the linoleum, shaking her pendulous breasts, which were slung in a white bowling blouse. Her bowling shoes pounded the floor purposefully, carrying the swinging breasts and rotating hips back and forth between the table and the stove.

So this was Patrolman Mancuso's aunt. Only Patrolman Mancuso could have something like that for an aunt, Ignatius snorted to himself.

"Whoo!" Mrs. Reilly screamed gaily. "Santa!"

"Watch this, kids," the gray-haired woman screamed back like a prize fight referee and began shaking lower and lower until she was almost on the floor.

"Oh, my God!" Ignatius said to the wind.

"You gonna bust a gut, girl," Mrs. Reilly laughed. "You gonna go through my good floor."

"Maybe you better stop, Aunt Santa," Patrolman Mancuso said morosely.

"Hell, I ain't stopping now. I just got here," the woman answered, rising rhythmically. "Who says a grammaw can't dance no more?"

Holding her arms outward, the woman bumped across the linoleum runway.

"Lord!" Mrs. Reilly said and guffawed, tipping the whiskey bottle to her glass. "What if Ignatius comes home and sees this?"

"Fuck Ignatius!"

"Santa!" Mrs. Reilly gasped, shocked but, Ignatius noticed, slightly pleased.

"You people cut it out," Miss Annie screamed through her shutters.

"Who's that?" Santa asked Mrs. Reilly.

"Cut it out before I ring up the cops," Miss Annie's muffled voice cried.

"Please stop," Patrolman Mancuso pleaded nervously.

Five

Darlene was pouring water into the half-filled liquor bottles behind the bar.

"Hey, Darlene, listen to this shit," Lana Lee commanded, folding the newspaper and weighting it down with her ashtray. "'Frieda Club, Betty Bumper, and Liz Steele, all of 796 St. Peter St., were arrested from El Caballo Lounge, 570 Burgundy St., last night and booked with disturbing the peace and creating a public nuisance. According to arresting officers, the incident started when an unidentified man made a proposal to one of the women. The woman's two companions struck the man, who fled from the lounge. The Steele woman threw a stool at the bartender, and the other two women menaced customers in the lounge with stools and broken beer bottles. Customers in the lounge said that the man who fled was wearing bowling shoes.' How's about that? People like that are ruining the Quarter. Some honest Joe tries to make off with one of those dykes and they try to beat him up. Once upon a time it was nice and straight around here. Now it's all dykes and fairies. No wonder business stinks. I can't stand dykes. I can't!"

"The only people we get in here at night anymore is plain-clothesmen," Darlene said. "How come they don't get a plain-clothesman after women like that?"

"This place is turning into a goddam precinct. All I'm putting on is a benefit show for the Policeman's Benevolent Association," Lana said disgustedly. "A lotta empty space and few cops throwing signals at each other. Half the time I gotta watch you, brain, to see you don't try to sell them a drink."

"Well, Lana," Darlene said. "How I'm supposed to know who's a cop? Everybody looks the same to me." She blew her nose. "I try to make a living."

"You tell a cop by his eyes, Darlene. They're very self-assured. I been in this business too long. I know every dirty cop angle. The marked bills, the phony clothes. If you can't tell by the eyes, then take a look at the money. It's full of pencil marks and crap."

"How I'm supposed to see the money? It's so dark in here I can hardly see the eyes even."

"Well, we're gonna have to do something about you. I don't want you sittin out here on my stools. You're gonna try to sell a double martini to the chief of police one of these nights."

"Then let me get on the stage and dance. I got a socko routine."

"Oh, shut up," Lana hollered. If Jones knew about the police in the place at night, then goodbye, discount porter. "Now look here, Darlene, don't tell that Jones we suddenly got the whole force in here at night. You know how colored people feel about cops. He might get scared and quit. I mean, I'm trying to help the boy out and keep him off the streets."

"Okay," Darlene said. "But I ain't making no money I'm so afraid the guy on the next stool is the police. You know what we need in here to make money?"

"What?" Lana asked angrily.

"What we need in here is a animal."

"A what? Jesus Christ."

"I ain cleanin up after no animal," Jones said, bumping his mop noisily against the legs of the barstools.

"Come on over and check under these stools," Lana called to him.

"Oh! Whoa! Where I miss a spot? Hey!"

"Look in the paper, Lana," Darlene said. "Almost every other club on the street's got them an animal."

Lana turned to the entertainment pages and through Jones' fog studied the nightclub ads.

"Well, little Darlene's on the ball. I guess you'd like to become the manager of this club, huh?"

"No, ma'm."

"Well, remember that," Lana said and ran a finger along the ads. "Look at this. They got a snake at Jerry's, got them some doves at the 104, a baby tiger, a chimp . . ."

"And that's where the people are going," Darlene said. "You gotta keep up with things in this business."

"Thanks a lot. Since it's your idea, you got any suggestions?"

"I suggest we vote unanimous agains changing over to a zoo."

"Keep on the floor," Lana said.

"We could use my cockatoo," Darlene said. "I been practicing a smash dance with it. The bird's very smart. You oughta hear that thing talk."

"In color bars peoples all the time tryina keep birds *out*."

"Give the bird a chance," Darlene pleaded.

"Whoa!" Jones said. "Watch out. Your orphan frien just pullin in. It's humanitaria time."

George was slouching through the door in a bulky red sweater, white denims, and beige flamenco boots with slim-pointed toes. On both his hands there were tatoos of daggers drawn with ball-point pencil.

"Sorry, George, nothing for the orphans today," Lana said quickly.

"See that? Well them orphan they better star applyin to the United Fun," Jones said and blew some smoke on the daggers. "We having trouble with salary as it is. Chariddy begin at home."

"Huh?" George asked.

"They sure keeping a buncha hoods in the orphanages these days," Darlene observed. "I wouldn't give him nothing,

Lana. He's operating some kinda shakedown racket, if you ast me. If this kid's a orphan, I'm the queen of England."

"Come here," Lana said to George and led him out onto the street.

"Whatsa matter?" George asked.

"I can't talk in front of those two jerks," Lana said. "Look, this new porter's not like the old one. This smartass has been asking me about this orphan crap since he first saw you. I don't trust him. I got cop trouble already."

"Then get yourself a new jig. There's plenty around."

"I couldn't get a blind Eskimo for the salary I'm paying him. I got him on something of a deal, like discount price. And he thinks if he tries to quit, I can get him arrested for vagrancy. The whole thing's a deal, George. I mean, in my line of business, you gotta keep your eye peeled for a bargain. Understand?"

"But what about me?"

"This Jones goes out to lunch from twelve to twelve-thirty. So you come around about twelve-forty-five."

"What am I supposed to do with them packages all afternoon? I can't do nothing till after three. I don't want to be carrying that stuff around."

"Go check it in the bus station. I don't care. Just be sure they're safe. I'll see you tomorrow."

Lana went back into the bar.

"I sure hope you told that kid off," Darlene said. "Somebody oughta report him to the Better Business Bureau."

"Whoa!"

"Come on, Lana. Give me and the bird a chance. We're boffo."

"It used to be the old Kiwanis types liked to come in and watch a cute girl shake it a little. Now it's gotta be with some kinda animal. You know what's wrong with people today?

They're sick. It's hard for a person to earn an honest buck."
Lana lit a cigarette and matched Jones cloud for cloud. "Okay.
We audition the bird. It's probably safer for you to be on my
stage with a bird than on my stools with a cop. Bring in the
goddam bird."

II

Mr. Gonzalez sat next to his little heater listening to the
sounds of the river, his peaceful soul suspended in a Nirvana
somewhere far above the two antennae of Levy Pants. His
senses subconsciously savored the clatter of rats and the smell
of old paper and wood and the possessed feeling that his pair
of baggy Levy Pants gave him. He exhaled a thin stream of
filtered smoke and aimed the cigarette's ashes like a
marksman directly at the center of his ashtray. The impossible had happened: life at Levy Pants had become even better.
The reason was Mr. Reilly. What fairy godmother had
dropped Mr. Ignatius J. Reilly on the worn and rotting steps
of Levy Pants?

He was four workers in one. In Mr. Reilly's competent
hands, the filing seemed to disappear. He was also quite kind
to Miss Trixie; there was hardly any friction in the office. Mr.
Gonzalez was touched by what he had seen the previous afternoon—Mr. Reilly on his knees changing Miss Trixie's socks.
Mr. Reilly was all heart. Of course, he was part valve, too.
But the constant conversation about the valve could be
accepted. It was the only drawback.

Looking happily about, Mr. Gonzalez noticed the results
of Mr. Reilly's handiwork in the office. Tacked to Miss
Trixie's desk was a large sign that said MISS TRIXIE with an
old-fashioned nosegay drawn in crayon in one corner.
Tacked to his desk was another sign that said SR. GONZALEZ

and was decorated with the crest of King Alfonso. A multi-sectioned cross was nailed to a post in the office, the LIBBY'S TOMATO JUICE and KRAFT JELLY on two sections awaiting what Mr. Reilly had said would be brown paint with some black streaks to suggest the grain of the wood. In several empty ice cream cartons on top of the filing cabinets beans were already sprouting little vines. The purple monkscloth drapes that hung from the window next to Mr. Reilly's desk created a meditative area in the office. There the sun cast a claret-colored glow over the three-foot plaster statue of St. Anthony that stood near the wastebasket.

There had never been a worker like Mr. Reilly. He was so dedicated, so interested in the business. He was even planning to visit the factory when his valve was better to see how he could improve conditions there. The other workers had always been so unconcerned, so slipshod.

The door opened slowly as Miss Trixie made her day's entrance, a large bag preceding her.

"Miss Trixie!" Mr. Gonzalez said in what was, for him, a very sharp tone.

"Who?" Miss Trixie cried frantically.

She looked down at her tattered nightgown and flannel robe.

"Oh, my goodness," she wheezed. "I thought I felt a little chilly outside."

"Go home right now."

"It's cold outside, Gomez."

"You can't stay at Levy Pants like that. I'm sorry."

"Am I retired?" Miss Trixie asked hopefully.

"No!" Mr. Gonzalez squeaked. "I just want you to go home and change. You only live around the block. Hurry up."

Miss Trixie shuffled through the door, banging it closed. Then she came in again to get the bag, which she had left on the floor, and banged out again.

By the time Ignatius arrived an hour later, Miss Trixie had not returned. Mr. Gonzalez listened to Mr. Reilly's heavy, slow tread on the stairs. The door was thrust open, and the marvelous Ignatius J. Reilly appeared, a plaid scarf as large as a shawl wound around his neck, one end of it stuffed down into his coat.

"Good morning, sir," he said majestically.

"Good morning," Mr. Gonzalez said with delight. "Did you have a nice ride here?"

"Only fair. I suspect that the driver was a latent speed racer. I had to caution him continually. Actually, we parted company with a degree of hostility on both sides. Where is our little distaff member this morning?"

"I had to send her home. She came to work this morning in her nightgown."

Ignatius frowned and said, "I do not understand why she was sent away. After all, we are quite informal here. We are one big family. I only hope that you have not damaged her morale." He filled a glass at the water cooler to water his beans. "You may not be surprised to see me appear one morning in my nightshirt. I find it rather comfortable."

"I certainly don't mean to dictate what you people should wear," Mr. Gonzalez said anxiously.

"I should hope not. Miss Trixie and I can only take so much."

Mr. Gonzalez pretended to look for something in his desk to avoid the terrible eyes that Ignatius had turned on him.

"I shall finish the cross," Ignatius said finally, removing two quarts of paint from the pouchlike pockets of his overcoat.

"That's wonderful."

"The cross is top priority at the moment. Filing, alphabetizing—all of that must wait until I have completed this project. Then, when I finish the cross, I am going to have to visit the factory. I suspect that those people are screaming for a compassionate ear, a dedicated guide. I may be able to aid them."

"Of course. Don't let me tell you what to do."

"I won't." Ignatius stared at the office manager. "At last my valve seems to permit a visit to the factory. I must not pass up this opportunity. If I wait, it may seal up for several weeks."

"Then you must go to the factory today," the office manager agreed enthusiastically.

Mr. Gonzalez looked at Ignatius hopefully, but he received no reply. Ignatius filed his overcoat, scarf, and cap in one of the file drawers and began working on the cross. By eleven o'clock he was giving the cross its first coat, meticulously applying the paint with a small watercolor brush. Miss Trixie was still AWOL.

At noon Mr. Gonzalez looked over the stack of papers on which he was working and said, "I wonder where Miss Trixie can be."

"You have probably broken her spirit," Ignatius replied coldly. He was dabbing at the rough edges of the cardboard with the brush. "However, she may appear for lunch. I told her yesterday that I was bringing her a luncheon meat sandwich. I have discovered that Miss Trixie considers luncheon meat a rather toothsome delicacy. I would offer you a sandwich, but I am afraid that there are only enough for Miss Trixie and me."

"That's quite all right." Mr. Gonzalez produced a wan smile and watched Ignatius open his greasy brown paper bag. "I'm going to have to work straight through lunch anyway to finish these statements and billings."

"Yes, you'd better. We must not allow Levy Pants to fall behind in the struggle for the survival of the fittest."

Ignatius bit into his first sandwich, tearing it in half, and chewed contentedly for a while.

"I do hope that Miss Trixie does appear," he said after he had finished the first sandwich and emitted a series of belches which sounded as if they had disintegrated his digestive tract. "My valve will not tolerate luncheon meat, I'm afraid."

While he was tearing the filling of the second sandwich from the bread with his teeth, Miss Trixie came in, her green celluloid visor facing the rear.

"Here she is," Ignatius said to the office manager through the big leaf of limp lettuce that was hanging from his mouth.

"Oh, yes," Mr. Gonzalez said weakly. "Miss Trixie."

"I imagined that the luncheon meat would activate her faculties. Over here, Mother Commerce."

Miss Trixie bumped into the statue of St. Anthony.

"I knew I had something on my mind all morning, Gloria," Miss Trixie said, taking the sandwich in her claws and going to her desk. Ignatius watched with fascination the elaborate process of gums, tongue, and lips that every piece of sandwich set into motion.

"You took a very long time to change," the office manager said to Miss Trixie, noting bitterly that her new ensemble was only a little more presentable than the robe and nightgown.

"Who?" Miss Trixie asked, sticking out a tongueful of masticated luncheon meat and bread.

"I said you took a long time to change."

"Me? I just left here."

"Will you please stop harassing her?" Ignatius demanded angrily.

"There was no need for the delay. She only lives down by the wharves somewhere," the office manager said and returned to his papers.

"Did you enjoy that?" Ignatius asked Miss Trixie when the last grimace of her lips had stopped.

Miss Trixie nodded and began industriously on a second

sandwich. But when she had at last eaten half, she slumped back in her chair.

"Oh, I'm full, Gloria. That was delicious."

"Mr. Gonzalez, would you care for the bit of sandwich that Miss Trixie can not eat?"

"No, thank you."

"I wish that you would take it. Otherwise, the rats will storm us *en masse*."

"Yes, Gomez, take this," Miss Trixie said, dropping the soggy half of uneaten sandwich on top of the papers on the office manager's desk.

"Now look what you've done, you old idiot!" Mr. Gonzalez screamed. "Damn Mrs. Levy. That's the statement for the bank."

"How dare you attack the spirit of the noble Mrs. Levy," Ignatius thundered. "I shall report you, sir."

"It took over an hour to prepare that statement. Look at what she's done."

"I want that Easter ham!" Miss Trixie snarled. "Where's my Thanksgiving turkey? I quit a wonderful job as cashier in a nickelodeon to come to work for this company. Now I guess I'll die in this office. I must say a worker gets shabby treatment around here. I'm retiring *right now*."

"Why don't you go wash your hands?" Mr. Gonzalez said to her.

"That's a good idea, Gomez," Miss Trixie said and tacked off to the ladies' room.

Ignatius felt cheated. He had hoped for a scene. While the office manager began making a copy of the statement, Ignatius returned to the cross. First, however, he had to lift Miss Trixie, who had returned and was kneeling directly beneath it and praying in the spot where Ignatius had been standing to paint. Miss Trixie hovered about him, leaving only to seal some envelopes for Mr. Gonzalez, to visit the bathroom several times, and to catnap. The office manager made the only noise in the office with his typewriter and adding machine, both of which Ignatius found slightly distracting. By one-thirty the cross was almost finished. It lacked only the little gold leaf letters that spelled GOD AND COMMERCE which Ignatius had ready to apply across the bottom of the cross. After the motto was applied, Ignatius stood back and said to Miss Trixie, "It is complete."

"Oh, Gloria, that's beautiful," Miss Trixie said sincerely. "Look at this, Gomez."

"Isn't that fine," Mr. Gonzalez said, studying the cross with tired eyes.

"Now to the filing," Ignatius said busily. "Then off to the factory. I cannot tolerate social injustice."

"Yes, you must go to the factory while your valve is operating," the office manager said.

Ignatius went behind the filing cabinets, picked up the accumulated and unfiled material, and threw it in the wastebasket. Noticing that the office manager was sitting at his desk with his hand over his eyes, Ignatius pulled out the first drawer of the files, and, turning it over, dumped its alphabetical contents into the wastebasket, too.

Then he lumbered off to the factory door, thundering past Miss Trixie, who had fallen to her knees again before the cross.

III

Patrolman Mancuso had tried a little moonlighting in his effort to apprehend someone, anyone for the sergeant. After dropping off his aunt from the bowling alley, he had stopped in the bar on his own to see what he could turn up. What had turned up was these three terrifying girls who had struck him. He touched the bandage on his head as he entered the precinct to see the sergeant, who had summoned him.

"What happened to you, Mancuso?" the sergeant screamed when he saw the bandage.

"I fell down."

"That sounds like you. If you knew anything about your job, you'd be in bars tipping us off on people like those three girls we brought in last night."

"Yes, sir."

"I don't know what whore give you the tip on this Night of Joy, but our boys have been in there almost every night and they haven't turned up anything."

"Well, I thought . . ."

"Shut up. You gave us a phony lead. You know what we do to people give us a phony lead?"

"No."

"We put them in the rest room at the bus station."

"Yes, sir."

"You stay in the booths there eight hours a day until you bring somebody in."

"Okay."

"Don't say 'okay.' Say 'yes, sir.' Now get outta here and go look in your locker. You're a farmer today."

IV

Ignatius opened "The Journal of a Working Boy" to the first unused sheet of Blue Horse looseleaf filler, officiously snapping the point of his ballpoint pen forward. The point of the Levy Pants pen did not catch on the first snap and slipped back into the plastic cylinder. Ignatius snapped more vigorously, but again the point slid disobediently back out of sight. Cracking the pen furiously on the edge of his desk, Ignatius picked up one of the Venus Medalist pencils lying on the floor. He probed the wax in his ears with the pencil and began to concentrate, listening to the sounds of his mother's preparations for an evening at the bowling alley. There were many staccato footfalls back and forth in the bathroom which meant, he knew, that his mother was attempting to accomplish several phases of her toilet at once. Then there were the noises that he had grown accustomed to over the years whenever his mother was preparing to leave the house: the plop of a hair brush falling into the toilet bowl, the sound of a box of powder hitting the floor, the sudden exclamations of confusion and chaos.

"Ouch!" his mother cried at one point.

Ignatius found the subdued and solitary din in the bathroom annoying and wished that she would finish. At last he heard the light click off. She knocked at his door.

"Ignatius, honey, I'm going."

"All right," Ignatius replied icily.

"Open the door, babe, and come kiss me goodbye."

"Mother, I am quite busy at the moment."

"Don't be like that, Ignatius. Open up."

"Run off with your friends, please."

"Aw, Ignatius."

"Must you distract me at every level. I am working on something with wonderful movie possibilities. Highly commercial."

Mrs. Reilly kicked at the door with her bowling shoes.

"Are you ruining that pair of absurd shoes that were bought with my hard-earned wages?"

"Huh? What's that, precious?"

Ignatius extracted the pencil from his ear and opened the door. His mother's maroon hair was fluffed high over her forehead; her cheekbones were red with rouge that had been spread nervously up to the eyeballs. One wild puff full of powder had whitened Mrs. Reilly's face, the front of her dress, and a few loose maroon wisps.

"Oh, my God," Ignatius said, "you have powder all over your dress, although that is probably one of Mrs. Battaglia's beauty hints."

"Why you always knocking Santa, Ignatius?"

"She appears to have been knocked a bit in her life already. Up rather than down. If she ever nears me, however, the direction will be reversed."

"Ignatius!"

"She also brings to mind the vulgarism 'knockers.'"

"Santa's a grammaw. You oughta be ashamed."

"Thank goodness Miss Annie's coarse cries restored peace the other night. Never in my life have I seen so shameless an orgy. And right in my very own kitchen. If that man were any sort of law enforcement officer, he would have arrested that 'aunt' right there on the spot."

"Don't knock Angelo, neither. He's got him a hard road, boy. Santa says he's been in the bathroom at the bus station all day."

"Oh, my God! Do I believe what I'm hearing? Please run along with your two cohorts from the Mafia and let me alone."

"Don't treat your poor momma like that."

"Poor? Did I hear poor? When the dollars are literally flowing into this home from my labors? And flowing out even more rapidly."

"Don't start that again, Ignatius. I only got twenty dollars out of you this week, and I almost had to get down on my knees and beg for it. Look at all them thing-a-ma-jigs you been buying. Look at that movie camera you brung home today."

"The movie camera will shortly be put to use. That harmonica was rather cheap."

"We never gonna pay off that man at this rate."

"That is hardly my problem. I don't drive."

"No, you don't care. You never cared for nothing, boy."

"I should have known that every time I open the door of my room I am literally opening a Pandora's Box. Doesn't Mrs. Battaglia want you to await her debauched nephew and her at the curb so that not one invaluable moment of bowling time will be lost?" Ignatius belched the gas of a dozen brownies trapped by his valve. "Grant me a little peace. Isn't it enough that I am harried all day long at work? I thought that I had adequately described to you the horrors which I must face daily."

"You know I appreciate you, babe," Mrs. Reilly sniffed. "Come on and gimme a little goodbye kiss like a good boy."

Ignatius bent down and lightly bussed her on the cheek.

"Oh, my God," he said, spitting out powder. "Now my mouth will feel gritty all night."

"I got too much powder on?"

"No, it's just fine. Aren't you an arthritic or something? How in the world can you bowl?"

"I think the exercise is helping me out. I'm feeling better."

A horn honked out on the street.

"Apparently your friend has escaped the bathroom," Ignatius snorted. "It's just like him to hang around a bus station. He probably likes to watch those Scenicruiser horrors arrive and depart. In his worldview the bus is apparently a good thing. That shows how retarded he is."

"I'll be in early, honey," Mrs. Reilly said, closing the miniature front door.

"I shall probably be misused by some intruder!" Ignatius screamed.

Bolting the door to his room, he grabbed an empty ink bottle and opened his shutters. He stuck his head out of the window and looked down the alley to where the little white

Rambler was visible in the darkness at the curb. With all of his strength, he heaved the bottle and heard it hit the roof of the car with greater sound effects than he had expected it to.

"Hey!" he heard Santa Battaglia shout as he silently closed the shutters. Gloating, he opened his looseleaf folder again and picked up his Venus Medalist.

Dear Reader,
A great writer is the friend and benefactor of his readers.
—Macaulay

Another working day is ended, gentle reader. As I told you before, I have succeeded in laying a patina, as it were, over the turbulence and mania of our office. All non-essential activities in the office are slowly being curtailed. At the moment I am busily decorating our throbbing hive of white-collared bees (three). The analogy of the three bees brings to mind three b's which describe most aptly my actions as an office worker: banish, benefit, beautify. There are also three b's which describe most aptly the actions of our buffoon of an office manager: bait, beg, blight, blunder, bore, boss, bother, bungle, burden, buzz. (In this case, I am afraid that the list gets somewhat out of hand.) I have come to the conclusion that our office manager serves no purpose other than one of obfuscation and hindrance. Were it not for him, the other clerical worker (La Dama del Comercio) and I would be quite peaceful and content, attending to our duties in an atmosphere of mutual consideration. I am certain that his dictatorial methods are, in part, responsible for Miss T.'s desire to retire.

I can at last describe to you our factory. This afternoon, feeling fulfilled after having completed the cross (Yes! It is completed and gives our office a needed spiritual dimension.), I set out to visit the clank and whirr and hiss of the factory.

The scene which met my eyes was at once compelling and repelling. The original sweatshop has been preserved for posterity at Levy Pants. If only the Smithsonian Institution, that grab-bag of our nation's refuse, could somehow vacuum-seal the Levy Pants factory and transport it to the capital of the United States of America, each worker frozen in an attitude of labor, the visitors to that questionable museum would defecate into their garish tourist outfits. It is a scene which combines the worst of Uncle Tom's Cabin and Fritz Lang's Metropolis; it is mechanized Negro slavery; it represents the progress which the Negro has made from picking cotton to tailoring it. (Were they in the picking stage of their evolution, they would at least be in the healthful outdoors singing and eating watermelons [as they are, I believe, supposed to do when in groups al fresco].) My intense and deeply felt convictions concerning social injustice were aroused. My valve threw in a hearty response.

(In connection with the watermelons, I must say, lest some professional civil rights organization be offended, that I have never been an observer of American folk customs. I may be wrong. I would imagine that today people grasp for the cotton with one hand while the other hand presses a transistor radio to the sides of their heads so that it can spew bulletins about used cars and Sofstyle Hair Relaxer and Royal Crown Hair Dressing and Gallo wine about their eardrums, a filtered menthol cigarette dangling from their lips and threatening to set the entire cotton field ablaze. Although residing along the Mississippi River [This river is famed in atrocious song and verse; the most prevalent motif is one which attempts to make of the river an ersatz father figure. Actually, the

Mississippi River is a treacherous and sinister body of water whose eddies and currents yearly claim many lives. I have never known anyone who would even venture to stick his toe in its polluted brown waters, which seethe with sewage, industrial waste, and deadly insecticides. Even the fish are dying. Therefore, the Mississippi as Father-God-Moses-Daddy-Phallus-Pops is an altogether false motif begun, I would imagine, by that dreary fraud, Mark Twain. This failure to make contact with reality is, however, characteristic of almost all of America's "art." Any connection between American art and American nature is purely coincidental, but this is only because the nation as a whole has no contact with reality. That is only one of the reasons why I have always been forced to exist on the fringes of its society, consigned to the Limbo reserved for those who do know reality when they see it.], I have never seen cotton growing and have no desire to do so. The only excursion in my life outside of New Orleans took me through the vortex to the whirlpool of despair: Baton Rouge. In some future installment, a flashback, I shall perhaps recount that pilgrimage through the swamps, a journey into the desert from which I returned broken physically, mentally, and spiritually. New Orleans is, on the other hand, a comfortable metropolis which has a certain apathy and stagnation which I find inoffensive. At least its climate is mild; too, it is here in the Crescent City that I am assured of having a roof over my head and a Dr. Nut in my stomach, although certain sections of North Africa [Tangiers, etc.] have from time to time excited my interest. The voyage by boat, however, would probably enervate me, and I am certainly not perverse enough to attempt air travel even if I were able to afford it. The Greyhound Bus Line is sufficiently menacing to make me accept my status quo. I wish that those

Scenicruisers would be discontinued; it would seem to me that their height violates some interstate highway statute regarding clearance in tunnels and so forth. Perhaps one of you, dear readers, with a legal turn of mind can dredge the appropriate clause from memory. Those things really must be removed. Simply knowing that they are hurtling somewhere on this dark night makes me most apprehensive.)

The factory is a large, barn-like structure that houses bolts of fabric, cutting tables, massive sewing machines, and furnaces that provide the steam for pressing. The total effect is rather surreal, especially when one sees Les Africains moving about attending to their tasks in this mechanized setting. The irony involved caught my fancy, I must admit. Something from Joseph Conrad sprang to my mind, although I cannot seem to remember what it was at the time. Perhaps I likened myself to Kurtz in The Heart of Darkness when, far from the trading company offices in Europe, he was faced with the ultimate horror. I do remember imagining myself in a pith helmet and white linen jodpurs, my face enigmatic behind a veil of mosquito netting.

The furnaces keep the place rather warm and toasty on these chill days, but in the summer I suspect that the workers once again enjoy the climate of their forebears, the tropic heat somewhat magnified by those great coal-burning steam-producing contrivances. I understand that the factory is not working at capacity currently, and I did observe that only one of these devices was operating, burning coal and what looked like one of the cutting tables. Also, I saw only one pair of trousers actually completed during the time that I spent there, although the factory workers were shambling about clutching all sorts of scraps of cloth. One woman, I noticed, was pressing some baby's clothing and another seemed to be making remarkable progress with the sections of fuscia satin which she was joining together on one of the large sewing machines. She appeared to be fashioning a rather colorful but nonetheless rakish evening gown. I must say that I admired the efficiency with which she whipped the material back and forth under the massive electric needle. This woman was apparently a skilled worker, and I thought it doubly unfortunate that she was not lending her talents to the creation of a pair of Levy Pants . . . pants. There was obviously a morale problem in the factory.

I looked for Mr. Palermo, the foreman of the factory, who is, incidentally, normally only a few steps from the bottle, as the many contusions that he has sustained from falling down among the cutting tables and sewing machines can testify, with no success. He was probably quaffing a liquid lunch in one of the many taverns in the vicinity of our organization; there is a bar on every corner in the neighborhood of Levy Pants, an indication that salaries in the area are abysmally low. On particularly desperate blocks there are three or four bars at every intersection.

In my innocence, I suspected that the obscene jazz issuing forth from the loud speakers on the walls of the factory was at the root of the apathy which I was witnessing among the workers. The psyche can be bombarded only so much by these rhythms before it begins to crumble and atrophy. Therefore, I found and turned off the switch which controlled the music. This action on my part led to a rather loud and defiantly boorish roar of protest from the collective workers, who began to regard me with sullen eyes. So I turned the music on again, smiling broadly and waving amiably in an attempt to acknowledge my poor judgment and to win the workers' confidence. (Their huge white eyes were already labeling me a "Mister Charlie." I would have to struggle to show them my almost psychotic dedication to helping them.)

Obviously continual response to the music had developed within them an almost Pavlovian response to the noise, a response which they believed was pleasure. Having spent countless hours of my life watching those blighted children on television dancing to this sort of music, I knew the physical spasm which it was supposed to elicit, and I attempted my own conservative version of the same on the spot to further pacify the workers. I must admit that my body moved with surprising agility; I am not without an innate sense of rhythm; my ancestors must have been rather outstanding at jigging on the heath. Ignoring the eyes of the workers, I shuffled about beneath one of the loud speakers, twisting and shouting, mumbling insanely, "Go! Go! Do it, baby, do it! Hear me talkin' to ya. Wow!" I know that I had recovered my ground with them when several began pointing to me and laughing. I laughed back to demonstrate that I, too, shared their high spirits. De Casibus Virorum Illustrium! Of the Fall of Great Men! My downfall occurred. Literally. My considerable system, weakened by the gyrations (especially in the region of the knees), at last rebelled, and I plummeted to the floor in a senseless attempt at one of the more egregiously perverse steps which I had witnessed on the television so many times. The workers seemed rather concerned and helped me up most politely, smiling in the friendliest fashion. I realized then that I had no more to fear concerning my faux pas in turning off their music.

In spite of all to which they have been subjected, Negroes are nonetheless a rather pleasant folk for the most part. I really have had little to do with them, for I mingle with my peers or no one, and since I have no peers, I mingle with no one. Upon speaking with several of the workers, all of whom seemed eager to speak with me, I discovered that they received even less pay than Miss Trixie.

In a sense I have always felt something of a kinship with the colored race because its position is the same as mine: we both exist outside the inner realm of American society. Of course, my exile is voluntary. However, it is apparent that many of the Negroes wish to become active members of the American middle class. I can not imagine why. I must admit that this desire on their part leads me to question their value judgments. However, if they wish to join the bourgeoisie, it is really none of my business. They may seal their own doom. Personally, I would agitate quite adamantly if I suspected that anyone were attempting to help me upward toward the middle class. I would agitate against the bemused person who was attempting to help me upward, that is. The agitation would take the form of many protest marches complete with the traditional banners and posters, but these would say, "End the Middle Class," "The Middle Class Must Go." I am not above tossing a small Molotov cocktail or two, either. In addition, I would studiously avoid sitting near the middle class in lunch counters and on public transportation, maintaining the intrinsic honesty and grandeur of my being. If a middle-class white were suicidal enough to sit next to me, I imagine that I would beat him soundly about the head and shoulders with one great hand, tossing, quite deftly, one of my Molotov cocktails into a passing bus jammed with middle-class whites with the other hand. Whether my siege were to last a month or a year, I am certain that ultimately everyone would let me alone after the total carnage and destruction of property had been evaluated.

I do admire the terror which Negroes are able to inspire in the hearts of some members of the white proletariat and only wish (This is a rather personal confession.) that I possessed the ability to similarly terrorize. The Negro terrorizes simply by being himself; I, however, must browbeat a bit in order to achieve the same end. Perhaps I should have been a Negro. I suspect that I would have been a rather large and terrifying one, continually pressing my ample thigh against the withered thighs of old white ladies in public conveyances a great deal and eliciting more than one shriek of panic. Then, too, if I were a Negro, I would not be pressured by my mother to find a good job, for no good jobs would be available. My mother herself, a worn old Negress, would be too broken by years of underpaid labor as a domestic to go out bowling at night. She and I could live most pleasantly in some moldy shack in the slums in a state of ambitionless peace, realizing contentedly that we were unwanted, that striving was meaningless.

However, I do not wish to witness the awful spectacle of the Negroes moving upward into the middle class. I consider this movement a great insult to their integrity as a people. But I am beginning to sound like the Beards and Parringtons and will soon totally forget Levy Pants, the commercial muse for this particular effort. A project for the future could be a social history of the United States from my vantage point; if The Journal of a Working Boy meets with any success at the book stalls, I shall perhaps etch a likeness of our nation with my pen. Our nation demands the scrutiny of a completely disengaged observer like your Working Boy, and I already have in my files a rather formidable collection of notes and jottings that evaluate and lend a perspective to the contemporary scene.

We must hasten back on the wings of prose to the factory and its folk, who prompted my rather lengthy digression. As I was telling you, they had just lifted me from the floor, my performance and subsequent pratfall the sources of a great feeling of camaraderie. I thanked them cordially, they meanwhile inquiring in their seventeenth-century English accents about my condition most solicitously. I was uninjured, and since pride is a Deadly Sin which I feel I generally eschew, absolutely nothing was hurt.

I then questioned them about the factory, for this was the purpose behind my visit. They were rather eager to speak with me and seemed even most interested in me as a person. Apparently the dull hours among the cutting tables make a visitor doubly welcome. We chatted freely, although the workers were generally non-committal about their work. Actually, they seemed more interested in me than in anything else; I was not bothered by their attentions and parried all of their questions blithely until they at last grew rather personal. Some of them who had from time to time straggled into the office asked pointed questions about the cross and the attendant decorations; one intense lady asked permission (which, of course, was granted) to gather some of her confreres about the cross occasionally to sing spirituals. (I abhor spirituals and those deadly nineteenth-century Calvinist hymns, but I was willing to suffer having my eardrums assaulted if a chorus or two would make these workers happy.) When I questioned them about wages, I discovered that their average weekly pay envelope contained less than thirty ($30) dollars. It is my considered opinion that someone deserves more than that in the way of a wage for simply staying in a place like the factory for five days a week, especially when the factory is one like the Levy Pants factory in which the leaking roof threatens to collapse at any moment. And who knows? Those people might have much better things to do than to loiter about Levy Pants, such as composing jazz or creating new dances or doing whatever those things are that they do with such facility. No wonder there was such apathy in the factory. Still it was incredible that the disparity between the doldrums of the production line and the fevered hustle of the office could be housed within the same (Levy Pants) bosom. Were I one of the factory workers (and I would probably be a large and particularly terrifying one, as I said earlier), I would long before have stormed the office and demanded a decent wage.

Here I must make a note. While I was desultorily attending graduate school, I met in the coffee shop one day a Miss Myrna Minkoff, a young undergraduate, a loud, offensive maiden from the Bronx. This expert from the universe of the Grand Concourse was attracted to the table at which I was holding court by the singularity and magnetism of my being. As the magnificence and originality of my worldview became explicit through conversation, the Minkoff minx began attacking me on all levels, even kicking me under the table rather vigorously at one point. I both fascinated and confused her; in short, I was too much for her. The parochialism of the ghettoes of Gotham had not prepared her for the uniqueness of Your Working Boy. Myrna, you see, believed that all humans living south and west of the Hudson River were illiterate cowboys or—even worse—White Protestants, a class of humans who as a group specialized in ignorance, cruelty, and torture. (I don't wish to especially defend White Protestants; I am not too fond of them myself.)

Soon Myrna's brutal social manner had driven my courtiers from the table, and we were left alone, all cold coffee and hot words. When I failed to agree with her braying and babbling, she told me that I was obviously anti-Semitic. Her logic was a combination of half-truths and clichés, her worldview a compound of misconceptions deriving from a history of our nation as written from the perspective of a subway tunnel. She dug into her large black valise and assaulted me (almost literally) with greasy copies of Men and Masses and Now! and Broken Barricades and Surge and Revulsion and various manifestos and pamphlets pertaining to organizations of which she was a most active member: Students for Liberty, Youth for Sex, The Black Muslims, Friends of Latvia, Children for Miscegenation, The White Citizens' Councils. Myrna was, you see, terribly engaged in her society; I, on the other hand, older and wiser, was terribly dis-engaged.

She had chiseled quite a bit of money from her father to go away to college to see what it was like "out there." Unfortunately, she found me. The trauma of our first meeting fed each other's masochism and led to an affair (platonic) of sorts. (Myrna was decidedly masochistic. She was only happy when a police dog was sinking its fangs into her black leotards or when she was being dragged feet first down stone steps from a Senate hearing.) I must admit that I always suspected Myrna of being interested in me sensually; my stringent attitude toward sex intrigued her; in a sense, I became another project of sorts. I did, however, succeed in thwarting her every attempt to assail the castle of my body and mind. Since Myrna and I confused most of the other students when we were apart, as a couple we were doubly confusing to the smiling Southern birdbrains who, for the most part, made up the student body. Campus rumor, I understand, linked us in the most unspeakably depraved intrigues.

Myrna's cure-all for everything from fallen arches to depression was sex. She promulgated this philosophy with disastrous effects to two Southern belles whom she took under her wing in order to renovate their backward minds. Heeding Myrna's counsel with the eager assistance of various young men, one of the simple lovelies suffered a nervous breakdown; the other attempted unsuccessfully to slash her wrists with a broken Coca-Cola bottle. Myrna's explanation was that the girls had been too reactionary to begin with, and with renewed vigor, she preached sex in every classroom and pizza parlor, almost getting herself raped by a janitor in the Social Studies building. Meanwhile, I tried to guide her toward the path of truth.

After several semesters Myrna disappeared from the college, saying in her offensive manner, "This place can't teach me anything I don't know." The black leotards, the matted mane of hair, the monstrous valise were all gone; the palmlined campus returned to its traditional lethargy and necking. I have seen that liberated doxy a few times since then, for, from time to time she embarks on an "inspection tour" of the South, stopping eventually in New Orleans to harangue me and to attempt to seduce me with the grim prison and chain and gang songs she strums on her guitar. Myrna is very sincere; unfortunately, she is also offensive.

When I saw her after her last "inspection tour" she was rather bedraggled. She had stopped throughout the rural South to teach Negroes folk songs she had learned at the Library of Congress. The Negroes, it seems, preferred more contemporary music and turned up their transistor radios loudly and defiantly whenever Myrna began one of her lugubrious dirges. Although the Negroes had tried to ignore her, the whites had shown great interest in her. Bands of crackers and rednecks had chased her from villages, slashed her tires, whipped her a bit about the arms. She had been hunted by bloodhounds, shocked by cattle prods, chewed by police dogs, peppered lightly with shotgun pellets. She had loved every minute of it, showing me quite proudly (and, I might add, suggestively) a fang mark on her upper thigh. My stunned and disbelieving eyes noted that on that occasion she was wearing dark stockings and not leotards. My blood, however, failed to rise.

We do correspond quite regularly, the usual theme of Myrna's correspondence tending to urge me to participate in lie-ins and wade-ins and sit-ins and such. Since, however, I do not eat at lunch counters and do not swim, I have ignored her advice. The subsidiary theme in the correspondence is one urging me to come to Manhattan so that she and I may raise our banner of twin confusion in that center of mechanized horrors. If I am ever really well, I may make the trip. At the moment that little musky Minkoff minx is probably in some tunnel far beneath the streets of the Bronx speeding in a subway train from a meeting on social protest to an orgy of folk singing or worse. Some day the authorities of our society will no doubt apprehend her for simply being herself. Incarceration will finally make her life meaningful and end her frustration.

A recent communication from her was bolder and more offensive than usual. She must be dealt with on her own level, and thus I thought of her as I surveyed the substandard conditions in the factory. Too long have I confined myself in Miltonic isolation and meditation. It is clearly time for me to step boldly into our society, not in the boring, passive manner of the Myrna Minkoff school of social action, but with great style and zest.

You will be witnesses to a certain courageous, daring, and aggressive decision on the part of the author, a decision which reveals a militancy, depth, and strength quite unexpected in so gentle a nature. Tomorrow I will describe in detail my answer to the Myrna Minkoffs of the world. The result may, incidentally, topple (all too literally) Mr. Gonzalez as a power within Levy Pants. That fiend must be dealt with. One of the more powerful civil rights organizations will no doubt cover me with laurels.

There is an almost unbearable pain needling my fingers as a result of these overabundant scribblings. I must lay down my pencil, my engine of truth, and bathe my crippled hands in some warm water. My intense devotion to the cause of justice has led to this lengthy diatribe, and I feel that my Levy circle-within-a-circle is zooming upward to new successes and heights.

Health note: Hands crippled, valve temporarily open (half-way)

Social note: Nothing today; Mother gone again, looking like a courtesan; one of her cohorts, you might like to know, has revealed his hopelessness by revealing a fetish for Greyhound buses.

I am going to pray to St. Martin de Porres, the patron saint of mulattoes, for our cause in the factory. Because he is also invoked against rats, he will perhaps aid us in the office, too.

Until later,
Gary, Your Militant Working Boy

V

Dr. Talc lit a Benson and Hedges, looking out of the window of his office in the Social Studies Building. Across the dark campus he saw some lights from the night classes in other buildings. All night he had been ransacking his desk for his notes on the British monarch of legend, notes hurriedly copied from a hundred-page survey of British history that he had once read in paperback. The lecture was to be given tomorrow, and it was now almost eight-thirty. As a lecturer Dr. Talc was renowned for the facile and sarcastic wit and easily digested generalizations that made him popular among the girl students and helped to conceal his lack of knowledge about almost everything in general and British history in particular.

But even Talc realized that his reputation for sophistication and glibness would not save him in the face of his being unable to remember absolutely anything about Lear and Arthur aside from the fact that the former had some children. He put his cigarette in the ashtray and began on the bottom drawer again. In the rear of the drawer there was a stack of old papers that he had not examined very thoroughly during his first search through the desk. Placing the papers in his lap, he thumbed through them one by one and found that they were, as he had imagined, principally unreturned essays that had accumulated over a period of more than five years. As he turned over one essay, his eye fell upon a rough, yellowed sheet of Big Chief tablet paper on which was printed with a red crayon:

Your total ignorance of that which you profess to teach merits the death penalty. I doubt whether you would know that St. Cassian of Imola was stabbed to death by his students with their styli. His death, a martyr's honorable one, made him a patron saint of teachers.

Pray to him, you deluded fool, you "anyone for tennis?" golf-playing, cocktail-quaffing pseudo-pedant, for you do indeed need a heavenly patron. Although

your days are numbered, you will not die as a martyr—
for you further no holy cause—but as the total ass which
you really are.

ZORRO

A sword was drawn on the last line of the page.

"Oh, I wonder whatever happened to him," Talc said aloud.

Six

Mattie's Ramble Inn was on a corner in the Carrollton section of the city where, after having run parallel for six or seven miles, St. Charles Avenue and the Mississippi River meet and the avenue ends. Here an angle is formed, the Avenue and its streetcar tracks on one side, the river and levee and railroad tracks on the other. Within this angle there is a separate little neighborhood. In the air there is always the heavy, cloying ordor of the alcohol distillery on the river, an odor that becomes suffocating on hot summer afternoons when the breeze blows in from the river. The neighborhood grew haphazardly a century or so ago and today looks hardly urban at all. As the city's streets cross St. Charles Avenue and enter this neighborhood, they gradually change from asphalt to gravel. It is an old rural town that has even a few barns, an alienated and microcosmic village within a large city.

Mattie's Ramble Inn looked like all the buildings on its block; it was low, unpainted, imperfectly vertical. Mattie's rambled slightly to the right, tilting toward the railroad tracks and the river. Its façade was almost invulnerable, covered as it was with tin advertising posters for a variety of beers and cigarettes and soft drinks. Even the screen on the door advertised a brand of bread. Mattie's was a combination bar and grocery, the grocery aspect limited to a sparse selection of goods, soft drinks, bread, and canned foods for the most part. Beside the bar there was an ice chest that cooled a few pounds of pickled meat and sausage. And there was no Mattie; Mr. Watson, the quiet, tan, *café au lait* owner, had sole authority over the restricted merchandise.

"The problem come from not havin no vocation skill," Jones was saying to Mr. Watson. Jones was perched on a wooden stool, his legs bent under him like ice tongs ready to pick up the stool and boldly carry it away before Mr. Watson's old eyes. "If I had me some trainin I wouldn be moppin no old whore flo."

"Be good," Mr. Watson answered vaguely. "Be well behave with the lady."

"Wha? Ooo-wee. You don understan at all, man. I got a job workin with a *bird*. How you like workin with a bird?" Jones aimed some smoke over the bar. "I mean, I'm glad that girl gettin a chance. She been workin for that Lee mother a long time. She need a break. But I bet that bird be makin more money than me. Whoa!"

"Be nice, Jones."

"Whoa! Hey, you really been brainwash," Jones said. "You ain got nobody to come in and mop your flo. How come? Tell me that."

"Don't get yourself in no trouble."

"Hey! You soun just like the Lee mother. Too bad you two ain met. She love you. She say, 'Hey, boy, you the kinda fool oldtimey nigger I been lookin for all my life.' She say, 'Hey, you so sweet, how's about waxin my floor and paintin my wall? You so darlin, how's about scrubbin my tawlet and polishin my shoe?' And you be sayin, 'Yes, ma'm, yes, ma'm. I'm well behave.' And you be bustin your ass fallin off a chandelier you been dustin and some other whore frien of her comin in so they can compare they price, and Lee star throwin some nickel at your feet and say, 'Hey boy, that sure a lousy show you puttin on. Han us back them nickel before we call a po-lice.' Ooo-wee."

"Didn that lady say she call a po-lice if you give her trouble?"

"She got me there. Hey! I think that Lee got some connection with the po-lice. She all the time tellin me about her frien on the force. She say she got such a high class place a po-lice never stick a foot in her door." Jones formed a thundercloud over the little bar. "She operatin *somethin* with that orphan crap, though. As soon as somebody like Lee say, 'Chariddy,' you know they somethin crooker in the air. And I know they somethin wron cause all of a sudden the Head Orphan stop showin up cause I'm axing plenty question. Shit! I like to fin out what goin on. I tire of bein caught in a trap payin me twenny dollar a week, workin with a bird as big as a eagle. I wanna get someplace, man. Whoa! I want me a air condition, some color TV, sit aroun drinkin somethin better than beer."

"You want another beer?"

Jones looked at the old man through his sunglasses and said, "You tryina sell me another beer, a poor color boy bustin his ass for twenny dollar a week? I think it about time you gimme a free beer with all the money you make sellin pickle meat and sof drink to po color peoples. You sen you boy to college with the money you been makin in here."

"He a schoolteacher now," Mr. Watson said proudly, opening a beer.

"Ain that fine. Whoa! I never go to school more than two year in my life. My momma out washing other people clothin, ain nobody talkin about school. I spen all my time rollin tire aroun the street. I'm rollin, momma washin, nobody learnin nothin. Shit! Who lookin for a tire roller to give them a job? I end up gainfully employ workin with a bird, got a boss probly sellin Spanish fly to orphan. Ooo-wee."

"Well, if conditions really bad . . ."

"'Really bad'? Hey! I'm workin in modren slavery. If I quit, I get report for bein vagran. If I stay, I'm gainfully employ on a salary ain even startin to be a minimal wage."

"I tell you what you can do," Mr. Watson said confidentially; leaning over the bar and handing Jones the beer. The other man at the bar bent toward them to listen; he had been silently following their conversation for several minutes. "You try you a little sabotage. That's the only way you fight that kinda trap."

"Wha you mean 'sabotage'?"

"You know, man," Mr. Watson whispered. "Like the maid ain bein paid enough to throw too much pepper in the soup by accident. Like the parkin lot attendant takin too much crap skid on some oil and crash a car into the fence."

"Whoa!" Jones said. "Like the boy workin in the supermarket suddenly get slippery fingers and drop a dozen aigs on the floor cause he ain been pay overtime. Hey!"

"Now you got it."

"We really plannin *big* sabotage," the other man at the bar said, breaking his silence. "We havin a big demonstration where I work."

"Yeah?" Jones asked. "Where?"

"At Levy Pant. We got this big old white man comin in the factory tellin us he like to drop a atom bum on top the company."

"It sound like you peoples havin more than sabotage," Jones said. "It sound like you havin a *war*."

"Be nice, be respectful," Mr. Watson told the stranger.

The man chuckled until his eyes filled with tears and he said, "This man say he prayin for the mulattas and the rats all over the world."

"Rats? Whoa! You peoples got a one-hunner-percen freak on your hand."

"He very smart," the man said defensively. "He very religious, too. He built him a big cross right in the office."

"Whoa!"

"He say, 'You peoples all be happier in the middle age. You

peoples gotta get you a cannon and some arrows, drop a nucular bum on top this place.'" The man laughed again. "We ain't got nothin better to do in that factory. He always interestin to listen to when he flappin his big moustache. He gonna lead us in a big demonstration he say make all the other demonstration look like a ladies' social."

"Yeah, and it sound like he gonna lead you peoples right into jail," Jones said, covering the bar with some more smoke. "He sound like a crazy white mother."

"He kinda strange," the man admitted. "But he work right in that office, and the manager in there, Mr. Gonzala, he think this guy pretty sharp. He let him do whatever he want. He even let him come back in the factory any time this guy want to. Plenty peoples ready to do demonstrate with him. He tell us he got permission from Mr. Levy hisself to have a demonstration, tell us Mr. Levy want us to demonstrate and get rid of Gonzala. Who know? Maybe they raise our wage. That Mr. Gonzala afred of him already."

"Tell me, man, what this white savior cat look like?" Jones asked with interest.

"He big and fat, got him a huntin cap he wearin all the time."

Jones's eyes widened behind his glasses.

"This huntin cap green? He got him a *green* cap?"

"Yeah. How you know that?"

"Whoa!" Jones said. "You peoples in plenty trouble. A police already lookin for that freak. He come in the Night of Joy one night, star tellin this Darlene gal about a bus."

"Well, whaddya know," the man said. "He tell us about a bus, too, tell us he go ridin into the har of darkness on a bus one time."

"He the same one. Stay away from that freak. He wanted by a po-lice. You po color peoples all get your ass throwed in jail. Whoa!"

"Well, I gotta ax him about that," the man said. "I sure don wanna get led on no demonstration by a convic."

II

Mr. Gonzalez was at Levy Pants early, as usual. He symbolically lit his little heater and a filtered cigarette with the same match, lighting two torches that signaled the start of another working day. Then he applied his mind to his early morning meditations. Mr. Reilly had added a new touch to the office the day before, streamers of mauve, gray, and tan crepe paper looped from light bulb to light bulb across the ceiling. The cross and signs and streamers in the office reminded the office manager of Christmas decorations and made him feel slightly sentimental. Looking happily into Mr. Reilly's area, he noticed that the bean vines were growing so healthily that they had even begun to twine downward through the handles of the file drawers. Mr. Gonzalez wondered how the file clerk managed to do his filing without disturbing the tender shoots. Pondering this clerical riddle, he was surprised to see Mr. Reilly himself burst like a torpedo through the door.

"Good morning, sir," Ignatius said brusquely, his scarf-shawl flying horizontally in his wake like the flag of some mobilized Scottish clan. A cheap movie camera was slung over his shoulder and under his arm he had a bundle which appeared to be a rolled-up bed sheet.

"Well you certainly are early today, Mr. Reilly."

"What do you mean? I always arrive at this time."

"Oh, of course," Mr. Gonzalez said meekly.

"Do you believe that I am here early for some purpose?"

"No. I . . ."

"Speak up, sir. Why are you so strangely suspicious? Your eyes are literally flickering with paranoia."

"What, Mr. Reilly?"

"You heard what I said," Ignatius answered and lumbered through the door to the factory.

Mr. Gonzalez tried to compose himself again but was disturbed by what sounded like a cheer from the factory. Perhaps, he thought, one of the workers had become a father or won something in a raffle. So long as the factory workers let him alone, he was willing to extend the same courtesy to them. To him they were simply part of the physical plant of Levy Pants not connected with "the brain center." They were not his to worry about; they were under the drunken control of Mr. Palermo. When he did find the proper courage, the office manager intended to approach Mr. Reilly in a most politic manner about the amount of time he was spending in the factory. However, Mr. Reilly had lately become somewhat distant and unapproachable, and Mr. Gonzalez dreaded the thought of a battle with him. His feet grew numb when he thought of one of those bear's paws landing squarely on the top of his head, driving him perhaps like a stake through the unpredictable flooring of the office.

Four of the male factory workers were embracing Ignatius around the Smithfield hams that were his thighs and, with considerable effort, were lifting him onto one of the cutting tables. Above the shoulders of his carriers Ignatius barked directions as if he were supervising the loading of the rarest and most precious of cargoes.

"Up and to the right, there!" he shouted down. "Up, up. Be careful. Slowly. Is your grip tight?"

"Yeah," one of the lifters answered.

"It feels rather loose. Please! I am deteriorating into a state of total anxiety."

The workers watched with interest as the lifters tottered back and forth under their burden.

"Now backward," Ignatius called nervously. "Backward until the table is directly beneath me."

"Don't you worry, Mr. R.," a lifter panted. "We aimin you right at that table."

"Apparently you are not," Ignatius replied, his body slamming into a post. "Oh, my God! My shoulder is dislocated."

A cry arose from the other workers.

"Hey, watch out with Mr. R.," someone screamed. "You men gonna bust his haid wide open."

"Please!" Ignatius cried. "Someone help! In another moment I shall probably be a broken heap."

"Look, Mr. R.," a lifter said breathlessly, "the table right behine us now."

"I shall probably be dumped into one of the furnaces before this misadventure terminates. I suspect that it would have been much wiser to address the group from floor level."

"Put your feets down, Mr. R. The table right under you."

"Slowly," Ignatius said, extending his big toe downward with great caution. "Well, so it is. All right. When I have steadied myself, you may release your hold upon my body."

Ignatius was at last vertically atop the long table, holding the bundled bed sheet over his pelvis to hide from his audience the fact that during the process of being lifted, he had become somewhat stimulated.

"Friends!" Ignatius said grandly and lifted the arm that was not holding the sheet. "At last the day is ours. I hope that you have all remembered to bring your engines of war." From the group around the cutting table there issued neither confirmation nor denial. "I mean the sticks and chains and clubs and so forth." Giggling in chorus, the workers waved some fence posts, broomsticks, bicycle chains, and bricks. "My God! You have really assembled a rather formidable and diffuse armory. The violence of our attack may surpass my expectations. However, the more definitive the blow, the more definitive the results. My cursory inspection of your arms, therefore, confirms my faith in the ultimate success of our crusade today. In our wake, we must leave a sacked and pillaged Levy Pants, we must fight fire with fire."

"What he say?" one worker asked another.

"We shall storm the office very shortly, thereby surprising the foe when his senses are still subject to the psychic mists of early morning."

"Hey, Mr. R., pardon me," a man called out from the crowd. "Somebody tell me you in trouble with a po-lice. Is that right?"

A wave of anxiety and uneasiness broke over the workers.

"What?" Ignatius screamed. "Where did you hear such slander. That is totally false. Some white supremacist, some upstate red-neck, perhaps even Gonzalez himself no doubt began that vile rumor. How dare you, sir. All of you must realize that our cause has many enemies."

While the workers were applauding him soundly, Ignatius wondered how that worker had learned of the mongoloid Mancuso's attempted arrest. Perhaps he had been standing in the crowd before the department store. That patrolman was the fly in everyone's ointment. However, the moment seemed to have been saved.

"Now this we will carry with us in the vanguard!" Ignatius shouted over the last sprinkled applause. He dramatically whipped from his pelvis the sheet, flapping it open. Among the yellow stains the word FORWARD was printed in high block letters in red crayon. Below this *Crusade for Moorish Dignity* was written in an intricate blue script.

"I wonder who been sleepin on that old thing," the intense woman with the spiritual bent, who was to be the leader of the choir, said. "Lord!"

Several other prospective rioters expressed the same curiosity in more explicitly physical terminology.

"Quiet now," Ignatius said, stomping one foot thunderously on the table. "Please! Two of the more statuesque women here will carry this banner between them as we march into the office."

"I ain puttin my hand on that," one woman answered.

"Quiet! Everyone!" Ignatius said furiously. "I am beginning to suspect that you people are not actually deserving of this cause. Apparently you are not prepared to make any of the ultimate sacrifices."

"How come we gotta take that old sheet with us?" someone asked. "I thought this suppose to be a demonstration dealin with wages."

"Sheet? What sheet!" Ignatius replied. "I am holding before you the proudest of banners, an identification of our purpose, a visualization of all that we seek." The workers studied the stains more intensely. "If you wish to simply rush into the office like cattle, you will have participated in nothing more than a riot. This banner alone gives form and credence to the agitation. There is a certain geometry involved in these things, a certain ritual which must be observed. Here, you two ladies standing there, take this between you and wave it thus with honor and pride, hands held high, et cetera."

The two women whom Ignatius indicated ambled slowly to the cutting table, gingerly took the banner with their thumbs and index fingers, and held it between them as if it were a leper's shroud.

"That looks even more impressive than I had imagined," Ignatius said.

"Don wave that thing around me, gal," someone said to the women, creating another ripple of giggles from the crowd.

Ignatius flipped his camera into action and aimed it at the banner and the workers. "Will all of you please wave your sticks and stones again?" The workers complied merrily.

Myrna would choke on her espresso when she saw this. "A bit more violently now. Brandish these weapons fiercely. Make faces. Scream. Perhaps some of you could jump up and down, if you don't mind."

They laughingly followed his directions, everyone, that is, but the two women who were sullenly holding the banner.

In the office Mr. Gonzalez was watching Miss Trixie bump into the door frame as she made her entrance for the day. At the same time he was wondering what the new and violent outburst from the factory meant.

Ignatius filmed the scene before him for a minute or two more, then he followed a post upward to the ceiling for what he imagined would be an interesting and rather recherché bit of cinematography suggesting aspiration. Envy would gnaw at Myrna's musky vitals. At the top of the post the camera focused upon several square feet of the rusted interior of the factory's roof. Then Ignatius handed the camera down to a worker and asked to be photographed. While the worker aimed the lens at him, Ignatius scowled and shook a fist, entertaining the workers greatly.

"All right now," he said benevolently when he had taken the camera back and flipped it off. "Let us control our riotous impulses for the moment and plan our stratagems. First, the two ladies here will precede us with the banner. Directly behind the banner comes the choir with some appropriate folk or religious melody. The lady in charge of the choir may choose the tune. Knowing nothing of your musical folkways, I shall leave the selection to you, although I wish that there had been time enough to teach all of you the beauties of some madrigal. I will only suggest that you choose a somewhat forceful melody. The remainder of you will compose the warriors' battalion. I shall follow the entire ensemble with my camera in order to record this memorable occasion. At some future date all of us may realize some additional revenues from the rental of this film to student organizations and other similarly appalling societies.

"Please remember this. Our first approach will be a peaceful and rational one. As we enter the office, the two ladies will carry the banner to the office manager. The choir will then form about the cross. The battalion will remain in the background until needed. Because we are dealing with Gonzalez himself, I suspect that the battalion will be called upon in short order. If Gonzalez fails to respond to the emotion of this spectacle, I shall call, 'Attack!' That will be the signal for your onslaught. Are there any questions?"

Someone said, "This a lotta shit," but Ignatius ignored the voice. There was a happy hush in the factory, most of the workers eager for the change of pace. Mr. Palermo, the foreman, appeared drunkenly between two of the furnaces for a moment and then disappeared.

"Apparently the battle plan is clear," Ignatius said when no questions were forthcoming. "Will the two ladies with the banner please take their positions over there by the door? Now the choir please form behind them and then the battalion." The workers formed rapidly, smiling and sticking one another with their engines of war. "Fine! The choir may now begin singing."

The lady with the spiritual bent blew a pitchpipe and the choir members began singing lustily, "Oh, Jesus, walk by my side, / Then I always, always be satisfied."

"That really sounds rather stirring," Ignatius observed. Then he shouted, "Forward!"

The formation obeyed so rapidly that before Ignatius could call anything else, the banner had already passed through the factory and was rising up the stairs to the office.

"Halt!" Ignatius screamed. "Someone come help me off this table."

> Oh, Jesus, you be my friend
> Right, oh, yeah, right up till the end.
> You take my hand
> And I feel grand
> Knowing you walking
> Hearing me talking
> I ain't complaining
> Though maybe it's raining
> When I'm with Jesus.

"Stop!" Ignatius called frantically, watching the last of the battalion file through the door. "Come back in here immediately."

The door swung closed. He got down on his hands and knees and crawled to the edge of the table. Then he swung around and, after a long while spent in maneuvering his extremities, managed to sit on the edge of the table. Noticing that his feet were swinging only a few inches from the floor, he decided to risk the jump. As he pushed himself free of the table and landed on the floor, the camera slid from his shoulder and hit the cement with a hollow, cracking sound. Disemboweled, its film entrails spilled onto the floor. Ignatius picked it up and flipped the switch that was supposed to set it in motion, but nothing happened.

> Oh, Jesus, you pay my bail
> When they put me in that old jail.
> Oh, oh, you always giving
> A reason for living.

"What are those maniacs singing?" Ignatius asked the empty factory while he tried to stuff foot upon foot of film into his pocket.

You never hurt me,
You never, never, never desert me.
I never sinning
I always winning
Now I got Jesus.

Ignatius, trailing unwound film, hustled to the door and entered the office. The two women were stonily displaying the back of the stained sheet to a confused Mr. Gonzalez. Their eyes closed, the choir members were chanting compulsively, lost in their melody. Ignatius pushed through the battalion loitering benignly on the fringes of the scene toward the desk of the office manager.

Miss Trixie saw him and asked, "What's happening, Gloria? What are all the factory people doing in here?"

"Run while you're able, Miss Trixie," he told her with great seriousness.

"Oh, Jesus, you give me peace/When you keeping away them po-lice."

"I can't hear you," Miss Trixie cried, grabbing his arm. "Is this a minstrel show?"

"Go dangle your withered parts over the toilet!" Ignatius screamed savagely.

Miss Trixie shuffled away.

"Well?" Ignatius asked Mr. Gonzalez, rearranging the two ladies so that the office manager could see the lettering on the other side of the sheet.

"What does this mean?" Mr. Gonzalez asked, reading the banner.

"Do you refuse to help these people?"

"Help them?" the office manager asked in a frightened voice. "What are you talking about, Mr. Reilly?"

"I am talking about the sin against society of which you are guilty."

"What?" Mr. Gonzalez's lower lip quivered.

"Attack!" Ignatius cried to the battalion. "This man is totally without charity."

"You ain give him a chance to say nothin," observed one of the discontented women holding the sheet. "You let Mr. Gonzalez talk."

"Attack! Attack!" Ignatius cried again, even more furiously. His blue and yellow eyes protruded and flashed.

Someone halfheartedly whizzed a bicycle chain over the top of the file cabinets and knocked the bean plants to the floor.

"Now look what you've done," Ignatius said. "Who told you to knock those plants over?"

"You say, 'Attagg,'" the owner of the bicycle chain answered.

"Stop that at once," Ignatius bellowed at a man who was apathetically making a vertical slash in the DEPARTMENT OF RESEARCH AND REFERENCE - I. REILLY, CUSTODIAN sign with a pen knife. "What do you people think you're doing?"

"Hey, you say, 'Attagg,'" several voices answered.

> In this lonesome place
> You give me grace
> Giving your light
> Through the long night.
> Oh, Jesus, you hearing my woe
> And I never, I never, never gonna let you go.

"Stop that awful song," Ignatius shouted at the choir. "Never has such egregious blasphemy fallen upon my ears."

The choir ceased its singing and looked hurt.

"I don't understand what you're doing," the office manager said to Ignatius.

"Oh, shut up your little pussymouth, you mongoloid."

"We goin back to the factory," the spokesman for the choir,

the intense lady, said angrily to Ignatius. "You a bad man. I *believe* a police looking for you."

"Yeah," several voices agreed.

"Now wait a moment," Ignatius begged. "Someone must attack Gonzalez." He surveyed the warriors' battalion. "The man with the brick, come over here at once and knock him a bit about the head."

"I ain't hittin nobody with this," the man with the brick said. "You probly got a po-lice record a mile long."

The two women dropped the sheet disgustedly on the floor and followed the choir, which was already beginning to file through the door.

"Where do you people think you're going?" Ignatius cried, his voice choked with saliva and fury.

The warriors said nothing and began to follow the choir and the two standard bearers out of the office. Ignatius waddled swiftly behind the warriors straggling in the rear and grabbed one of them by the arm, but the man swatted at him as if he were a mosquito and said, "We got enough trouble without gettin throwed in jail."

"Come back in here! We're not finished. You can get Miss Trixie if you want," Ignatius cried frantically to the disappearing battalion, but the procession continued to move silently and determinedly farther down the stairs into the factory. Finally, the door swung closed on the last of the crusaders for Moorish dignity.

III

Patrolman Mancuso looked at his watch. He had been in the rest room a full eight hours. It was time to check his costume in at the precinct and go home. He had arrested no one all day and, in addition, he seemed to be catching a cold. It was chilly and damp in that booth. He sneezed and tried to open the door, but it wouldn't give. He shook it, fumbled with the lock, which appeared to be stuck. After a minute or so of rattling and pushing, he called, "Help!"

IV

"Ignatius! So you got yourself fired."

"Please, Mother, I am near the breaking point." Ignatius stuck the bottle of Dr. Nut under his moustache and drank noisily, making great sounds of sucking and gurgling. "If you are planning now to be a harpy, I shall certainly be pushed over the brink."

"A little job in a office and you can't hold it down. With all your education."

"I was hated and resented," Ignatius said, casting a hurt expression at the brown walls of the kitchen. He pulled his tongue from the mouth of the bottle with a thump and belched some Dr. Nut. "Ultimately it was all Myrna Minkoff's fault. You know how she makes trouble."

"Myrna Minkoff? Don't gimme that foolishness, Ignatius. That girl's in New York. I know you, boy. You musta really pulled some boo-boos at that Levy Pants."

"My excellence confused them."

"Gimme that paper, Ignatius. We gonna take a look at them want ads."

"Is that true?" Ignatius thundered. "Am I going to be thrown out again into the abyss? Apparently you have bowled all the charity out of your soul. I must have at least a week in bed, with service, before I shall again be whole."

"Speaking of bed, what happened to your sheet, boy?"

"I certainly wouldn't know. Perhaps it was stolen. I have warned you about intruders."

"You mean somebody broke into this house just to take one of your dirty sheets?"

"If you were a bit more conscientious about doing the laundry, the description of that sheet would be somewhat different."

"Okay, hand over that paper, Ignatius."

"Are you really going to attempt to read aloud? I doubt whether my system could bear that trauma at the moment. Anyway, I am looking at a very interesting article in the science column about mollusks."

Mrs. Reilly snatched the paper from her son, leaving two little scraps of it in his hands.

"Mother! Is this offensive display of ill manners one of the results of your association with those bowling Sicilians?"

"Shut up, Ignatius," his mother said, leafing compulsively toward the classified section of the newspaper. "Tomorrow morning you getting on that St. Charles trolley with the birds."

"Huh?" Ignatius asked absently. He was wondering what he could write to Myrna now. The film seemed to have been ruined, too. Explaining the disaster of the Crusade in a letter would be impossible. "What was that you said, mother of mine?"

"I said you gettin on that trolley with the birds," Mrs. Reilly screamed.

"That sounds appropriate."

"When you come home again, you gonna have you a job."

"Apparently Fortuna has decided upon another downward spin."

"What?"

"Nothing."

V

Mrs. Levy lay prone on the motorized exercising board, its several sections prodding her ample body gently, nudging and kneading her soft, white flesh like a loving baker. Winding her arms under the table, she held it tightly.

"Oh," she moaned softly and happily, nibbling on the section beneath her face.

"Turn that thing off," her husband's voice said somewhere behind her.

"What?" Mrs. Levy raised her head and looked dreamily around. "What are you doing here? I thought you were staying in town for the races."

"I changed my mind, if it's okay with you."

"Sure, it's okay with me. Do whatever you want. Don't let me tell you what to do. Have yourself a ball. See if I care."

"Pardon me. I'm sorry I tore you away from the board."

"Let's leave the board out of this, if you don't mind."

"Oh, I'm sorry if I insulted it."

"Just leave my board out of it. That's all I said. I'm trying to be nice. I don't start the arguments around here."

"Turn the damn thing on again and shut up. I'm going to take a shower."

"You see? You're very excited over nothing. Don't take all your guilt feelings out on me."

"What guilt feelings? What have I done?"

"You know what it is, Gus. You know how you've thrown your life away. A whole business down the drain. A chance to go nationwide. Your father's sweat and blood handed to you on a silver platter."

"Ugh."

"A growing concern failing."

"Listen, I have a headache from trying to save that

business today. That's why I didn't go to the races."

After having fought with his father for almost thirty-five years, Mr. Levy had decided that he would spend the rest of his life trying not to be bothered. But he was bothered every day that he was at Levy's Lodge by his wife simply because she resented his not wanting to be bothered by Levy Pants. And in staying away from Levy Pants, he was bothered even more by the company because something was always going wrong there. It would all be simpler and less bothersome if he would have really operated Levy Pants and put in an eight hour day as manager. But just the name "Levy Pants" gave him heartburn. He associated it with his father.

"What did you do, Gus? Sign a few letters?"

"I fired somebody."

"Really? Big deal. Who? One of the furnace stokers?"

"You remember I told you about that big kook, the one that ass Gonzalez hired?"

"Oh. Him." Mrs. Levy rolled about on the exercising board.

"You should see what he did to that place. Paper streamers hanging from the ceiling. A big cross tacked up in the office. As soon as I walk in today, he comes up to me and starts complaining that somebody from the factory knocked his bean plants to the floor."

"Bean plants? He thought Levy Pants was a truck garden?"

"Who knows what went on in that head. He wants me to fire the one who knocked over his plants and this other guy he says cut up his sign. He says the factory workers are a bunch of rowdies who have no respect for him. He says they're out to get him. So I go back in the factory to find Palermo, who of course is not there, and what do I find? All those workers have bricks and chains lying all over the place. They're all very emotionally worked up, and they tell me this guy Reilly, that's the big slob, made them bring

163

all that crap so they could attack the office and beat up Gonzalez."

"What?"

"He'd been telling them they were underpaid and over-worked."

"I think he's right," Mrs. Levy said. "Just yesterday Susan and Sandra wrote something about that in their letter. Their little friends at college told them that, from what they'd said about their father, he sounded like a plantation owner living on slave labor. The girls were very excited. I meant to mention it to you, but I had so much trouble with that new hair designer that it slipped my mind. They want you to raise the salaries of those poor people or they won't come home again."

"Who do those two think they are?"

"They think they're your daughters, in case you forgot. All they want is to respect you. They said you have to improve conditions at Levy Pants if you want to see them again."

"What's their big interest in colored people all of a sudden? The young men gave out already?"

"Now you're attacking the girls again. You see what I mean? That's why I can't respect you either. If one of your daughters was a horse and the other a baseball player, you couldn't do enough for them."

"If one of them was a horse and the other a baseball player, we'd be better off, believe me. They could turn in a profit."

"I'm sorry," Mrs. Levy said, flipping the board on again. "I can't listen to any more of this. I'm too disillusioned already. I'll hardly be able to bring myself to write the girls about this."

Mr. Levy had seen his wife's letters to the girls, emotional, irrational brainwashing editorials that could have made Patrick Henry out to be a Tory, that brought the girls home on holidays bristling with hostility against their father for the thousands of injustices he had committed against their mother. With him cast as a Klansman firing a young crusader, Mrs. Levy could really write a flaming broadside. The material at hand was too good.

"This guy was a real psycho," Mr. Levy said.

"To you character is a psychosis. Integrity is a complex. I've heard it all before."

"Look, I probably wouldn't have fired him if one of the factory workers hadn't told me he heard this kook is wanted by the police. That really made up my mind fast. I have enough trouble with that company without having a kooky police character working in there."

"Don't give me that. It's too typical. To somebody like you, crusaders and idealists are always beatniks and criminals. It's your defense against them. But thanks for telling me. It will add to the realism of the letter."

"I've never fired anybody in my life," Mr. Levy said. "But I can't keep somebody the police are looking for. We might get in trouble."

"Please." Mrs. Levy gestured warningly from her board. "That young idealist must be floundering somewhere at this very moment. It will break the girls' hearts, just as it's breaking mine. I'm a woman of great character and integrity and refinement. You've never appreciated that. I've been debased through my association with you. You've made everything seem so cheap, me included. I've become very hardened."

"So I ruined you too, huh?"

"I was a very warm and loving girl at one time with high hopes. The girls knew that. I thought you'd make Levy Pants nationwide." Mrs. Levy's head bounced up and down, up and down. "Look. Now it's just a little run-down concern with a few outlets. Your daughters are disillusioned. I'm disillusioned. That young man you fired is disillusioned."

"You want me to kill myself?"

"You make your own decisions. You always have. I've just existed for your pleasure. I'm just another old sports car. Use me when you wish. I don't care."

"Oh, shut up. Nobody wants to use you for anything."

"You see that? You're always attacking. It's insecurity, guilt complexes, hostility. If you were proud of yourself and of the way you treat other people, you'd be pleasant. Just take Miss Trixie as another example. Look at what you've done to her."

"I've never done anything to that woman."

"That's just it. She's alone, afraid."

"She's almost dead."

"Since Susan and Sandra are gone, I feel a guilt complex myself. What am I doing? Where is my project? I am a woman of interests, ideals." Mrs. Levy sighed. "I feel so useless. You've caged me in with hundreds of material objects that don't satisfy the real me." Her bouncing eyes looked coldly at her husband. "Bring me Miss Trixie and I won't write that letter."

"What? I don't want that senile bag out here. Whatever happened to your bridge club? The last time you didn't write a letter you got a new dress. Settle for that. I'll buy you a ball gown."

"It's not enough that I've kept that woman active. She needs personal help."

"You've already used her as a guinea pig for that correspondence course you took. Why not let her alone. Let Gonzalez retire her."

"Do that and you'll kill her. Then she'll really feel unwanted. You'll have a death on your hands."

"Oh, boy."

"When I think of my own mother. On the beach in San Juan every winter. A tan, a bikini. Dancing, swimming, laughing. Boy friends."

"She has heart failure every time a wave knocks her down.

166

What she doesn't lose in the casinos she spends on the house doctor at the Caribe Hilton."

"You don't like my mother because she's on to you. She was right. I should have married a doctor, somebody with ideals." Mrs. Levy bounced sadly. "It really doesn't matter to me very much anymore. Suffering has only strengthened me."

"How much would you suffer if somebody pulled the wires out of that goddam exercising board?"

"I told you already," Mrs. Levy said angrily. "Leave the board out of this. Your hostility's getting the upper hand. Take my advice, Gus. Go see that analyst in the Medical Arts building, the one that helped Lenny pull his jewelry shop out of the red. He cured Lenny of that complex he had about selling rosaries. Lenny swears by that doctor. Now he's got some kind of exclusive agreement with a bunch of nuns who peddle the rosaries in about forty Catholic schools all over the city. The money's rolling in. Lenny's happy. The sisters are happy. The kids are happy."

"That sounds great."

"Lenny's put in a beautiful line of statues and religious accessories."

"I bet he's happy."

"He is. You should be the same. Go see that doctor before it's too late, Gus. For the girls' sake you should be helped. I don't care."

"I'm sure you don't."

"You're a very mixed-up person. Sandra, personally, is much happier since she was psychoanalyzed. Some doctor at the college helped her out."

"I'm sure he did."

"Sandra may have a setback when she hears of what you did to that young activist. I know the girls will at last turn against you completely. They're warm and compassionate, just like I was before I was brutalized."

"Brutalized?"

"Please. Not another word of sarcasm." An aquamarine-nailed gesture warned from the bouncing and undulating board. "Do I get Miss Trixie or do the girls get the letter?"

"You get Miss Trixie," Mr. Levy said finally. "You'll probably try to bounce her on that board and break her hip."

"Leave the board out of this!"

Seven

Paradise Vendors, Incorporated, was housed in what had formerly been an automobile repair shop, the dark ground floor of an otherwise unoccupied commerical building on Poydras Street. The garage doors were usually open, giving the passerby an acrid nostrilful of boiling hot dogs and mustard and also of cement soaked over many years by automobile lubricants and motor oils that had dripped and drained from Harmons and Hupmobiles. The powerful stench of Paradise Vendors, Incorporated, sometimes led the overwhelmed and perplexed stroller to glance through the open door into the darkness of the garage. There his eye fell upon a fleet of large tin hot dogs mounted on bicycle tires. It was hardly an imposing vehicular collection. Several of the mobile hot dogs were badly dented. One crumpled frankfurter lay on its side, its one wheel horizontal above it, a traffic fatality.

Among the afternoon pedestrians who hurried past Paradise Vendors, Incorporated, one formidable figure waddled slowly along. It was Ignatius. Stopping before the narrow garage, he sniffed the fumes from Paradise with great sensory pleasure, the protruding hairs in his nostrils analyzing, cataloging, categorizing, and classifying the distinct odors of hot dog, mustard, and lubricant. Breathing deeply, he wondered whether he also detected the more delicate odor, the fragile scent of hot dog buns. He looked at the white-gloved hands of his Mickey Mouse wristwatch and noticed that he had eaten lunch only an hour before. Still the intriguing aromas were making him salivate actively.

He stepped into the garage and looked around. In a corner an old man was boiling hot dogs in a large institutional pot whose size dwarfed the gas range upon which it rested.

"Pardon me, sir," Ignatius called. "Do you retail here?"

The man's watering eyes turned toward the large visitor.

"What do you want?"

"I would like to buy one of your hot dogs. They smell rather tasty. I was wondering if I could buy just one."

"Sure."

"May I select my own?" Ignatius asked, peering down over the top of the pot. In the boiling water the frankfurters swished and lashed like artificially colored and magnified paramecia. Ignatius filled his lungs with the pungent, sour aroma. "I shall pretend that I am in a smart restaurant and that this is the lobster pond."

"Here, take this fork," the man said, handing Ignatius a bent and corroded semblance of a spear. "Try to keep your hands out of the water. It's like acid. Look what it's done to the fork."

"My," Ignatius said to the old man after having taken his first bite. "These are rather strong. What are the ingredients in these."

"Rubber, cereal, tripe. Who knows? I wouldn't touch one of them myself."

"They're curiously appealing," Ignatius said, clearing his throat. "I thought that the vibrissae about my nostrils detected something unique while I was outside."

Ignatius chewed with a blissful savagery, studying the scar on the man's nose and listening to his whistling.

"Do I hear a strain from Scarlatti?" Ignatius asked finally.

"I thought I was whistling 'Turkey in the Straw.'"

"I had hoped that you might be familiar with Scarlatti's work. He was the last of the musicians," Ignatius observed and resumed his furious attack upon the long hot dog. "With

170

your apparent musical bent, you might apply yourself to something worthwhile."

Ignatius chewed while the man began his tuneless whistling again. Then he said, "I suspect that you imagine 'Turkey in the Straw' to be a valuable bit of Americana. Well, it is not. It is a discordant abomination."

"I can't see that it matters much."

"It matters a great deal, sir!" Ignatius screamed. "Veneration of such things as 'Turkey in the Straw' is at the very root of our current dilemma."

"Where the hell do you come from? Whadda you want?"

"What is your opinion of a society that considers 'Turkey in the Straw' to be one of the pillars, as it were, of its culture?"

"Who thinks that?" the old man asked worriedly.

"Everyone! Especially folk singers and third-grade teachers. Grimy undergraduates and grammar schoolchildren are always chanting it like sorcerers." Ignatius belched. "I do believe that I shall have another of these savories."

After his fourth hot dog, Ignatius ran his magnificent pink tongue around his lips and up over his moustache and said to the old man, "I cannot recently remember having been so totally satisfied. I was fortunate to find this place. Before me lies a day fraught with God knows what horrors. I am at the moment unemployed and have been launched upon a quest for work. However, I might as well have had the Grail set as my goal. I have been rocketing about the business district for a week now. Apparently I lack some particular perversion which today's employer is seeking."

"No luck, huh?"

"Well, during the week, I have answered only two ads. On some days I am completely enervated by the time I reach Canal Street. On these days I am doing well if I have enough spirit to straggle into a movie palace. Actually, I have seen every film that is playing downtown, and since they are all offensive enough to be held over indefinitely, next week looks particularly bleak."

The old man looked at Ignatius and then at the massive pot, the gas range, and the crumpled carts. He said, "I can hire you right here."

"Thank you very much," Ignatius said condescendingly. "However, I could not work here. This garage is particularly dank, and I'm susceptible to respiratory ailments among a variety of others."

"You wouldn't be working in here, son. I mean as a vendor."

"What?" Ignatius bellowed. "Out in the rain and snow all day long?"

"It don't snow here."

"It has on rare occasions. It probably would again as soon as I trudged out with one of these wagons. I would probably be found in some gutter, icicles dangling from all of my orifices, alley cats pawing over me to draw the warmth from my last breath. No, thank you, sir. I must go. I suspect that I have an appointment of some sort."

Ignatius looked absently at his little watch and saw that it had stopped again.

"Just for a little while," the old man begged. "Try it for a day. How's about it? I need vendors bad."

"A day?" Ignatius repeated disbelievingly. "A day? I can't waste a valuable day. I have places to go and people to see."

"Okay," the old man said firmly. "Then pay me the dollar you owe for them weenies."

"I am afraid that they will all have to be on the house. Or on the garage or whatever it is. My Miss Marple of a mother discovered a number of theater tickets stubs in my pockets last night and has given me only carfare today."

"I'll call in the police."

"Oh, my God!"

"Pay me! Pay me or I'll get the law."

The old man picked up the long fork and deftly placed its two rotting tongs at Ignatius' throat.

"You are puncturing my imported muffler," Ignatius screamed.

"Gimme your carfare."

"I can't walk all the way to Constantinople Street."

"Get a taxi. Somebody at your house can pay the driver when you get there."

"Do you seriously think that my mother will believe me if I tell her that an old man held me up with a fork and took my two nickels?"

"I'm not gonna be robbed again," the old man said, spraying Ignatius with saliva. "That's all that happens to you in the hot dog trade. Hot dog vendors and gas station attendants always get it. Holdups, muggings. Nobody respects a hot dog vendor."

"That is patently untrue, sir. No one respects hot dog vendors more than I. They perform one of our society's few worthwhile services. The robbing of a hot dog vendor is a symbolic act. The theft is not prompted by avarice but rather by a desire to belittle the vendor."

"Shut your goddam fat lip and pay me."

"You are quite adamant for being so aged. However, I am not walking fifty blocks to my home. I would rather face death by rusty fork."

"Okay, buddy, now listen to me. I'll make a bargain with you. You go out and push one of these wagons for an hour, and we'll call it quits."

"Don't I need clearance from the Health Department or something? I mean, I might have something beneath my fingernails that is very debilitating to the human system. Incidentally, do you get all of your vendors this way? Your hiring practices are hardly in step with contemporary policy.

I feel as if I've been shanghaied. I am too apprehensive to ask how you go about firing your employees."

"Just don't ever try to rob a hot dog man again."

"You've just made your point. Actually, you have made two of them, literally in my throat and muffler. I hope that you are prepared to compensate for the muffler. There are no more of its kind. It was made in a small factory in England that was destroyed by the Luftwaffe. At the time it was rumored that the Luftwaffe was directed to strike directly at the factory in order to destroy British morale, for the Germans had seen Churchill wrapped in a muffler of this sort in a confiscated newsreel. For all I know, this may be the same one that Churchill was wearing in that particular Movietone. Today their value is somewhere in the thousands. It can also be worn as a shawl. Look."

"Well," the old man said finally, after watching Ignatius employ the muffler as a cummerbund, a sash, a cloak, and a pair of kilts, a sling for a broken arm, and a kerchief, "you ain't gonna do too much damage to Paradise Vendors in one hour."

"If the alternatives are jail or a pierced Adam's apple, I shall happily push one of your carts. Though I can't predict how far I'll go."

"Don't get me wrong, son. I ain't a bad guy, but you can only take so much. I spent ten years trying to make Paradise Vendors a reputable organization, but that ain't easy. People look down on hot dog vendors. They think I operate a business for bums. I got trouble finding decent vendors. Then when I find some nice guy, he goes out and gets himself mugged by hoodlums. How come God had to make it so tough for you?"

"We must not question His ways," Ignatius said.

"Maybe not, but I still don't get it."

"The writings of Boethius may give you some insight."

"I read Father Keller and Billy Graham in the paper every single day."

"Oh, my God!" Ignatius spluttered. "No wonder you are so lost."

"Here," the old man said, opening a metal locker near the stove. "Put this on."

He took what looked like a white smock out of the locker and handed it to Ignatius.

"What is this?" Ignatius asked happily. "It looks like an academic gown."

Ignatius slipped it over his head. On top of his overcoat, the smock made him look like a dinosaur egg about to hatch.

"Tie it at the waist with the belt."

"Of course not. These things are supposed to freely flow about the human form, although this one seems to provide little leeway. Are you sure that you don't have one in a larger size?

"Upon close scrutiny, I notice that this gown is rather yellow about the cuffs. I hope that these stains about the chest are ketchup rather than blood. The last wearer of this might have been stabbed by hoodlums."

"Here, put on this cap." The man gave Ignatius a little rectangle of white paper.

"I am certainly not wearing a paper cap. The one that I have is perfectly good and far more healthful."

"You can't wear a hunting cap. This is the Paradise vendor's uniform."

"I will not wear that paper cap! I am not going to die of pneumonia while playing this little game for you. Plunge the fork into my vital organs, if you wish. I will not wear that cap. Death before dishonor and disease."

"Okay, drop it," the old man sighed. "Come on and take this cart here."

"Do you think that I am going to be seen on the streets

with that damaged abomination?" Ignatius asked furiously, smoothing the vendor's smock over his body. "Give me that shiny one with the white sidewall tires."

"Awright, awright." the old man said testily. He opened the lid on the little well in the cart and with a fork slowly began transferring hot dogs from the pot to the little well in the cart. "Now I give you a dozen hot dogs." He opened another lid in the top of the metal bun. "I'm putting a package of buns in here. Got that?" He closed that lid and pulled upon a little side door cut in the shining red tin dog. "In here they got a little can of liquid heat keeps the hot dogs warm."

"My God," Ignatius said with some respect. "These carts are like Chinese puzzles. I suspect that I will continually be pulling at the wrong opening."

The old man opened still another lid cut in the rear of the hot dog.

"What's in there? A machine gun?"

"The mustard and ketchup's in here."

"Well, I shall give this a brave try, although I may sell someone the can of liquid heat before I get too far."

The old man rolled the cart to the door of the garage and said, "Okay, buddy, go ahead."

"Thank you so much," Ignatius replied and wheeled the big tin hot dog out onto the sidewalk. "I will be back promptly in an hour."

"Get off the sidewalk with that thing."

"I hope that you don't think I am going out into the traffic."

"You can get yourself arrested for pushing one of them things on the sidewalk."

"Good," Ignatius said. "If the police follow me, they might prevent a robbery."

Ignatius pushed slowly away from the headquarters of Paradise Vendors through the heavy pedestrian traffic that moved to either side of the big hot dog like waves on a ship's prow. This was a better way of passing time than seeing personnel managers, several of whom, Ignatius thought, had treated him rather viciously in the last few days. Since the movie houses were now off limits due to lack of funds, he would have had to drift, bored and aimless, around the business district until it seemed safe to return home. The people on the street looked at Ignatius, but no one bought. After he had gone half a block, he began calling, "Hot dogs! Hot dogs from Paradise!"

"Get in the street, pal," the old man cried somewhere behind him.

Ignatius turned the corner and parked the wagon against a building. Opening the various lids, he prepared a hot dog for himself and ravenously ate it. His mother had been in a violent mood all week, refusing to buy him any Dr. Nut, pounding on his door when he was trying to write, threatening to sell the house and move into an old folks' home. She described to Ignatius the courage of Patrolman Mancuso, who, against heavy odds, was *fighting* to retain his job, who *wanted* to work, who was making the best of his torture and exile in the bathroom at the bus station. Patrolman Mancuso's situation reminded Ignatius of the situation of Boethius when he was imprisoned by the emperor before being killed. To pacify his mother and to improve conditions at home, he had given her *The Consolation of Philosophy*, an English translation of the work that Boethius had written while unjustly imprisoned and had told her to give it to Patrolman Mancuso so that he might peruse it while sealed in his booth. "The book teaches us to accept that which we cannot change. It describes the plight of a just man in an unjust society. It is the very basis for medieval thought. No doubt it will aid your patrolman during his moments of crisis," Ignatius had said benevolently. "Yeah?" Mrs. Reilly had asked. "Aw, that's sweet, Ignatius. Poor Angelo'll be glad to get this." For about a day, at least, the present to Patrolman Mancuso had brought a temporary peace to life on Constantinople Street.

When he had finished the first hot dog, Ignatius prepared and consumed another, contemplating other kindnesses that might postpone his having to go to work again. Fifteen minutes later, noticing that the supply of hot dogs in the little well was visibly diminishing, he decided in favour of abstinence for the moment. He began to push slowly down the street, calling again, "Hot dogs!"

George, who was wandering up Carondelet with an armload of packages wrapped in plain brown paper, heard the cry and went up to the gargantuan vendor.

"Hey, stop. Gimme one of these."

Ignatius looked sternly at the young boy who had placed himself in the wagon's path. His valve protested against the pimples, the surly face that seemed to hang from the long well-lubricated hair, the cigarette behind the ear, the aquamarine jacket, the delicate boots, the tight trousers that bulged offensively in the crotch in violation of all rules of theology and geometry.

"I am sorry," Ignatius snorted. "I have only a few frankfurters left, and I must save them. Please get out of my way."

"Save them? Who for?"

"That is none of your business, you waif. Why aren't you in school? Kindly stop molesting me. Anyway, I have no change."

"I got a quarter," the thin white lips sneered.

"I cannot sell you a frank, sir. Is that clear?"

"Whatsa matter with you, friend?"

"What's the matter with *me*? What's the matter with *you*? Are you unnatural enough to want a hot dog this early in the afternoon? My conscience will not let me sell you one. Just look at your loathsome complexion. You are a growing boy

178

whose system needs to be surfeited with vegetables and orange juice and whole wheat bread and spinach and such. I, for one, will not contribute to the debauchery of a minor."

"Whadda you talking about? Sell me one of them hot dogs. I'm hungry. I ain't had no lunch."

"No!" Ignatius screamed so furiously that the passersby stared. "Now get away from me before I run over you with this cart."

George pulled open the lid of the bun compartment and said, "Hey, you got plenty stuff in here. Fix me a weenie."

"Help!" Ignatius screamed, suddenly remembering the old man's warnings about robberies. "Someone is stealing my buns! Police!"

Ignatius backed up the cart and rammed it into George's crotch.

"Ouch! Watch out there, you nut."

"Help! Thief!"

"Shut up, for Christ's sake," George said and slammed the door. "You oughta be locked up, you big fruit. You know that?"

"What?" Ignatius screamed. "What impertinence was that?"

"You big crazy fruit," George snarled more loudly and slouched away, the taps on his heels scraping the sidewalk. "Who wants to eat anything your fruity hands touched?"

"How dare you scream obscenities at me. Someone grab that boy," Ignatius said wildly as George disappeared into the crowds of pedestrians farther down the street. "Someone with some decency grab that juvenile delinquent. That filthy little minor. Where is his respect? That little guttersnipe must be lashed until he collapses!"

A woman in the group around the mobile hot dog said, "Ain't that awful? Where they get them hot dog vendors from?"

"Bums. They all bums," someone answered her.

"Wine is what it is. They all crazy from wine if you ast me. They shouldn't let people like him out on the street."

"Is my paranoia getting completely out of hand," Ignatius asked the group, "or are you mongoloids really talking about me?"

"Let him alone," someone said. "Look at them eyes."

"What's wrong with my eyes?" Ignatius asked viciously.

"Let's get outta here."

"Please do." Ignatius replied, his lips quivering, and prepared another hot dog to quiet his trembling nervous system. With shaking hands, he held the foot of red plastic and dough to his mouth and slipped it in two inches at a time. The active chewing massaged his throbbing head. When he had shoved in the last millimeter of crumb, he felt much calmer.

Grabbing the handle again, he shoved off up Carondelet Street, waddling slowly behind the cart. True to his promise to make it around the block, he turned again at the next corner and stopped by the worn granite walls of Gallier Hall to consume two more of the Paradise hot dogs before continuing on the last leg of his journey. When Ignatius turned the final corner and saw again the PARADISE VENDORS, INC., sign hanging out over the sidewalk of Poydras Street at an angle, he broke into a relatively brisk trot that brought him panting through the doors of the garage.

"Help!" Ignatius breathed pitifully, bumping the tin hot dog over the low cement sill of the garage.

"What happened, pal? I thought you was supposed to stay out a whole hour."

"We're both fortunate that I have returned at all. I am afraid that they have struck again."

"Who?"

"The syndicate. Whoever they are. Look at my hands."

Ignatius shoved two paws into the man's face. "My entire nervous system is on the brink of revolt against me for subjecting it to such trauma. Ignore me if I suddenly go into a state of shock."

"What the hell happened?"

"A member of the vast teen-age underground besieged me on Carondelet Street."

"You was robbed?" the old man asked excitedly.

"Brutally. A large and rusty pistol was placed at my temples. Actually, was pressed directly upon a pressure point, causing the blood to stop circulating on the left side of my head for quite a while."

"On Carondelet Street at this time of day? Nobody stopped it?"

"Of course no one stopped it. People encourage this sort of thing. They probably derive some sort of pleasure from the spectacle of a poor and struggling vendor's being publicly humiliated. They probably respected the boy's initiative."

"What did he look like?"

"A thousand other youths. Pimples, pompadour, adenoids, the standard adolescent equipment. There might have been something else like a birthmark or trick knee. I really can't recall. After the pistol had been thrust against my head, I fainted from lack of circulation in the brain and from fright. While I was lying in a heap on the sidewalk, he apparently ransacked the wagon."

"How much money did he get?"

"Money? No money was stolen. After all, there was no money to steal, for I had not been able to vend even one of these delicacies. He stole the hot dogs.

"Yes. However, he apparently didn't take them all. When I had recovered, I checked the wagon. There are still one or two left, I think."

"I never heard of nothing like this."

"Perhaps he was very hungry. Perhaps some vitamin deficiency in his growing body was screaming for appeasement. The human desire for food and sex is relatively equal. If there are armed rapes, why should there not be armed hot dog thefts? I see nothing unusual in the matter."

"You're full of bullshit."

"I? The incident is sociologically valid. The blame rests upon our society. The youth, crazed by suggestive television programs and lascivious periodicals had apparently been consorting with some rather conventional adolescent females who refused to participate in his imaginative sexual program. His unfulfilled physical desires therefore sought sublimation in food. I, unfortunately, was the victim of all of this. We may thank God that this boy has turned to food for an outlet. Had he not, I might have been raped right there on the spot."

"He took all but four," the old man said, peering down into the well in the hot dog. "That son of a bitch, I wonder how he could carry all them hot dogs away."

"I really don't know," Ignatius said. Then he added indignantly, "I awaked to find the lid of the cart open. Of course no one would help me up. My white smock stamped me as a vendor, an untouchable."

"How about making another try?"

"What? In my present condition, do you seriously expect me to take to the streets again and hustle? My ten cents is going to be deposited in the hands of St. Charles streetcar conductor. The remainder of the day I intend to spend in a hot tub trying to recapture some semblance of normality."

"Then how about coming back tomorrow, pal, and trying it again?" the old man asked hopefully. "I really need vendors."

Ignatius pondered the proposal for some time, scrutinizing the scar on the old man's nose and belching gassily. At least he would be working. That should satisfy his mother. The work offered little supervision and harassment. Ending his meditations with a clearing of the throat, he belched, "If I am functioning in the morning, I shall perhaps return. I cannot predict the hour at which I will arrive, but, more or less, I imagine that you can expect to see me."

"That's fine, son," the old man said. "Call me Mr. Clyde."

"I shall," Ignatius said and licked at a crumb that he had discovered in the corner of his mouth. "Incidentally, Mr. Clyde, I shall be wearing this smock home to prove to my mother that I am employed. You see, she drinks rather heavily, and she needs reassurance that money from my labors will be forthcoming in order that her supply of spirits won't be cut off. My life is a rather grim one. One day I shall perhaps describe it to you in detail. For the moment, however, you must know a thing or two about my valve."

"*Valve?*"

"Yes."

II

Jones was blindly running a sponge along the bar. Lana Lee had gone on a shopping trip, her first one in a long time, locking the cash register loudly and warningly before leaving. After he had wet the bar a little, Jones tossed the sponge back into the bucket, took a seat in a booth, and tried to look at the latest *Life* Darlene had given him. He lit a cigarette, but the cloud of smoke made the magazine even more invisible. The best reading light in the Night of Joy was the small one on the cash register, so Jones went over to the bar and flipped it on. He was just beginning a study in-depth of a cocktail party scene in a Seagram's V. O. advertisement when Lana Lee pushed into the bar.

"I thought I shouldn't leave you in here alone," she said, opening a bag and taking out a box of classroom chalk which she put in the cabinet under the bar. "What the hell are you doing with my cash register? Get back on my floor."

"I already finish on your flo. I turnin into a expert on flos. I think color cats got sweepin and moppin in they blood, it come natural. It sorta like eatin and breathin now to color peoples. I bet you give some little color baby one-year-old a broom in he han, he star sweepin his ass off. Whoa!"

Jones returned to the advertisement while Lana locked the cabinet again. Then she looked at the long tracks of dust on the floor that made it look as if Jones had plowed rather than mopped it. There were linear streaks of clean floor for the furrows, and linear streaks of dust, the hillocks. Although Lana did not know it, this was Jones's attempt at some subtle sabotage. He had some larger plans for the future.

"Hey, you there. Take a look at my goddam floor."

Jones reluctantly looked through his sunglasses and saw nothingness.

"Whoa! You got a fine flo. Ooo-wee. Everthin in the Night of Joy firs rate."

"You see all that crap?"

"For twenty dollar a week, you gotta expec a little crap. The crap star disappearin when the wage goin up aroun fifty or sigsty."

"I want performance when I put out money," Lana said angrily.

"Listen, you ever try livin on my kinda wage? You think color peoples get grossries and clothin at a specia price? What you thinkin about half the time you sittin up here playin with your penny? Whoa! Where I live, you know how peoples buy cigarette? Them peoples cain affor a whole pack, they buy they cigarette separate two cent apiece. You think a color mother got it easy? Shit. I ain foolin. I gettin pretty tire of bein vagran or tryina keep my ass alive on this kinda wage."

"Who took you off the streets and gave you a job when

the cops was about to lock you up for vagrancy? You might think about that sometime when you're goofing off behind them goddam glasses."

"Goofin off? Shit. Goofin off ain cleanin up this mother-fuckin cathouse. They somebody in here sweepin and moppin up all the shit your po, stupor customer drippin on the flo. I feel sorry for them po peoples comin in here thinkin they gonna have theirself some fun, probly gettin knockout drop in they drink, catchin the clap off the ice cube. Whoa! And talkin about puttin out money it seem to me maybe you be puttin out a little more now that your orphan frien stop comin aroun. Since you cut out the chariddy, maybe you slip me some of the United Fun money."

Lana said nothing. She clipped the receipt for the box of chalk to her ledger book so that she could list it in the column of itemized deductions that always accompanied her income tax returns. She had already bought a used globe of the world. That, too, was stored in the cabinet. All she needed now was a book. When she saw George next, she would ask him to bring her one. He must have some kind of book left over from the days before he had dropped out of high school.

Lana had taken some time to assemble the little collection of props. While the plainclothesmen had been coming in at night, she had been too worried and preoccupied to attend to this project for George. There had been the major problem of Darlene, the vulnerable point in Lana's wall of protection against undercover policemen. But now, the plainclothesmen had gone away as suddenly as they had appeared. Lana had spotted each one as soon as he had entered, and with Darlene safely off the stools and practicing with her bird, the plain-clothesmen had nothing to go on. Lana had seen to it that they were actively ignored by everyone. It took experience to be able to spot a cop. But a person who could spot a cop could also avoid a lot of trouble.

There were only two things to be settled. One was getting the book. If George wanted her to have a book, he could get it for her himself. Lana wasn't about to buy a book, even a used one. The other was getting Darlene back on the stools now that the plainclothesmen were gone. Having someone like Darlene on commission was better than having her on salary. And what Lana had seen Darlene do on the stage with the bird told her that, for the moment, the Night of Joy might do better if it decided not to cater to the animal trade.

"Where's Darlene?" Lana asked Jones. "I got a little message for her and that bird."

"She telephone and say she be in sometime this afternoon to do some more rehearsin," Jones said to the advertisement he was researching. "She say she takin her bird to the veternaria firs, she think it losin some of its feather."

"Yeah?"

Lana started to plan the ensemble with the globe, the chalk, and the book. If the thing had commercial possibilities, it should be done with a certain finesse and quality. She envisioned several arrangements that would combine grace and obscenity. There was no need to be too raw. After all, she was appealing to kids.

"Here we come," Darlene called happily from the door. She tripped into the bar in slacks and a pea jacket, carrying a covered birdcage.

"Well, don't plan to stay too long," Lana answered. "I got some news for you and your friend."

Darlene put the cage on the bar and uncovered a huge, scrofulous rose cockatoo that looked, like a used car, as if it had passed through the hands of many owners. The bird's crest dipped, and it cried horribly, "Awwk."

"Okay, get it out, Darlene. You go back to your stool starting tonight."

"Aw, Lana," Darlene moaned. "Whatsa matter? We been

doing good in rehearsal. Just wait'll we iron out the kinks. This act is gonna be a boffo smash."

"To tell you the truth, Darlene, I'm afraid of you and that bird."

"Look, Lana." Darlene took off her pea jacket and showed the manager the tiny rings attached to the side of her slacks and blouse with safety pins. "You see these things? That's what's gonna make the act smooth. I been practicing with it in my apartment. It's a new angle. He grabs at those rings with his beak and rips my clothes off. I mean, these rings is just for rehearsal. When I get my costume made, the rings are gonna be sewed on top of a hook and eye so when he grabs, the costume pops open. I'm telling you, Lana. It's gonna be a smash hit sensation."

"Listen, Darlene, it was safer when you just had that goddam thing flying around your head or whatever it did."

"But now it's gonna be a real part of the turn. It's gonna *pull* . . ."

"Yeah, and it might pull your tits off. All I need in this place is a goddam accident and a ambulance to drive away my customers and ruin my investment. Or maybe this bird gets it in his head to fly out in the audience and pull out somebody's eyes. No, to be frank, I don't trust you and a bird, Darlene. Safety first."

"Aw, Lana." Darlene was heartbroken. "Give us a chance. We just getting good."

"No. Beat it. Take that thing off my bar before it takes a shit." Lana threw the cover over the birdcage. "The you-know-whats are gone and you can go back to your stool."

"I think maybe I'll tell you-know-who about the you-know-whats and make you-know-who scared and quit."

Jones looked up from an advertisement and said, "If you peoples be talkin all this double-talk, I cain read. Whoa. Who the 'you-know-whats' and who 'you-know-who?'"

"Get off that stool, jailbait, and get on my floor."

"That bird been travelin to Night of Joy practicin and tryin," Jones said from his cloud, smiling. "Shit. You gotta give it a chance, cain treat it like it's color peoples."

"That's right," Darlene agreed sincerely.

"Since we cuttin off the orphan chariddy and we not extendin it to the porter help, maybe we oughta give a little to a po, strugglin gal gotta hustle on commission. Hey!" Jones had seen the bird flap around on the stage while Darlene tried to dance. He had never seen a worse performance; Darlene and the bird qualified as legitimate sabotage. "Maybe it need a little polishin here and there, a little twistin and rockin, some more slippin and slidin, but I think that ack very good. Ooo-wee."

"You see that?" Darlene said to Lana. "Jones oughta know. Colored people got plenty rhythm."

"Whoa!"

"I don't wanna scare somebody with a story about some people."

"Oh, shut up, Darlene," Lana screamed.

Jones covered the two with some smoke and said, "I think Darlene and that there bird very unusual. Whoa! I think you be attractin plenny new peoples in this place. What other club got them a ball eagle on the stage?"

"You jerks think there's really a bird trade we could tap?" Lana asked.

"Hey! I sure they a bird trade. White peoples always got parrakeets and canayries they smoochin. Wait till them peoples fin out what kinda bird the Night of Joy offerin. You be havin a doorman in front this place. You be gettin the society trade. Whoa!" Jones created a dangerous-looking nimbus that seemed ready to burst. "Darlene and that bird jus gotta eye-rom out a few rough spot. Shit. The gal jus startin in show biz. She need a break."

188

"That's right," Darlene said. "I'm just startin out in show biz. I need a break."

"Shut up, stupid. You think you can get that bird to strip you?"

"Yes, ma'm," Darlene said enthusiastically. "Suddenly it come to me. I was sitting in my apartment watching it play on its rings, and I said to myself, 'Darlene, how come you don't stick some rings on your clothes?'"

"Shut your moron up," Lana said. "Okay, let's see what it can do."

"Whoa! Now you talkin. All kinda mother be showin up to see this act."

III

"Santa, I hadda call you, honey."

"What's wrong, Irene babe?" Mrs. Battaglia's froggy baritone asked feelingly.

"It's Ignatius."

"What he's done now, sweetheart? Tell Santa."

"Wait a minute. Let me see if he's still in that tub." Mrs. Reilly listened apprehensively to the great liquid thrashings coming from the bathroom. One whalelike snort floated out into the hall through the peeling bathroom door. "It's okay. He's still in there. I can't lie to you, Santa. My heart's broke."

"Aw."

"Ignatius comes home about a hour ago dressed up like a butcher."

"Good. He's got him another job, that big fat bum."

"But not in a butcher shop, honey," Mrs. Reilly said, her voice heavy with grief. "He's a hot dog vendor."

"Aw, come on," Santa croaked. "A hot dog vendor? You mean out on the streets?"

"Out on the streets, honey, like a bum."

"Bum is right, girl. Even worst. Read the police notices in the paper sometimes. They all a bunch of vagrants."

"Ain't that awful!"

"Somebody oughta punch that boy in the nose."

"When he first comes in, Santa, he makes me guess what kinda job he's got. First, I guess, 'butcher,' you know?"

"Of course."

"So he says, very insolent, 'Guess again. You ain't even close.' I keep guessing for about five minutes until I can't think of no more jobs where you'd be wearing one of them white uniforms. The he finally says, 'Wrong every time. I got me a job selling weenies.' I almost passed out, Santa, right on the kitchen floor. Wouldn't thata been fine, me with my head broke open on the linoleum?"

"He wouldn't care, not that one."

"Not him."

"Never in a million years."

"He don't care about his poor momma," Mrs. Reilly said. "With all his education, mind you. Selling weenies out on the street in the broad daylight."

"So what you told him, girl?"

"I didn't tell him nothing. By the time I got my mouth open, he runs off to the bathroom. He's still locked up in there splashing water all over the floor."

"Hold on a minute, Irene. I got one of my little grandchirren over here for the day," Santa said and screamed at someone at her end of the line: "Get the hell away from that stove, Charmaine, and go play out on the banquette before I bust you right in the mouth."

A child's voice made some reply.

"Lord," Santa continued calmly to Mrs. Reilly. "Them kids is sweet, but sometimes I just don't know. Charmaine! Get the hell outside and go play on your bike before I come slap your face off. Hold the line, Irene."

Mrs. Reilly heard Santa put the telephone down. Then a child screamed, a door slammed, and Santa was back on the line.

"Christ, I tell you true, Irene, that child won't listen to nobody! I'm trying to cook her some spaghettis and daube, and she keeps on playing in my pot. I wish them sisters at her school would beat up on her a little. You know Angelo. You shoulda seen how them sisters beat up on him when he was a kid. One sister throwed him right into a blackboard. That's how come Angelo's such a sweet, considerate man today."

"The sisters loved Ignatius. He was such a darling child. He used to win all them little holy pictures for knowing his catechism."

"Them sisters shoulda knocked his head in."

"When he useta come home with all them little holy pictures," Mrs. Reilly sniffed, "I sure never thought then he'd end up selling weenies in the broad daylight." Mrs. Reilly coughed nervously and violently into the telephone. "But tell me, sweetheart, how Angelo's making out?"

"His wife Rita rings me up a little while ago to tell me she thinks he's coming down with pneumonia from being stuck in that toilet all the time. I tell you true, Irene, that Angelo's getting as pale as a ghost. The cops sure don't treat that boy right. He loves the force. When he graduated from the cops' academy, you woulda thought he just made it outta the Ivory League. He was sure proud."

"Yeah, poor Angelo looks bad," Mrs. Reilly agreed. "He's got him a bad cough, that boy. Well, maybe he'll feel a little better after he reads that thing Ignatius give me to give him. Ignatius says it's inspirational literature."

"Yeah? I wouldn't trust no 'inspirational literature' I got from that Ignatius. It's prolly fulla dirty stories."

"Suppose somebody I know sees him with one of them wagons."

"Don't be ashamed, babe. It ain't your fault you got a brat on your hands," Santa grunted. "What you need is a man in that house, girl, to set that boy straight. I'm gonna find that nice old man ast about you."

"I don't want a nice old man. All I want is a nice child."

"Don't you worry. Just leave it to Santa. I'll fix you up. The man runs the fish market says he don't know the man's name. But I'll find out. As a matter of fact, I think I seen him walking down St. Ferdinand Street the other day."

"He ast about me?"

"Well, Irene, I mean I didn't get a chance to talk to him. I don't even know if it was the same man."

"You see that? That old man don't care neither."

"Don't talk like that, girl. I'll ask over by the beer parlor. I'll hang around Sunday mass. I'll find out his name."

"That old man don't care for me."

"Irene, they's no harm in meeting him."

"I got enough problems with Ignatius. It's the disgrace, Santa. Suppose Miss Annie, the next door lady, sees him with one of them wagons. She's awready about to get us put under a peace bond. She's all the time spying in that alley behind her shutters."

"You can't worry about people, Irene," Santa advised. "The people on my block got dirty mouths. If you can live down here in St. Ode of Cluny Parish, you can live anyplace. Vicious is the word, believe me. I got one woman on my block's gonna get a brick right in her face if she don't shut up about me. Somebody told me she's been calling me a 'merry widow.' But don't you worry. I'm gonna get her good. I think she's running with some man works at the shipyards, anyways. I think I'm gonna write her husband a little anonymous letter to straighten out that girl."

"I know what it is, sugar. Remember I lived down there on Dauphine when I was a girl. The anonymous letters my poppa useta get . . . about *me*. Vicious. I always thought my cousin, that poor spinster girl, was writing them."

"Which cousin was that?" Santa asked with interest. Irene Reilly's relatives always had gory biographies that were worth hearing.

"That was the one knocked a pot of berling water on her arm when she was a child. She was kinda scalded looking. You know what I mean? I always seen her writing away at the kitchen table at her momma's house. She was prolly writing about me. She was very jealous when Mr. Reilly started seeing me."

"That's the way it goes," Santa said. A scalded relative was a dull figure in Irene's dramatic gallery. Then she said hoarsely and cheerfully, "I'll have a little party with you and Angelo and his wife, if she'll come."

"Aw, that's sweet, Santa, but I don't feel much like a party these days."

"It'll do you good to shake yourself a little, girl. If I can find out about that old man, I'll invite him over too. You and him can dance."

"Well, if you see the old man, babe, tell him Miss Reilly said, 'Hello.'"

Behind the bathroom door Ignatius was lying passively in the tepid water pushing the plastic soap dish back and forth across the surface with one finger and listening now and then to his mother on the telephone. Occasionally he held the soap dish down until it filled with water and sank. Then he would feel for it on the bottom of the tub, empty it, and sail it again. His blue and yellow eyes rested on an unopened manila envelope on the top of the toilet. For quite a while Ignatius had been trying to decide whether or not he would open the envelope. The trauma of having found employment had affected his value negatively, and he was waiting until the warm water in which he wallowed like a pink hippopotamus had a calming effect upon his system. Then he would attack the envelope. Paradise Vendors should prove to be a pleasant employer. He would spend his time parked somewhere by the river accumulating notes for the Journal. Mr. Clyde had a certain paternal quality that Ignatius liked; the old man, the scarred and wizened mogul of the frankfurter, would be a welcome new character in the Journal.

At last Ignatius felt relaxed enough and, raising his dripping bulk out of the water, picked up the envelope.

"Why must she use this sort of envelope?" he asked angrily, studying the little circle of a Planetarium Station, New York, postmark on the thick tan paper. "The contents are probably written in marking pencil or worse."

He tore the envelope open, wetting the paper, and pulled out a folded poster that said in large letters:

LECTURE! LECTURE!
M. Minkoff speaks boldly about
"Sex in Politics: Erotic Liberty
as a Weapon Against Reactionaries"
8 p.m. Thursday, the 28th
Y.M.H.A. – Grand Concourse
Admission: $1.00 - OR - Sign M. Minkoff's Petition Which Aggressively Demands More and Better Sex for All and a Crash Program for Minorities! (The petition will be mailed to Washington.) Sign now and save America from sexual ignorance, chastity, and fear. Are you committed enough to help in this bold and crucial movement?

"Oh, my God!" Ignatius spurted through his dripping moustache. "Are they letting her speak in public now? What in the world does the title of this ludicrous lecture mean?" Ignatius read the poster again, viciously. "At any rate, I know that she will speak boldly, and in a perverse way I wish that I could hear that little minx babbling before an audience. This time she has outdone herself in offending taste and decency."

Following a handwritten arrow at the bottom of the poster and the word *over*, Ignatius complied and looked at the other side of the poster, where Myrna had written something:

Sirs:

What is wrong, Ignatius? I have not heard from you. Well, I don't really blame you for not writing. I guess I came on a little strong in my last letter, but it was only because your paranoid fantasy disturbed me, rooted as it possibly was in your unhealthy attitude toward sex. You know that ever since I first met you I have directed pointed questions at you in order to clarify your sexual inclinations. My only desire was to aid you in finding your true self-expression and contentment through satisfying, natural orgasm. I respect your mind and I have always accepted your eccentric tendencies and that is why I want to see you reach the plateau of perfect mental-sexual balance. (A good, explosive orgasm would cleanse your being and bring you out of the shadows.) Just don't be angry at me about the letter.

I will explain this poster a little later in this letter because I imagine you are interested in knowing how this bold, dedicated lecture came about. First, though, I must tell you that the movie is off, so if you were planning to play the landlord, forget it. Basically, we had trouble with funds. I could not milk another drachma out of my father, so Leola, the Harlem find, got very hostile about salary (or lack of it) and finally dropped a remark or two that sounded a little anti-Semitic to me. Who needs a girl who isn't dedicated enough to work gratis in a project that would benefit her race? Samuel has decided to become a forest ranger in Montana because he is planning a

*dramatic allegory set in a dark woods (Ignorance and
Custom) and he wants to get the feel of the forest. From
what I know of Samuel, he will be a big flop as a
ranger, but the allegory, I know, will be challenging and
controversial, full of unpleasant truths. Wish him well. He
is fantastic.*

*To get back to the lecture. At last it seems that I am
finding a platform for my philosophy, etc. It all happened
in a strange way. A few weeks ago I was at a party that
some friends were giving for this very real boy who had
just returned from Israel. He was unbelievable. I mean
that.*

Ignatius emitted a little Paradise gas.

*For hours and hours he sang these folk songs he had picked
up over there; really significant songs that proved my
theory that music should basically be an instrument of
social protest and expression. He kept us all in that
apartment for hours and hours listening and asking for
more. Later we all started talking—on many levels—and I
let him know what was on my mind in general.*

"Ho, hum," Ignatius yawned violently.

*He said, "Why are you keeping all of this to yourself,
Myrna? Why haven't you let the world in on this?" I told
him that I often spoke in discussion groups and in my
group therapy group. I also told him about these letters of
mine to the editor that have been printed in* The New
Democracy *and* Man and Masses *and* Now!

"Get out of that tub, boy," Ignatius heard his mother
scream outside the door of the bathroom.

"Why?" he asked. "Are you going to use it?"

"No."

"Then please go away."

"You been in there too long."

"Please! I am attempting to read a letter."

"A letter? Who wrote you a letter?"

"My dear friend, Miss Minkoff."

"The last thing you said was she got you fired outta Levy Pants."

"Well, she did. However, it might have been a favor in disguise. My new work may prove rather agreeable."

"Ain't that awful," Mrs. Reilly said sadly. "You get fired outta a two-bit clerk job in a factory and now you selling weenies in the streets. Well, I'll tell you one thing, Ignatius, you better not get fired by the weenie man. You know what Santa said?"

"I'm sure that it was rather perceptive and incisive, whatever it was. I would imagine that it is rather difficult to comprehend her assaults upon the Mother tongue."

"She said somebody oughta punch you right in the nose."

"Coming from her, that's rather literate."

"What that Myrna's doing now?" Mrs. Reilly asked suspiciously. "How come she's writing so much? She needed a good bath, that girl."

"Myrna's psyche is only capable of dealing with water in an oral context."

"What?"

"Will you please stop shrieking like a fishmonger and run along? Don't you have a bottle of muscatel baking in the oven? Now let me alone. I'm very nervous."

"Nervous? You been in that hot water over an hour."

"It's hardly hot anymore."

"Then get out the tub."

"Why is it so important to you that I leave this tub? Mother,

I really don't understand you at all. Isn't there something that, as a housekeeper, you feel compelled to do at the moment? I noticed this morning that the lint in the hallway is forming into spheres almost as large as baseballs. Clean the house. Telephone for the correct time. Do something. Lie down and take a nap. You're looking rather peaked these days."

"Of course I am, boy. You breaking your poor momma's heart. What would you do if I dropped dead?"

"Well, I am not going to participate in this idiotic conversation. Carry on a monologue out there if you wish. Quietly. I must concentrate upon the new offenses that M. Minkoff has conceived in this letter."

"I can't take it no more, Ignatius. You gonna find me laying in the kitchen one of these days with a stroke. Just watch, boy. You gonna be all alone in the world. Then you gonna fall on your knees and pray to God for the way you treated your poor dear mother."

From the bathroom there came only silence. Mrs. Reilly waited for at least a splash of water or a rustle of paper, but the bathroom door might as well have been the door of a tomb. After a minute or two of fruitless waiting, she walked off down the hall toward the oven. When Ignatius heard the oven door creak open he returned to the letter.

He said, "With that voice and personality, you should be appearing before the people in prison." This guy was really amazing; in addition to his tough mind, he was a real mensch. He was so gentlemanly and thoughtful I could hardly believe it. (Especially after dealing with Samuel, who is dedicated and unafraid but all a little too loud and something of a clod.) I never met anybody so dedicated to fighting reactionary ideas and prejudice as this folk singer. His very best friend was a Negro abstractionist, he said, who made magnificent smears of protest and defiance

*across the canvas, sometimes slashing the canvas to shreds
with a knife. He handed me this brilliant pamphlet that
showed in detail how the Pope is trying to assemble a
nuclear armory; it really opened my mind, and I forwarded
it to the editor of* The New Democracy *to aid him in
his battle against the Church. But this guy also had this
big thing against WASPS. Like he hated them. I mean, this
fellow was sharp.*

*The next day I got a telephone call from him. Would I
lecture to this social action group he was going to form
somewhere in Brooklyn Heights? I was overcome. In this
world of dog eat dog, it is rare to find a friend . . . a really
sincere friend . . . or so I thought. Well, to make my point
as briefly as possible, I had learned the hard way that the
lecture circuit is something like show business: the casting
couch and that routine. Get what I mean?*

"Do I believe this egregious offense against good taste that
I am reading?" Ignatius asked the floating soap dish. "This
girl is without shame entirely!"

*Again I have been awakened to the fact that my body
appeals to some people more than my mind.*

"Ho hum," Ignatius sighed.

*Personally, I feel like exposing this phony "folk singer" who
I guess is preying on some other dedicated young girl
liberal at this moment. Somebody I know said she heard
this "folk singer" guy is really a Baptist from Alabama.
Boy, what a fraud he was. So then I checked on this
pamphlet he had given me and discovered that it was
printed by the Klan. This will give you some idea of the
ideological subtleties which we have to deal with today. It*

sounded like a good liberal pamphlet to me. Now I have had to humiliate myself by writing to the editor of The New Democracy to tell him that the pamphlet, although challenging, was written by the wrong people. Well, the WASPS struck back and got me this time. The incident reminded me of the time in Poe Park when this squirrel I was feeding turned out to really be a rat which at first glance could have passed for a squirrel any day. So live and learn. This phony gave me an idea. You can always learn something from crumbs. I decided to ask up here at the Y if I could get the auditorium one night. After a while, they said o.k. Of course, the audience up here at the Bronx 'Y' will probably be a little parochial, but if I make good in the lecture, I might one day end up speaking down at the Lex. Ave. 'Y' where great thinkers like Norman Mailer and Seymour Krim are always airing their views. It won't hurt to try.

I hope that you are working on your personality problems, Ignatius. Is the paranoia getting any worse? The basis for the paranoia, I think, is the fact that you're always sealed up in that room and have become suspicious of the outside world. I don't know why you insisted on living way down there with the alligators. In spite of the complete overhaul that your mind is crying for, you have a brain that could really grow and flower here in N.Y. As it is, you are thwarting yourself and your mentality. The last time I saw you, when I was passing through from Mississippi, you were in pretty bad shape. You've probably regressed completely by now living in that substandard old house with only your mother for company. Aren't your natural impulses crying for release? A beautiful and meaningful love affair would transform you, Ignatius. I know it would. Great Oedipus bonds are encircling your brain and destroying you.

*I don't imagine that your sociological or political ideas are
getting any more progressive either. Have you abandoned
your project to form a political party or nominate a
candidate for president by divine right? I remember that
when I finally met you and challenged your political
apathy, you came up with this idea. I knew that it was a
reactionary project, but it at least showed that you were
developing some political consciousness. Please write to me
about the matter. I am very concerned. We need a three-
party system in this country, and I think that day by day
the fascists are growing in strength. This Divine Right
Party is the sort of fringe-group scheme that would syphon
off a large part of the fascist support.*

*Well, let me stop. I hope the lecture is a success. You,
especially, would benefit from its message. By the way, if
you ever do activate the Divine Right movement, I can give
you some help in organizing a chapter up here. Please get
out of the house, Ignatius, and enter into the world around
you. I am worried about your future. You have always been
one of my most important projects and I am interested in
hearing of your current mental condition, so please get
out of the pillows and write.*

M. Minkoff

Later, his puckered pink skin wrapped in the old flannel
robe that a safety pin held around his hips, Ignatius sat at the
desk in his room filling his fountain pen. In the hall his mother
was speaking to someone else on the telephone saying, "And
I used every last cent of the insurance money his poor old
Grammaw Reilly left just to keep him in college. Ain't that
awful? All that money down the drain." Ignatius belched and
opened a drawer to search for the stationery that he believed
he still had; there he found the yo-yo that he had bought from
the Filipino who had been selling them in the neighborhood

a few months ago. On one side of the yo-yo there was a palm tree which the Filipino had carved at Ignatius' request. Ignatius spun the yo-yo downward, but the string snapped and it rattled across the floor and under the bed where it landed on a pile of Big Chief tablets and old magazines. Removing the piece of string that hung from his finger, he dug into the drawer again and found a sheet of paper with a Levy Pants letterhead.

Beloved Myrna:

I have received your offensive communication. Do you seriously think that I am interested in your tawdry encounters with such sub-humans as folk singers? In every letter of yours I seem to find some reference to the sleaziness of your personal life. Please confine yourself to discussing issues and such; thereby you will at least avoid obscenity and offense. I did think, however, that the symbolism of the rat and squirrel or rat-squirrel or squirrel-rat was evocative and rather excellent.

On the dark night of that dubious lecture, the sole member of your audience will probably be some desperately lonely old male liberarian who saw a light in the window of the lecture hall and hopefully came in to escape the cold and the horrors of his personal hell. There in the hall, his stooped figure sitting alone before the podium, your nasal voice echoing among the empty chairs and hammering boredom, confusion, and sexual reference deeper and deeper into the poor wretch's bald skull, confounded to the point of hysteria, he will doubtlessly exhibit himself, waving his crabbed organ like a club in despair against the grim sound that drones on and on over his head. If I were you, I would cancel the lecture immediately; I am certain that the 'Y' management would be only too glad to accept your withdrawal, especially if they have had a chance to see that tasteless poster which is now no doubt tacked to every telephone pole in the Bronx.

The comments upon my personal life were uncalled for and revealed a shocking lack of taste and decency.

Actually, my personal life has undergone a metamorphosis: I am currently connected in a most vital manner with the food merchandising industry, and therefore I doubt quite seriously whether I shall have much time in the future to correspond with you.

Busily,
Ignatius

Eight

"Let her alone," Mr. Levy said. "Look, she's trying to sleep."

"Let her alone?" Mrs. Levy propped up Miss Trixie on the yellow nylon couch. "Do you realize, Gus, that this is the tragedy of this poor woman's life. She's always been alone. She needs someone. She needs love."

"Ugh."

Mrs. Levy was a woman of interests and ideals. Over the years she had given herself freely to bridge, African violets, Susan and Sandra, golf, Miami, Fanny Hurst and Hemingway, correspondence courses, hairdressers, the sun, gourmet foods, ballroom dancing, and, in recent years, Miss Trixie. She had always had to settle for Miss Trixie at a distance, an unsatisfactory arrangement for carrying out the program outlined in the psychology correspondence course, the final examination of which she had failed resoundingly. The correspondence school had even refused to give her an F. But now that Mrs. Levy had played her card correctly in the game dealing with the firing of the young idealist, she had Miss Trixie in the wrinkled flesh, visor, sneakers, and all. Mr. Gonzalez had gladly given the assistant accountant an indefinite vacation.

"Miss Trixie," Mrs. Levy said sweetly. "Wake up."

Miss Trixie opened her eyes and wheezed, "Am I retired?"

"No, darling."

"What?" Miss Trixie snarled. "I thought I was retired!"

"Miss Trixie, you think that you're old and tired. This is very bad."

"Who?"

"You."

"Oh. I am. I am very tired."

"Don't you see?" Mrs. Levy asked. "It's all in your mind. You have this age psychosis. You're still a very attractive woman. You must say to yourself, 'I am still attractive. I am a very attractive woman.'"

Miss Trixie exhaled a grunting snore into Mrs. Levy's lacquered hair.

"Will you please let her alone, Dr. Freud?" Mr. Levy said angrily, looking up from a *Sports Illustrated*. "I almost wish Susan and Sandra were home so you could play with them. Whatever happened to your canasta circle?"

"Don't talk to me, you failure. How can I play canasta when there's a psycho in distress?"

"Psycho? The woman's senile. We had to stop at about thirty gas stations on the way over here. Finally I got tired of getting out of the car and showing her which was the Men's and which was the Women's, so I let her pick them herself. I worked out a system. The law of averages. I laid money on her and she came out about fifty-fifty."

"Don't tell me any more," Mrs. Levy cautioned. "Not another word. It's too typical. Permitting this anal compulsive to flounder like that."

"Isn't Lawrence Welk on?" Miss Trixie asked suddenly.

"No, dear. Relax."

"It *is* Saturday."

"He'll be on. Don't worry. Now tell me, what do you dream about."

"I can't remember at the moment."

"Try," Mrs. Levy said, making some sort of note on her date book with a rhinestoned automatic pencil. "You must try, Miss Trixie. Darling, your mind is warped. You're like a cripple."

"I may be old, but I'm not crippled," Miss Trixie said wildly.

"Look, you're exciting her, Florence Nightingale," Mr.

Levy said. "With all you know about psychoanalysis, you're going to ruin whatever's left in that head of hers. All she wants is to retire and sleep."

"You've already wrecked your life. Don't do the same to hers. This case can't be retired. She must be made to feel wanted and needed and loved . . ."

"Turn on your goddam exercising board and let her take a nap!"

"I thought we agreed to let the board out of this."

"Let her alone. Let me alone. Go ride your exercycle."

"Quiet, please!" Miss Trixie croaked and rubbed her eyes.

"We must talk pleasantly in front of her," Mrs. Levy whispered. "Loud voices, arguing, will only make her more insecure."

"I'll buy that. Keep quiet. And get that senile bag out of my rumpus room."

"That's right. Think about yourself as usual. If your father could only see you today." Mrs. Levy's aqua lids rose in horror. "A motheaten playboy looking for kicks."

"Kicks?"

"Now you people shut up," Miss Trixie warned. "I must say it was a dark day when I was brought out here. It was much nicer in there with Gomez. Nice and quiet. If this is some sort of an April Fool, I don't think it's funny." She looked at Mr. Levy through rheumy eyes. "You're the bird that fired my friend Gloria. Poor Gloria. The kindest person ever worked in that office."

"Oh, no!" Mrs. Levy sighed. Then she turned on her husband. "So you only fired one person, is that right? What about this Gloria? One person treats Miss Trixie like a human being. One person is her friend. Do you know this? Do you care? Oh, no. Levy Pants might as well be on Mars for all you care. You walk in from the track one day and kick Gloria out."

"Gloria?" Mr. Levy asked. "I didn't fire any Gloria!"

"Yes, you did!" Miss Trixie piped. "I saw it with my very own eyes. Poor Gloria was the soul of kindness. I remember Gloria gave me socks and luncheon meat."

"Socks and luncheon meat?" Mr. Levy whistled through his teeth. "Oh, boy."

"That's right," Mrs. Levy shouted. "Make fun of this neglected creature. Just don't tell me whatever else you did at Levy Pants. I couldn't bear it. I won't tell the girls about Gloria. They wouldn't understand a heart like yours. They're too innocent."

"No, you'd better not try to tell them about Gloria," Mr. Levy said angrily. "Any more of this foolishness and you'll be down on the beach in San Juan with your mother, laughing, and swimming and dancing."

"Are you threatening me?"

"Now quiet!" Miss Trixie snarled more loudly. "I want to go back to Levy Pants right this very minute."

"You see that?" Mrs. Levy asked her husband. "You hear that desire to work. And you want to crush her by retiring her. Gus, please. Get help. You're going to end badly."

Miss Trixie was reaching for the bag of scraps that she had brought as luggage.

"Okay, Miss Trixie," Mr. Levy said as if he were summoning a pet cat. "Let's go get in the car."

"Thank goodness," Miss Trixie sighed.

"Take your hands off her!" Mrs. Levy screamed.

"I haven't even gotten up from my chair," her husband answered.

Mrs. Levy shoved Miss Trixie down on the couch again and said, "Now stay there. You need help."

"Not from you people," Miss Trixie wheezed. "Let me up."

"Let her up."

"Please." Mrs. Levy held up a warning hand, plump and ringed. "Don't worry about this neglected creature I've taken under my wing. Don't worry about me either. Forget your little daughters. Get in your sports car and ride. There's a regatta this afternoon. Look. You can see the sails from the picture window I had installed with your father's hard-earned money."

"I'll get even with you people," Miss Trixie was snarling on the couch. "Don't worry. You'll find out."

She tried to rise, but Mrs. Levy had pinned her to the yellow nylon.

II

His cold was getting worse and worse, and each cough caused a vague pain in his lungs that lingered on for moments after the cough had seared his throat and chest. Patrolman Mancuso wiped his mouth clean of saliva and tried to clear the phlegm from his throat. One afternoon he had had such a bad case of claustrophobia that he almost fainted in the booth. Now it seemed that he was ready to faint from the dizziness that the cold had induced. He leaned his head against the side of the booth for a moment and closed his eyes. Red and blue clouds floated across his eyelids. He had to capture some character and get out of that rest room before his ague got so bad that the sergeant had to carry him to and from the booth every day. He had always hoped to win honor on the force, but what honor was there in dying of pneumonia in a bus station rest room? Even his relatives would laugh. What would his children say to their friends at school?

Patrolman Mancuso looked at the tiles on the floor. They were out of focus. He felt panic. Then he stared at them more closely and saw that the haze was only the moisture that formed a gray film over almost every surface in the rest room.

He looked again at *The Consolation of Philosophy*, which was opened on his lap, and turned a limp, damp page. The book was making him more depressed. The guy who wrote it was going to be tortured by the king. The preface had said so. Now all this time the guy was writing this thing, he was going to end up with something driven down into his head. Patrolman Mancuso felt sorry for the guy and felt obliged to read what he had written. So far he had only covered only about twenty pages and was beginning to wonder whether this Boethius was something of a gambler. He was always talking about fate and odds and the wheel of fortune. Anyway, it wasn't the kind of book that exactly made you look up to the brighter side.

After a few sentences Patrolman Mancuso's mind began to wander. He looked out through the crack in the door of the booth, which he always left open an inch or two so that he could see who was using the urinals, the lavatories, and the paper-towel box. There at the lavatories was the same boy that Patrolman Mancuso had been seeing every day, it seemed. He watched the delicate boots moving back and forth from the lavatory to the paper-towel dispenser. The boy leaned against a lavatory and began drawing on the back of his hands with a ballpoint pen. There might be something in this, Patrolman Mancuso thought.

He opened the booth and went up to the boy. Coughing, he tried to say pleasantly, "What's that you're writing on your hand, pal?"

George looked at the monocle and the beard at his elbow and said, "Get the hell away from me before I kick your nuts in."

"Cawd the police," Patrolman Mancuso taunted.

"No," George answered. "Just get away. I ain't making trouble."

"You afred udda police?"

George wondered who this nut was. He was as bad as that hot dog vendor.

"Look, kookie, move it. I don't want no trouble with the cops."

"You dote?" Patrolman Mancuso asked happily.

"No, and neither does a screwball like you," George said, looking at the watering eye behind the monocle and the moistness at the mouth of the beard.

"You udder arrest," Patrolman Mancuso coughed.

"What? Boy, are you out of it."

"Patrodeman Madcuso. Uddercover." A badge flashed in front of George's pimples. "Cubb alogg wid me."

"What the hell are you arresting me for? I'm just standing here," George protested nervously. "I ain't done nothing. What is this?"

"You udder suspiciudd."

"Suspicion of what?" George asked in panic.

"Aha!" Patrolman Mancuso slobbered. "You rilly afred."

He reached out to grab George by the arm and handcuff him, but George snatched *The Consolation of Philosophy* from under Patrolman Mancuso's arm and slammed it into the side of his head. Ignatius had bought a large, elegant, limited edition of the English translation, and all fifteen dollars of its price hit Patrolman Mancuso in the head with the force of a dictionary. Patrolman Mancuso bent over to pick up the monocle, which had fallen from his eye. When he straightened up again, he saw the boy scraping rapidly out of the door of the rest room with the book in his hand. He wanted to run after him, but his head was throbbing too badly. He returned to his booth to rest and grew even more depressed. What could he tell Mrs. Reilly about the book?

George opened the locker in the waiting room of the bus terminal as quickly as he could and took out the brown-paper packages he had stored. Without closing the locker door, he ran out onto Canal Street and jogged metallically toward the central business district, looking over his shoulder for the beard and monocle. There was no beard anywhere behind him.

This was really bad luck. That undercover agent would be prowling the bus station all afternoon looking for him. And what about tomorrow? The bus station was no longer safe; it was off-limits.

"Damn Miss Lee," George said aloud, still walking as fast as he could. If she weren't so tight, this wouldn't have happened. She could have fired the jig, and he could have kept on picking up his packages at the old time, two o'clock. As it was, he had almost been arrested. And it was all because he had to go check the stuff in the bus station, all because he was stuck with the stuff now for two hours every afternoon. Where did you put stuff like that? You could get tired of carrying that stuff around all afternoon. Mother was home all the time, so you couldn't go around there with it.

"Tight bitch," George mumbled. He tucked the packages higher up under his arm and realized that he was also carrying the book he had taken from the undercover agent. Stealing from a cop. That was good, too. Miss Lee had asked him to bring her the book she needed. George looked at the title, *The Consolation of Philosophy*. Well, she had a book now.

III

Santa Battaglia tasted a spoonful of the potato salad, cleaned the spoon with her tongue, and placed the spoon neatly on a paper napkin next to the plate of salad. Sucking some pieces of parsley and onion from between her teeth, she said to the picture of her mother on the mantelpiece, "They gonna love that. Nobody makes a good potatis salad like Santa."

The parlor was almost ready for the party. On top of the old console radio there were two fifths of Early Times and a six-bottle carton of Seven-Up. The phonograph she had borrowed from her niece sat on the mopped linoleum in the center of the room, the cord rising to the chandelier where it was plugged in. Two gïant-sized bags of potato chips rested in either corner of the red plush sofa. A fork stuck out of the open bottle of olives that she had placed on a tin tray on top of the covered and folded rollaway bed.

Santa grabbed the picture on the mantelpiece, a photograph of an ancient and hostile-looking woman in a black dress and black stockings standing in a dark alley paved with oyster shells.

"Poor momma," Santa said feelingly, giving the picture a loud, wet kiss. The grease on the glass that covered the photograph showed the frequency of these affectionate onslaughts. "You sure had it hard, kid." The little black coals of Sicilian eyes glared almost animatedly at Santa from the snapshot. "The only picture of you I got, momma, and you standing in a alley. Ain't that a shame."

Santa sighed at the unfairness of it all and slammed the picture down on the mantelpiece among the bowl of wax fruit and the bouquet of paper zinnias and the statue of the Virgin Mary and the figurine of the Infant of Prague. Then she went back to the kitchen to get some ice cubes and one of the kitchen chairs. After she had returned with the chair and a little picnic cooler of ice cubes, she arranged her best jelly glasses on the mantelpiece before her mother's picture. The proximity of the picture made her grab it and kiss it again, the ice cube in her mouth cracking against the glass.

"I say a prayer for you every day, babe," Santa told the snapshot incoherently, balancing the ice cube on her tongue. "You better believe they's a candle burning for you over in St. Ode's."

Someone knocked at the front shutters. In putting the picture down hurriedly, Santa tipped it over on its face.

"Irene!" Santa screamed when she opened the door and saw the hesitant Mrs. Reilly on the front steps and her nephew, Patrolman Mancuso, standing down on the banquette. "Come on in, sweetheart darling. You sure looking cute."

"Thanks, honey," Mrs. Reilly said. "Whoo! I forgot how long it takes to drive down here. Me and Angelo been in that car almost a hour."

"Id's the traffig is whad id is," Patrolman Mancuso offered.

"Listen to that cold," Santa said. "Aw, Angelo. You better tell them men at the precinct to take you out that toilet. Where's Rita?"

"She diddit feel like cubbig. She's got her a headache."

"Well, no wonder, locked up in that house with them kids all day long," Santa said. "Aw, she oughta get out, Angelo. What's wrong with that girl?"

"Nerbs," Angelo answered sadly. "She's got nerbous trouble."

"Nerves is terrible," Mrs. Reilly said. "You know what happened, Santa? Angelo lost the book Ignatius give him. Ain't that a shame. I don't mind about the book, but don't never tell Ignatius about it. We'll really have us a fight on our hands."

Mrs. Reilly put her finger to her lips to indicate that the book must forever be a secret.

"Well, gimme your coat, girl," Santa said eagerly, almost tearing Mrs. Reilly's old purple woolen topper off. She was determined that the ghost of Ignatius J. Reilly would not haunt her party as it had haunted so many evenings of bowling.

"You got you a nice place here, Santa," Mrs. Reilly said respectfully. "It's clean."

"Yeah, but I want to get me some new linoleum for the parlor. You ever used them paper curtains, honey? They don't look too bad. I seen some nice ones up by Maison Blanche."

"I bought some nice paper curtains for Ignatius' room once, but he tore them off the window and crumpled them up. He says they an abortion. Ain't that awful?"

"Everybody to his own taste," Santa observed quickly.

"Ignatius don't know I come here tonight. I told him I was going to a novena."

"Angelo, fix Irene here a nice drink. Take a little whiskey yourself, help out that cold. I got some cokes in the kitchen."

"Ignatius don't like novenas neither. I don't know what that boy likes. Personally, I'm getting kinda fed up on Ignatius, even if he is my own child."

"I fixed us a good potatis salad, girl. That old man tells me he likes a good potatis salad."

"You oughta see them big uniforms he's giving me to launder. And all the directions I get on how to wash them. He sounds like he's selling soap powder on the TV. Ignatius acts like he's really made good pushing that wagon around downtown.

"Look at Angelo, babe. He's fixing us a nice drink."

"You got any aspirins, honey?"

"Aw, Irene! What kinda party pooper I got on my hands? Take a drink. Wait till the old man comes. We gonna have us a nice time. Look, you and the old man can dance right in front the phonograph."

"Dance? I don't feel like dancing with no old man. Besides, my feet swole up this afternoon while I was ironing them uniforms."

"Irene, you can't disappoint him, girl. You shoulda seen his face when I invited him out in front the church. Poor old man. I bet nobody ast him out."

"He wanted to come, huh?"

"Wanted to come? He ast me should he wear a suit."

"And what you told him, honey?"

"Well, I said, 'Wear whatever you want, mister.'"

"Well, that's nice." Mrs. Reilly looked down at her green

taffeta cocktail dress. "Ignatius ast me why I was wearing a cocktail dress to go to a novena. He's sitting in his room right now writing some foolishness. I says, 'What's that you writing now, boy?' And he say, 'I'm writing about being a weenie vendor.' Ain't that terrible? Who want to read a story like that? You know how much he brought home from that weenie place today? Four dollars. How I'm gonna pay off that man?"

"Look. Angelo fixed us a nice hi-ball."

Mrs. Reilly took a jelly glass from Angelo and drank half of it in two gulps.

"Where you got that nice high-fly from, darling?"

"What you mean?" Santa asked.

"That gramaphone you got in the middle of the floor."

"That's my little niece's. She's precious. Just graduated outta St. Odo High and she's awready got her a good saleslady job."

"You see that?" Mrs. Reilly said excitedly. "I bet she's making better than Ignatius."

"Lord, Angelo," Santa said. "Stop that coughing. Go lay down in the back and rest up till the old man comes."

"Poor Angelo," Mrs. Reilly said after the patrolman had left the room. "He sure a sweet boy. You two sure been good friends to me. And to think we all met when he tried to arrest Ignatius."

"I wonder how come that old man ain't showed up yet."

"Maybe he's not coming, Santa." Mrs. Reilly finished her drink. "I'm gonna make me another one, if you don't mind, sugar. I got problems."

"Go ahead, babe. I'm gonna take your coat back in the kitchen and see how Angelo's making out. I sure got two happy people at my party so far. I hope that old man don't fall down and break his leg on the way over."

After Santa had left, Mrs. Reilly filled her glass with bourbon and added a jigger of Seven-Up. She picked up the spoon, tasted the potato salad, and, cleaning the spoon with her lips, put it back on the paper napkin. The family in the other half of Santa's double house was beginning to stage what sounded like a riot. Sipping her drink, Mrs. Reilly put her ear to the wall and tried to filter some meaning out of the loud shouting.

"Angelo's taking some cough medicine," Santa said as she returned to the parlor.

"You sure got you good walls in this building, babe," Mrs. Reilly said, unable to comprehend the gist of the argument on the other side of the wall. "I wish me and Ignatius lived here. Miss Annie wouldn't have nothing to complain about."

"Where's that old man?" Santa asked the front shutters.

"Maybe he ain't gonna come."

"Maybe he forgot."

"That's the way it is with old folks, honey."

"He ain't that *old*, Irene."

"How old is he?"

"Someplace in his late sixties, I guess."

"Well, that ain't too old. My poor old Tante Marguerite, the one I told you them kids beat up on to get fifty cents out her coin purse, she going on eighty." Mrs. Reilly finished her drink. "Maybe he went to see a nice picture show or something. Santa, you mind if I make me another drink."

"Irene! You gonna be on the floor, girl. I ain't gonna introduce no drunk to this nice old man."

"I'll make me a small one. I got nerves tonight."

Mrs. Reilly slopped a great deal of whiskey into her glass and sat down again, crushing one of the bags of potato chips.

"Oh, Lord, what I done now?"

"You just smashed them potato chips," Santa said a little angrily.

"Aw, they all crumbs now," Mrs. Reilly said, pulling the bag from beneath her. She studied the flattened cellophane.

"Listen, Santa, what time you got? Ignatius says he's sure the burgulars is striking tonight and for me to get in early."

"Oh, take it easy, Irene. You just got here."

"To tell you the truth, Santa, I don't think I want to meet this old man."

"Well, it's too late now."

"Yeah, but what me and this old man gonna do?" Mrs. Reilly asked apprehensively.

"Aw, relax, Irene. You making *me* nervous. I'm sorry I axt you over." Santa pulled Mrs. Reilly's drink down from her lips for a moment. "Now listen to me. You had arthritus very bad. The bowling's helping that out. Right? You was stuck home with that crazy boy every night until Santa come along. Right? Now listen to Santa, precious. You don't wanna end up all alone with that Ignatius on your hands. This old man looks like he's got him a little money. He dresses neat. He knows you from somewhere. He likes you." Santa looked Mrs. Reilly in the eye. "This old man can pay off your debt!"

"Yeah?" Mrs. Reilly hadn't thought of this before. The old man suddenly became a little more attractive. "He's clean?"

"Sure he's clean," Santa said angrily. "You think I'm trying fix my friend up with a bum?"

Someone knocked lightly at the shutters on the front door.

"Oh, I bet that's him," Santa said eagerly.

"Tell him I hadda go, honey."

"Go? Where you goint to, Irene? The man's right by the front door."

"He is, huh?"

"Lemme go take a look."

Santa opened the door and pushed the shutters outward.

"Hey, Mr. Robichaux," she said into the night to someone whom Mrs. Reilly couldn't see. "We been waiting for you. My friend Miss Reilly here's been wondering where you was. Come on in out the cold."

"Yeah, Miss Battaglia, I'm sorry I'm a little late, but I had to take my little granchirren around the neighborhood. They raffling some rosaries for the sisters."

"I know," Santa said. "I bought a chance from a little kid just the other day. They beautiful rosaries. A lady I know won the outboard motor the sisters was raffling last year."

Mrs. Reilly sat frozen on the sofa staring into her drink as if she had just discovered a roach floating in it.

"Irene!" Santa cried. "What you doing, girl? Say 'hello' to Mr. Robichaux."

Mrs. Reilly looked up and recognized the old man whom Patrolman Mancuso had arrested in front of D. H. Holmes.

"Glad to meet you," Mrs. Reilly said to her drink.

"Maybe Miss Reilly don't remember," Mr. Robichaux told Santa, who was beaming happily, "But we met before."

"To think you two are old friends." Santa said happily. "It's sure a small world."

"Ay-yi-yi," Mrs. Reilly said, her voice choked with misery. "Eh, la la."

"You remember," Mr. Robichaux said to her. "It was down-town by Holmes. That policeman tried to take in your boy and he took me in instead."

Santa's eyes opened wide.

"Oh yeah," Mrs. Reilly said. "I think I remember now. A little."

"It wasn't your fault though, Miss Reilly. It's them police. They all a bunch of communiss."

"Not so loud," Mrs. Reilly cautioned. "They got thin walls in this building." She moved her elbow and knocked her empty glass off the arm of the sofa. "Oh, Lord. Santa, maybe you oughta go tell Angelo to run along. I can get me a taxi. Tell him he can run out the back way. It's easier for him. You know?"

"I see whatcha mean, honey." Santa turned to Mr. Robichaux. "Listen, when you seen my friend and me down by the bowling alley, you didn't see no man with us, huh?"

"You ladies was all alone."

"Wasn't that the night A. got himself arrested?" Mrs. Reilly whispered to Santa.

"Oh, yeah, Irene. You come by for me in that car of yours. You remember the fender came loose entirely right in front the bowling alley."

"I know. I got it in the backseat. Ignatius is the one made me wreck that car, he got me so nervous from the backseat."

"Aw, no," Mr. Robichaux said. "The one thing I can't stand is a poor loser or a bad sport."

"If somebody does me dirt," Santa continued, "I try to turn the other cheek. You know what I mean? That's the Christian way. Ain't that right, Irene?"

"That's right, darling," Mrs. Reilly agreed halfheartedly. "Santa, sweet, you got some nice aspirins?"

"Irene!" Santa said angrily. "You know, Mr. Robichaux, now suppose you saw that cop that took you in."

"I hope I never see him again," Mr. Robichaux said with emotion. "He's a dirty communiss. Them people want to set up a police state."

"Yeah, but just supposing. Wouldn't you forgive and forget?"

"Santa," Mrs. Reilly interrupted, "I think I'm gonna run in the kitchen and see if you got some nice aspirins."

"It was the disgrace," Mr. Robichaux said to Santa. "My whole family heard about it. The police called up my daughter."

"Aw, that ain't nothing," Santa said. "Everybody gets took in some time in they life. You see her?" Santa picked up the photograph lying face down on the mantelpiece and showed it to her two guests. "My poor dear momma. The police took her out the Lautenschlaeger Market four times for disturbing the peace." Santa paused to give the snapshot a moist kiss. "You think she cared? Not her."

"That's your momma?" Mrs. Reilly asked interestedly. "She had it hard, huh? Mothers got a hard road to travel, believe me."

"So, as I was saying," Santa continued, "I wouldn't feel bad about getting arrested. Policeman got them a hard line of work. Sometimes they make a mistake. They only human, after all."

"I always been a decent citizen," Mrs. Reilly said. "I wanna go wrench out my glass in the zink."

"Oh, go sit down, Irene. Lemme talk to Mr. Robichaux."

Mrs. Reilly went over to the old console radio and poured herself a glass of Early Times.

"I'll never forget that Patrolman Mancuso," Mr. Robichaux was saying.

"Mancuso?" Santa asked with great surprise. "I got plenty relatives with that very same name. As a matter of fact, one of them's on the force. As a matter of fact, he's here now."

"I think I hear Ignatius calling me. I better go."

"Calling you?" Santa asked. "Whadda you mean, Irene? Ignatius is six miles away uptown. Look, we ain't even give Mr. Robichaux a drink. Fix him a drink, kid, while I go get Angelo." Mrs. Reilly studied her drink furiously in the hope of turning up a roach or at least a fly. "Gimme that coat, Mr. Robichaux. Whatcha friends call you?"

"Claude."

"Claude, I'm Santa. And that there's Irene. Irene, say 'hello.'"

"Hello," Mrs. Reilly said automatically.

"You two make friends while I'm gone," Santa said and disappeared into the other room.

"How's that fine big boy of yours?" Mr. Robichaux asked to end the silence that had fallen.

"Who?"

"Your son."

"Oh, him. He's okay." Mrs. Reilly's mind flew back to Constantinople Street where she had left Ignatius writing in his room and mumbling something about Myrna Minkoff.

Through the door, Mrs. Reilly had heard Ignatius saying to himself, "She must be lashed until she drops."

There was a long silence broken only by the violent sipping noises that Mrs. Reilly made on the rim of her glass.

"You want some nice potato chips?" Mrs. Reilly finally asked, for she found that the silence made her even more ill at ease.

"Yeah, I think I would."

"They right in the bag next to you." Mrs. Reilly watched Mr. Robichaux open the cellophane package. His face and his gray gabardine suit both seemed to be neat and freshly pressed. "Maybe Santa needs some help. Maybe she went and fell down."

"She just left the room a minute ago. She'll be back."

"These floors are dangerous," Mrs. Reilly observed, studying the shiny linoleum intently. "You could slip down and crack your skull wide open."

"You gotta be careful in life."

"Ain't that the truth. Me, I'm always careful."

"Me, too. It pays to be careful."

"It sure does. That's what Ignatius said just the other day," Mrs. Reilly lied. "He says to me, 'Momma, it sure pays to be careful, don't it?' And I says to him, 'That's right, son. Take care.'"

"That's good advice."

"I'm all the time giving Ignatius advice. You know? I'm always trying to help him out."

"I bet you a good momma. I seen you and that boy downtown plenty times, and I always thought what a fine-looking big boy he was. He kinda stands out, you know?"

"I try with him. I say, 'Be careful, son. Watch you don't slip down and crack your skull open or fracture a arm.'" Mrs. Reilly sucked at the ice cubes a bit. "Ignatius learned safety at my knee. He's always been grateful for that."

"That's good training, believe me."

"I tell Ignatius, I say, 'Take care when you cross the street, son.'"

"You gotta watch out in traffic, Irene. You don't mind if I call you by your first name, huh?"

"Feel free."

"Irene's a pretty name."

"You think so? Ignatius says he don't like it." Mrs. Reilly crossed herself and finished her drink. "I sure got a hard road, Mr. Robichaux. I don't mind telling you."

"Call me Claude."

"As God is my witness, I got a awful cross to bear. You wanna nice drink?"

"Yeah, thanks. Not too strong, though. I'm not a drinking man."

"Oh, Lord," Mrs. Reilly sniffed, filling two glasses to the rim with whiskey. "When I think of all I take. Sometimes I could really have me a good cry."

With that, Mrs. Reilly burst into loud, wild tears.

"Aw, don't cry," Mr. Robichaux pleaded, completely confused by the tragic turn the evening was apparently taking.

"I gotta do something. I gotta call the authorities to come take that boy away," Mrs. Reilly sobbed. She paused to take a mouthful of Early Times. "Maybe they put him in a detention home or something."

"Ain't he thirty years old?"

"My heart's broke."

"Ain't he writing something?"

"Some foolishness nobody never gonna feel like reading. Now him and that Myrna writing insults to each other. Ignatius is telling me he's gonna get that girl good. Ain't that awful? Poor Myrna."

Mr. Robichaux, unable to think of anything to say, asked, "Why don't you get a priest to talk to your boy?"

"A priest?" Mrs. Reilly wept. "Ignatius won't listen to no priest. He calls the priest in our parish a heretic. They had a big fight when Ignatius' dog died." Mr. Robichaux could find no comment for that enigmatic statement. "It was awful. I thought I'd get throwed out the Church. I don't know where that boy gets his ideas from. It's a good thing his poor poppa's dead. He'd be breaking his poor father's heart with that weenie wagon."

"What weenie wagon?"

"He's out on the streets pushing a weenie wagon all over."

"Oh. He's got him a job now."

"A job?" Mrs. Reilly sobbed. "It's all over my neighborhood. The lady next door's been asking me a million questions. All Constantinople Street's talking about him. When I think of all the money I spent on that boy's education. You know, I thought chirren was supposed to comfort you in your old age. What kinda comfort Ignatius is giving me?"

"Maybe your boy went to school too long," Mr. Robichaux advised. "They got plenty communiss in them colleges."

"Yeah?" Mrs. Reilly asked with interest, dabbing at her eyes with the skirt of her green taffeta cocktail dress, unaware that she was showing Mr. Robichaux the wide runs in her stockings at the knee. "Maybe that's what's wrong with Ignatius. It's just like a communiss to treat his momma bad."

"Ax that boy what he thinks of democracy some time."

"I sure will," Mrs. Reilly said happily. Ignatius was just the type to be a communist. He even looked like one a little. "Maybe I can scare him."

"That boy shouldn't be giving you trouble. You got a very fine character. I admire that in a lady. When I reconnized you down by the bowling alley with Miss Battaglia, I says to myself, 'I hope I can meet her some time.'"

"You said that?"

"I admired your integrity, standing up for that boy in front that dirty cop, especially if you got troubles with him at home. That takes courage."

"I wisht I woulda let Angelo take him away. None of this other stuff woulda happened. Ignatius woulda been locked up safe in jail."

"Who's Angelo?"

"There! I hadda go open my big mouth. What I said, Claude?"

"Something about Angelo."

"Lord, lemme go see if Santa's okay. Poor thing. Maybe she burnt herself on the stove. Santa's all the time getting herself burnt. She don't take care around the fire, you know."

"She woulda screamed if she was burnt."

"Not Santa. She's got plenty courage, that girl. You won't hear a word outta her. It's that strong Italian blood."

"Christ Awmight!" Mr. Robinchaux screamed, jumping to his feet. "That's him!"

"What?" Mrs. Reilly asked in panic, and, looking around, saw Santa and Angelo standing in the doorway of the room. "You see, Santa. I knew this was gonna happen. Lord, my nerves is shot already. I shoulda stayed home."

"If you wasn't a dirty cop, I'd punch you right in the nose," Mr. Robichaux was screaming at Angelo.

"Aw, take it easy, Claude," Santa said calmly. "Angelo here didn't mean no harm."

"He ruint me, that communiss."

Patrolman Mancuso coughed violently and looked depressed. He wondered what terrible thing would happen to him next.

"Oh, Lord, I better go," Mrs. Reilly said despairingly. "The last thing I need is a fight. We'll be all over the newspaper. Ignatius'll really be happy then."

"How come you brought me here?" Mr. Robichaux asked Santa wildly. "What is this?"

"Santa, honey, you wanna call me a nice taxi?"

"Aw, shut up, Irene," Santa answered. "Now listen, Claude, Angelo says he's sorry he took you in."

"That don't mean nothing. It's too late to feel sorry. I was disgraced in front my granchirren."

"Don't be mad at Angelo," Mrs. Reilly pleaded. "It was all Ignatius' fault. He's my own flesh and blood, but he sure does look funny when he goes out. Angelo shoulda locked him up."

"That's right," Santa added. "Listen at what Irene's telling you, Claude. And watch out you don't step on my poor little niece's phonograpy."

"If Ignatius woulda been nice to Angelo, none of this woulda happened," Mrs. Reilly explained to her audience. "Just look at the cold poor Angelo's got. He's got him a hard road, Claude."

"You tell him, girl," Santa said. "Angelo got that cold on account of he took you in, Claude." Santa waved a stubby finger at Mr. Robichaux a little accusingly. "Now he's stuck in a toilet. Next thing they gonna kick him off the force."

Patrolman Mancuso coughed sadly.

"Maybe I got a little excited," Mr. Robichaux conceded.

"I shouldn't of toog you id," Angelo breathed. "I got nerbous."

"It was all my fault," Mrs. Reilly said, "for trying to protect that Ignatius. I should of let you lock him away, Angelo." Mrs. Reilly turned her white, powdery face to Mr. Robichaux. "Mr. Robichaux, you don't know Ignatius. He makes trouble every-place he goes."

"Somebody oughta punch that Ignatius in the nose," Santa said eagerly.

"Somebody oughta punch him in the mouth," Mrs. Reilly added.

"Somebody oughta beat up on that Ignatius," Santa said. "Now come on. Everybody make friends."

"Okay," Mr. Robichaux said. He took Angelo's blue-white hand and shook it limply.

"Ain't that nice," Mrs. Reilly said. "Come sit on the sofa, Claude, and Santa can play her precious little niece's high-fly."

While Santa put a Fats Domino record on the phonograph, Angelo, sniffling and looking a little confused, sat down on the kitchen chair across from Mrs. Reilly and Mr. Robichaux.

"Now ain't this nice," Mrs. Reilly screamed brightly over the deafening piano and bass. "Santa, honey, you wanna turn that down a little?"

The thumping rhythm decreased slightly in volume.

"Okay," Santa shouted at her guests. "Now everybody make friends while I go get us some plates for my good potatis salad. Hey, come on, Irene and Claude. Let's see you kids shake a leg."

The two little coal-black eyes scowled down at her from the mantelpiece as she stomped gaily out of the room. The three guests, drowned in the pounding beat of the phonograph, silently studied the rose-colored walls and the floral patterns on the linoleum. Then, suddenly, Mrs. Reilly screamed to the two gentleman, "You know what? Ignatius was running the water in the tub when I left, and I bet he forgot to turn it off." When no one answered, she added, "Mothers got a hard road."

Nine

"We got a complaint on you from the Board of Health, Reilly."

"Oh, is that all? From the expression on your face, I thought that you were having some sort of epileptic seizure," Ignatius said to Mr. Clyde through his mouthful of hot dog and bun, bumping his wagon into the garage. "I am afraid to guess what the complaint could be or how it could have originated. I assure you that I have been the very soul of cleanliness. My intimate habits are above reproach. Carrying no social diseases, I don't see what I could possibly transmit to your hot dogs that they do not already have. Look at these fingernails."

"Don't gimme none of your bullshit, you fat bum." Mr. Clyde ignored the paws that Ignatius had extended for inspection. "You only been on the job a few days. I got guys working for me for years never been in trouble with the Board."

"No doubt they're more foxy than I."

"They got this man was checking on you."

"Oh," Ignatius said calmly and paused to chew on the tip of the hot dog that was sticking from his mouth like a cigar butt. "So that's who that obvious appendage of officialdom was. He looked like an arm of the bureaucracy. You can always tell employees of the government by the total vacancy which occupies the space where most other people have faces."

"Shut up, you big slob. Did you pay for that weenie you eating?"

"Well, indirectly. You may subtract it from my miserable wage." Ignatius watched as Mr. Clyde jotted some numbers on a pad. "Tell me, what archaic sanitary taboo have I violated?

I suspect that it's some falsification on the part of the inspector."

"The Board says they seen the vendor with Number Seven . . . that's you . . ."

"So it is. Thrice-blessed Seven! I'm guilty on that count. They've already pinned something on me. I imagined that Seven would ironically be an unlucky cart. I want another cart as soon as possible. Apparently I am pushing a jinx about the streets. I am certain that I can do better with some other wagon. A new cart, a new start."

"Will you listen to me?"

"Well, if I really must. I should perhaps warn you that I am about to faint from anxiety and general depression, though. The film I saw last night was especially grueling, a teen-age beach musical. I almost collapsed during the singing sequence on surfboard. In addition, I suffered through two nightmares last night, one involving a Scenicruiser bus. The other involved a girl of my acquaintance. It was rather brutal and obscene. If I described it to you, you would no doubt become frightened."

"They seen you picking a cat out the gutter on St. Joseph Street."

"Is that the best that they can do? What an absurd lie," Ignatius said and with a flip of his tongue pulled in the last visible portion of the hot dog.

"What was you doing on St. Joseph Street? That's all warehouses and wharfs out there. They's no people on St. Joseph. That's not even on our routes."

"Well, I didn't know that. I had only feebly shambled out there to rest a while. Occasionally a pedestrian happened along. Unfortunately for us, they did not seem to be in hot dog moods."

"So you *was* there? No wonder you not selling nothing. And I guess you was playing with that goddam cat."

"Now that you mention it, I do seem to remember a domesticated animal or two in the vicinity."

"So you was playing with the cat."

"No, I was not 'playing' with the cat. I only picked it up to fondle it a bit. It was a rather appealing calico. I offered it a hot dog. However, the cat refused to eat it. It was an animal with some taste and decency."

"You realize what a serious violation that is, you big ape?"

"No, I am afraid I don't," Ignatius said angrily. "It has apparently been taken for granted that the cat was unclean. How do we know that? Cats are notoriously sanitary, continuously licking at themselves when they suspect that there is the slightest cause for offense. That inspector must have some prejudice against cats. This cat hasn't been given a chance."

"We not talking about this cat!" Mr. Clyde said with such vehemence that Ignatius was able to see the purple veins swelling around the whitened scar on his nose. "We talking about you."

"Well, *I* certainly am clean. We've already discussed that. I just wanted to see that the cat got a fair hearing. Sir, am I going to be endlessly harassed? My nerves are nearing total decay already. When you checked my fingernails a moment ago, I hope that you noticed the frightening vibration of my hands. I would hate to sue Paradise Vendors, Incorporated, to pay the psychiatrist's fees. Perhaps you do not know that I am not covered by any hospitalization plan. Paradise Vendors, of course, is too paleolithic to consider offering its workers such benefits. Actually, sir, I am growing quite dissatisfied with conditions at this disreputable firm."

"Why, what's wrong?" Mr. Clyde asked.

"Everything, I'm afraid. On top of that, I don't feel at all appreciated."

"Well, at least you show up every day. I'll give you that."

"That is only because I would be beaten senseless with a

baked wine bottle if I dared stay at home. Opening the door of my home is like intruding into the den of a lioness. My mother is becoming increasingly abusive and vicious."

"You know, Reilly, I don't wanna fire you," Mr. Clyde said in a paternal tone. He had heard the sad tale of vendor Reilly: the drunken mother, the damages that had to be paid, the threat of penury for both son and mother, the mother's lascivious friends. "I'm gonna fix you up with a new route and give you another chance. I got some merchandising gimmicks maybe help you out."

"You may send a map of my new route to the mental ward at Charity Hospital. The solicitous nuns and psychiatrists there can help me decipher it between shock treatments."

"Now shut up."

"You see that? You've destroyed my initiative already," Ignatius belched. "Well, I do hope that you have selected a scenic route, preferably something in a park area where there are ample seating accommodations for sufferers from tired, stunned feet. When I rose this morning, my ankles gave way. Fortunately I grabbed for the bedpost in time. Otherwise, I would have landed on the floor in a broken heap. My tarsi are apparently about to throw in the towel completely."

Ignatius limped around Mr. Clyde to illustrate, his desert boots scuffing along the oily cement.

"Stop that, you big slob. You ain't crippled."

"Not completely as of yet. However, various small bones and ligaments are beginning to wave a white flag of surrender. My physical apparati seem to be preparing to announce a truce of some sort. My digestive system has almost ceased functioning altogether. Some tissue has perhaps grown over my pyloric valve, sealing it forever."

"I'm gonna put you down in the French Quarter."

"What?" Ignatius thundered. "Do you think that I am going to perambulate about in that sinkhole of vice? No, I am afraid that the Quarter is out of the question. My psyche would crumble in that atmosphere. Besides, the streets are very narrow and dangerous there. I could easily be struck down in traffic or be wedged against a building."

"Take it or leave it, you fat bastard. That's the last chance you get." Mr. Clyde's scar was beginning to whiten again.

"It is? Well, please don't have another seizure. You may tumble into that vat of franks and scald yourself. If you insist, I imagine that I shall have to trundle my franks down into Sodom and Gomorrah."

"Okay. Then it's settled. You come in tomorrow morning, we'll fix you up with some gimmicks."

"I can't promise you that many hot dogs will be sold in the Quarter. I will probably be kept busy every moment protecting my honor against those fiends who live down there."

"You get mostly the tourist trade in the Quarter."

"That's even worse. Only degenerates go touring. Personally, I have been out of the city only once. By the way, have I ever told you about that particular pilgrimage to Baton Rouge? Outside the city limits there are many horrors."

"No. I don't wanna hear about it."

"Well, too bad for you. You might have gained some valuable insights from the traumatic tale of that trip. However, I am glad that you do not want to hear of it. The psychological and symbolic subtleties of the journey probably wouldn't be comprehended by a Paradise Vendors mentality. Fortunately, I've written it all down, and at some time in the future, the more alert among the reading public will benefit from my account of that abysmal sojourn into the swamps to the inner station of the ultimate horror."

"Now listen here, Reilly."

"In the account I struck upon an especially suitable simile in comparing the Scenicruiser bus to a loop-the-loop in a surrealistic amusement park."

"Now shut up!" Mr. Clyde screamed, waving his fork menacingly. "Let's go over your receipts for today. How much did you sell?"

"Oh, my God," Ignatius sighed. "I knew that we'd get to that sooner or later."

The two haggled over the profits for several minutes. Ignatius had actually spent the morning sitting at Eads Plaza watching the harbor traffic and jotting some notes about the history of shipping and Marco Polo in a Big Chief tablet. Between notes, he had contemplated means of destroying Myrna Minkoff but had reached no satisfactory conclusion. His most promising scheme had involved getting a book on munitions from the library, constructing a bomb, and mailing it in plain paper to Myrna. Then he remembered that his library card had been revoked. The afternoon had been wasted on the cat; Ignatius had tried to trap the cat in the bun compartment and take it home for a pet. But it had escaped.

"It seems to me that you would be generous enough to give some sort of discount to your own employees," Ignatius said importantly after an audit of the day's receipts showed that, upon subtracting the cost of the hot dogs he had eaten, his take-home pay for the day was exactly a dollar and twenty-five cents. "After all, I am becoming your best customer."

Mr. Clyde stuck the fork in Vendor Reilly's muffler and ordered him out of the garage, threatening him with dismissal if he didn't show up early to begin working the French Quarter.

Ignatius flapped off to the trolley in a dark mood and rode uptown belching Paradise gas so violently that, although the car was crowded, no one would sit next to him.

When he walked into the kitchen, his mother greeted him by falling to her knees and saying, "Lord, tell me how come you sent me this terrible cross to bear? What I done, Lord? Tell me. Send me a sign. I been good."

"Stop that blasphemy this moment," Ignatius screamed. Mrs. Reilly was questioning the ceiling with her eyes, seeking an answer among the grease and cracks. "What a greeting I receive after a discouraging day battling for my very existence on the streets of this savage town."

"What's them bo-bos on your hand?"

Ignatius looked at the scratches he had received in trying to persuade the cat to remain in the bun compartment.

"I had a rather apocalyptic battle with a starving prostitute," Ignatius belched. "Had it not been for my superior brawn, she would have sacked my wagon. Finally she limped away from the fray, her glad rags askew."

"Ignatius!" Mrs. Reilly cried tragically. "Every day it seems you getting worst and worst. What's happening to you?"

"Get your bottle out of the oven. It must be done by now."

Mrs. Reilly looked at her son slyly and asked, "Ignatius, you sure you not a communiss?"

"Oh, my God!" Ignatius bellowed. "Every day I am subjected to a McCarthyite witchhunt in this crumbling building. No! I told you before. I am not a fellow traveler. What in the world has put that into your head?"

"I read someplace in the paper where they got plenty communiss at college."

"Well, fortunately I didn't meet them. Had they crossed my path, they would have been beaten to within an inch of their lives. Do you think that I want to live in a communal society with people like that Battaglia acquaintance of yours, sweeping streets and breaking up rocks or whatever it is people are always doing in those blighted countries? What I want is a good, strong monarchy with a tasteful and decent king who has some knowledge of theology and geometry and to cultivate a Rich Inner Life."

"A king? You want a king?"

"Oh, stop babbling at me."

"I never heard of nobody wanted a king."

"Please!" Ignatius pounded a paw into the oilcloth on the kitchen table. "Sweep the porch, visit Miss Annie, call the Battaglia bawd, practice with your bowling ball out in the alley. Let me alone! I am in a very bad cycle."

"What you mean, 'cycle'?"

"If you do not stop molesting me, I shall christen the prow of your broken Plymouth with the bottle of wine in the oven," Ignatius snorted.

"Fighting with some poor girl in the street," Mrs. Reilly said sadly. "Ain't that awful. And right in front a weenie wagon. Ignatius, I think you need help."

"Well, I am going to watch television," Ignatius said angrily. "The Yogi Bear program is coming on."

"Wait a minute, boy." Mrs. Reilly rose from the floor and pulled a small manila envelope out of a pocket in her sweater. "Here. This come for you today."

"Oh?" Ignatius asked with interest, seizing the little tan envelope. "I imagine that you have memorized its contents by now."

"You better stick your hands in the sink and wrench out them scratches."

"They can wait," Ignatius said. He ripped at the envelope. "M. Minkoff has apparently responded to my missive with a rather frantic urgency. I told her off quite viciously."

Mrs. Reilly sat down and crossed her legs, swinging her white socks and old black patent leather pumps sadly while her son's blue and yellow eyes scanned the unfolded Macy's bag on which the letter was written.

Sirs:

Well, at last I heard from you, Ignatius. And a sick, sick letter it was. I won't go into the "Levy Pants" letterhead on that stationery. It is probably your idea of an anti-Semitic

*prank. It's a good thing that I'm above attack on that level.
I never thought that you would stoop so low. Live and
learn.*

*Your comments about the lecture showed a very petty
jealousy I didn't expect from someone who claims to be so
broad and non-committed. Already the lecture is beginning to
interest several dedicated people I know. One person who has
promised to come (and bring several sharp friends, too) is a
brilliant new contact I made during rush hour on the Jerome
Avenue line. His name is Ongah, and he is an exchange
student from Kenya who is writing a dissertation at N. Y. U.
on the French symbolists of the 19th cent. Of course, you
would not understand or like a brilliant and dedicated guy
like Ongah. I could listen to him talk for hours. He is serious
and does not come on with all of that pseudo stuff like you
always did. What Ongah says is meaningful. Ongah is real
and vital. He is virile and aggressive. He rips at reality and
tears aside concealing veils.*

"Oh, my God!" Ignatius slobbered. "The minx has been
raped by a Mau-Mau."

"What's that?" Mrs. Reilly asked suspiciously.

"Go turn on the television set and warm it up," Ignatius
said absently and returned to his furious reading of the letter.

*He is not a bit like you, as you can imagine. He is also a
musician and a sculptor and spends every minute in some
real and meaningful activity, creating and sensing. His
sculpture almost leaps out and grabs you, it is so filled
with life and being.*

*At least your letter let me know that you are still alive,
if you can call what you do 'living.' What were all these
lies about being connected with the "food merchandising
industry?" Is this some attack on my father's restaurant*

*supply business? If so, that didn't get to me either because
my father and I have been at ideological odds for years.
Let's face it, Ignatius. Since I saw you last, you have done
nothing but lie around rotting in your room. Your hostility
to my lecture is a manifestation of your feelings of failure,
nonaccomplishment, and mental (?) impotence.*

"This liberal doxy must be impaled upon the member of
a particularly large stallion," Ignatius mumbled furiously.
"What? What's that, boy?"

*Ignatius, a very bad crack-up is on the way. You must do
something. Even volunteer work at a hospital would snap
you out of your apathy, and it would probably be non-
taxing on your valve and other things. Get out of that
womb-house for at least an hour a day. Take a walk,
Ignatius. Look at the trees and birds. Realize that life is
surging all around you. The valve closes because it thinks it
is living in a dead organism. Open your heart, Ignatius,
and you will open your valve.*

*If you are having any sex fantasies, describe them in
detail in your next letter. I may be able to interpret their
meaning for you and help you through this psycho-sexual
crisis you are having. When I was at college, I told you
many times that you would undergo a psychotic phase of
this sort.*

*I thought you might be interested in knowing that I've
just read in* Social Revulsion *that Louisiana has the
highest illiteracy rate in the U.S. Come out from under the
mess before it's too late. I really don't mind what you wrote
about the lecture. I understand your condition, Ignatius.
The members of my group therapy group are all following
your case with interest (I have told it to them chapter by
chapter beginning with the paranoid fantasy, adding*

certain background commentaries), and they are all rooting
for you. If I were not so busy with the lecture, I would
take off on a long-overdue inspection tour and come to see
you personally. Hold on until we meet again.

M. Minkoff

Ignatius folded the letter violently; then he rolled the folded
Macy's bag into a ball and heaved it into the garbage pail.
Mrs. Reilly looked at her son's reddened face and asked,
"What that girl wants? What she's doing nowadays?"

"Myrna is preparing to bray at some unfortunate Negro.
In public."

"Ain't that awful. You sure pick up with fine friends,
Ignatius. Them colored people already got it hard, boy. They
got a hard road, too. Life's hard, Ignatius. You'll learn."

"Thank you very much," Ignatius said in a businesslike
manner.

"You know that poor old colored lady sells them pralines
in front the cemetery? Aw, Ignatius. I really feel sorry for her.
The other day I seen her wearing a little cloth coat full of
holes, and it was cold out. So I says to her, I says, 'Hey, honey,
you gonna catch your death of cold wearing that little cloth
coat full of holes.' And she says . . ."

"Please!" Ignatius shouted furiously. "I am not in the mood
for a dialect story."

"Ignatius, listen to me. That lady's pitiful, yeah. She says,
'Oh, I don't mind the cold, sugar. I'm used to it.' Ain't that
brave?" Mrs. Reilly looked emotionally at Ignatius for agreement but was treated only to a sneering moustache. "Ain't
that something. So, you know what I done, Ignatius. I give
her a quarter and I says, 'Here, darling, go buy you a trinket
for your little granchirren.'"

"What?" Ignatius exploded. "So that is where our profits
are going. While I am almost reduced to begging on the

streets, you are flinging our money away at frauds. That woman's clothing is all a ruse. She has a wonderful, lucrative location at that cemetery. Doubtlessly she makes ten times more than I do."

"Ignatius! She's all broke down," Mrs. Reilly said sadly. "I wish you was as brave as she is."

"I see. Now I am being compared to a degenerate old female fraud. Worse, I am losing in the comparison. My own mother daring to malign me so." Ignatius thrust a paw onto the oilcloth. "Well, I have had enough of this. I'm going into the parlor to watch the Yogi Bear program. Between wine breaks, bring me a snack of some sort. My valve is screaming for appeasement."

"Shut up over there," Miss Annie screamed through her shutters as Ignatius gathered his smock about him and swept into the hall contemplating his most important problem: organizing a new assault against the minx's effrontery. The civil rights assault had failed because of defections in the ranks. There must be other assaults which could be launched in the fields of politics and sex. Preferably politics. The strategy deserved his full attention.

II

Lana Lee was on a barstool, her legs crossed in tan suede trousers, her muscular buttocks pinning the stool to the floor and commanding it to support her in perfectly vertical form. When she moved slightly, the great muscles of her nether cheeks rippled to life to prevent the stool from leaning and tottering even an inch. The muscles rippled around the cushion of the stool and grabbed it, holding it erect. Long years of practice and usage had made her rump an unusually versatile and dexterous thing.

Her body had always amazed her. She had received it free of charge, yet she had never bought anything that had helped her as much as that body had. At these rare moments when Lana Lee grew sentimental or even religious, she thanked God for His goodness in forming a body that was also a friend. She repaid the gift by giving it magnificent care, expert service and maintenance that was given with the emotionless precision of a mechanic.

Today was Darlene's first dress rehearsal. A few minutes earlier Darlene had arrived with a large dress box and disappeared backstage. Lana looked at Darlene's gadget on the stage. A carpenter had made a stand that looked like a hatrack but instead of hooks there were large rings attached to the top of the stand and three rings on chains hung from the top at different heights. What Lana had seen of the act so far was not promising, but Darlene said that the costuming would transform the performance into a thing of beauty. Lana couldn't complain all things considered, she was glad that she had let Darlene and Jones talk her into permitting Darlene to perform. She was getting the act cheap, and she had to admit that the bird was very good, a skilled and professional performer who almost made up for the act's human deficiencies. The other clubs along the street might get the tiger, chimp, and snake trade. The Night of Joy had the bird trade in the bag, and Lana's peculiar knowledge of one aspect of humanity told her that the bird trade might indeed be very large.

"Okay, Lana, we're ready," Darlene called offstage.

Lana looked over at Jones, who was sweeping out the booths in a cloud of cigarette smoke and dust and said, "Put the record on."

"Sorry. Recor playin star at thirty a week. Whoa!"

"Put down that broom and get on that phonograph before I call up the precinct," Lana hollered at him.

"And you get off your stool and get on that phonograph

before I call up the precinc and ax them po-lice mothers make a search for your orphan frien who disappear. Ooo-wee."

Lana studied Jones's face, but his eyes were invisible behind the smoke and dark glasses.

"What was that?" she asked finally.

"The only thing you ever be givin the orphan is siphlus. Whoa! Don gimme no shit about no motherfuckin record player. As soon as I crack open this orphan case, I callin a po-lice myself. I sick and tire of workin in this cathouse below the minimal wage and getting intimidatia all the time."

"Hey, kids, where's our music?" Darlene's voice called eagerly.

"What can you prove to the cops?" Lana asked Jones.

"Hey! Then they *is* somethin crooker with the orphans. Whoa! I knowed it all along. Well, if you ever plannin to call up a po-lice about me, I plannin to call up a po-lice about you. Phones at po-lice headquarters really be hummin. Ooo-wee. Now lemme in peace with my sweepin and moppin. Recor playin pretty advance for color peoples. I probably break your machine."

"I'd like to see a jailbait vagrant like you trying to get the cops to believe you, especially when I tell them you been dipping into my cash register."

"What's happening?" Darlene inquired from behind the little curtain.

"The only thing I been dippin in around here is a mop bucket fulla dirty water."

"It's my word against yours. The police already got their eyes on you. All they need is to get the word about you from an old pal of theirs like me. Which one you think they'll believe?" Lana looked at Jones and saw that his silence had answered her question. "Now get on the phonograph."

Jones threw his broom into a booth and put on the record of *Stranger in Paradise*.

"Okay, everybody, here we come," Darlene called, bumping on stage with the cockatoo on her arm. She was wearing a low-cut orange satin evening dress, and at the peak of her upswept hair there was a large artificial orchid. She made several clumsily lascivious motions over toward the stand while the cockatoo swayed unsteadily on her arm. Holding onto the top of the stand with one hand, she made a grotesque pass at the pole with her pelvis and sighed, "Oh."

The cockatoo was placed in the lowest ring, and with beak and claw began to climb up to the next highest ring. Darlene bumped and ground around the pole in a sort of orgiastic frenzy until the bird was on a level with her waist. Then she offered the bird the ring sewed in the side of her gown. He grabbed at it with his beak and the gown popped open.

"Oh," Darlene sighed, bumping down to the edge of the little stage to show the audience the lingerie that showed through the opening. "Oh. Oh."

"Whoa!"

"Stop it, stop it," Lana screamed and, leaping from her stool, snapped off the phonograph.

"Hey, what's the matter?" Darlene asked in an offended voice.

"It stinks is what's the matter. For one thing, you're dressed up like a streetwalker. I want a nice, refined act in my club. I got a decent business, stupid."

"Whoa!"

"You look like a whore in that orange dress. And what's all these sounds you're making like a slut? You look like a drunk nympho passing out in a alley."

"But Lana . . ."

"The bird's okay. You stink." Lana stuck a cigarette between her coral lips and lit it. "We gotta rethink the whole act. You look like your motor's broke or something. I know this business. Stripping's an insult to a woman. The kinda creeps come in here don't wanna see a tramp get insulted."

"Hey!" Jones aimed his cloud at Lana Lee's. "I thought you say nice, refine peoples comin here at night."

"Shut up," Lana said. "Now listen, Darlene. Anybody can insult a tramp. These jerks wanna see a sweet, clean virgin get insulted and stripped. You gotta use your *head* for Chrissake, Darlene. You gotta be *pure*. I want you to be like a nice, refined girl who's surprised when the bird starts grabbing at your clothes."

"Who says I'm not refined?" Darlene asked angrily.

"Okay. You're refined. Then be refined on my stage. That's what gives a turn *drama*, goddammit."

"Ooo-wee. Night of Joy be winnin a Academy Awar with this ack. The bird get one, too."

"Get back on my floor."

"Right away, Scarla O'Horror."

"Wait a minute," Lana screamed in the best tradition of the director in a musical movie. She had always enjoyed the theatrical aspects of her profession: performing, posing, composing tableaux, directing acts. "That's it."

"That's what?" Darlene asked.

"An idea, moron," Lana answered, holding her cigarette before her lips and speaking through it as if it were a director's megaphone. "*Now* see this act. You're gonna be a southern belle type, a big sweet virgin from the Old South who's got this pet bird on the old plantation."

"Say, I like that," Darlene said enthusiastically.

"Of course you do. Now listen to me." Lana's mind began to whirl. This act could be her theatrical masterpiece. That bird had star quality. "We get you a big plantation dress, crinoline, lace. A big hat. A parasol. Very refined. Your hair's on your shoulders in curls. You're just coming in from a big ball where a lot of southern gentlemen were trying to feel you up over the fried chicken and hog jowls. But you cooled them all. Why? Because you're a lady, dammit. You come onstage.

The ball's over, but you still got your honor. You got your little pet with you to tell it goodnight, and you say to it, 'There was plenty beaux at that ball, honey, but I still got my honor.' Then the goddam bird starts grabbing at your dress. You're shocked, you're surprised, you're innocent. But you're too refined to stop it. Got it?"

"That's great," Darlene said.

"That's drama," Lana corrected. "Okay, let's give it a try. Music, maestro."

"Whoa! Now we really back on the plantation." Jones slid the needle across the first few grooves of the record. "I'm pretty stupor to open my mouth in this miser cathouse."

Darlene minced out on the stage, sashaying demurely, and making a rosebud of her mouth, said, "There sure was plenty balls at that beau, honey, but . . ."

"Stop!" Lana hollered.

"Give me a chance," Darlene pleaded. "It's my first time. I been practicing being an exotic, not a actress."

"You can't remember one simple line like that?"

"Darlene got Night of Joy nerves." Jones clouded the area in front of the stage. "It come from low wage and high intimidatia. The bird be gettin it, too, pretty soon, be snarlin and clawin and fallin off its stan. Whoa!"

"Darlene's your pal, huh? I see she's always passing you magazines," Lana said angrily. This Jones was really starting to get under her lotioned skin. "This act is mostly your idea, Jones. You sure you wanna see her get a chance on the stage?"

"Sure. Whoa! Somebody gotta get ahead in this place. Anyway, this ack got plenny class, bring in a lotta trade. I be gettin a raise. Hey!" Jones smiled a yellow crescent that opened the lower part of his face. "I got all my hope pin on that bird."

Lana had an idea that would help business and hurt Jones. She'd let him go too far already.

"Good," Lana said to him. "Now listen to me, Jones. You wanna help out Darlene here. You think this act is good, huh? I remember you said Darlene and the bird was gonna bring in so much business I'd need a doorman. Well, I got a doorman. You."

"Hey! I ain comin around here at night below the minimal wage."

"You're coming out on opening night," Lana said evenly. "You gonna be out front on the sidewalk. We're gonna rent you a costume. Real Old South doorman. You attract the people in here. Understand? I wanna see a full house for your pal and her bird."

"Shit. I quittin this motherfuckin bar. Maybe you gettin Scarla O'Horror and her ball eagle on the stage, but you ain gettin a fiel han out front, too."

"The precinct is gonna be gettin a certain report."

"Maybe they be gettin another orphan repor, too."

"I don't think so."

Jones knew that this was true. Finally, he said, "Okay. I be here on openin night. I bring in some peoples. I bring in some peoples shut down your place for good. I be bringin in peoples like that fat mother got him the green cap."

"I wonder where he went to," Darlene said.

"Shut up and lemme hear you say your lines," Lana hollered at her. "Your friend here wants to see you get ahead. He's gonna help you out, Darlene. Show him how good you are."

Darlene cleared her throat and enunciated carefully, "There sure was plenty beaux at the bowl, honey, but I still got me honor."

Lana grabbed Darlene and the bird off the stage and pushed them out into the alley. Jones listened to the loud sounds of argument and pleading coming from the alley and heard one plop of a slap land on someone's face.

He went behind the bar to get a glass of water and contemplated means of sabotage that could finish Lana Lee forever. Outside, the cockatoo was squawking and Darlene was crying, "I ain't no actress, Lana. I already told you."

Looking down for a moment, Jones saw that Lana Lee had absentmindedly left the door open on the little cabinet under the bar. All afternoon she had been preoccupied with previewing Darlene's dress rehearsal. Jones knelt down and, for the first time in the Night of Joy, took off his sunglasses. At first his eyes had to adjust to the brighter but still dim light that revealed crusted dirt on the floor behind the bar. He looked into the little cabinet, and there he saw neatly stacked about ten packages wrapped in plain paper. Piled in the corner were a globe, a box of chalk, and a large, expensive-looking book.

He did not want to sabotage his discovery by taking anything from the cabinet. Lana Lee, with her hawk eyes and bloodhound nose, would notice that right away. He thought for a moment, then he took the pencil from the cash register and, running his hand down the side of the stacked packages, wrote as minutely as possible on the side of each package the address of the Night of Joy. Like a note in a bottle, the address might bring some reply, perhaps from a legitimate and professional saboteur. An address on a package wrapped in plain brown paper was as damaging as a fingerprint on a gun, Jones thought. It was something that shouldn't be there. He stacked the packages back carefully, straightening the pile to its original symmetry. Then he placed the pencil on the cash register and finished his water. He studied the door of the cabinet and decided that it was open at about the same angle at which he had found it.

He came from behind the bar and resumed his desultory sweeping just as Lana, Darlene, and the bird, looking like a small unruly mob, burst in from the alley. Darlene's orchid was hanging, and the bird's few feathers were ruffled. Lana Lee, though, was still well groomed and looked as though some cyclone had miraculously missed only her.

"Okay now, Darlene," Lana said, grabbing Darlene by the shoulders. "What the hell are you supposed to say?"

"Whoa! You sure a understandin director. If you be makin big movies, half the peoples in it be dead."

"Shut up and get on my floor," Lana said to Jones and shook Darlene a little. "Now say it right, stupid."

Darlene sighed hopelessly and said, "There sure was plenty bones at that ball, honey, but I still got my honor."

III

Patrolman Mancuso leaned against the sergeant's desk and wheezed, "You gotta tage me oud thad badroom. I can breed no more."

"What?" The sergeant looked at the wan figure before him, at the watery pink eyes behind the bifocals, at the dry lips through the white goatee. "What's wrong with you, Mancuso? Why can't you stand up like a man? Getting a cold. Men on the force don't catch cold. Men on the force are *strong*."

Patrolman Mancuso coughed wetly into the goatee.

"You haven't picked up nobody out that bus station. Remember what I told you? You stay there until you bring me somebody."

"I'b getting pneumodia."

"Take some cold tablets. Get outta here and bring me somebody."

"My at says if I stay iddat badroom, I'b gudda die."

"Your aunt? A grown man like you's gotta listen to his aunt? Jesus. What kinda people you know, Mancuso? Old ladies who go sit in strip joints all alone, aunts. You probly belong to a ladies' sodality or something. *Stand up straight.*" The sergeant studied the miserable figure that was shaking with the aftereffects of a dangerous cough. He didn't want to be responsible for a death. It would be better to give Mancuso a probationary period and kick him off the force. "Okay. Don't go back to the bus station. Get out on the streets again and get some sunshine. But listen here. I'm giving you two weeks. If you don't bring in nobody by then, you're off the force. You understand me, Mancuso?"

Patrolman Mancuso nodded, sniffling.

"I'b gudda try. I'b gudda brig you subbody."

"Stop leaning over me," the sergeant screamed. "I don't wanna catch your cold. Stand up. Get outta here. Go take some pills and orange juice. Jesus."

"I'b gudda brig you subbody," Patrolman Mancuso wheezed again, this time even more unconvincingly than the first. Then he drifted off in his novel costume, the sergeant's ultimate practical joke on him. He was wearing a baseball cap and a Santa Claus outfit.

IV

Ignatius ignored his mother's pounding on his door and crying in the hall about the fifty cents in wages that he had brought home for the day's work. Sweeping the Big Chief tablets, yo-yo, and rubber glove from his desk, he opened the journal and began to write:

> *Dear Reader,*
> *A good book is the precious life-blood of a master-spirit,*
> *embalmed and treasured up on purpose for a life beyond.*
> *—Milton*

The perverted (and I suspect quite dangerous) mind of Clyde has devised still another means of belittling my rather invincible being. At first I thought that I might have found a surrogate father in the czar of sausage, the mogul of meat. But his resentment and jealousy of me are increasing daily; no doubt they will ultimately overwhelm him and destroy his mind. The grandeur of my physique, the complexity of my worldview, the decency and taste implicit in my carriage, the grace with which I function in the mire of today's world—all of these at once confuse and astound Clyde. Now he has relegated me to working in the French Quarter, an area which houses every vice that man has ever conceived in his wildest aberrations, including, I would imagine, several modern variants made possible through the wonders of science. The Quarter is not unlike, I would imagine, Soho and certain sections of North Africa. However, the residents of the French Quarter, blessed with American "Stick-to-it-tiveness" and "Know-how," are probably straining themselves at this moment to equal and surpass in variety and imagination the diversions enjoyed by the residents of those other world areas of human degradation.

Clearly an area like the French Quarter is not the proper environment for a clean-living, chaste, prudent, and impressionable young Working Boy. Did Edison, Ford, and Rockefeller have to struggle against such odds?

Clyde's fiendish mind has not stopped at so simple an abasement, however. Because I am allegedly handling what Clyde calls "the tourist trade," I have been caparisoned in a costume of sorts.

(Judging from the customers I have had on this first day with the new route, the "tourists" seem to be the same old vagrants I was selling to in the business district. In a stupor induced by Sterno, they have doubtlessly stumbled

down into the Quarter and thus, to Clyde's senile mind, qualify as "tourists." I wonder whether Clyde has even had an opportunity to see the degenerates and wrecks and drifters who buy and apparently subsist on Paradise products. Between the other vendors—totally beaten and ailing itinerants whose names are something like Buddy, Pal, Sport, Top, Buck, and Ace—and my customers, I am apparently trapped in a limbo of lost souls. However, the simple fact that they have been resounding failures in our century does give them a certain spiritual quality. For all we know, they may be—these crushed wretches—the saints of our age: beautifully broken old Negroes with tan eyes; downtrodden drifters from wastelands in Texas and Oklahoma; ruined share-croppers seeking a haven in rodent-infested urban rooming houses.

(Nevertheless, I do hope that in my dotage, I will not have to rely upon hot dogs for sustenance. The sale of my writings may bring some profit. If need be, I could always turn to the lecture circuit, following behind the ghastly M. Minkoff, whose offenses against taste and decency have already been described in detail to you readers, in order to clear away the boulders of ignorance and obscenity which she will have strewn among the various lecture halls of the nation. Perhaps, however, there will be some person of quality in her first audience who will wrest her from the podium and lash her a bit about her erogenous zones. In spite of whatever spiritual qualities it may possess, skid row is definitely sub-standard in the matter of physical comfort, and I seriously doubt whether my substantial and well-formed physique would easily adapt to sleeping in alleys. I would definitely tend to hang over park benches. Therefore, my size itself is a safeguard against my ever sinking too low within the structure of our civilization. [After all, I do not believe that one must necessarily scrape bottom, as it were, in order to view his society subjectively. Rather than moving vertically downward, one may move horizontally outward toward a point of sufficient detachment where a modicum of creature comforts are not necessarily precluded. I was there—on the very rim of our age—when my mother's cataclysmic intemperance, as you well know, catapulted me into the fever of contemporary existence. To be quite honest, I must say that since then things have been getting worse and worse. Conditions have deteriorated. Minkoff, my passionless flame, has turned upon me. Even my mother, the agent of my destruction, has begun to bite the hand that feeds her. My cycle is dipping lower and lower. Oh, Fortuna, you capricious sprite!] Personally, I have found that a lack of food and comfort, rather than ennobling the spirit, creates only anxiety within the human psyche and channels all of one's better impulses only toward the end of procuring something to eat. Even though I do have a Rich Inner Life, I must have some food and comfort also.)

But back to the matter at hand: Clyde's vengeance. The vendor who formerly had the Quarter route wore an improbable pirate's outfit, a Paradise Vendor's nod to New Orleans folklore and history, a Clydian attempt to link the hot dog with Creole legend. Clyde forced me to try it on in the garage. The costume, of course, had been made to fit the tubercular and underdeveloped frame of the former vendor, and no amount of pulling and pushing and inhaling and squeezing would get it onto my muscular body. Therefore, a compromise of sorts was made. About my cap I tied the red sateen pirate's scarf. I screwed the one golden earring, a large novelty store hoop of an earring, onto my left earlobe. I affixed the black plastic cutlass to the side of my white vendor's smock with a safety pin. Hardly an impressive pirate, you will say.

However, when I studied myself in the mirror, I was forced to admit that I appeared rather fetching in a dramatic way. Brandishing the plastic cutlass at Clyde, I cried, "Walk the plank, Admiral!" This, I should have known, was too much for his literal and sausage-like mind. He grew most alarmed and proceeded to attack me with his spear-like fork. We lunged about in the garage like two swashbucklers in an especially inept historical film for several moments, fork and cutlass clicking against each other madly. Realizing that my plastic weapon was hardly a match for a long fork wielded by a maddened Methuselah, realizing that I was seeing Clyde at his worst, I tried to end our little duel. I called out pacifying words; I entreated; I finally surrendered. Still Clyde came, my pirate costume so great a success that it had apparently convinced him that we were back in the golden days of romantic old New Orleans when gentlemen decided matters of hot dog honor at twenty paces. It was then that a light dawned in my intricate mind. I know that Clyde was really trying to kill me. He would have the perfect excuse: self defense. I had played right into his hands. Fortunately for me, I fell to the floor. I had backed into one of the carts, lost my always precarious balance, and had fallen down. Although I struck my head rather painfully against the cart, I cried pleasantly from the floor, "You win, sir." Then I silently paid homage to dear old Fortuna for snatching me from the jaws of death by rusty fork.

I quickly rolled my cart out of the garage and set out for the Quarter. Along the way, many pedestrians gave my semi-costume favorable notice. My cutlass slapping against my side, my earring dangling from my lobe, my red scarf shining in the sun brightly enough to attract a bull, I strode resolutely across town, thankful that I was still alive, armoring myself against the horrors that awaited me in the Quarter. Many a loud prayer rose from my chaste pink lips, some of thanks, some of supplication. I prayed to St. Mathurin, who is invoked for epilepsy and madness, to aid Mr. Clyde (Mathurin is, incidentally, also the patron saint of clowns). For myself, I sent a humble greeting to St. Medericus, the Hermit, who is invoked against intestinal disorders. Meditating upon the call from the grave which I had almost received, I began to think about my mother, for I have always wondered what her reaction would be were I to die in the cause of paying for her misdeeds. I can see her at the funeral, a shoddy, low-cost affair held in the basement of some dubious funeral parlor. Insane with grief, tears boiling from her reddened eyes, she would probably tear my corpse from the coffin, screaming drunkenly, "Don't take him! Why do the sweetest flowers wither and fall from the stem?" The funeral would probably degenerate into a circus, my mother constantly poking her fingers into the two holes dug in my neck by Mr. Clyde's rusty fork, crying an illiterate Grecian cry of curses and vengeance. There would be a certain amount of spectacle involved in the proceedings, I imagine. However, with my mother acting as director, the inherent tragedy would soon become melodrama. Snatching the white lily from my lifeless hands, she would break it in half and wail to the throng of mourners, well-wishers, celebrants, and sightseers, "As this lily was, so was Ignatius. Now they are both snatched and broken." As she threw the lily back into the coffin, her feeble aim would send it flying directly into my whitened face.

For my mother I sent a prayer flying to St. Zita of Lucca, who spent her life as a house servant and practiced many austerities, in the hope that she would aid my mother in fighting her alcoholism and nighttime roistering.

Strengthened by my interlude of worship, I listened to

the cutlass slapping against my side. It seemed, like some weapon of morality, to be spurring me toward the Quarter, each plastic slap saying, "Take heart, Ignatius. Thou hast a terrible swift sword." I was beginning to feel rather like a Crusader.

At last I crossed Canal Street pretending to ignore the attention paid me by all whom I passed. The narrow streets of the Quarter awaited me. A vagrant petitioned for a hot dog. I waved him away and strode forth. Unfortunately, my feet could not keep pace with my soul. Below my ankles, the tissues were crying for rest and comfort, so I placed the wagon at the curb and seated myself. The balconies of the old buildings hung over my head like dark branches in an allegorical forest of evil. Symbolically, a Desire bus hurtled past me, its diesel exhaust almost strangling me. Closing my eyes for a moment to meditate and thereby draw strength, I must have fallen asleep, for I remember being rudely awakened by a policeman standing next to me prodding me in the ribs with the toe of his shoe. Some musk which my system generates must be especially appealing to the authorities of the government. Who else would be accosted by a policeman while innocently awaiting his mother before a department store? Who else would be spied upon and reported for picking a helpless stray of a kitten from a gutter? Like a bitch in heat, I seem to attract a coterie of policemen and sanitation officials. The world will someday get me on some ludicrous pretext; I simply await the day that they drag me to some air-conditioned dungeon and leave me there beneath the florescent lights and sound-proofed ceiling to pay the price for scorning all that they hold dear within their little latex hearts.

Rising to my full height—a spectacle in itself—I looked down upon the offending policeman and crushed him with *a comment which, fortunately, he failed to understand. Then I wheeled the wagon farther into the Quarter. Because it was early afternoon, there were few people stirring on the streets. I guessed that the residents of the area were still in bed recovering from whatever indecent acts they had been performing the night before. Many no doubt required medical attention: a stitch or two here and there in a torn orifice or a broken genital. I could only imagine how many haggard and depraved eyes were regarding me hungrily from behind the closed shutters. I tried not to think about it. Already I was beginning to feel like an especially toothsome steak in a meat market. However, no one called enticingly from the shutters; those devious mentalities throbbing away in their dark apartments were apparently more subtle seducers. I thought that a note, at least, might flutter down. A frozen orange juice can came flying out of one of the windows and barely missed me. I stooped over and picked it up in order to inspect the empty tin cylinder for a communication of some sort, but only a viscous residue of concentrated juice trickled out on my hand. Was this some obscene message? While I was pondering the matter and staring up at the window from which the can had been hurled, an old vagrant approached the wagon and pleaded for a frankfurter. Grudgingly I sold him one, ruefully concluding that, as always, work was interfering at a crucial moment.*

By now, of course, the window from which the can had been sent flying was closed. I rolled farther down the street, staring at the closed shutters for a sign of some sort. Wild laughter issued from more than one building as I passed. Apparently the deluded occupants therein were indulging in some obscene diversion which amused them. I tried to close my virgin ears to their horrid cackling.

A group of tourists wandered along the streets, their

cameras poised, their glittering eyeglasses shining like sparklers. Noticing me, they paused and, in sharp Midwestern accents which assailed my delicate eardrums like the sounds of a wheat thresher (however unimaginably horrible that must sound), begged me to pose for a photograph. Pleased by their gracious attentions, I acquiesced. For minutes they snapped away as I obliged them with several artful poses. Standing before the wagon as if it were a pirate's vessel, I brandished my cutlass menacingly for one especially memorable pose, my other hand holding the prow of the tin hot dog. As a climax, I attempted to climb atop the wagon, but the solidity of my physique proved too taxing for that rather flimsy vehicle. It began to roll from beneath me, but the gentlemen in the group were kind enough to grab it and assist me down. At last this affable group bade me farewell. As they wandered down the street madly photographing everything in sight, I heard one kindly lady say, "Wasn't that sad? We should have given her something." Unfortunately, none of the others (doubtless right-wing conservatives all) responded to her plea for charity very favorably, thinking, no doubt, that a few cents cast my way would be a vote of confidence for the welfare state. "He would only go out and spend it on more liquor," one of the other women, a shriveled crone whose face bespoke WCTU affiliation, advised her friends with nasal wisdom and an abundance of harsh r's. Apparently the others sided with the WCTU drab, for the group continued down the street.

I must admit that I would not have turned down an offering of some sort. A Working Boy can use every penny that he can get his ambitious and striving hands on. In addition, those photographs could earn those corn-belt clods a fortune in some photographic contest. For a moment, I considered running behind these tourists, but

just then an improbable satire on a tourist, a wan little
figure in Bermuda shorts panting under the weight of a
monstrous apparatus with lenses that certainly must have
been a CinemaScope camera, called out a greeting to me.
Upon closer inspection, I noted that it was, of all people,
Patrolman Mancuso. I, of course, ignored the Machiavel's
faint mongoloid grin by pretending to tighten my earring.
Apparently he has been released from his imprisonment in
the rest room. "How you doing?" he persisted illiterately.
"Where is my book?" I demanded terrifyingly. "I'm still
reading it. It's very good," he answered in terror. "Profit by
its lesson," I cautioned. "When you have completed it, I
shall ask you to submit to me a written critique and
analysis of its message to humanity!" With that order still
ringing magnificently in the air, I strode proudly off down
the street. Then, realizing that I had forgotten the wagon, I
returned grandly to retrieve it. (That wagon is a terrible
liability. I feel as if I am stuck with a retarded child who
deserves constant attention. I feel like a hen sitting on one
particularly large tin egg.)

Well, here it was almost two o'clock, and I had sold
exactly one hot dog. Your Working Boy would have to
bustle if success was to be his goal. The occupants of the
French Quarter obviously did not place frankfurters high
on their list of delicacies, and the tourists were not
apparently coming to colorful and picturesque old N. O. to
gorge themselves upon Paradise products. Clearly I am
going to have what is known in our commercial terminology as a merchandising problem. The evil Clyde has in
vengeance given me a route that is a "White Elephant,"
a term which he once applied to me during the course of
one of our business conferences. Resentment and jealousy
have again struck me down.

In addition, I must devise some means of handling M.

256

Minkoff's latest effronteries. Perhaps the Quarter will provide me with some material: a crusade for taste and decency, for theology and geometry, perhaps.

Social note: A new film featuring my favorite female star, whose recent circus musical excess stunned and overwhelmed me, is opening shortly at one of the downtown movie palaces. I must somehow get to see it. Only my wagon stands in the way. Her new film is billed as a "sophisticated" comedy in which she must certainly reach new heights of perversion and blasphemy.

Health note: Astonishing weight increase, due no doubt to the anxiety which my dear mother's increasing unpleasantness is causing me. It is a truism of human nature, that people learn to hate those who help them. Thus, my mother has turned on me.

Suspendedly,
Lance, Your Besieged Working Boy

V

The lovely girl smiled hopefully at Dr. Talc and breathed, "I just love your course. I mean, it's grand."

"Oh, well," Talc replied delightedly. "That's very kind of you. I'm afraid the course is rather general . . ."

"Your approach to history is so vital, so contemporary, so refreshingly unorthodox."

"I do believe that we must cast aside some of the old forms and approaches." Talc's voice was important, pedantic. Should he invite this charming creature to have a drink with him? "History is, after all, an evolutionary thing."

"I *know*," the girl said, opening her eyes wide enough so that Talc could lose himself in their blueness for a moment or two.

"I only wish to interest my students. Let's face it. The average student is not interested in the history of Celtic Britain. For that matter, neither am I. That's why, even if I do admit it myself, I always sense a sort of rapport in my classes."

"I *know*." The girl brushed gracefully against Talc's expensive tweed sleeve in reaching for her purse. Talc tingled at her touch. This was the sort of girl who should be attending college, not ones like that dreadful Minkoff girl, that brutal and slovenly girl who had almost been raped by one of the janitors just outside of his office. Dr. Talc shuddered at the very thought of Miss Minkoff. In class she had insulted and challenged and vilified him at every turn, egging the Reilly monster to join in the attack. He would never forget those two; no one on the faculty ever would. They were like two Huns sweeping down on Rome. Dr. Talc idly wondered if they had married each other. Each certainly deserved the other. Perhaps they had both defected to Cuba. "Some of those historical characters are so dull."

"That's very true," Talc agreed, eager to join any campaign against the figures of English history, who had been the scourges of his existence for so many years. Simply keeping track of all of them gave him a headache. He paused to light a Benson and Hedges and cleared some of the phlegm of English history from his throat. "They all made so many foolish mistakes."

"I *know*." The girl looked into her compact mirror. Then her eyes hardened and her voice grew a little surly. "Well, I don't want to waste your time with all this historical chatter. I wanted to ask you what happened to that report that I handed in about two months ago. I mean, I'd like to get some idea of what kind of grade I'm going to get in this course."

"Oh, yes," Dr. Talc said vaguely. His hopeful bubble burst. Under their skins students were all alike. The lovely girl had turned into steely-eyed businesswoman checking, adding the profits of her grades. "You handed in a report, did you?"

"I most certainly did. It was in a yellow binder."

"Let me see if I can find it then." Dr. Talc got up and began to look through piles of various antique term papers, reports, and examinations on the top of the bookcase. As he was rearranging the stacks, and old sheet of wide-lined tablet paper folded into an airplane fell out of one binder and glided to the floor. Talc had not noticed the plane, only one of the many that had come sailing through his transom and window one semester a few years earlier. As it landed, the girl picked it up and, seeing that there was writing on the yellowed paper, unfolded the glider.

"Talc: You have been found guilty of misleading and perverting the young. I decree that you be hung by your underdeveloped testicles until dead. zorro" The girl reread the red crayon message, and as Talc continued to press his search on top of the bookcase, she opened her purse, dropped in the airplane, and snapped the clasp.

Ten

Gus Levy was a nice guy. He was also a regular fellow. He had friends among promoters and trainers and coaches and managers across the country. At any arena or stadium or track Gus Levy could count on knowing at least one person connected with the place. He knew owners and ticket sellers and players. He even got a Christmas card every year from a peanut vendor who worked the parking lot across from Memorial Stadium in Baltimore. He was very well liked.

Levy's Lodge was where he went between seasons. He had no friends there. At Christmas the only sign of the season at Levy's Lodge, the only barometer of Yuletide spirit was the appearance of his daughters, who descended upon him from college with demands for additional money coupled with threats to disavow his paternity forever if he continued to mistreat their mother. For Christmas, Mrs. Levy always compiled not a gift list but rather a list of the injustices and brutalities she had suffered since August. The girls got this list in their stockings. The only gift Mrs. Levy asked of the girls was that they attack their father. Mrs. Levy loved Christmas.

Now Mr. Levy was waiting at the lodge for spring practice to begin. Gonzalez had his reservations to Florida and Arizona in order. But at Levy's Lodge it was like Christmas all over again, and what was going on in Levy's Lodge could have been postponed until he left for the practice camps, Mr. Levy thought.

Mrs. Levy had stretched Miss Trixie across his favorite couch, the yellow nylon one, and was rubbing skin cream into the old woman's face. Now and then Miss Trixie's tongue would flap out and sample a bit of cream from her upper lip.

"I'm getting nauseous from watching that," Mr. Levy said. "Can't you take her outside? It's a nice day."

"She likes this couch," Mrs. Levy answered. "Let her have some enjoyment. Why don't *you* go outside and wax your sports car?"

"Silence!" Miss Trixie snarled with the stupendous false teeth that Mrs. Levy had just bought her.

"Listen to that," Mr. Levy said. "She's really running this place."

"So she's asserting herself. Does that bother you? The teeth have given her a little self-confidence. Of course, you begrudge the woman even that. I'm beginning to understand why she's so insecure. I've found out that Gonzalez ignores her all day, makes her feel unwanted in about a hundred different ways. Subconsciously she hates Levy Pants."

"Who doesn't?" said Miss Trixie.

"Sad, sad," was all that Mr. Levy answered.

Miss Trixie grunted and some air whistled through her lips.

"Now let's cut this out," Mr. Levy said. "I've let you play a lot of ridiculous games around here. This one doesn't even make sense. If you want to open a funeral parlor, I'll set you up. But not in my rumpus room. Now wipe that goo off her face and let me drive her back to town. Let me have some peace while I'm in this house."

"So. You're angry all of a sudden. At least you're having a normal response. That's unusual for you."

"Are you doing this just to make me angry? You can make me angry without all this. Now let her alone. All she wants is to retire. It's like torturing a dumb animal."

"I am a very attractive woman," Miss Trixie mumbled in her sleep.

"Listen to that!" Mrs. Levy cried happily. "And you want to throw her out in the snow? I'm just getting through to her. She's like a symbol of everything you haven't done."

Suddenly Miss Trixie leaped up, snarling, "Where's my eyeshade?"

"This is going to be good," Mr. Levy said. "Wait till she sinks those five-hundred-dollar teeth in you."

"Who took my eyeshade?" Miss Trixie demanded fiercely. "Where am I? Take your hands off me."

"Darling," Mrs. Levy began, but Miss Trixie had fallen asleep on her side, her creamed face smearing the couch.

"Look, Fairy Godmother, how much have you spent on this little game already? I'm not paying to have that couch recovered."

"That's right. Spend all your money on the horses. Let this human flounder."

"You'd better take those teeth out of her mouth before she bites off her tongue. Then she'll really be stuck."

"Speaking of tongue, you should have heard all that she told me about Gloria this morning." Mrs. Levy made a gesture that indicated acceptance of injustice and tragedy. "Gloria was the soul of kindness, the first person in years who took an interest in Miss Trixie. Then out of the blue you walk in and kick Gloria out of her life. I think it's given her a very bad trauma. The girls would love to know about Gloria. They'd ask you some questions, believe me."

"I bet they would. You know, I think you're really going out of your mind. There is *no* Gloria. If you keep on talking to your little protégé there, she's going to take you with her right into the twilight zone. When Susan and Sandra come home for Easter, they'll find you bouncing on that board with a paper bag full of rags in your arms."

"Oh, oh. I see. Mere guilt about this Gloria incident. Fighting, resentment. It's all going to end very badly, Gus.

Please skip one of your tournaments and go see Lenny's doctor. The man works miracles, believe me."

"Then ask him to take Levy Pants off our hands. I talked to three realtors this week. Every one of them said it was the most unsalable property they'd ever seen."

"Gus, did I hear correctly? Did I hear you say something about selling your heritage?" Mrs. Levy screamed.

"Quiet!" Miss Trixie snarled. "I'll get you people. Wait and see. You'll get it. I'll get even."

"Oh, shut up," Mrs. Levy shouted at her and pressed her back to the couch, where she promptly dozed off.

"Well, one guy," Mr. Levy continued calmly, "this very aggressive-looking agent, gave me some hope. Like all the others, he said, 'Nobody wants a clothing factory today. The market's dead. Your place is outmoded. Thousands for repairs and modernization. It's got a railroad switch line, but light goods like clothes are going by truck today, and the place is badly located for trucks. Across town from the highways. Southern garment business folding. Even the land's not worth much. The whole area is becoming a slum.' And on and on. But this one agent said maybe he could interest some super-market chain in buying the factory for a store. Well, that sounded good. Then the hitch came in. There's no parking area around Levy Pants, the neighborhood's living median or something is too low to support a big market, and on and on again. He said the only hope was renting it out as a ware-house, but again warehouse revenues are not high and the place is badly located for a warehouse. Something about high-ways again. So don't worry. Levy Pants is still ours, like a chamberpot we inherited."

"A chamberpot? Your father's sweat and blood is a cham-berpot? I see your motive. Destroy the last monument to your father's accomplishments."

"Levy Pants is a monument?"

"Why I ever wanted to work there I'll never know," Miss Trixie said angrily from among the pillows where Mrs. Levy had her pinioned. "Thank goodness poor Gloria got out of there in time."

"Pardon me, ladies," Mr. Levy said, whistling through his teeth. "You two can discuss Gloria alone."

He got up and went into the whirlpool bath. While the water swirled and jetted around him, he wondered how he might somehow be able to dump Levy Pants in the lap of some poor buyer. It must have some uses. A skating rink? A gym? A Negro cathedral? Then he wondered what would happen if he carried Mrs. Levy's exercising table to the seawall and dumped it into the Gulf. He dried himself carefully, put on his terry-cloth robe, and went back into the rumpus room to get his dope sheet.

Miss Trixie was sitting up on the couch. Her face had been cleaned. Her mouth was an orange smear. Her weak eyes were accentuated by shadow. Mrs. Levy was adjusting a coiffed black wig over the old woman's thin hair.

"What in the world are you doing to me now?" Miss Trixie was wheezing at her benefactress. "You'll pay for this."

"Do you believe it?" Mrs. Levy asked her husband proudly, all traces of hostility gone from her voice. "Just look at that."

Mr. Levy couldn't believe it. Miss Trixie looked exactly like Mrs. Levy's mother.

II

In Mattie's Ramble Inn, Jones poured a glassful of beer and sank his long teeth into the foam.

"That Lee woman ain't treatin you right, Jones," Mr. Watson was telling him. "One thing I don like to see a colored man make fun of hisself for being colored. That what she be doin with you fix up like a plantation darky."

"Whoa! Color cats got it har enough without peoples bustin out laughin cause they color. Shit. I make my mistake when I tell that Lee mother a po-lice tell me to get a job. I shoulda tell her them fair employmen peoples sendin me over, scare that gal a little."

"You better go to the po-lice and tell them you quittin at that place but you gonna fin you another job."

"Hey! I ain walkin in no precinc and flappin my mouth at no po-lice. Them po-lice take one look at me, throw my ass in jail. Whoa! Color peoples cain fin no job, but they sure can fin a openin in jail. Goin in jail the bes way you get you somethin to eat regular. But I rather starve *outside*. I rather mop a whore floor than go to jail and be makin plenny license plate and rug and leather belt and shit. I jus was stupor enough to get my ass snatch up in a trap at that Night of Joy. I gotta figure this thing out myself."

"I still say you go to the po-lice and tell them you be between job a little while."

"Yeah. And maybe I be between job about fifdy year. I ain seen no peoples screamin for unskill color cats. Ooo-wee. Somebody like that Lee bastar know plenny po-lice. Otherwise that B-drinker, knockout drop cathouse be close down long ago. I ain takin no chance going to no Lee frien in the po-lice and sayin, 'Hey, man, I jus be vagran a little while.' He say, 'Okay, boy, you be servin jus a little while, too.' Whoa!"

"Well, how the sabotage comin along."

"Pretty poor. Lee make me work overtime on the floor the other day, she see the crap gettin a little thicker so pretty soon her poor, stupor customer be up to they ankle in dus. Shit. I tol you I wrote a address on one of her orphan package, so if she still distributin for the United Fun maybe we be gettin some answer on that. I sure like to see wha that address bringin in. Maybe it'll be bringin in a po-lice. Whoa!"

"It pretty clear you not gettin nowhere. Go talk to the po-lice, man. They understand your story."

"I *scare* of the po-lice, Watson. Ooo-wee. You be scare, too, if you was jus standin in Woolsworth and some po-lice drag you off. Especially when Lee probly goin roun the whirl with half the po-lice on the force. Whoa!" Jones sent up what looked like a cloud, a radioactive one which gradually sent some fallout down onto the bar and the cooler filled with pickled meat. "Say, whatever happen to that dumb mother was in here that day, the one workin for Levy Pant? You ever seen him aroun again?"

"The man talking about demonstratin?"

"Yeah, the cat got him that fat white freak for a leader, the one tellin them poor color peoples they suppose to drop a nucular bum on top they factory, kill theirselves and get what's left of their ass throwed in jail."

"I ain't seen him since."

"Shit. I like to fin out where that fat freak hidin out. Maybe I call up Levy Pant and ax for him. I like to drop him in the Night of Joy like a nucular bum. Seem like he the kin make that Lee mother shit in her drawer. Whoa! If I gonna be a doorman, I gonna be the mos sabotagin doorman ever guarded a plantation. Ooo-wee. The cotton fiel be burn to the groun before I'm through."

"Watch out, Jones. Don be gettin yourself in no trouble."

"Whoa!"

III

Ignatius was beginning to feel worse and worse. His valve seemed to be glued, and no amount of bouncing was opening it. Great belches ripped out of the gas pockets of his stomach

266

and tore through his digestive tract. Some escaped noisily. Others, weaning belches, lodged in his chest and caused massive heartburn.

The physical cause for this health decline was, he knew, the too strenuous consuming of Paradise products. But there were other, subtler reasons. His mother was becoming increasingly bold and overtly antagonistic; it was becoming impossible to control her. Perhaps she had joined some fringe group of the far right wing that was making her belligerent and hostile. At any rate, she certainly had been carrying on a witchhunt in the brown kitchen recently, asking him all sorts of questions concerning his political philosophy. Which was strange. His mother had always been notably apolitical, voting only for candidates who seemed to have been kind to their mothers. Mrs. Reilly had been solidly behind Franklin Roosevelt for four terms not because of the New Deal, but because his mother, Mrs. Sara Roosevelt, seemed to have been respected and well treated by her son. Mrs. Reilly had also voted for the Truman woman standing before her Victorian house in Independence, Missouri, and not specifically for Harry Truman. To Mrs. Reilly, Nixon and Kennedy had meant Hannah and Rose. Motherless candidates confused her, and in motherless elections she stayed at home. Ignatius could not understand her sudden, clumsy effort to protect the American Way against her son.

Then there was Myrna, who had been appearing to him in a series of dreams that was taking the form of the old Batman serials that he had seen at the Prytania as a child. One chapter followed the other. In one gruesome chapter, he had been standing on a subway platform, reincarnated as St. James, the Less, who was martyred by the Jews. Myrna appeared through a turnstile carrying a NON-VIOLENT CONGRESS FOR THE SEXUALLY NEEDY placard and began heckling him. "Jesus will come to the fore, skins or not,"

Ignatius-St. James prophesied grandly. But Myrna, sneering, pushed him with the placard onto the tracks before the speeding subway train. He had awakened just as the train was about to crush him. The M. Minkoff dreams were getting worse than the old, terrifying Scenicruiser dreams in which Ignatius, magnificent on the upper deck, had ridden doomed buses over the rails of bridges and into collisions with jets taxiing along airport runways.

By night he was plagued by dreams and by day by the impossible route that Mr. Clyde had given him. No one in the French Quarter, it seemed, was interested in hot dogs. So his take-home pay was getting smaller, and his mother, in turn, was getting surlier. When and how would this vicious cycle end?

He had read in the morning paper that a ladies' art guild was having a hanging of its paintings in Pirate's Alley. Imagining that the paintings would be offensive enough to interest him for a while, he pushed his wagon up onto the flagstones of the Alley toward the variety of artwork dangling from the iron pickets of the fence behind the Cathedral. On the prow of the wagon, in an attempt to attract business among the Quarterites, Ignatius taped a sheet of Big Chief paper on which he had printed in crayon: TWELVE INCHES (12) OF PARADISE. So far no one had responded to its message.

The Alley was filled with well-dressed ladies in large hats. Ignatius pointed the prow of the wagon into the throng and pushed forward. A woman read the Big Chief statement and screamed, summoning her companions to draw aside from the ghastly apparition that had appeared at their art show.

"Hot dogs, ladies?" Ignatius asked pleasantly.

The ladies' eyes studied the sign, the earring, the scarf, the cutlass, and pleaded for him to move along. Rain for their hanging would have been bad enough. But *this*.

"Hot dogs, hot dogs," Ignatius said a little angrily. "Savories from the hygienic Paradise kitchens."

He belched violently during the silence that followed. The ladies pretended to study the sky and the little garden behind the Cathedral.

Ignatius lumbered over to the picket fence, abandoning the hopeless cause espoused by the wagon, and viewed the oil paintings and pastels and watercolors strung there. Although the style of each varied in crudity, the subjects of the paintings were relatively similar: camellias floating in bowls of water, azaleas tortured into ambitious flower arrangements, magnolias that looked like white windmills. Ignatius scrutinized the offerings furiously for a while all by himself, for the ladies had stepped back from the fence and had formed what looked like a protective little grouping. The wagon, too, stood forlorn on the flagstones, several feet from the newest member of the art guild.

"Oh, my God!" Ignatius bellowed after he had promenaded up and down along the fence. "How dare you present such abortions to the public."

"Please move along, sir," a bold lady said.

"Magnolias don't look like that," Ignatius said, thrusting his cutlass at the offending pastel magnolia. "You ladies need a course in botany. And perhaps geometry, too."

"You don't *have* to look at our work," an offended voice said from the group, the voice of the lady who had drawn the magnolia in question.

"Yes, I do!" Ignatius screamed. "You ladies need a critic with some taste and decency. Good heavens! Which one of you did this camellia? Speak up. The water in this bowl looks like motor oil."

"Let us alone," a shrill voice said.

"You women had better stop giving teas and brunches and settle down to the business of learning how to draw," Ignatius thundered. "First, you must learn how to handle a brush. I would suggest that you all get together and paint someone's house for a start."

"Go away."

"Had you 'artists' had a part in the decoration of the Sistine Chapel, it would have ended up looking like a particularly vulgar train terminal," Ignatius snorted.

"We don't intend to be insulted by a coarse vendor," a spokeswoman for the band of large hats said haughtily.

"I see!" Ignatius screamed. "So it is you people who slander the reputation of the hot dog vendor."

"He's mad."

"He's so common."

"So coarse."

"Don't encourage him."

"We don't want you here," the spokeswoman said tartly and simply.

"I should imagine not!" Ignatius was breathing heavily. "Apparently you are afraid of someone who has some contact with reality, who can truthfully describe to you the offenses which you have committed to canvas."

"Please leave," the spokeswoman ordered.

"I shall." Ignatius grabbed the handle of his cart and pushed off. "You women should all be on your knees begging forgiveness for what I have seen here on this fence."

"The city is certainly going down when *that's* out on the streets," a woman said as Ignatius waddled off down the Alley.

Ignatius was surprised to feel a small rock bounce off the back of his head. Angrily, he shoved the wagon along the flagstones until he was near the end of the alley. There he parked the wagon in a little passageway so that it would be out of sight. His feet hurt, and while he was resting he didn't want anyone to bother him by asking for a hot dog. Even though business couldn't be worse, there were times when a person had to be true to himself and consider his welfare first. Much more of this vending and his feet would be bloody stumps.

Ignatius squatted uncomfortably on the side steps of the Cathedral. His recently increased weight and the bloating caused by the inoperative valve made any position other than standing or lying down somewhat awkward. Removing his boots, he began to inspect his great slabs of feet.

"Oh, dear," a voice said above Ignatius. "What am I seeing? I come out to see this dreadful, tacky art exhibit, and what do I find as Exhibit Number One? It's the ghost of Lafitte, the pirate. No. It's Fatty Arbuckle. Or is it Marie Dressler? Tell me soon or I'll die."

Ignatius looked up and saw the young man who had bought his mother's hat in the Night of Joy.

"Get away from me, you fop. Where is my mother's hat?"

"Oh, that," the young man sighed. "I'm afraid it was destroyed at a really wild gathering. Everyone dearly loved it."

"I'm sure that they did. I won't ask you just how it was desecrated."

"I wouldn't remember anyway. Too many martinis that night for little *moi*."

"Oh, my God."

"What in God's name are you doing in that bizarre outfit? You look like Charles Laughton in drag as the Queen of the Gypsies. What *are* you supposed to be? I really want to know."

"Move along, you coxcomb," Ignatius belched, the gassy eructations echoing between the walls of the Alley. The women's art guild turned its hats toward the source of the volcanic sound. Ignatius glared at the young man's tawny velvet jacket and mauve cashmere sweater and the wave of blonde hair that fell over the forehead of his sharp, glittering face. "Get away from me before I strike you down."

"Oh, my goodness," the young man laughed in short,

merry, childish breaths that made his downy jacket quiver. "You really are insane, aren't you?"

"How dare you!" Ignatius screamed. He unpinned his cutlass and began to strike the young man's calves with the plastic weapon. The young man giggled and danced about in front of Ignatius to avoid the thrusts, his lithe movements making him a difficult target. Finally he danced across the Alley and waved to Ignatius. Ignatius picked up one of his elephantine desert boots and flung it at the pirouetting figure.

"Oh," the young man squealed. He caught the shoe and threw it back at Ignatius, whom it hit squarely in the face.

"Oh, my God! I've been disfigured."

"Shut up."

"I can easily have you booked for assault."

"If I were you, I'd stay as far away from the police as possible. What do you think they'd say when they saw that outfit, Mary Marvel? And booking *me* with assault? Let's be a little realistic. I'm surprised that they're permitting you to go cruising at all in that fortune-teller's ensemble." The young man clicked his lighter open, lit a Salem, and clicked it closed. "And with those bare feet and that toy sword? Are you kidding?"

"The police will believe anything I tell them."

"Get with it, please."

"You may be locked away for several years."

"Oh, you really are on the moon."

"Well, I certainly don't have to sit here listening to you," Ignatius said, putting on his suede boots.

"Oh!" the young man shrieked happily. "That look on your face. Like Bette Davis with indigestion."

"Don't talk to me, you degenerate. Go play with your little friends. I am certain that the Quarter is crawling with them."

"How is that dear mother of yours?"

"I don't want to hear her sainted name cross your decadent lips."

"Well, since it already has, is she all right? She's so sweet and dear, that woman, so unspoiled. You're very lucky."

"I will not discuss her with you."

"If that's the way you want to be, all right. I just hope that she doesn't know that you're flouncing around the streets like some sort of Hungarian Joan of Arc. That earring. It's so Magyar."

"If you want a costume like this, then buy one," Ignatius said. "Let me alone."

"I know that something like that couldn't be bought anywhere. Oh, but it would bring the house down at a party."

"I suspect that the parties you attend must be true visions of the apocalypse. I knew that our society was coming to this. In a few years, you and your friends will probably take over the country."

"Oh, we're planning to," the young man said with a bright smile. "We have connections in the highest places. You'd be surprised."

"No, I wouldn't. Hroswitha could have predicted this long ago."

"Who in the world is that?"

"A sibyl of a medieval nun. She has guided my life."

"Oh, you're truly fantastic," the young man said gleefully. "And although I didn't think it would be possible, you've gained weight. Where will you ever end? There's something so unbelievably tacky about your obesity."

Ignatius rose to his feet and stabbed the young man in the chest with his plastic cutlass.

"Take that, you offal," Ignatius cried, digging the cutlass into the cashmere sweater. The tip of the cutlass broke off and fell to the flagstone walk.

"Oh, dear," the young man shrieked. "You'll tear my sweater, you big crazy thing."

Down the Alley the women's art guild members were removing their paintings from the fence and folding their aluminum lawn chairs like Arabs in preparation for stealing away. Their annual outdoor exhibit had been ruined.

"I am the avenging sword of taste and decency," Ignatius was shouting. As he slashed at the sweater with his broken weapon, the ladies began to dash out the Royal Street end of the Alley. A few stragglers were snatching at their magnolias and camellias in panic.

"Why did I ever stop to talk to you, you maniac?" the young man asked in a vicious and breathless whisper. "This is my very finest sweater."

"Whore!" Ignatius cried, scraping the cutlass across the young man's chest.

"Oh, isn't this horrible."

He tried to run away, but Ignatius had been holding his arm firmly with the hand that was not wielding the cutlass. Slipping a finger through Ignatius' hoop earring, the young man pulled downward, breathing to Ignatius, "Drop that sword."

"Good grief." Ignatius dropped the sword onto the flagstones. "I think that my ear is broken."

The young man released the earring.

"Now you've done it!" Ignatius slobbered. "You will rot in a federal prison for the remainder of your life."

"Just look at my sweater, you disgusting monster."

"Only the most flamboyant offal would be seen in a miscarriage like that. You must have some shame or at least some taste in dress."

"You awful creature. You huge *thing*."

"I will probably spend several years at the Eye, Ear, Nose, and Throat Hospital having this attended to," Ignatius said, fingering his ear. "You may expect to receive some rather staggering medical bills each month. My corps of attorneys will contact you in the morning wherever it is that you carry on your questionable activities. I shall warn them beforehand that they may expect to see and hear anything. They are all brilliant attorneys, pillars of the community, aristocratic Creole scholars whose knowledge of the more surreptitious forms of living is quite limited. They may even refuse to see you. A considerably lesser representative may be sent to call upon you, some junior partner whom they've taken in out of pity."

"You awful, terrible animal."

"However, to save you the anxiety of awaiting this phalanx of legal luminaries to arrive at your spider web of an apartment, I shall consent to accepting a settlement now, if you wish. Five or six dollars should suffice."

"My sweater cost me forty dollars," the young man said. He felt the worn portion that had been scraped by the cutlass. "Are you prepared to pay for it?"

"Of course not. Never become involved in an altercation with a pauper."

"I can easily sue you."

"Perhaps we should both drop the idea of legal recourse. For an event so auspicious as a courtroom trial, you would probably get completely carried away and appear in a tiara and evening gown. An old judge would grow quite confused. Both of us would doubtlessly be found guilty on some trumped up charge."

"You revolting beast."

"Why don't you run along and partake in some dubious recreation that appeals to you," Ignatius belched. "Look, there's a sailor drifting along Chartres Street. He looks rather lonely."

The young man glanced down to the Chartres Street end of the Alley.

"Oh, him," he said. "That's only Timmy."

"Timmy?" Ignatius asked angrily. "Do you know him?"

"Of course," the young man said in a voice heavy with boredom. "He's one of my dearest, *oldest* friends. He's not a sailor at all."

"What?" Ignatius thundered. "Do you mean that he is impersonating a member of the armed forces of this country?"

"That's not all he impersonates."

"This is extremely serious." Ignatius frowned and the red sateen scarf rode down on his hunting cap. "Every soldier and sailor that we see could simply be some mad decadent in disguise. My God! We may all be trapped in some horrible conspiracy. I knew that something like this was going to happen. The United States is probably totally defenseless!"

The young man and the sailor waved at each other familiarly, and the sailor drifted out of sight around the front of the Cathedral. Following a few steps behind the sailor, Patrolman Mancuso appeared at the end of Pirate's Alley wearing a beret and goatee.

"Oh!" the young man shrieked gaily, watching Patrolman Mancuso stalking the sailor. "It's that marvelous policeman. Don't they know that everyone in the Quarter knows who he is?"

"Do you know him, too?" Ignatius asked guardedly. "He's a very dangerous man!"

"Everyone knows him. Thank goodness he's back again. We were beginning to wonder what had happened to him. We love him dearly. Oh, I simply wait to see what new disguise they put on him. You should have seen him a few weeks ago before he had disappeared, he was just too much in that cowboy outfit." The young man exploded in wild laughter. "He could hardly walk in these boots, his ankles kept giving way. Once he stopped me on Chartres when I was going truly mad with your mother's W.P.A. hat. Then he stopped me again on Dumaine and tried to start a conversation. That day he was wearing horn-rimmed glasses and a crew sweater, and he told me that he was a Princeton student down here on a vacation. He's just fabulous. I'm so glad the police have returned him to the people who truly appreciate him. I'm sure he was being wasted wherever he was recently. Oh, that accent of his. Some people like him best as the British tourist. That is choice. But I've always preferred his southern colonel. It's really a matter of taste, I guess. We've had him arrested twice for making indecent proposals. That's always wonderfully confusing to the police. I do hope that we haven't gotten him in too much trouble, for he's close to our hearts."

"He is thoroughly evil," Ignatius observed. Then he said, "I wonder how many of our 'military' are simply people like your friend, disguised tarts."

"Who knows? I wish they all were."

"Of course," Ignatius said in a thoughtful, serious voice, "this could be a worldwide deception." The red sateen scarf rode up and down. "The next war could turn out to be one massive orgy. Good grief. How many of the military leaders of the world may simply be deranged old sodomites acting out some fake fantasy role? Actually, this might be quite beneficial to the world. It could mean an end to war forever. This could be the key to lasting peace."

"It certainly could," the young man said pleasantly. "Peace at any price."

Two nerve ends in Ignatius' mind met and formed an immediate association. Perhaps he had found a means of assaulting the effrontery of M. Minkoff.

"The power-crazed leaders of the world would certainly be surprised to find that their military leaders and troops were only masquerading sodomites who were only too eager to meet the masquerading sodomite armies of other nations in order to have dances and balls and learn some foreign dance steps."

"Wouldn't that be wonderful? The government would pay us to travel. How divine. We would bring an end to world strife and renew people's hope and faith."

"Perhaps you are the hope for the future," Ignatius said, dramatically pounding one paw into the other. "There certainly doesn't seem to be anything else very promising on the horizon."

"We would also help to end the population explosion."

"Oh, my God!" The blue and yellow eyes flashed wildly. "Your method would probably be more satisfying and acceptable than the rather stringent birth control tactics which I have always advocated. I must dedicate some space to this in my writings. This subject deserves the attention of a profound thinker who has a certain perspective on the world's cultural development. I am certainly glad that you have given me this valuable new insight."

"Oh, what a fun day this has been. You're a gypsy. Timmy's a sailor. The marvelous policeman's an artist." The young man sighed. "It's just like Mardi Gras, and I feel so left out. I think I'll go home and throw something on."

"Wait just a moment," Ignatius said. He couldn't permit this opportunity to slip through his swollen fingers.

"I'll put on some clogs. I'm in my Ruby Keeler phase," the young man told Ignatius gaily. Then he began to sing, "'You go home and get your scanties, I'll go home and get my panties, and away we'll go. Oh-ho-ho. Off we're gonna shuffle, shuffle off to Buffalo-ho-ho . . .'"

"Stop that offensive performance," Ignatius ordered angrily. These people must be whipped into line.

The young man did a little soft shoe around Ignatius and said, "Ruby was such a darling. I watch her old movies on television religiously. 'And for just a silver quarter, we can tip the pullman porter, turn the lights down low, oh-ho-ho, off we're gonna shuffle, shuffle off to . . .'"

"Please be serious for a moment. Stop fluttering around here."

"*Moi?* Fluttering? What do you want, Gypsy Woman?"

"Have you people considered forming a political party and running a candidate?"

"Politics? Oh, Maid of Orleans. How dreary."

"This is very important!" Ignatius shouted worriedly. He would show Myrna how to inject sex into politics. "Although I had never considered it before, you may hold the key to the future."

"Well, what do you want to do about it, Eleanor Roosevelt?"

"You must start a party organization. Plans must be made."

"Oh, please," the young man sighed. "All this man's talk is making my mind reel."

"We may be able to save the world!" Ignatius bellowed in an orator's voice. "Good heavens. Why haven't I thought of this before?"

"This kind of conversation depresses me more than you could possibly imagine," the young man told him. "You're beginning to remind me of my father, and what could be more depressing than that?" The young man sighed. "I'm afraid I'll have to be running along. It's costume time."

"No!" Ignatius grabbed the lapel of the young man's jacket.

"Oh, my goodness," the young man breathed, putting his hand to his throat. "Now I'll be on pills all night."

"We must organize immediately."

"I can't tell you how much you're depressing me."

"There must be a large organizational meeting to kick off the campaign."

"Wouldn't that be something like a party?"

"Yes, in a way. However, it would have to express your purpose."

"Then it might be sort of fun. You can't imagine how drab, drab the parties have been lately."

"This is not to be a party, you ass."

"Oh, we'll be very serious."

"Good. Now listen to me. I must come to lecture to you people so that you will be set upon the correct path. I have a rather extensive knowledge of political organization."

"Marvelous. And you must wear that fantastic costume. I can assure you that you'll get everyone's undivided attention," the young man shrieked, covering his mouth with a hand. "Oh, my dear, what a wild gathering it could be."

"There is no time to be lost," Ignatius said sternly. "The apocalypse is near at hand."

"We'll have it next week at my place."

"You must have some red, white, and blue bunting," Ignatius advised. "Political meetings always have that."

"I'll have yards and yards of it. What a decorating job lies ahead. I'll have to get some close friends in to help me."

"Yes, do that," Ignatius said excitedly. "Begin organizing at every level."

"Oh, I never guessed that you would be such a fun person to know. You were so hostile in that dreadful, tacky bar."

"My being has many facets."

"You amaze me." The young man stared at Ignatius' outfit. "To think that they're letting you run around loose. In a way, I respect you."

"Thank you very much." Ignatius' voice was smooth, pleased. "Most fools don't comprehend my worldview at all."

"I wouldn't imagine so."

"I suspect that beneath your offensively and vulgarly effemi-nate façade there may be a soul of sorts. Have you read widely in Boethius?"

"Who? Oh, heavens no. I never even read newspapers."

"Then you must begin a reading program immediately so

that you may understand the crises of our age," Ignatius said solemnly. "Begin with the late Romans, including Boethius, of course. Then you should dip rather extensively into early Medieval. You may skip the Renaissance and the Enlightenment. That is mostly dangerous propaganda. Now that I think of it, you had better skip the Romantics and the Victorians, too. For the contemporary period, you should study some selected comic books."

"You're fantastic."

"I recommend Batman especially, for he tends to transcend the abysmal society in which he's found himself. His morality is rather rigid, also. I rather respect Batman."

"Oh, look, there's Timmy again," the young man said. The sailor was passing on Chartres Street in the opposite direction. "Doesn't he ever get tired of the same old route? Back and forth, back and forth. Look at him. It's winter and he's still wearing his summer whites. Of course he doesn't realize that he's a sitting duck for the shore patrol. You can't imagine how stupid and foolish that boy is."

"His face did appear rather clouded," Ignatius said. The artist in the beret and goatee passed Chartres, busily following the sailor by several feet. "Oh, my God! That ludicrous law officer will ruin everything. He's the fly in everyone's ointment. Perhaps you should run along and get the deranged sailor off the street. If the naval authorities apprehend him, they will discover that he is an imposter, and our political strategy will be undone. Spirit that clown away before he wrecks the most fiendish political coup in the history of western civilization."

"Oh!" the young man shrieked happily. "I'll go back and tell him about it. When he hears what he's almost done, he'll scream and faint."

"Now don't slacken in your preparations," Ignatius warned.

"I'll work myself to exhaustion," the young man said gaily.

"Ward meetings, voter registration, pamphlets, committees. We'll start the kickoff rally around eightish. I'm on St. Peter Street, the yellow stucco building just off Royal. You can't miss it. Here's my card."

"Oh, my God!" Ignatius mumbled, looking at the austere little calling card. "You can't really be named Dorian Greene."

"Yes, isn't that wild?" Dorian asked languidly. "If I told you my real name, you'd never speak to me again. It's so common I could die just thinking of it. I was born on a wheat farm in Nebraska. You can take it from there."

"Well, at any rate, I am Ignatius J. Reilly."

"That isn't too dreadful. I sort of imagined you as a Horace or Humphrey or something like that. Well, don't fail us. Practice your speech. I guarantee a large crowd, everyone is almost dead from ennui and general depression, so they'll be fighting for invitations. Give me a tinkle and we'll iron out the exact date."

"Be sure to stress the importance of this historic conclave," Ignatius said. "We shall want no fly-by-nights in this core group."

"There may be a few costumes. That's what's so wonderful about New Orleans. You can masquerade and Mardi Gras all year round if you want to. Really, sometimes the Quarter is like one big costume ball. Sometimes I can't tell friend from foe. But if you oppose costumes, I'll tell everyone, although their little hearts will snap with disappointment. We haven't had a good party in months."

"I would not oppose a few tasteful and decent maskers," Ignatius said at last. "They may add the proper international atmosphere to the meeting. Politicians always seem to want to shake hands with mongoloids in ethnic and native costumes. Now that I think of it, you may encourage a costume or two. We do not want any female impersonators, however. I don't believe that politicians care to be seen with them particularly. They cause resentment among rural voters, I suspect."

"Now let me run along and find that silly Timmy. I'll frighten him to death."

"Beware of that Machiavel of a policeman. If he gets wind of the plot, we're lost."

"Oh, if I weren't so glad to see him back on the beat, I'd telephone the police and have him arrested immediately for soliciting. You don't know the wonderful expression that man used to get on his face when the squad car arrived to take him off. And the arresting officers. It was too priceless. But we'll all be so grateful to have him back. No one will dare mistreat him now. So long, Gypsy Mother."

Dorian skipped off down the alley to find the decadent mariner. Ignatius looked toward Royal Street and wondered what had happened to the women's art guild. He lumbered over to the passageway where his cart was hidden, prepared a hot dog, and prayed that some customers would happen along before the day was over. Sadly he realized how low Fortuna had spun his wheel. He had never imagined that he would one day be praying that people buy hot dogs from him. At least he had a magnificent new scheme ready for launching against M. Minkoff. The thought of the kickoff rally cheered him greatly. This time the minx would be totally confounded.

IV

It was all a matter of storage. From almost one to three every afternoon George was stuck with the packages. One afternoon he had gone to a movie, but even there in the dark watching a double bill of two nudist colony films he wasn't comfortable. He was afraid to put the packages down on an adjoining seat, especially in a theater like that one. Holding them in his lap, he was reminded of the burden throughout the three hours of tanned flesh that filled the screen. On the other days he had carried them around with him during boring wanderings through the business district and the Quarter. But by three o'clock he was so tired from the marathon of strolling that he hardly had the enthusiasm to negotiate his day's business; and in two hours of being carried, the wrapping on the packages got damp and started to break. If one of those packages broke open on the street, he could plan to spend the next few years in a juvenile detention home. Why had that undercover agent tried to arrest him in the rest room? He hadn't done a thing. That agent must have had some sort of detective ESP.

Finally George thought of a place that would at least guarantee him some rest and a chance to sit down, St. Louis Cathedral. He sat in one of the pews next to a bank of vigil lights and decorated his hands, his packages stacked beside him. When his hands were done, he picked a missal from the rack before him and looked through it, refreshing his dim knowledge of the mechanics of the Mass by studying the drawings of the celebrant as he moved through the devotions. The Mass was really very simple, George thought. Until it was time to leave he flipped back and forth through the missal. Then he gathered up his packages and went out onto Chartres Street.

A sailor leaning against a lamppost winked at him. George acknowledged the greeting with an obscene gesture of his tatooed hands and slouched off down the street. As he passed Pirate's Alley, he heard screaming. There in the Alley the crazy hot dog vendor was trying to stab a fairy with a plastic knife. That vendor was really far out. George paused for a second to look at the earring and scarf that were heaving and bobbing while the fairy shrieked. That vendor probably didn't know what day it was or what month or even what year. He must have thought today was Mardi Gras.

Just in time George saw the rest room undercover agent coming down the street behind the sailor. He looked like a beatnik. George ran behind one of the arches of the ancient Spanish governmental building, the Cabildo, and dashed through the arcade out onto St. Peter Street, where he continued running until he reached Royal and headed uptown to the bus lines.

Now the undercover agent was prowling around the Cathedral. George had to give it to the cops. They were really on the ball. Christ. A guy didn't have a chance.

So his mind returned to the matter of storage. He was beginning to feel like some escaped convict hiding out from the cops. Where now? He climbed on an outbound Desire bus and pondered the matter while the bus swung around and headed out on Bourbon Street, passing by the Night of Joy. Lana Lee was out on the sidewalk giving the jig some directions about a poster he was putting up in the glass case on the front of the bar. The jig flipped a cigarette that would have set Miss Lee's hair on fire if it hadn't been aimed by a master marksman. As it was, the butt sailed over Miss Lee's head with about an inch to spare. These jigs were really getting smart. George would have to ride into one of their neighborhoods one of these nights and toss a few eggs. He and his friends hadn't done that in a long time, driving along in someone's souped-up car and splattering whatever jigs were stupid enough to be standing out on the sidewalk.

But back to the matter of storage. The bus crossed Elysian Fields before George came up with anything. There it was. It had been before him all the time and he just hadn't realized it. He could have kicked himself in the shins with the stiletto toes of his flamenco boots. He saw a nice, roomy, weather-tight metal compartment, a mobile safety deposit box that no undercover agent in the world, however crafty, would think of opening, a safe vault operated by the biggest patsy in the world: the bun compartment in that oddball vendor's wagon.

Eleven

"Aw, look," Santa said, holding the newspaper close to her eyes. "They got a cute picture show on in the neighborhood with little Debbie Reynolds."

"Aw, she's sweet," Mrs. Reilly said. "You like her, Claude?"

"Who's that?" Mr. Robichaux asked pleasantly.

"Little Debra Reynolds," Mrs. Reilly answered.

"I don't think I can place her. I don't go to the show much."

"She's darling," Santa said. "So petite. You ever seen her in that cute picture where she played Tammy, Irene?"

"Ain't that the picture where she went blind?"

"No, girl! You must be thinking of the wrong show."

"Oh, I know who I was thinking of, precious. I was thinking of June Wyman. She was sweet, too."

"Aw, she was good," Santa said. "I remember that picture where she played the dummy who got herself raped."

"Lord, I'm glad I didn't go see that show."

"Aw, it was wonderful, babe. Very dramatic. You know? The look on that poor dummy's face when she got raped. I'll never forget it."

"Anybody want more coffee?" Mr. Robichaux asked.

"Yeah, gimmee some there, Claude," Santa said, folding the newspaper and throwing it on top of the refrigerator. "I'm sure sorry Angelo couldn't make it. That poor boy. He told me he's gonna be working day and night on his own so he can bring somebody in. He's out someplace tonight, I guess. You oughta heard what his Rita been telling me. It seems Angelo went out an bought a lot of expensive clothes he can wear so maybe he can attract some character. Ain't

287

that a shame. That just shows you how much that boy loves the force. If they was to kick him out, it'd break his heart. I sure hope he takes in some bum."

"Angelo's got him a hard road to travel," Mrs. Reilly said absently. She was thinking of the PEACE TO MEN OF GOOD WILL sign that Ignatius had tacked to the front of their house after he had come home from work. Miss Annie had immediately started an inquisition about that as soon as it had appeared, screaming questions through her shutters. "What you think about somebody wants peace, Claude?"

"That sounds like a communiss to me."

Mrs. Reilly's worst fears were realized.

"Who wants peace?" Santa asked.

"Ignatius got a sign up in front the house about peace."

"I mighta known," Santa said angrily. "First that boy wants a king, now he wants peace. I'm telling you, Irene. For your own good. That boy's gotta be put away."

"He ain't wearing no earring. I ask him and he says, 'I ain't wearing no earring, momma.'"

"Angelo don't lie."

"Maybe he just got him a small one."

"A earring's a earring to me. Ain't that right, Claude?"

"That's right," Claude answered Santa.

"Santa, honey, that's a sweet little Blessed Virgin you got on top that T.V.," Mrs. Reilly said to get them off the earring topic.

Everyone looked at the television set next to the refrigerator, and Santa said, "Ain't that nice, though? It's a little Our Lady of the Television. It's got a suction cup base so I don't knock it over when I'm banging around in the kitchen. I bought it by Lenny's."

"Lenny's got everything," Mrs. Reilly said. "It looks like it's made outta nice plastic, too, don't break."

"Well, how you kids liked that dinner?"

"It was delicious," Mr. Robichaux said.

"It was wonderful," Mrs. Reilly agreed. "I ain't had me a good meal in a long time."

"Aarff," Santa belched. "I think I put too much garlic in them stuffed eggplants, but I got a heavy hand with garlic. Even my granchirren tell me, they say, 'Hey, maw-maw, you sure got a heavy hand with garlic.'"

"Ain't that sweet," Mrs. Reilly said of the gourmet grandchildren.

"I thought the eggplants was fine," Mr. Robichaux said.

"I'm only happy when I'm scrubbing my floors and cooking my food," Santa told her guests. "I love to fix a big pot of meatballs or jumbalaya with shrimps."

"I like to cook," Mr. Robichaux said. "It helps out my daughter sometimes."

"I bet it does," Santa said. "A man who can cook is a big help around the house, believe me." She kicked Mrs. Reilly under the table. "A woman's got a man that likes to cook is a lucky girl."

"You like to cook, Irene?" Mr. Robichaux asked.

"You talking to me, Claude?" Mrs. Reilly had been wondering what Ignatius looked like in an earring.

"Come back out the clouds, girl," Santa ordered. "Claude here was axing you if you like to cook."

"Yeah," Mrs. Reilly lied. "I like to cook okay. But sometimes it gets so hot in that kitchen, especially in the summer. You don't get no breezy out that alley. Ignatius likes to eat junk, anyways. You give Ignatius a few bottles of Dr. Nut and plenty bakery cakes, and he's satisfied."

"You oughta get you a letrit range," Mr. Robichaux said. "I bought my daughter one. It don't get hot like a gas stove."

"Where you getting all this money from, Claude?" Santa asked interestedly.

"I got me a nice pension from the railroad. I was with

them for forty-five years, you know. They gimme a beautiful gold pin when I retired."

"Ain't that nice," Mrs. Reilly said. "You made good, huh, Claude?"

"Then," Mr. Robichaux said, "I got me a few little rental properties around my house. I was always putting a little of my salary aside to invest in properties. Property's a good investment."

"It sure is," Santa said, rolling her eyes wildly at Mrs. Reilly. "Now you well fixed, huh?"

"I'm pretty comfortable. But you know sometimes I get tired of living with my daughter and her husband. I mean, they're young. They got they own family. They are very nice to me, but I'd rather have my own home. You know what I mean?"

"If I was you," Mrs. Reilly said, "I'd stay where I was. If your little daughter don't mind having you around, you got you a nice setup. I wisht I had me a nice child. Be grateful for what you got, Claude."

Santa ground the heel of her shoe into Mrs. Reilly's ankle.

"Ouch!" Mrs. Reilly cried.

"Lord, I'm sorry, babe. Me and my big feet. Big feet's always been my problem. They can hardly fit me down by the shoe store. That clerk sees me coming, and he says, 'Lord, here comes Miss Battaglia again. What I'm gonna do?'"

"Your feet ain't so big," Mrs. Reilly observed, looking under the kitchen table.

"I just got them squshed up in this little pair of shoes. You oughta see them things when I'm barefoot, girl."

"I got bum feet," Mrs. Reilly told the other two. Santa made a sign for Mrs. Reilly not to discuss her deficiencies, but Mrs. Reilly was not to be silenced. "Some days I can't hardly walk. I think they went bad when Ignatius was little and I useta have to carry him around. Lord but he was slow walking. Always falling down. He was sure heavy, too. Maybe that's how I got my arthuritis."

"Listen, you two," Santa said quickly so that Mrs. Reilly would not describe some new, horrible deficiency. "Why don't we go see that cute little Debbie Reynolds?"

"That would be nice," Mr. Robichaux said. "I never go to the show."

"You wanna go see a show?" Mrs. Reilly asked. "I don't know. My feet."

"Aw, come on, girl. Let's get out the house. It smells like garlic in here."

"I think Ignatius told me this movie ain't no good. He sees every picture that comes out, that boy."

"Irene!" Santa said angrily. "You all the time thinking of that boy, and with all the trouble he's giving you. You better wake up, babe. If you had any sense, you woulda had that boy locked away at Charity Hospital a long time ago. They'd turn a hose on him. They'd stick a letrit socket in that boy. They'd show that Ignatius. They'd make him behave himself."

"Yeah?" Mrs. Reilly asked with interest. "How much that cost?"

"It's all for free, Irene."

"Socialized medicine," Mr. Robichaux observed. "They probly got communiss and fellow travelers working in that place."

"They got nuns operating the place, Claude. Lord, where you all the time getting this communiss stuff from?"

"Maybe them sisters been fooled," Mr. Robichaux said.

"Ain't that awful," Mrs. Reilly said sadly. "Them poor sisters. Operating for a buncha communiss."

"I don't care who's operating the place," Santa said. "If it's free and they lock people away, Ignatius oughta be there."

"Once Ignatius started talking to them people, they'd maybe get mad and lock him up for good," Mrs. Reilly said, but she was thinking that even that alternative wasn't too unattractive. "Maybe he wouldn't listen to the doctors."

"They'd make him listen. They'd beat him in the head, they'd lock him up in a straitjacket, they'd pump some water on him," Santa said a little too eagerly.

"You gotta think about yourself, Irene," Mr. Robichaux said. "That son of yours is gonna put you in your grave."

"That's it. You tell her, Claude."

"Well," Mrs. Reilly said, "We'll give Ignatius a chance. Maybe he'll make good yet."

"Selling weenies?" Santa asked. "Lord." She shook her head. "Well, lemme go dump these dishes in the zink. Come on, let's go see that precious Debbie Reynolds."

A few minutes later, after Santa had stopped in the parlor to kiss her mother goodbye, the three of them set out for the theater. The day had been a balmy day; a south wind had been blowing steadily from the Gulf. Now the evening was still warm. Heavy odors of Mediterranean cooking floated across the congested neighborhood from the opened kitchen windows in every apartment building and double house. Each resident seemed to be making some contribution, however small, to the general cacophany of dropping pots, booming television sets, arguing voices, screaming children, and slamming doors.

"St. Odo Parish is really at it tonight," Santa commented thoughtfully as the three slowly strolled down the narrow sidewalk between the curb and the steps of the double houses built in solid, straight rows down each block. The streetlights shone on the treeless stretches of asphalt and cement and continuous old slate roofs. "It's even worst in the summertime. Everybody's out on the streets till ten-eleven o'clock."

"Don't tell *me*, precious," Mrs. Reilly said as she hobbled dramatically between her friends. "Remember I'm from Dauphine Street. We useta put the kitchen chairs out on the banquette and set there till midnight sometimes waiting for the house to cool off. And the things the people down here say! Lord."

"Vicious is what it is," Santa agreed. "Dirty mouths."

"Poor poppa," Mrs. Reilly said. "He was so poor. Then when he went and got his hand caught in that fanbelt, the people in the neighborhood had the nerve to say he musta been drunk. The anonymous letters we got about that. And my poor old Tante Boo-boo. Eighty years old. She was burning a candle for her poor departed husband and it fall off the night table and sets her mattress on fire. The people said she was smoking in bed."

"I believe people innocent until they proven guilty."

"That's the same way I feel, Claude," Mrs. Reilly said. "Just the other day I says to Ignatius, 'Ignatius, I think people innocent until they prove guilty.'"

"Irene!"

They crossed St. Claude Avenue during a lull in the heavy traffic and walked along the other side of the avenue under the neon lights. As they were passing a funeral parlor, Santa stopped to talk to one of the mourners standing out on the sidewalk.

"Say, Mister, who they got laid out in there?" she asked the man.

"They waking old lady Lopez," the man answered.

"You don't say. She the wife of that Lopez ran the little market over on Frenchman Street?"

"That's the one."

"Aw, I'm sorry to hear that," Santa said. "What she died from?"

"Heart trouble."

"Ain't that a shame," Mrs. Reilly said emotionally. "Poor girl."

"Well, if I was dressed," Santa told the man, "I'd go in and pay my respects. Me and my friends here just on our way to a picture show. Thank you."

As they walked along, Santa described to Mrs. Reilly the many sadnesses and tribulations that had comprised old lady Lopez's dismal existence. Finally Santa said, "I think I'll send her family a Mass."

"Lord," Mrs. Reilly said, overcome by old lady Lopez's biography, "I think I'll send a Mass, too, for the repose of that poor woman's soul."

"Irene!" Santa screamed. "You don't even know them people."

"Well, that's true," Mrs. Reilly agreed weakly.

When they arrived at the theater, there was some discussion between Santa and Mr. Robichaux over who was going to buy the tickets. Mrs. Reilly said that she would if she didn't have to meet a payment on Ignatius' trumpet before the week was out. Mr. Robichaux was adamant, though, and Santa at last let him have his way.

"After all," Santa said to him as he handed tickets to the two ladies, "you the one's got all the money."

She winked at Mrs. Reilly, whose mind had wandered again to that sign that Ignatius refused to explain to her. During most of the movie Mrs. Reilly thought about Ignatius' rapidly decreasing salary, the payment on the trumpet, the payment on the wrecked building, the earring, and the sign. Only Santa's happy exclamations of "Ain't she precious!" and "Just take a look at that cute dress she's got, Irene!" brought Mrs. Reilly back to what was happening on the screen. Then something else drew her from her meditations about her son and her problems, both of which were really the same thing. Mr. Robichaux's hand had gently covered and was now holding hers. Mrs. Reilly was too afraid to move. Why did movies always seem to make the men she had known—Mr. Reilly and Mr. Robichaux—amorous? She stared blindly at the screen, on which she saw not Debbie Reynolds cavorting in color but rather Jean Harlow taking a bath in black and white.

Mrs. Reilly was wondering if she could easily wrench her hand out of Mr. Robichaux's and bolt from the theater when Santa cried, "Just watch it, Irene, I betcha little Debbie's gonna have her a baby!"

"A what?" Mrs. Reilly screamed wildly, bursting into crazy, loud tears that didn't subside until the frightened Mr. Robichaux took her maroon head and placed it carefully on his shoulder.

II

Dear Reader,
Nature has sometimes made a fool; but a coxcomb is always of man's own making.

—Addison

As I was wearing the soles of my desert boots down to a mere sliver of crepe rubber on the old flagstone banquettes of the French Quarter in my fevered attempt to wrest a living from an unthinking and uncaring society, I was hailed by a cherished old acquaintance (deviate). After a few minutes of conversation in which I established most easily my moral superiority over this degenerate, I found myself pondering once more the crises of our times. My mentality, uncontrollable and wanton as always, whispered to me a scheme so magnificent and daring that I shrank from the very thought of what I was hearing. "Stop!" I cried imploringly to my god-like mind. "This is madness." But still I listened to the counsel of my brain. It was offering me the opportunity to Save the World Through Degeneracy. There on the worn stones of the Quarter I enlisted the aid of this wilted flower of a human in gathering his associates in foppery together behind a banner of brotherhood.

Our first step will be to elect one of their number to some very high office—the presidency, if Fortuna spins us kindly. Then they will infiltrate the military. As soldiers, they will all be so continually busy in fraternizing with one another, tailoring their uniforms to fit like sausage skins, inventing new and varied battle dress, giving cocktail parties, etc., that they will never have time for battle. The one whom we finally make Chief of Staff will want only to attend to his fashionable wardrobe, a wardrobe which, alternately, will permit him to be either Chief of Staff or debutante, as the desire strikes him. In seeing the success of their unified fellows here, perverts around the world will also band together to capture the military in their respective countries. In those reactionary countries in which the deviates seem to be having some trouble in gaining control, we will send aid to them as rebels to help them in toppling their governments. When we have at last overthrown all existing governments, the world will enjoy not war but global orgies conducted with the utmost protocol and the most truly international spirit, for these people do transcend simple national differences. Their minds are on one goal; they are truly united; they think as one.

None of the pederasts in power, of course, will be practical enough to know about such devices as bombs; these nuclear weapons would lie rotting in their vaults somewhere. From time to time the Chief of Staff, the President, and so on, dressed in sequins and feathers, will entertain the leaders, i.e., the perverts, of all the other countries at balls and parties. Quarrels of any sort could easily be straightened out in the men's room of the redecorated United Nations. Ballets and Broadway musicals and entertainments of that sort will flourish everywhere and will probably make the common folk happier than did the grim, hostile, fascistic pronouncements of their former leaders.

Almost everyone else has had an opportunity to run the world. I cannot see why these people should not be given their chance. They have certainly been the underdog long enough. Their movement into power will be, in a sense, only a part of the global movement toward opportunity, justice, and equality for all. (For example, can you name one good, practicing transvestite in the Senate? No! These people have been without representation long enough. Their plight is a national, a global disgrace.)

Degeneracy, rather than signaling the downfall of a society, as it once did, will now signal peace for a troubled world. We must have new solutions to new problems.

I shall act as a sort of mentor and guide for the movement, my not inconsiderable knowledge of world history, economics, religion, and political strategy acting as a reservoir, as it were, from which these people can draw rules of operational procedure. Boethius himself played a somewhat similar role in degenerate Rome. As Chesterton has said of Boethius, "Thus he truly served as a guide, philosopher, and friend to many Christians; precisely because, while his own times were corrupt, his own culture was complete."

This time I shall really confound Myrna minx. The scheme is too breathtaking for the literal, liberal minx mind mired in a claustrophobic clutch of clichés. The Crusade for Moorish Dignity, my brilliant first attack upon the problems of our times, would have been a rather grand and decisive coup had it not been for the basically bourgeois worldview of the rather simple people who were members of the vanguard. This time, however, I shall be working with people who eschew the insipid

297

philosophy of the middle class, people who are willing to assume controversial positions, to follow their cause, however unpopular it may be, however it may threaten the smugness of the middle class.

Does M. Minkoff want sex in politics? I shall give her sex in politics—and plenty of it! No doubt she will be too overcome to respond to the originality of my project. At the very least, she will seethe with envy. (That girl must be attended to. Such effrontery cannot go unchecked.)

A debate between Pragmatism and Morality rages in my brain. Is the glorious end, Peace, worth the awesome means, Degeneracy? Like two figures in the medieval Morality play, Pragmatism and Morality spar in the boxing ring of my brain. I cannot await the outcome of their furious debate: I am too obsessed with Peace. (If any perceptive film producers are interested in buying the movie rights to this Journal, I might here make a note on the filming of this debate. A musical saw would provide excellent background accompaniment, and the hero's eyeball may be superimposed upon the debate scene in a most symbolic manner. Certainly some attractive new discovery could be found in a drugstore or a motel or in whatever den people are "discovered" to play the Working Boy. The film may be made in Spain, Italy, or some other interesting land which the cast may wish to see, such as North America.)

Sorry. Those of you who are interested in the latest bleak frankfurter news will find none. My mind is too preoccupied with the magnificence of this design. Now I must communicate with M. Minkoff and make some jottings for my lecture at the kickoff rally.

Social note: My truant mother is gone again, which is really rather fortunate. Her vigorous assaults and blistering attacks against my being are negatively affecting my valve. She said that she was going out to attend a Crowning of

*the May Queen at some church, but since it isn't May, I
tend to doubt her veracity.*

*The "sophisticated comedy" featuring my number one
female film favorite is opening at a downtown palace
momentarily. Somehow I must be there on opening day. I
can only imagine the film's latest horrors, its flaunting of
vulgarity in the face of theology and geometry, taste and
decency. (I do not understand this compulsion of mine for
seeing movies; it almost seems as if movies are "in my
blood.")*

*Health note: My stomach is getting out of bounds; the
seams of my vendor's smock are creaking ominously.*

Until later,

Tab, Your pacifist Working Boy

III

Mrs. Levy helped the renovated Miss Trixie up the steps and
opened the door.

"This is Levy Pants!" Miss Trixie snarled.

"You're back again where you're wanted and needed,
darling." Mrs. Levy spoke as if she were comforting a child.
"And how you've been missed. Every day Mr. Gonzalez has
been on the phone begging for you. Isn't it wonderful to
know that you're so vital to a business?"

"I thought I was retired." The massive teeth snapped like
a bear trap. "You people have tricked me!"

"Now are you happy?" Mr. Levy asked his wife. He was
walking behind them carrying one of Miss Trixie's bags of
scraps. "If she had a knife on her, I'd be taking you to the
hospital right now."

"Listen to the fire in her voice," Mrs. Levy said. "So
vigorous. It's unbelievable."

Miss Trixie tried to break away from Mrs. Levy as they entered the office, but her pumps did not give her the traction that she was used to with sneakers, and she only wobbled.

"She's *back?*" Mr. Gonzalez cried heartbrokenly.

"Can you believe your eyes?" Mrs. Levy asked him.

Mr. Gonzalez was forced to look at Miss Trixie, whose eyes were weak pools edged with blue shadow. Her lips had been extended in an orange line that almost reached her nostrils. Near the earrings a few gray wisps of hair escaped from beneath the black wig, which was slightly awry. The short skirt revealed withered, bowed legs and small feet that made the pumps look like snowshoes. Whole days of napping under a sunlamp had baked Miss Trixie to a golden brown.

"She certainly looks fit," Mr. Gonzalez said. His voice was false and he smiled a broken smile. "You've done her a wonderful service, Mrs. Levy."

"I am a very attractive woman," Miss Trixie babbled.

Mr. Gonzalez laughed nervously.

"Now listen here," Mrs. Levy said to him. "Part of this woman's trouble is that kind of attitude. Ridicule she doesn't need."

Mr. Gonzalez tried unsuccessfully to kiss Mrs. Levy's hand.

"I want you to make her feel wanted, Gonzalez. This woman still has a sharp mind. Give her work that will exercise those faculties of hers. Give her more authority. She desperately needs an active role in this business."

"Definitely," Mr. Gonzalez agreed. "I've said that myself all along. Haven't I, Miss Trixie."

"Who?" Miss Trixie snarled.

"I've always wanted you to assume more responsibility and authority," the office manager screamed. "Isn't that correct?"

"Oh, shut up, Gomez." Miss Trixie's teeth clattered like castanets. "Have you bought me that Easter ham yet? Answer me that."

"All right. You've had your fun. Let's go," Mr. Levy said to his wife. "Come on. I'm getting depressed."

"Just a moment," Mr. Gonzalez said. "I have some mail for you."

As the office manager went to his desk to get the mail, there was a crash in the rear of the office. Everyone, aside from Miss Trixie who had begun napping on her desk, turned around and looked in the filing department. There an extremely tall man with long black hair was picking up a file drawer that had fallen to the floor. He stuffed the filing roughly back into the drawer and slammed the drawer into its slot in the files.

"That's Mr. Zalatimo," Mr. Gonzalez whispered. "He's only been with us for a few days, and I don't think he's going to work out. I don't think we'll want to include him in the Levy Pants plan."

Mr. Zalatimo looked confusedly at the filing cabinets and scratched himself. Then he opened another drawer and fumbled through its contents with one hand while the other scratched at his armpit through his threadbare knitted shirt.

"Would you care to meet him?" the office manager asked.

"No thanks," Mr. Levy said. "Where do you find the people that work in this place, Gonzalez? I never see people like this anywhere else."

"He looks like a gangster to me," Mrs. Levy said. "You don't keep any cash around here, do you?"

"I think Mr. Zalatimo's honest," the office manager whispered. "He only has trouble alphabeting." He handed Mr. Levy a sheaf of mail. "These are mostly confirmations on your hotel reservations for spring practice. There's a letter in there from Abelman. It's addressed to you and not the company, and it's marked personal, so I thought you'd better open it. It's been around for a few days."

"What does that crack want now?" Mr. Levy said angrily.

"Maybe he wonders what happened to a brilliant, growing concern," Mrs. Levy observed. "Maybe he wonders what happened since Leon Levy died. Maybe this Abelman has some words of advice to a playboy. Read it, Gus. It will be your work for Levy Pants for the week."

Mr. Levy looked at the envelope, on which "personal" had been written three times in red ballpoint. He opened it and found a letter on which some attachment had been stapled.

Dear Gus Levy,

We were shocked and grievously injured to receive the attached letter. We have been a faithful outlet for your merchandise for thirty years and have heretofore always had the warmest affectionate feelings for your firm. Maybe you remember the wreath we sent when your father died for which we spared no expense.

This will be very short. After many nights without sleep, we have given the original letter to our lawyer, who is instigating a libel suit for $500,000. This may do a little to compensate for our hurt feelings.

Get a lawyer. We will see you in court like gentlemen. No more threats, please.

> *Very best wishes,*
> *I. Abelman,*
> *Manager, Abelman's Dry Goods*

Mr. Levy turned cold as he flipped the page and read the Thermofaxed copy of the letter to Abelman's. It was incredible. Who would go to the trouble of writing things like that? "Mr. I. Abelman, Mongoloid, Esq."; "your total lack of contact with reality"; "your blighted worldview"; "you may feel the sting of the lash across your pitiful shoulders." Worst of all, the "Gus Levy" signature looked fairly authentic. Abelman must be kissing the original right now and smacking his lips.

To somebody like Abelman that letter was like a savings bond, a blank draft on a bank.

"Who wrote this?" Mr. Levy demanded, giving the letter to Mr. Gonzalez.

"What is it, Gus? A problem? Are you having a problem? That's one of your problems. You never tell me your problems."

"Oh, my goodness!" Mr. Gonzalez squeaked. "This is horrible."

"Silence!" Miss Trixie snapped.

"What is it, Gus? Something you didn't handle correctly? Some authority you delegated to somebody else?"

"Yes, it's a problem. It's a problem that means we could lose the shirts off our backs."

"What?" Mrs. Levy grabbed the letters from Mr. Gonzalez. She read them and became a hag. Her lacquered curls turned into snakes. "Now you've done it. Anything to get back at your father, to ruin his business. I knew it was going to end like this."

"Oh, shut up. I never write the letters around here."

"Susan and Sandra will have to quit college. They'll be selling themselves to sailors and gangsters like that one there."

"Huh?" Mr. Zalatimo asked, sensing that he was being discussed.

"You're *sick*," Mrs. Levy shouted at her husband.

"Quiet!"

"And will I be any better off?" Mrs. Levy's aquamarine lids were trembling. "What will become of me? Already my life has been wrecked. What happens to me now? Prowling in garbage cans, following the fleet. My mother was right."

"Quiet!" Miss Trixie demanded, this time much more fiercely. "You people are the noisiest I've ever met."

Mrs. Levy had collapsed in a chair, sobbing something about going out to sell Avon products.

"What do you know about this, Gonzalez?" Mr. Levy asked the office manager whose lips had turned white.

"I don't know a thing," Mr. Gonzalez piped. "It's the first time I've seen that letter."

"You write the correspondence around here."

"I didn't write *that*." His lips were quivering. "I wouldn't do something like that to Levy Pants!"

"No, I know you wouldn't." Mr. Levy tried to think. "Somebody really had it in for us."

Mr. Levy went over to the files, pushed the scratching Mr. Zalatimo aside, and opened the files in the A's. There was no Abelman folder. The drawer was completely empty. He opened several other drawers, but half of them were empty, too. What a way to begin fighting a libel suit.

"What do you people do with the filing?"

"I was wondering about that myself," Mr. Zalatimo said vaguely.

"Gonzalez, what was the name of that big kook you had working in here, the big fat one with the green cap?"

"Mr. Ignatius Reilly. He handled the letter to go out." Who had composed that awful thing?

"Hey," Jones's voice said over the telephone, "you people still got a fat mother with a green cap workin there at Levy Pant? A big white guy got him a moustache?"

"No we don't," Mr. Gonzalez answered in a shrill voice and slammed the phone down.

"Who was that?" Mr. Levy asked.

"Oh, I don't know. Someone for Mr. Reilly." The office manager wiped his forehead with a handkerchief. "The one who tried to make the factory workers kill me."

"Reilly?" Miss Trixie said. "That wasn't Reilly, that was . . ."

"The young idealist?" Mrs. Levy sobbed. "Who wanted him?"

"I don't know," the office manager answered. "It sounded like a Negro voice to me."

"Well, I guess so," Mrs. Levy said. "He's out trying to help some other unfortunates right now. It's encouraging to know that his idealism is still intact."

Mr. Levy had been thinking of something, and he asked the office manager, "What was the name of that kook?"

"Reilly. Ignatius J. Reilly."

"It was?" Miss Trixie said with interest. "That's strange. I always thought it . . ."

"Miss Trixie, please," Mr. Levy said angrily. That Reilly blimp was working for the company at the time that that letter to Abelman was dated. "Do you think that that Reilly would write a letter like that?"

"Maybe," Mr. Gonzalez said. "I don't know. I had high hopes for him until he tried to get that worker to brain me."

"That's right," Mrs. Levy moaned. "Try to pin it on the young idealist. Put him away where his idealism won't bother you. People like the young idealist don't deal in underhanded things like that. Wait until Susan and Sandra hear about this." Mrs. Levy made a gesture that indicated that the girls would clearly go into a state of shock. "Negroes are calling here to get his counsel. You're about to frame him. I can't take much more of this, Gus. I can't, I can't!"

"Then do you want *me* to say I wrote that?"

"Of course not!" Mrs. Levy screamed at her husband. "I'm supposed to end in the poorhouse? If the young idealist wrote it, he goes to jail for forgery."

"Say, what's going on?" Mr. Zalatimo asked. "Is this dump gonna close down or what? I mean, I'd like to know."

"Shut up, gangster," Mrs. Levy answered wildly, "before we pin it on you."

"Huh?"

"Will you keep quiet? You're getting everything confused," Mr. Levy said to his wife. Then he turned to the office manager. "Get me this Reilly's phone number."

Mr. Gonzalez awakened Miss Trixie and asked her for a phone book.

"*I* keep all of the phone books," Miss Trixie snapped. "And no one is going to use them."

"Then look up a Reilly on Constantinople Street for us."

"Well, all right, Gomez," Miss Trixie snarled. "Hold your horses." She took the three hoarded office telephone books out of some recess in her desk, and, studying the pages with a magnifying glass, gave them a number.

Mr. Levy dialed it and a voice answered, "Good morning. Regal Cleaners."

"Give me one of those phone books," Mr. Levy hollered.

"No," Miss Trixie rasped, slapping her hand down on the stack of books, guarding them with her newly enameled nails. "You'll only lose it. I'll find the right number. I must say you people are very impatient and excitable. Staying at your house took ten years off my life. Why can't you let poor Reilly alone? You already kicked him out over nothing."

Mr. Levy dialed the second number that she gave him. A woman who sounded slightly intoxicated answered and told him that Mr. Reilly wouldn't be home until late in the afternoon. Then she started crying, and Mr. Levy got depressed and thanked her and hung up.

"Well, he's not at home," Mr. Levy told the audience in the office.

"Mr. Reilly always seemed to have the best interests of Levy Pants at heart," the officer manager said sadly. "Why he started that riot I'll never know."

"For one thing because he had a police record."

"When he came to apply, I certainly didn't think he was a police character." The office manager shook his head. "He seemed so refined."

Mr. Gonzalez watched Mr. Zalatimo probing his long index

finger high into one of his nostrils. What would this one do? His feet tingled with fear.

The factory door banged open and one of the workers screamed, "Hey, Mr. Gonzalez, Mr. Palerma just burn his hand on one of them furnace door."

There were sounds of disorder in the factory. A man was cursing.

"Oh, my goodness," Mr. Gonzalez cried. "Quiet the workers. I'll be there in a minute."

"Come on," Mr. Levy said to his wife. "Let's get out of here. I'm getting heartburn."

"Just a moment." Mrs. Levy gestured to Mr. Gonzalez. "About Miss Trixie. I want you to give her a welcome every morning. Give her meaningful work to do. In the past her insecurity probably made her afraid of taking any responsible work. I think she's over that now. Basically she has a deep seated hatred of Levy Pants that I've analyzed as being rooted in fear. The insecurity and fear have led to hatred."

"Of course," the office manager said, half listening. The factory sounded bad.

"Go see about the factory, Gonzalez," Mr. Levy said. "I'll get in touch with Reilly."

"Yes, sir." Mr. Gonzalez made a deep bow to them and dashed out of the office.

"Okay." Mr. Levy was holding the door open. Just come near Levy Pants and you were subjected to all sorts of annoyances and depressing influences. You couldn't leave the place alone for a minute. Anyone who wanted to take it easy and not be bothered had better not have a company like Levy Pants. Gonzalez didn't even know what kind of mail was going out of the office. "Come on, Dr. Freud. Let's go."

"Look how calm you are. It doesn't matter to you that Abelman is about to sue our lives away if he can." The aquamarine lids trembled. "Aren't you going to get the idealist?"

"Some other time. I've had enough for one day."

"Meanwhile Abelman has Scotland Yard at our throats."

"He's not even home." Mr. Levy didn't feel like speaking with the crying woman again. "I'll call him tonight from the coast. There's nothing to worry about. They can't sue me for a half million for a letter I didn't write."

"Oh, no? I'm sure somebody like Abelman could. I can just see that lawyer he's got. Crippled from chasing ambulances. Mutilated from being caught in fires he's started for insurance money."

"Well, you'll take the bus back to the coast if you don't hurry up. I'm getting indigestion from this office."

"All right, all right. You can't spare a minute of your wasted life for this woman, can you?" Mrs. Levy indicated the loudly snoring Miss Trixie. She shook Miss Trixie's shoulder. "I'm going, darling. Everything is going to be fine. I've spoken to Mr. Gonzalez and he's delighted to see you again."

"Quiet!" Miss Trixie ordered. Her teeth snapped menacingly.

"Come on before I have to take you to get a rabies shot," Mr. Levy said angrily and grabbed his wife through her fur coat.

"Just look at this place." A gloved hand gestured to the dingy office furniture, to the warped floors, to the crepe paper streamers still hanging from the days when I. J. Reilly was custodian of the files, to Mr. Zalatimo who was kicking at the wastebasket in alphabetical frustration. "Sad, sad. A business down the drain, unhappy young idealists stooping to forgery to get even."

"Get out of here, you people," Miss Trixie snarled, slapping her palm on the desk.

"Listen to the conviction in that voice," Mrs. Levy said proudly as her round, furry figure was being hauled through the door. "I've worked a miracle."

The door closed and Mr. Zalatimo came over to Miss

Trixie, absently scratching himself. He tapped her on the shoulder and asked, "Say, lady, maybe you can help me out with this. What would you say comes first, *Willis* or *Williams?*"

Miss Trixie glared at him for a moment. Then she sank her teeth into his hand. In the factory Mr. Gonzalez heard Mr. Zalatimo's screaming. He didn't know whether to desert the seared Mr. Palermo and see what had happened or to stay in the factory, where the workers had begun dancing with one another under the loudspeakers. Levy Pants demanded a lot of a person.

In the sports car, as they drove through the salt marshes that led back to the coast, Mrs. Levy, pulling her blowing fur up closer around her neck said, "I'm establishing a Foundation."

"I see. Suppose Abelman's lawyer gets the money out of us."

"He won't. The young idealist is trapped," she said calmly. "A police record, inciting a riot. His character references will stink."

"Oh. Suddenly you agree that your young idealist is a criminal."

"He obviously was all alone."

"But you wanted to get your hands on Miss Trixie."

"That's right."

"Well, there will be no Foundation."

"Susan and Sandra will hate to know that your bum's attitude toward the world almost ruined them, that because you won't even take the time to supervise your own company, we have somebody suing us for half a million. The girls will really resent that. The least that you've always given them has been material comfort. Susan and Sandra will hate to know that they could have ended up as prostitutes or worse."

"They might at least have made some money at it. As it is, they're all for free."

"Please, Gus. Not another word. Even my brutalized spirit

has some sensitivity left. I can't let you slander my girls like that." Mrs. Levy sighed contentedly. "This Abelman business is the most dangerous of all your mistakes and errors and evasions through the years. The girls' hair will curl when they read of it. Of course, I won't frighten them if you don't want me to."

"How much do you want for this Foundation?"

"I haven't decided yet. I've been composing the rules and regulations."

"May I ask what this Foundation is going to be called, Mrs. Guggenheim? The Susan and Sandra slush fund?"

"It will be called the Leon Levy Foundation, in honor of your father. I have to do something to honor your father's name for all that you haven't done to honor it. The awards will commemorate the memory of that great man."

"I see. In other words, you'll be tossing laurels at old men outstanding only for their unequaled meanness."

"Please, Gus." Mrs. Levy held up a gloved hand. "The girls have been thrilled by my reports on the Miss Trixie project. The Foundation will really give them faith in their name. I must do all I can to make up for your complete failure as a parent."

"Getting an award from the Leon Levy Foundation will be a public insult. Your hands will be really full of libel suits then, libel suits from the recipients. Forget it. Whatever happened to bridge? Other people are still playing it. Can't you go play golf at Lakewood anymore? Take some more dancing lessons. Take Miss Trixie with you."

"To be quite honest with you, Miss Trixie was beginning to bore me the last few days."

"So that's why the rejuvenation course ended all of a sudden."

"I've done all I can for that woman. Susan and Sandra are proud that I've tried to keep her active so long."

"Well, there will be no Leon Levy Foundation."

"Do you resent it? There's resentment in your voice. I can hear it. There's hostility. Gus, for your own sake. That doctor in the Medical Arts building. Lenny's savior. Before it's too late. Now I'll have to watch over you every minute to see to it that you get in touch with that idealist criminal as soon as possible. I know you. You'll put it off, and Abelman will have a van out in front of Levy's Lodge taking everything away."

"Including your exercising board."

"I've already told you!" Mrs. Levy screamed. "Leave the board out of this!" She adjusted her ruffled furs. "Now get to that Reilly psycho before Abelman comes down here and starts taking the hub caps off this sports car. With somebody like that, Abelman has no case. Lenny's doctor can analyze Reilly, and the state will put him away someplace where he can't try to wreck people. Thank goodness Susan and Sandra won't know that they almost ended up selling roach tablets from door to door. Their hearts would break if they knew how carelessly their own father handled their welfare."

IV

George had set up his stakeout on Poydras Street across from the Paradise Vendors, Incorporated, garage. He had remembered the name on the wagon and looked up the address of the vending firm. All morning he had waited for the big vendor, who had never shown up. Perhaps he had been fired for stabbing the fairy in Pirate's Alley. At noon George had left his outpost and gone down to the Quarter to get the packages from Miss Lee. Now he was back on Poydras wondering whether the vendor was going to show. George had decided to try to be nice to him, to hand him a few dollars right away. Hot dog vendors must be poor. He'd appreciate a few bucks. This vendor was a perfect front man. He would never know what was coming off. He had a good education, though.

At last, sometime after one o'clock, a white smock billowed off the trolley and whipped into the garage. A few minutes later the oddball vendor wheeled his wagon out onto the sidewalk. He was still wearing the earring, scarf, and cutlass, George noticed. If he put them on in the garage, they must be part of his sales gimmick. You could tell by the way that he talked, though, that he had gone to school a long time. That was probably what was wrong with him. George had been wise enough to get out of school as soon as possible. He didn't want to end up like that guy.

George watched him push the wagon a few feet down the block, stop, and tape a piece of tablet paper to the front of his wagon. George would use psychology on him; he'd play up to the vendor's education. That and the money should make him rent out his bun compartment.

Then an old man stuck his head out of the garage, ran up behind the vendor, and struck him across the back with a long fork.

"Get moving, you ape," the old man shouted. "You're already late. It's already afternoon. Today you're gonna bring in a profit or else."

The vendor said something coolly and quietly. George couldn't understand it, but it lasted a long time.

"I don't care if your mother takes dope," the old man answered. "I don't wanna hear no more bullshit about that automobile accident and your dreams and your goddam girl friend. Now get outta here, you big baboon. I want five dollars minimum from you today."

With a push from the old man, the vendor rolled to the corner and disappeared onto St. Charles. After the old man returned to the garage, George slouched off in pursuit of the wagon.

Unaware that he was being trailed, Ignatius pushed his cart

312

against the traffic down St. Charles toward the Quarter. He had stayed up so late the night before working on his lecture for the kickoff rally that he hadn't been able to move from his yellowed sheets until almost noon, and then it had only been his mother's violent pounding and screaming that had awakened him. Now that he was out on the streets, he had a problem. Today the sophisticated comedy was opening at the RKO Orpheum. He had been able to bleed ten cents out of his mother for carfare home, although she had even begrudged him that. Somehow he had to sell five or six hot dogs quickly, park the wagon somewhere, and get to that theater so that his disbelieving eyes could drink in every blasphemous technicolored moment.

Lost in speculation about means for raising the money, Ignatius did not notice that for quite some time his car had been traveling in a straight and unswerving line. When he attempted to pull closer to the curb, the cart would not incline to the right at all. Stopping, he saw that one of the bicycle tires had lodged in the groove of a streetcar track. He tried to bump the cart out of the groove; it was too heavy to be easily bounced. He bent and tried to lift the cart on one side. As he slipped his hands beneath the big tin bun, he heard through the light mist the grinding of an approaching streetcar. The hard little bumps appeared on his hands, and his valve, after wavering for a moment of frantic decision, slammed closed. Wildly Ignatius pulled upward on the tin bun. The bicycle tire shot up out of the tracks, rose upward, balanced for a second in the air, and then became horizontal as the cart turned over loudly on its other side. One of the little lids in the tin bun opened and deposited a few steaming hot dogs on the street.

"Oh, my God!" Ignatius mumbled to himself, watching the silhouette of the streetcar forming a half-block away. "What vicious trick is Fortuna playing on me now?"

313

Deserting the wreck, Ignatius lumbered down the tracks toward the streetcar, the white muu-muu of a uniform swishing around his ankles. The olive and copper trolley car ground slowly toward him, leisurely pitching and rocking. The motorman, seeing the huge, spherical, white figure panting in the center of the tracks, slid the car to a halt and opened one of the front windows.

"Pardon me, sir," the earring called up to him. "If you will wait a moment, I shall attempt to right my listing craft."

George saw his opportunity. He ran over to Ignatius and said cheerily, "Come on, prof, let's you and me get this off the street."

"Oh, my God!" Ignatius thundered. "My pubescent nemesis. What a promising day this appears to be. I am apparently to be run over by a streetcar and robbed simultaneously, thereby setting a Paradise record. Get away, you depraved urchin."

"You grab that end and I'll get this one."

The streetcar clanged at them.

"Oh, all right," Ignatius said finally. "Actually, I would be perfectly happy to let this ridiculous liability lie here on its side."

George took one end of the bun and said, "You better close that little door before more of them weenies falls out."

Ignatius kicked the little door closed, as if he were playing to win in a professional football game, neatly severing a protruding hot dog into two six-inch sections.

"Take it easy, prof. You gonna break your wagon."

"Shut up, you truant. I didn't ask you to make conversation."

"Okay," George said, shrugging. "I mean, I'm just tryna help you out."

"How could you possibly help me?" Ignatius bellowed, baring a tan fang or two. "Some authority of society is probably hot on the scent of your suffocating hair tonic right now. Where did you come from? Why are you following me?"

"Look, you want me to help you pick up this pile of junk?"

"Pile of junk? Are you talking about this Paradise vehicle?"

The streetcar clanged at them again.

"Come on," George said. "*Up.*"

"I hope you realize," Ignatius said as he breathlessly lifted the wagon, "that our association is only the result of an emergency."

The cart bounced back onto its two bicycle tires, the contents of the tin bun rattling against its sides.

"Okay, prof, there you go. Glad I could help you out."

"In case you haven't noticed, you waif, you are about to be hooked on the cowcatcher of that streetcar."

The streetcar rolled by them slowly so that the conductor and motorman could study Ignatius' costume more closely.

George grabbed one of Ignatius' paws and stuck two dollars in it.

"Money?" Ignatius asked happily. "Thank God." He quickly pocketed the two bills. "I'd rather not ask the obscene motive for this. I'd like to think that you're attempting to make amends in your simple way for slandering me on my dismal first day with this ludicrous wagon."

"That's it, prof. You said it better than I ever could. You're a really educated guy."

"Oh?" Ignatius was very pleased. "There may be some hope for you yet. Hot dog?"

"No, thanks."

"Then pardon me while I have one. My system is petitioning for appeasement." Ignatius looked down into the well of his wagon. "My God, the hot dogs are quite disordered."

While Ignatius was slamming doors and plunging his paws down into the well, George said, "Now I helped you out, prof. Maybe you can do the same for me."

"Perhaps," Ignatius said disinterestedly, biting into the hot dog.

"You see these?" George indicated the brown paper packages he was carrying under his arms. "These are school supplies. Now this is my problem. I gotta pick them up from the distributor at lunchtime, but I can't deliver them to the schools until after school's closed. So I gotta carry them around for almost two hours. You understand? What I'm looking for is a place to put these things in the afternoon. Now I could meet you someplace about one and put them in your bun compartment and come get them out sometime before three."

"How bogus," Ignatius belched. "Do you seriously expect me to believe you? Delivering school supplies after the schools are closed?"

"I'll pay you a couple of bucks every day."

"You will?" Ignatius asked with interest. "Well, you will have to pay me a week's rent in advance. I don't deal in small sums."

George opened his wallet and gave Ignatius eight dollars.

"Here. With the two you already got, that makes ten for the week."

Ignatius happily pocketed the new bills and ripped one of the packages from George's arms, saying, "I must see what it is that I'm storing. You're probably selling goof balls to infants."

"Hey!" George shouted. "I can't deliver the stuff if it's opened."

"Too bad for you." Ignatius fended off the boy and tore off the brown wrapping. He saw a stack of what looked like postcards. "What are these? Visual aids for civics or some other equally stultifying high school subject?"

"Gimme that, you nut."

"Oh, my God!" Ignatius stared at what he saw. Once in high school someone had shown him a pornographic photograph, and he had collapsed against a water cooler, injuring his ear. This photograph was far superior. A nude woman was sitting on the edge of a desk next to a globe of the world. The suggested onanism with the piece of chalk intrigued Ignatius. Her face was hidden behind a large book. While George evaded indifferent slaps from the unoccupied paw, Ignatius scrutinized the title on the cover of the book: Anicius Manlius Severinus Boethius, *The Consolation of Philosophy.* "Do I believe what I am seeing? What brilliance. What taste. Good grief."

"Give that back," George pleaded.

"This one is *mine*," Ignatius gloated, pocketing the top card. He handed the torn package back to George and looked at the piece of torn wrapping between his fingers. There was an address on it. He pocketed that, too. "Where in the world did you get these? Who is this brilliant woman?"

"None of your business."

"I see. A secret operation." Ignatius thought of the address on the piece of paper. He would do his own investigating. Some destitute woman intellectual was doing anything for a dollar. Her worldview must be quite incisive, if her reading material were any guide. It could be that she was in the same situation as the Working Boy, a seer and philosopher cast into a hostile century by forces beyond her control. Ignatius must meet her. She might have some new and valuable insights. "Well, in spite of my misgivings, I shall make my cart available to you. However, you must watch the cart this afternoon. I have a rather urgent appointment."

"Hey, what is this? How long you gonna be?"

"About two hours."

"I gotta get uptown by three o'clock."

"Well, you shall be a little late this afternoon," Ignatius said angrily. "I am already lowering my standards by associating with you and fouling up my bun compartment. You should be glad that I haven't turned you in. I have on the

317

police force a brilliant friend, a sly undercover agent, Patrolman Mancuso. He is just looking for the sort of break a case like yours would offer. Fall to your knees and be grateful for my benevolence."

Mancuso? Wasn't that the name of the undercover agent who had stopped him in the rest room. George got very nervous.

"What does this undercover pal of yours look like?" George sneered in an attempt at bravery.

"He is small and elusive." Ignatius' voice was cunning. "He is given to many disguises. He is a veritable will-o'-the-wisp, scurrying here and there in his never-ending search for marauders. For a while he chose the covert of a bathroom but now is out on the streets where he remains at my beck and call every minute."

George's throat filled with something that choked him.

"This is a frame-up," he swallowed.

"That's enough from you, you guttersnipe. Encouraging the degeneration of some noble woman scholar," Ignatius barked. "You should be kissing the hem of my uniform in gratitude for my not advising Sherlock Mancuso of your evil goods. Meet me before the RKO Orpheum in two hours!"

Ignatius billowed grandly off down Common Street. George put his two packages in the bun compartment and sat down on the curb. This was really luck meeting a pal of Mancuso's. The big vendor really had him. He looked furiously at the wagon. Now he wasn't only stuck with the packages. He was stuck with a big hot dog wagon.

Ignatius tossed money at the cashier and literally lunged into the Orpheum, waddling down the aisle toward the footlights. His timing had been perfect. The second feature was just beginning. The boy with the magnificent photographs was definitely a find. Ignatius wondered if he could blackmail him into watching the wagon every afternoon. The urchin had certainly responded to his mention of a friend on the police force.

Ignatius snorted at the movie credits. All of the people involved in the film were equally unacceptable. A set designer, in particular, had appalled him too many times in the past. The heroine was even more offensive than she had been in the circus musical. In this film she was a bright young secretary whom an aged man of the world was trying to seduce. He flew her in a private jet to Bermuda and installed her in a suite. On their first night together she broke out in a rash just as the libertine was opening her bedroom door.

"Filth!" Ignatius shouted, spewing wet popcorn over several rows. "How dare she pretend to be virgin. Look at her degenerate face. Rape her!"

"They sure got some funny people at matinees," a lady with a shopping bag said to her companion. "Just take a look at him. He's got on a earring."

Then there was a soft-focus love scene, and Ignatius began to lose control. He could feel the hysteria overtaking him. He tried to be silent, but he found that he couldn't.

"They're photographing them through several thicknesses of cheesecloth," he spluttered. "Oh, my God. Who can imagine how wrinkled and loathsome those two really are? I think I'm getting nauseated. Can't someone in the projection booth turn off the electricity? Please!"

He rattled his cutlass loudly against the side of his seat. An old usherette came down the aisle and tried to grab the cutlass from him, but Ignatius wrestled with her, and she slid to the carpet. She got up and hobbled away.

The heroine, believing her honor to be in question, had a series of paranoid fantasies in which she was lying on a bed with her libertine. The bed was pulled through the streets and floated across a swimming pool at the resort hotel.

"Good grief. Is this smut supposed to be comedy?" Ignatius

demanded in the darkness. "I have not laughed once. My eyes can hardly believe this highly discolored garbage. That woman must be lashed until she drops. She is undermining our civilization. She is a Chinese Communist agent sent over to destroy us. Please! Someone with some decency get to the fuse box. Hundreds of people in this theater are being demoralized. If we're all lucky, the Orpheum may have forgotten to pay its electrical bill."

As the film ended Ignatius cried, "Under her All-American face she is really Toyko Rose!"

He wanted to stay for another showing, but he remembered the waif. Ignatius didn't want to ruin a good thing. He needed that boy. Weakly he climbed over the four empty popcorn boxes that had accumulated before his seat during the movie. He was completely enervated. His emotions were spent. Gasping, he staggered up the aisle and out onto the sunlit street. There, by the cab stand at the Roosevelt Hotel, George was keeping a surly watch over the wagon.

"Jesus," he sneered. "I thought you was never coming outta there. What kinda appointment you had? You just went to see a movie."

"Please," Ignatius sighed. "I've just been through trauma. Run along. I'll meet you at one sharp tomorrow at Canal and Royal."

"Okay, prof." George took his packages and started to slouch away. "Keep your mouth shut, huh?"

"We shall see," Ignatius said sternly.

He ate a hot dog with trembling hands and peeked down into his pocket at the photograph. From above the woman's figure looked even more matronly and reassuring. Some broken professor of Roman history? A ruined medievalist? If only she would have shown her face. There was an air of solitude, of detachment, of solitary sensual and scholarly pleasure that appealed to him greatly. He looked at the scrap of wrapping paper, at the crude, tiny address. Bourbon Street. The undone woman was in the hands of commercial exploiters. What a challenging character for the Journal. That particular work, Ignatius thought, was rather lacking in the sensual department. It needed a good injection of lip-smacking innuendo. Perhaps the confessions of this woman would perk it up a bit.

Ignatius rolled down into the Quarter and, for a wild and very fleeting moment, pondered an affair. How Myrna would gnaw at her espresso cup rim in envy. He would describe every lush moment with this scholarly woman. With her background and Boethian worldview, she would take a very stoic and fatalistic view of whatever sexual gaucheries and blunders he committed. She would be understanding. "Be kind," Ignatius would sigh to her. Myrna probably attacked sex with the vehemence and seriousness that she brought to social protest. How anguished she would be when Ignatius described his tender pleasures.

"Do I dare?" Ignatius asked himself, bumping the wagon absentmindedly into a parked car. The handle sank into his stomach and he belched. He would not tell the woman how he came across her. First, he would discuss Boethius. She would be overwhelmed.

Ignatius found the address and said, "Oh, my God! The poor woman is in the hands of fiends." He studied the façade of the Night of Joy and lumbered up to the poster in the glass case. He read:

ROBERTA E. LEE
presents

Harlett O'Hara,
the Virgin-ny Belle
(and pet!)

321

Who was Harlett O'Hara? Even more important, what kind of pet? Ignatius was intrigued. Afraid of attracting the wrath of the Nazi proprietress, he sat down uncomfortably on the curb and decided to wait.

Lana Lee was watching Darlene and the bird. They were almost ready to open. Now if only Darlene could get that line straight. She wandered away from the stage, gave Jones some additional directions about cleaning under the stools, and went to look out of the porthole of glass in the padded door. She'd seen enough of the act for one afternoon. The act was really pretty good in its own way. George was really bringing in the money with the new merchandise. Things were looking good. Too, Jones seemed to be broken in at last.

Lana pushed the door open and hollered out into the street, "Hey, you. Get off my curb, you character."

"Please," a rich voice answered from the street, pausing to think of some excuse. "I am only resting my rather broken feet."

"Go rest them someplace else. Get that crappy wagon away from in front my business."

"Let me assure you that I did not choose to collapse here before your gas chamber of a den. I did not return here of my own volition. My feet have simply ceased to function. I am paralyzed."

"Go get paralyzed down the block. All I need is you hanging around here again to ruin my investment. You look like a queer with that earring. People'll think this is a gay bar. Go on."

"People will never make that mistake. Without a doubt you operate the most dismal bar in the city. May I interest you in purchasing a hot dog?"

Darlene came to the door and said, "Well, look who it is. How's your poor momma?"

"Oh, my God," Ignatius bellowed. "Why did Fortuna lead me to this spot?"

"Hey, Jones," Lana Lee called. "Quit knocking that broom and come chase this character away."

"Sorry. Bouncer wage star at fifty dollar a week."

"You sure treat your poor momma cruel," Darlene said out the door.

"I don't imagine that either of you ladies has read Boethius," Ignatius sighed.

"Don't talk to him," Lana said to Darlene. "He's a fucking smart-aleck. Jones, I'll give you about two seconds to come out here before I get you picked up on a vagrancy rap along with this character. I'm getting fed up with smartasses in general."

"Goodness knows what storm trooper will descend upon me and beat me senseless," Ignatius observed coolly. "You can't frighten me. I've already had my trauma for the day."

"Ooo-wee!" Jones said when he looked out the door. "The green cap mother. In person. Live."

"I see that you've wisely decided to hire a particularly terrifying Negro to protect you against your enraged and cheated customers," the green cap mother said to Lana Lee.

"Hustle him off," Lana said to Jones.

"Whoa! How you hustle off a elephan?"

"Look at those dark glasses. No doubt his system is swimming in dope."

"Get the hell back in there," Lana said to Darlene, who was staring at Ignatius. She pushed Darlene and said to Jones, "Okay. Get him."

"Get out your razor and slash me," Ignatius said as Lana and Darlene went in. "Throw lye in my face. Stab me. You wouldn't realize, of course, that it was my interest in civil rights which led to my becoming a crippled vendor of franks. I lost a particularly successful position because of my stand on the racial question. My broken feet are the indirect result of my sensitive social conscience."

"Whoa! Levy Pant kick your ass out for tryina get all them po color people throwed in jail, huh?"

"How do you know about that?" Ignatius asked guardedly. "Were you involved in that particularly abortive coup?"

"No. I hear peoples talkin aroun."

"You did?" Ignatius asked interestedly. "No doubt they made some mention of my carriage and bearing. Thus, I am recognizable. I hardly suspected that I have become a legend. Perhaps I abandoned that movement too hastily." Ignatius was delighted. This was developing into a bright day after many bleak ones. "I have probably become a martyr of sorts." He belched. "Would you care for a hot dog? I extend the same courteous service to all colors and creeds. Paradise Vendors has been a pioneer in the field of public accommodations."

"How come a white cat like you, talkin so good, sellin weenies?"

"Please blow your smoke elsewhere. My respiratory system, unfortunately, is below par. I suspect that I am the result of particularly weak conception on the part of my father. His sperm was probably emitted in a rather offhand manner."

This was luck, Jones thought. The fat mother dropped out of the sky just when he needed him most.

"You mus be outa your min man. You oughta have you a good job, big Buick, all that shit. Whoa! Air condition, color TV . . ."

"I have a very pleasant occupation," Ignatius answered icily. "Outdoor work, no supervision. The only pressure is on the feet."

"If I go to college I wouldn be draggin no meat wagon aroun sellin peoples a lotta garbage and shit."

"Please! Paradise products are of the very highest quality." Ignatius rapped his cutlass against the curb. "Anyone employed by that dubious bar is not in a position to question another's occupation."

"Shit, you think I like the Night of Joy? Ooo-wee. I wanna get someplace. I like to get someplace good, be gainfully employ, make me a livin wage."

"Just as I suspected," Ignatius said angrily. "In other words, you want to become totally bourgeois. You people have all been brainwashed. I imagine that you'd like to become a success or something equally vile."

"Hey, now you gettin me. Whoa!"

"I really don't have the time to discuss the errors of your value judgments. However, I would like some information from you. Do you by any chance have a woman in that den who is given to reading?"

"Yeah. She all the time slippin me somethin to read, tellin me I be improvin myself. She pretty decent."

"Oh, my God." The blue and yellow eyes flashed. "Is there any way that I can meet this paragon?"

Jones wondered what this was all about. He said, "Whoa! You wanna see her, you come around some night, see her dancin with her pet."

"Good grief. Don't tell me that she is this Harlett O'Hara."

"Yeah. She Harla O'Horror all right."

"Boethius plus a pet," Ignatius mumbled. "What a discovery."

"She be openin in a coupla three days, man. You oughta get your ass down here. This the very fines ack I ever seen. Whoa!"

"I can only imagine," Ignatius said respectfully. Some brilliant satire on the decadent Old South being cast before the unaware swine in the Night of Joy audience. Poor Harlett. "Tell me. What sort of pet does she have?"

"Hey! I cain tell you that, man. You gotta see for yourself. This ack a big surprise. Harla got somethin to say, too. This ain jus a reglar strip ack. Harla talkin."

Good heavens. Some incisive commentary which no one in her audiences could fully comprehend. He must see Harlett. They must communicate.

"There is one thing I would like to know, sir," Ignatius said. "Is the Nazi proprietress of this cesspool around here every night?"

"Who? Miss Lee? No." Jones smiled at himself. The sabotage was working too perfectly. The fat mother really wanted to come to the Night of Joy. "She say Harla O'Horror so perfec, she so fine, she don't havta be comin aroun at night to supervise. She say jus as soon Harla be openin, she leavin for a vacation in Califonia. Whoa!"

"What luck," Ignatius slobbered. "Well, *I* shall be here to see Miss O'Hara's act. You may secretly reserve a ringside table for me. I must see and hear everything she does."

"Ooo-wee. You be real welcome, man. Drag your ass over in a coupla days. We give you the fines service in the house."

"Jones, are you talking to that character or what?" Lana demanded from the door.

"Don't worry," Ignatius told her. "I'm leaving. Your henchman has terrified me completely. I shall never make the mistake of even passing by this vile pigsty."

"Good," Lana said and swung the door closed.

Ignatius gloated at Jones conspiratorially.

"Hey, listen," Jones said. "Before you be leavin, tell me somethin. Wha you think a color cat can do to stop bein vagran or employ below the minimal wage?"

"Please." Ignatius fumbled through his smock to find the curb and raise himself. "You can't possibly realize how confused you are. Your value judgments are all wrong. When you get to the top or wherever it is that you want to go, you'll have a nervous breakdown or worse. Do you know of any Negroes with ulcers? Of course not. Live contentedly in some hovel. Thank Fortuna that you have no Caucasian parent hounding you. Read Boethius."

"Who? Read wha?"

"Boethius will show you that striving is ultimately meaningless, that we must learn to accept. Ask Miss O'Hara about him."

"Listen. How you like bein vagran half the time?"

"Wonderful. I myself was a vagrant in happier, better days. If only I were in your shoes. I would stir from my room only once a month to fumble for my relief check in the mailbox. Realize your good fortune."

The fat mother was really a freak. The poor people at Levy Pants were lucky that they hadn't ended up in Angola.

"Well be sure you come aroun in a coupla nights." Jones blew a cloud at the earring. "Harla be doin her stuff."

"I shall be there with bells on," Ignatius said happily. How Myrna would gnash her teeth.

"Whoa!" Jones walked around to the front of the wagon and studied the sheet of Big Chief paper. "Look like somebody been playin tricks on you."

"That is only a merchandising gimmick."

"Ooo-wee. You better check it again."

Ignatius lumbered around to the prow and saw that the waif had decorated the TWELVE INCHES (12") OF PARADISE sign with a variety of genitals.

"Oh, my God!" Ignatius ripped off the sheet covered with the ballpoint grafitti. "Have I been pushing this about?"

"I be out front lookin for you," Jones said. "Hey!"

Ignatius waved a happy paw and waddled off. At last he had a reason for earning money: Harlett O'Hara. He aimed the denuded prow of the wagon toward the Algiers ferry ramp, where the longshoremen gathered in the afternoons. Calling, entreating, he guided the wagon into the crowd of men and succeeded in selling all of his hot dogs, courteously and effusively squirting ketchup and mustard on his sold goods with all the energy of a fireman.

What a brilliant day. The signs from Fortuna were more than promising. A surprised Mr. Clyde received cheery greetings and ten dollars from vendor Reilly, and Ignatius, his smock filled with bills from the waif and the mogul of frankfurters, billowed onto the trolley with a glad heart.

He entered the house and found his mother talking quietly on the telephone.

"I been thinking about what you said," Mrs. Reilly was whispering into the phone. "Maybe it ain't such a bad idea after all, babe. You know what I mean?"

"Of course it ain't," Santa answered. "Them people at Charity can let Ignatius take him a little rest. Claude ain't gonna want no Ignatius around, sweetheart."

"He likes me, huh?"

"Likes you? He called up this morning to ax me if I thought you was ever gonna remarry. Lord. I says, 'Well, Claude, you gotta pop the question.' Whoee. You two having a worldwin courtship if I ever seen one. That poor man's desperate from loneliness."

"He's sure considerate," Mrs. Reilly breathed into the mouthpiece. "But sometimes he makes me nervous with all them communiss."

"What in the world are you babbling about?" Ignatius thundered in the hall.

"Christ," Santa said. "It sound like that Ignatius come in."

"Ssh," Mrs. Reilly said into the phone.

"Well, listen, sweetheart. Once Claude gets married, he'll stop thinking about them communiss. His mind isn't occupied is what's wrong with him. You give him some loving."

"Santa!"

"Good grief," Ignatius spluttered. "Are you speaking with that Battaglia strumpet?"

"Shut up, boy."

"You better knock that Ignatius in the head," Santa said.

"I wisht I was strong enough, sweetheart," Mrs. Reilly answered.

"Oh, Irene, I almost forgot to tell you. Angelo come around this morning for a cup of coffee. I hardly reconnized him. You oughta seen him in that wool suit. He looked like Mrs. Astor's horse. Poor Angelo. He's sure trying hard. Now he's going to all the high-class bars, he says. He better get him some character."

"Ain't that awful," Mrs. Reilly said sadly. "What Angelo's gonna do if he gets himself kicked off the force? And him with three chirren to support."

"There are a few challenging openings at Paradise Vendors for men with initiative and good taste," Ignatius said.

"Listen at that nut," Santa said. "Aw, Irene. You better ring up the Charity, honey."

"We gonna give him another chance. Maybe he'll hit the jackpot."

"I don't know why I bother talking to you, girl," Santa sighed hoarsely. "I'll see you tonight then about seven. Claude says he's gonna come over here. Come pick us up and we'll take us a nice ride out to the lake for some of them good crabs. Whoo! You kids sure lucky you got me for a chaperone. You two need one, especially with that Claude around."

Santa guffawed in a voice huskier than usual and hung up.

"What in the world do you and that old bawd babble about?" Ignatius asked.

"Shut up!"

"Thank you. I see that things about here are as cheerful as ever."

"How much money you brought in today? A quarter?" Mrs. Reilly screamed. She leaped up and stuck her hand into one of the pockets of the smock and pulled out the brilliant photograph. "Ignatius!"

"Give that to me," Ignatius thundered. "How dare you besmirch that magnificent image with your vintner's hands."

Mrs. Reilly peeked at the photograph again and then closed

her eyes. A tear crept out from beneath her closed eyelids. "I knew when you started selling them weenies you was gonna be hanging around with people like this."

"What do you mean, 'people like this'?" Ignatius asked angrily, pocketing the photograph. "This is a brilliant, misused woman. Speak of her with respect and reverence."

"I don't wanna speak at all," Mrs. Reilly sniffed, her lids still sealed. "Go sit in your room and write some more of your foolishness." The telephone rang. "That must be that Mr. Levy. He already rang up here twice today."

"Mr. Levy? What does that monster want?"

"He wouldn't tell me. Go on, crazy. Answer that. Pick up that phone."

"Well, I certainly don't want to speak with him," Ignatius thundered. He picked up the telephone, and in an assumed voice rich with Mayfair accents said, "Yus?"

"Mr. Reilly?" a man asked.

"Mr. Reilly is not here."

"This is Gus Levy." In the background, a woman's voice was saying, "Let's see what you're going to say. Another chance down the drain, a psycho escaped."

"I'm terribly sorry," Ignatius enunciated. "Mr. Reilly was called out of town this afternoon on rather crucial business. Actually, he is at the state mental hospital in Mandeville. Since being so viciously dismissed by your concern, he has had to commute back and forth regularly from Mandeville. His ego is badly bruised. You may yet receive his psychiatrists' bills. They are rather staggering."

"He cracked up?"

"Violently and totally. We had something of a time with him here. The first time that he went to Mandeville, he had to be transported in an armored car. As you know, his physique is rather grand. This afternoon, however, he left in a state patrol ambulance."

"Can he have visitors at Mandeville?"

"Of course. Drive out to see him. Bring him some cookies."

Ignatius slammed the telephone down, pressed a quarter into the palm of his still sniffling, blinded mother, and waddled to his room. Before opening the door, he stopped to straighten the PEACE TO MEN OF GOOD WILL sign that he had tacked to the peeling wood.

All signs were pointing upward; his wheel was revolving skyward.

Twelve

There had been a flurry of excitement. The wild blowing of the postman's whistle, the chugging postal truck out on Constantinople Street, his mother's excited screaming, Miss Annie's calling to the postman that his whistle had frightened her—all had interrupted Ignatius' dressing for the kickoff rally. He signed the postal delivery receipt and rushed back to his room, locking his door.

"What is it, boy?" Mrs. Reilly asked in the hall.

Ignatius looked at the AIR MAIL SPECIAL DELIVERY stamping on the manila envelope and at the little hand-written pleas, "Urgent" and "Rush."

"Oh, my goodness," he said happily. "The Minkoff minx must be beside herself."

He tore open the envelope and pulled out the letter.

Sirs:
Did you really send me this telegram, Ignatius?
MYRNA FORM PEACE PARTY CENTRAL COMMITTEE NORTH-EASTERN ZONE AT ONCE STOP ORGANIZE AT EVERY LEVEL STOP RECRUIT SODOMITES ONLY STOP SEX IN POLITICS STOP DETAILS WILL FOLLOW STOP IGNATIUS NATIONAL CHAIRMAN STOP
What does this mean, Ignatius? Do you really want me to recruit fags? Who wants to be a registered Sodomite? Ignatius, I am very worried. Are you hanging around with some queers? I could have guessed that this would happen. The paranoid fantasy of the arrest and accident was the first clue. Now the whole thing is out in the open. Your

normal sexual outlets have been blocked for so long that now the sexual overflow is seeping out into the wrong channels. Since the fantasy, which was the beginning of it all, you have been undergoing a period of crisis which is culminating in overt sexual aberration. I could tell that you were going to flip sooner or later. Now it has happened. My group therapy group will really be depressed when they hear that your case has taken a turn for the worse. Please leave that decaying city and come north. Call me collect if you want to and we can talk over this problem of sexual orientation that you are having. You must have therapy soon or you will become a screaming queen.

"How dare she?" Ignatius bellowed.

Whatever happened to the Divine Right party? I had several people who were all ready to join. I don't know if they'll go for this Sodomite business, although I can see that we might use this Sodomite party to drain off the fringe-group fascists. Maybe we could split the right wing in half. Still I don't think this is a good idea at all. Suppose non-Sodomites want to join and we refuse. We will be accused of being prejudiced, and the whole thing will flop. The lecture was not exactly a success, I'm afraid. It went over all right—right over the people's heads. There were two or three middle aged people in the audience who tried to heckle me with these very hostile remarks, but a couple of my friends from the group therapy group challenged them hostility for hostility and finally drove those reactionaries out of the auditorium. Just as I suspected, I was a little too advanced for the neighborhood audience. Ongah did not show up, that crumb. As far as I'm concerned, they can send him back to Africa. I really

*thought that guy had something on the ball. Apparently
he's very apathetic politically. He promised me he would be
there, that schmuck. Ignatius, this Sodomite plan does not
sound very practical at all. In addition, I think it is only a
dangerous manifestation of your declining mental health. I
don't know how I can tell my group therapy group about
this weird development—however predictable it might have
been. The group has been really pulling for you all along.
Some are even identifying with you. If you go, they might
go, too. I need immediate communication from you. Please
call collect anytime after 6 P.M. I am very, very worried.*

M. Minkoff

"She's totally confounded," Ignatius said happily. "Wait
until she hears of my apocalyptic meeting with Miss O'Hara."

"Ignatius, what's that you got?"

"A communication from Myrna minx."

"What that girl wants?"

"She's threatening suicide unless I swear that my heart is
hers alone."

"Ain't that awful. I bet you been telling that poor girl a
lota lies. I know you, Ignatius."

Behind the door there were sounds of dressing; something
that sounded like a piece of metal fell to the floor.

"Where you going to?" Mrs. Reilly asked the peeling paint.

"Please, Mother," a basso profundo voice answered. "I'm
rather rushed. Stop bothering me, please."

"You might as well stay at home all day long for all the
money you bringing in," Mrs. Reilly screamed at the door.
"How I'm gonna meet the note I gotta pay that man?"

"I wish that you would let me alone. I am addressing a
political meeting tonight, and I must organize my thoughts."

"A political meeting? Ignatius! Ain't that wonderful. Maybe
you'll make good in politics, boy. You got you a fine voice.

What club, honey? The Crescent City Democrats? The Old Regulars?"

"The party is secret at the moment, I'm afraid."

"What kinda political party's secret?" Mrs. Reilly asked suspiciously. "Are you gonna talk with a buncha communiss?"

"Ho hum."

"Somebody gimme some pamphlets on the communiss, boy. I been reading all about the communiss. Don't try to fool me, Ignatius."

"Yes, I saw one of those pamphlets in the hall this afternoon. You either dropped it there on purpose so that I could benefit from its message or you tossed it there accidentally during your regular afternoon wine orgy in the belief that it was a particularly elephantine bit of confetti. I imagine that your eyes have some trouble focusing at about two in the afternoon. Well, I read through the pamphlet. It's almost completely illiterate. Goodness knows where you get such garbage. Probably from the old woman who sells pralines at the cemetery. Well, I am not a communist, so let me alone."

"Ignatius, don't you think maybe you'd be happy if you went and took you a little rest at Charity?"

"Are you referring to the psychiatric ward by any chance?" Ignatius demanded in a rage. "Do you think that I am insane? Do you suppose that some stupid psychiatrist could even attempt to fathom the workings of my psyche?"

"You could just rest, honey. You could write some stuff in your little copybooks."

"They would try to make me into a moron who liked television and new cars and frozen food. Don't you understand? Psychiatry is worse than communism. I refuse to be brainwashed. I won't be a robot!"

"But, Ignatius, they help out a lot of people got problems."

"Do you think that I have a problem?" Ignatius bellowed. "The only problem that those people have anyway is that they don't like new cars and hair sprays. That's why they are put away. They make the other members of the society fearful. Every asylum in this nation is filled with poor souls who simply cannot stand lanolin, cellophane, plastic, television, and subdivisions."

"Ignatius, that ain't true. You remember old Mr. Becnel used to live down the block? They locked him up because he was running down the street naked."

"Of course he was running down the street naked. His skin could not bear any more of that dacron and nylon clothing that was clogging his pores. I've always considered Mr. Becnel one of the martyrs of our age. The poor man was badly victimized. Now run along to the front door and see if my taxi has arrived."

"Where you getting money for a taxi?"

"I keep a few pennies stuffed in my mattress," Ignatius answered. He had blackmailed another ten dollars out of the urchin, also forcing the waif to watch the wagon while he spent the afternoon at Loew's State watching a film about drag-racing teenagers. The guttersnipe was definitely a discovery, a gift sent by Fortuna to make amends for all of her bad spins. "Go peek through the shutters."

The door creaked open and Ignatius appeared in his pirate finery.

"Ignatius!"

"I thought that you might react like that. Therefore I have kept all of this paraphernalia stashed at Paradise Vendors, Incorporated."

"Angelo was right," Mrs. Reilly cried. "You been out on the streets dressed up like a Mardi Gras all this time."

"A scarf here. A cutlass there. One or two deft and tasteful suggestions. That's all. The total effect is rather fetching."

"You can't go out like that," Mrs. Reilly hollered.

"Please. Not another hysterical scene. You'll dislodge all

of the thoughts which are developing in my mind in connection with the lecture."

"Get back in that room, boy." Mrs. Reilly began beating Ignatius on the arms. "Get back in there, Ignatius. I ain't fooling this time, boy. You can't disgrace me like that."

"Good heavens! Mother, stop that. I'll be in no condition for my speech."

"What kinda speech you gonna make? Where you going to, Ignatius? Tell me, boy?" Mrs. Reilly slapped her son flatly in the face. "You ain't leaving this house, crazy."

"Oh, my God, Are you going mad? Get away from me this instant. I hope that you've noticed that scimitar dangling from my uniform."

A slap struck Ignatius in the nose: another landed on his right eye. He waddled down the hall, pushed the long shutters open, and ran out into the yard.

"Come back in this house," Mrs. Reilly screamed from the front door. "You ain't going no where, Ignatius."

"I dare you to come out in that shredded nightgown and get me!" Ignatius answered defiantly and stuck out his massive pink tongue.

"Get back in here, Ignatius."

"Hey, knock it off, you two," Miss Annie shouted from behind her front shutters. "My nerves is shot to hell."

"Take a look at Ignatius," Mrs. Reilly called to her. "Ain't that awful?"

Ignatius was waving to his mother from the brick sidewalk, his earring catching the rays of the streetlight.

"Ignatius, come in here like a good boy," Mrs. Reilly pleaded.

"I awready got me a headache from the goddam postman's whistle," Miss Annie threatened loudly. "I'm gonna ring up the cops in about one minute."

"Ignatius," shouted Mrs. Reilly, but it was too late. A taxi

337

was cruising down the block. Ignatius flagged it down just as his mother, forgetting the disgrace of the shredded night-gown, ran down to the curb. Ignatius slammed the rear door right in his mother's maroon hair and barked an address at the driver. He stabbed at his mother's hands with the cutlass and ordered the driver to move along immediately. The taxi sped off, churning up some pebbles in the gutter that stung Mrs. Reilly's legs through the torn rayon gown. She watched the red taillights for a moment, then she ran back into the house to telephone Santa.

"Going to a costume party, pal?" the driver asked Ignatius as they turned onto St. Charles Avenue.

"Watch where you're going and speak when you're spoken to," Ignatius thundered.

During the ride the driver said nothing else, but Ignatius practiced his speech loudly in the back seat, rapping his cutlass against the front seat to emphasize certain key points.

At St. Peter Street he got out and first heard the noise, dim yet frenetic singing and laughing coming from the three-story yellow stucco building. Some prosperous Frenchman had built the house in the late 1700s to house a menage of wife, children, and spinster *tantes*. The *tantes* had been stored up in the attic along with the other excess and unattractive furni-ture, and from the two little dormer windows in the roof they had seen what little of the world they believed existed outside of their own *monde* of slanderous gossip, needlework, and cyclical recitations of the rosary. But the hand of the professional decorator had exorcised whatever ghosts of the French bourgeoisie might still haunt the thick brick walls of the building. The exterior was painted a bright canary yellow; the gas jets in the reproduction brass lanterns mounted on either side of the carriageway flickered softly, their amber flames rippling in reflection on the black enamel of the gate and shutters. On the flagstone paving beneath both lanterns there were old plantation pots in which Spanish daggers grew and extended their sharply pointed stilettos.

Ignatius stood before the building regarding it with extreme distaste. His blue and yellow eyes denounced the resplendent façade. His nose rebelled against the very noticeable odor of fresh enamel. His ears shrank from the bedlam of singing, cackling, and giggling that was going on behind the closed black patent leather shutters.

Testily clearing his throat, he looked at the three brass doorbells and at the little white cards above each:

> Billy Truehard
> Raoul Frayle   - 3A
> Frieda Club
> Betty Bumper
> Liz Steele   - 2A
> Dorian Greene   - 1A

He jabbed a finger into the bottom bell and waited. The frenzy behind the shutters abated very slightly. A door opened somewhere down the carriageway, and Dorian Greene came walking toward the gate.

"Oh, dear," he said when he saw who was out on the sidewalk. "Where in the world have you been? I'm afraid that the kickoff rally is fast getting out of hand. I have tried unsuccessfully once or twice to call the group to order, but apparently feelings are running rather high."

"I hope you've done nothing to dampen their morale," Ignatius said gravely, tapping his cutlass impatiently on the iron gate. He noticed somewhat angrily that Dorian was walking toward him a little unsteadily; this was not what he had expected.

"Oh, what a gathering," Dorian said as he opened the gate. "Everyone is simply letting his hair down."

Dorian did a rapid and uncoordinated pantomime to illustrate this.

"Oh, my God!" Ignatius said. "Stop that appalling obscenity."

"Several people will be completely ruined after this evening. There's going to be a mass exodus for Mexico City in the morning. But then Mexico City is so wonderfully wild."

"I certainly hope that no one has tried to inflict any warmongering resolutions upon the gathering."

"Oh, goodness, no."

"I'm relieved to hear that. Heaven knows what opposition we may have to face even at the outset. We may have some 'enemy within.' Word may have leaked out to the whole military combine of the nation and, for that matter, the world."

"Well, come along, Gypsy Queen, let's get inside."

As they walked down the carriageway, Ignatius said, "This building is repellingly flamboyant." He looked at the pastel lamps concealed behind the palms along the walls. "Who's responsible for this abortion?"

"I, of course, Magyar Maiden. I own the building."

"I should have known. May I ask where the money comes from to support this decadent whimsy of yours?"

"From my dear family out there in the wheat," Dorian sighed. "They send me large checks every month. In return I simply guarantee them that I'll stay out of Nebraska. I left there under something of a cloud, you see. All that wheat and those endless plains. I can't tell you how depressing it all was. Grant Wood romanticized it, if anything. I went East for college and then came here. Oh, New Orleans is such freedom."

"Well, at least we have a gathering place for our coup. Now that I've seen the place, however, I would have preferred your renting an American Legion hall or something equally appropriate. This place looks more like the setting for some perverted activity like a tea dance or a garden party."

"Do you know that a national home decorating magazine

wants to do a four-page color spread on this building?" Dorian asked.

"If you had any sense, you would realize that that is the ultimate insult," Ignatius snorted.

"Oh, Girl with the Golden Earring, you are driving me out of my mind. Look, here's the door."

"Just a moment," Ignatius said cautiously. "What is that awful noise? It sounds as if someone's being sacrificed."

They stood in the pastel light of the carriageway listening. Somewhere in the patio a human was crying in distress.

"Oh, dear, what are they doing now?" Dorian's voice was impatient. "Those little fools. They never can behave themselves."

"I would suggest that we investigate," Ignatius said, his voice a conspiratorial whisper. "Some obsessed military officer may have slipped into the meeting incognito and may be trying to extricate our secrets from some faithful party member by means of torture. The dedicated military will stoop to anything. It could even be some foreign agent."

"Oh, what fun!" Dorian shrieked.

He and Ignatius tripped and waddled to the patio. There someone was crying for help in the slave quarters. The door of the slave quarters was slightly ajar, but Ignatius threw himself against it anyway, shattering several panes of glass.

"Oh, my God!" he screamed when he saw what was before him. "They've struck!"

He looked at the little sailor shackled and chained to the wall. It was Timmy.

"Do you see what you've done to my door?" Dorian was asking behind Ignatius.

"The enemy is among us," Ignatius said wildly. "Who tattled? Tell me. Someone is on to us."

"Oh, get me out of here," the little sailor pleaded. "It's awfully dark."

"You little fool," Dorian spat at the sailor. "Who chained you in here?"

"It was that terrible Billy and Raoul. They're so awful, those two. They brought me out here to show me how you're redecorating the slave quarters, and the next thing I knew they locked me in these dirty chains and ran back into the party."

The little sailor rattled his chains.

"I've just had this place redone," Dorian said to Ignatius. "Oh, my door."

"Where are those agents?" Ignatius demanded, unpinning his cutlass and waving it about. "We must apprehend them before they leave this building."

"Please get me out. I can't stand the dark."

"It's your fault that this door is broken," Dorian hissed at the deranged mariner. "Playing games with those two tramps from upstairs."

"He broke the door."

"What can you expect from him? Just look at him."

"Are you two deviates talking about me?" Ignatius asked angrily. "If you're going to get this excited about a door, I seriously doubt whether you'll survive for long in the vicious arena of politics."

"Oh, get me out of here. I'm going to *scream* if I stay in these tacky chains much longer."

"Oh, shut up, Nellie," Dorian snapped, slapping Timmy across his pink cheeks. "Get out of my house and go back on the streets where you belong."

"Oh!" the sailor cried. "What a terrible thing to say."

"Please," Ignatius cautioned. "The movement must not be sabotaged by internal strife."

"I did think that I had at least one friend left," the sailor said to Dorian. "I see I was wrong. Go ahead. Slap me again if it gives you so much pleasure."

"I wouldn't even touch you, you little tramp."

"I doubt whether any hack, under pressure, could pen such atrocious melodrama," Ignatius observed. "Now stop all of this, you two degenerates. Exercise at least a little taste and decency."

"Slap me!" the sailor shrieked. "I know you're dying to do it. You'd love to hurt me, wouldn't you?"

"Apparently he won't settle down until you've agreed to inflict at least a little physical injury upon him," Ignatius told Dorian.

"I wouldn't put a finger on his stupid slut body."

"Well, we must do something to silence him. My valve can take only so much of this deranged mariner's neuroses. We shall have to politely drop him from the movement. He simply does not measure up. Anyone can smell that heavy musk of masochism which he exudes. It's stinking up the slave quarters at this very moment. In addition, he appears rather drunk."

"You hate me, too, you big monster," the sailor screamed at Ignatius.

Ignatius tapped Timmy soundly on the head with his cutlass, and the seafarer emitted a little moan.

"Goodness knows what debased fantasy he's having," Ignatius commented.

"Oh, hit him again," Dorian chirped happily. "What fun!"

"Please let me out of these awful chains," the sailor pleaded. "My sailor suit's getting all rusty."

While Dorian was unlocking the shackles with a key he took from over the door, Ignatius said, "You know, manacles and chains have functions in modern life which their fevered inventors must never have considered in an earlier and simpler age. If I were a suburban developer, I would attach at least one set to the walls of every new yellow brick ranch style and Cape Cod split level. When the suburbanites grew tired of television and Ping-Pong or whatever they do in their little homes, they could chain one another up for a while. Everyone would love it. Wives would say, 'My husband put me in chains last night. It was wonderful. Has your husband done that to you lately?' And children would hurry eagerly home from school to their mothers who would be waiting to chain them. It would help the children to cultivate the imagination denied them by television and would appreciably cut down on the incidence of juvenile delinquency. When father came in from work, the whole family could grab him and chain him for being stupid enough to be working all day long to support them. Troublesome old relatives would be chained in the carport. Their hands would be released only once a month so they could sign over their Social Security checks. Manacles and chains could build a better life for all. I must give this some space in my notes and jottings."

"Oh, my dear," Dorian sighed. "Don't you ever shut up?"

"My arms *are* all rusty," Timmy said. "Just wait till I get my hands on that Billy and Raoul."

"Our little convention seems to be getting rather unwieldy," Ignatius said of the mad noises issuing from Dorian's apartment. "Apparently feeling about the issues is striking more than one nerve center."

"Oh, heavens, I'd rather not look," Dorian said, pushing the glass-paneled wisp of a French provincial door open.

Inside Ignatius saw a seething mass of people. Cigarette and cocktail glasses held like batons flew in the air directing the symphony of chatter, shrieking, singing, and laughing. From the bowels of a huge stereophonic phonograph the voice of Judy Garland was fighting its way through the din. A small band of young men, the only stationary ones in the room, stood before the phonograph as if it were an altar. "Divine!" "Fantastic!" "So human!" they were saying of the voice from their electric tabernacle.

His blue and yellow eyes traveled from this rite to the rest of the room, where the other guests were attacking one another with conversation. Herringbones and madras and lamb's wool and cashmere flashed past in a blur as hands and arms rent the air in a variety of graceful gestures. Fingernails, cuff links, pinky rings, teeth, eyes—all glittered. In the center of one knot of elegant guests a cowboy with a little riding crop flicked the crop at one of his fans, producing a response of exaggerated screaming and pleased giggling. In the center of another knot stood a lout in a black leather jacket who was teaching judo holds, to the great delight of his epicene students. "Oh, do teach me that," someone near the wrestler screamed after an elegant guest had been twisted into an obscene position and then thrown to the floor to land with a crash of cuff links and other, assorted jewelry.

"I only invited the better people," Dorian said to Ignatius.

"Good gracious," Ignatius spluttered. "I can see that we're going to have a great deal of trouble capturing the conservative rural red-neck Calvinist vote. We are going to have to rebuild our image along lines other than those I see here."

Timmy, who was watching the black leather lout twist and dump eager partners sighed, "How fun."

The room itself was what decorators would probably call *severe*. The walls and high ceilings were white, and the room itself was sparsely furnished with a few pieces of antique furniture. The only voluptuous element in the large room was the champagne-colored velvet drapes tied back with white ribbons. The two or three antique chairs had apparently been chosen for their bizarre design and not for their ability to seat anyone, for they were delicate suggestions, hints at furniture with cushions barely capable of accommodating a child. A human in such a room was expected not to rest or sit or even relax, but rather pose, thereby transforming himself into a human furnishing that would complement the decor as well as possible.

After Ignatius had studied the decor, he said to Dorian,

"The only functional item in here is that phonograph, and that is obviously being misused. This is a room with no soul." He snorted loudly, in part over the room and in part over the fact that no one in the room had even noticed him, even though he complemented the decor as well as a neon sign would have. The participants in the kickoff rally seemed much more concerned about their own private fates this evening than they were about the fate of the world. "I notice that no one in this whitened sepulcher of a room has so much as even looked at us. They haven't even nodded to their host, whose liquor they are consuming and whose year-round air conditioning they are taxing with all of those overpowering colognes. I feel rather like an observer at a catfight."

"Don't worry about them. They've been simply dying for a good party for months. Come. You must see the decoration that I've made." He took Ignatius over to the mantel-piece and showed him a bud vase containing one red, one white, and one blue rose. "Isn't that wild? It's better than all of that tacky crepe paper. I did buy some crepe paper, but nothing that I could do with it satisfied me."

"This is a floral abortion," Ignatius commented irritably and tapped the vase with his cutlass. "Dyed flowers are unnatural and perverse and, I suspect, obscene also. I can see that I am going to have my hands full with you people."

"Oh, talk, talk, talk," Dorian moaned. "Then let's go into the kitchen. I want you to meet the ladies' auxiliary."

"Is that true? An auxiliary?" Ignatius asked greedily. "Well, I must compliment you upon your foresightedness."

They entered the kitchen where, except for two young men who were having an emotional argument in a corner, all was quiet. Seated at a table were three women drinking from beer cans. They regarded Ignatius squarely. The one who was crushing a beer can in her hand stopped and tossed the can into a potted plant next to the sink.

"Girls," Dorian said. The three beer girls raised a raucous Bronx cheer. "This is Ignatius Reilly, a new face."

"Put it there, Fats," the girl who had been crushing the can said. She grabbed Ignatius' paw and worked it over as if it, too, were a prospect for crushing.

"Oh, my God!" Ignatius screamed.

"That's Frieda," Dorian explained. "And they're Betty and Liz."

"How do you do," Ignatius said, slipping his hands into the pockets of his smock to prevent any further handshaking. "I'm sure that you'll be of invaluable help to our cause."

"Where did you pick him up?" Frieda asked Dorian while her two companions studied Ignatius and nudged each other.

"Mr. Greene and I met through my mother," Ignatius answered grandly for Dorian.

"No kidding," Frieda said, "Your mother must be a very interesting person."

"Hardly," Ignatius replied.

"Well, grab yourself a beer, Tubby," Frieda said. "I wish we had it in bottles. Betty here could open you one with her teeth. She's got teeth like an iron claw." Betty made an obscene gesture at Frieda. "And one of those days she's going to get them all knocked down her fucking throat."

Betty hit Frieda on the head with an empty can.

"You're asking for it," Frieda said, raising one of the kitchen chairs.

"Now stop it," Dorian spat. "If you three can't behave, you can just leave right now."

"Personally," Liz said, "we're getting very bored just sitting here in the kitchen."

"Yeah," Betty screamed. She grabbed a rung of the chair that Frieda was holding over her head, and she and Frieda began wrestling for possession of it. "How come we have to sit out here?"

"Put that chair down this minute," Dorian said.

"Yes, please," Ignatius added. He had retreated to a corner. "Someone will be injured."

"Like *you*," Liz said. She heaved an unopened beer can at Ignatius, who ducked.

"Good heavens!" Ignatius said. "I think I shall return to the other room."

"Beat it, bigass," Liz said to him. "You're using up all the air in here."

"Girls!" Dorian was screaming at the wrestling Frieda and Betty, whose T-shirts were growing damp. They were huffing and heaving around the room with the chair, mashing each other against the wall and sink.

"Okay, cut it out," Liz screamed at her friends. "These people are going to think you're crude."

She picked up another chair and got between the two contestants. Then she slammed her chair down onto the one that Frieda and Betty were wrestling over, knocking the girls aside. The two chairs rattled and clattered to the floor.

"Who told you to butt in?" Frieda demanded of Liz, grabbing her by her cropped hair.

Dorian, stumbling over the chairs, tried to push the girls back to the table, snapping, "Now sit down there and be decent."

"This party stinks," Betty said, "Where's the action?"

"How come you invited us down here if all we're gonna do is sit here in this frigging kitchen?" Frieda demanded.

"You'll only start brawling in there. You know it. I thought it would be a neighborly thing to do to ask you down out of courtesy. I don't want any trouble. This is the nicest party we've had in months."

"Okay," Frieda growled. "We'll sit out here like ladies." The girls punched one another about the arms in agreement. "After all, we're only paying tenants. Go in there and be nice to that phony cowboy, the one that sounds like Jeanette MacDonald, the one that tried to bitch us on Chartres Street the other day."

"He's a very fine and friendly person," Dorian said. "I'm sure he didn't see you girls."

"He saw us all right," Betty said. "We copped him on the head."

"I'd like to kick his superior balls in," Liz said.

"Please," Ignatius said importantly. "All I see about me is strife. You must close ranks and present a unified front."

"What's with him?" Liz asked, opening the beer can she had thrown at Ignatius. A spray of foam shot out and wet Ignatius on his distended Paradise product stomach.

"Well, I've had enough of this," Ignatius said angrily.

"Good," Frieda said. "Shove off."

"The kitchen is our territory tonight," Betty said. "We decide who uses it."

"I certainly am interested in seeing the first sherry party that the auxiliary gives," Ignatius snorted and lumbered to the door. As he was exiting, an empty beer can struck the door frame near his earring. Dorian followed him out and closed the door. "I can't imagine how you decided to besmirch the movement by inviting those rowdies here."

"I had to," Dorian explained. "If you don't invite them to a party, they break in anyway. Then they're even worse. They're really fun girls when they're in a good mood, but they had some trouble with the police recently, and they're taking it out on everyone."

"They shall be dropped from the movement immediately!"

"Anything you say, Magyara," Dorian sighed. "I myself feel a little sorry for the girls. They used to live in California, where they had a grand time. Then there was an incident about assaulting a bodybuilder at Muscle Beach. They had been Indian arm wrestling with the boy, or so they say, and then it seems that things got out of hand. They literally had to flee southern California and dash across the desert in that magnificent German automobile of theirs. I have given them sanctuary. In many respects they're wonderful tenants. They guard my building better than any watchdog could. They have loads of money that they get from some aging movie queen."

"Really?" Ignatius asked with interest. "Perhaps I was hasty about dropping them. Political movements must get their money from whatever source they can. The girls have, no doubt, a charm which their blue jeans and boots obscure." He looked over the seething mass of guests. "You must get these people quiet. We must bring them to order. There is crucial business at hand."

The cowboy, the phony bitch, was tickling an elegant guest with his riding crop. The black leather lout was pinning an ecstatic guest to the floor. Everywhere there were screams, sighs, shrieks. Lena Horne was now singing within the phonograph. "Clever," "Crisp," "Terribly cosmo," the group around the phonograph was saying reverently. The cowboy broke away from his aroused fans and began to synchronize his lips to the lyrics on the record, slinking around the floor like a chanteuse in boots and stetson. With a barrage of squeals, the guests gathered around him, leaving the black leather lout with no one to torture.

"You must stop all of this," Ignatius shouted to Dorian, who was winking at the cowboy. "Aside from the fact that I am witnessing a most egregious offense against taste and decency, I am also beginning to smother from the stench of glandular emissions and cologne."

"Oh, don't be so drab. They're just having fun."

"I am very sorry," Ignatius said in a businesslike tone. "I am here tonight on a mission of the utmost seriousness. There is a girl who must be attended to, a bold and forward minx of a trollop. Now turn off that offensive music and quiet these sodomites. We must get down to brass tacks."

"I thought you were going to be fun. If you're just going to be tacky and dreary, then you'd better leave."

"I shall not leave! No one can deter me. Peace! Peace! Peace!"

"Oh, dear. You *are* serious about this, aren't you?"

Ignatius broke away from Dorian and rushed across the room, pushing through the elegant guests, and unplugged the phonograph. As he turned around, he was greeted by the guests' emasculated version of an Apache war cry.

"Beast." "Madman." "Is this what Dorian promised?" "That fantastic Lena." "The outfit—grotesque. And that earring. Oh, my." "That was my very favorite song." "Horrible." "How unbelievably gross." "So monstrously huge." "A bad, bad dream."

"Silence!" Ignatius bellowed over their enraged babbling. "I am here tonight my friends, to show you how you may save the world and bring peace."

"He's truly mad." "Dorian, what a bad joke." "Where in the world did he come from?" "Not even vaguely attractive." "Filthy." "Depressing." "Someone turn on that delicious record again."

"The challenge," Ignatius continued at full volume, "is placed before you. Will you turn your singular talents to saving the world, or will you simply turn your backs on your fellow man?"

"Oh, how awful!" "Not at all amusing." "I'll have to leave if this tacky charade continues." "In such poor taste." "Someone turn on that record again. Dear, dear Lena." "Where is my coat?" "Let's go to a smart bar." "Look, I've spilled my martini on my most priceless jacket." "Let's go to a smart bar."

"The world today is in a state of grave unrest," Ignatius screamed against the mewing and hissing. He paused for a moment to glance down in his pocket at some notes he had scribbled on a piece of Big Chief paper. Instead he pulled out the torn and dogeared photograph of Miss O'Hara. Several guests saw it and schrieked. "We must prevent the apocalypse. We must fight fire with fire. Therefore, I turn to you."

"Oh, what in heaven's name is he talking about?" "This is making me so depressed." "Those eyes, they're frightening." "Let's go to a smart bar." "Let's go to San Francisco."

"Silence, you perverts!" Ignatius cried. "Listen to me."

"Dorian," the cowboy pleaded in a lyric soprano. "Make him keep quiet. We were having such fun, such a grand, gay time. Oh, he's not even amusing."

"That's, right," an extremely elegant guest, whose taut face was brown with suntan makeup, said. "He's truly awful. So depressing."

"Must we listen to all of this?" another guest asked, waving his cigarette as if it were a magic wand which would make Ignatius disappear. "Is this a trick of some kind, Dorian? You know that we dearly love parties with a motif, but *this*. I mean, I never even watch the news on television. I've been working all day in that shop, and I don't want to come to a party and have to hear all of this sort of thing. Let him talk later if he really has to. His remarks are in such terrible taste."

"So inappropriate," the black leather lout sighed, turning suddenly fey.

"All right," Dorian said. "Turn on the record. I thought it might be fun." He looked at Ignatius, who was snorting loudly. "I'm afraid, my dears, that it turned out to be a terrible, terrible bomb."

"Wonderful." "Dorian's magnificent." "There's the plug." "I love Lena." "I truly think that this is her very best recording." "So smart. Those special lyrics." "I saw her in New York once. Magnificent." "Play *Gypsy* next. I adore Ethel." "Oh, good, it's coming on."

There Ignatius stood like the boy on the burning deck. The

music rose from the tabernacle once again. Dorian fled to speak with a group of his guests, actively ignoring Ignatius, as was everyone else in the room. Ignatius felt as alone as he had felt on that dark day in high school when in a chemistry laboratory his experiment had exploded, burning his eyebrows off and frightening him. The shock and terror had made him wet his pants, and no one in the laboratory would notice him, not even the instructor, who hated him sincerely for similar explosions in the past. For the remainder of that day, as he walked soggily around the school, everyone had pretended that he was invisible. Ignatius, feeling just as invisible standing there in Dorian's living room, began feinting at some imaginary opponent with his cutlass to relieve his self-consciousness.

Many were now singing with the record. Two began dancing near the phonograph. The dancing spread like a forest fire, and soon the floor was filled with couples who swayed and dipped around the Gibraltar of a wallflower, Ignatius. As Dorian swept past in the arms of the cowboy, Ignatius tried futilely to attract his attention. He attempted even to stick the cowboy with his cutlass, but the two were a wily and elusive dance team. Just as he was about to evanesce completely, Frieda, Liz, and Betty burst in from the kitchen.

"We couldn't take that kitchen any more," Frieda said to Ignatius. "After all, we're human beings, too." She gave Ignatius a light rabbit punch to the stomach. "Looks like you're left out, Fats."

"Just what do you mean?" Ignatius asked haughtily.

"Looks like your costume's not going over too well," Liz observed.

"Pardon me, ladies. I must leave."

"Hey, don't go, Tubby," Betty said. "Somebody'll ask you. They're just trying to bitch you. Don't give up the ship. They'd bitch their own mother."

At that moment, Timmy, who had slipped out to the slave

quarters again to look for his missing charm bracelet and, he hoped, more games with the chains, appeared in the living room. He wandered over to Ignatius and asked wistfully, "Do you want to dance?"

"There. You see?" Frieda said to Ignatius.

"I want to see this," Liz shouted. "Let's see you two do the limbo. Come on. I'll get a broom we can use for the pole."

"Oh, my God!" Ignatius said. "Please. I don't dance."

"Oh, come on," Timmy said. "I can teach you. I love to dance. I'll lead."

"Go ahead, bigass," Betty threatened.

"No. It would be impossible. The cutlass, the smock. Someone would be injured. I came here to speak, not dance. I don't dance. I never dance. I have never danced in my life."

"Well, you're going to dance now," Frieda told him. "You don't want to hurt this sailor's feelings."

"I am not dancing!" Ignatius barked. "I have never danced, and I certainly am not going to begin with some drunken deviate."

"Oh, don't be so straight," Timmy sighed.

"I have always had a rather substandard sense of balance," Ignatius explained. "We will plunge to the floor a broken heap. This deranged mariner will be crippled or worse."

"Tubby looks like a troublemaker," Frieda said to her friends. "Right?"

With a wink from Frieda, the three girls attacked Ignatius. One wrapped a square leg around his; the other kicked him in the back of the knee; the third pushed him backward onto the cowboy, who was whirling in the vicinity. Ignatius steadied himself by grabbing the cowboy, who broke from Dorian's horrified grasp and toppled to the floor. As the cowboy landed, the needle jumped from the record and the music stopped. But in its place there began a chorus of shrieking and screaming from the guests.

"Oh, Dorian, get him out!" an elegant shrieked in panic.

There was a metallic crash of rings, bracelets, and cuff links as some of the guests pressed together in a corner.

"Hey, you knocked that bitch of a cowboy over like a tenpin," Frieda screamed admiringly at Ignatius, who was still flailing his arms to regain his balance.

"Nice work, Fats," Liz said.

"Let's aim him at somebody else," Betty said to her companions.

"What have you done, you huge beastly thing?" Dorian cried at Ignatius.

"This is an outrage," Ignatius was shouting. "I have not only been ignored and vilified at this gathering. I have been viciously attacked within the walls of your cobweb of a home. I hope that you carry liability insurance. If not, you may well lose this flamboyant property once my legal advisors have attended to you."

Dorian was down on his knees, fanning the cowboy, whose lids were beginning to flutter.

"Make him leave, Dorian," the cowboy sobbed. "He almost *killed* me."

"I had thought you might be different and funny," Dorian hissed at Ignatius. "As it is, you have proved to be the most awful thing that has ever been in my house. From the moment that you broke the door, I should have realized that it would end like this. What did you do to this dear boy?"

"My trousers are *filthy*," the cowboy shrieked.

"I was savagely attacked and pushed onto that coxcomb cowpoke."

"Don't try to lie, Fats," Frieda said. "We saw the whole thing. He was jealous, Dorian. He wanted to dance with you."

"Awful." "Make him go." "Ruining the party." "So monstrous." "Dangerous." "Total loss."

"Get out!" Dorian cried.

"We'll handle him," Frieda said.

"All right," Ignatius said grandly as the three girls sank their stubby hands into his smock and started propelling him toward the door. "You have made your choice. Live in a world of war and bloodshed. When the bomb drops, do not come to me. I shall be in my shelter!"

"Can it," Betty said.

The three girls hustled Ignatius through the door and down the carriageway.

"Thank Fortuna I'm dissociating myself from this movement," Ignatius thundered. The girls had knocked the scarf down over one eye and he was having trouble seeing where he was going. "You distempered people hardly have voter appeal."

They pushed him through the gate and onto the sidewalk. The Spanish dagger plants at the gate pricked his calves painfully and he stumbled forward.

"Okay, buster," Frieda called through the gate as she closed it. "We're giving you a ten minutes headstart. Then we start combing the Quarter."

"We better not find your fat ass," Liz said.

"Shove off, Tubby," Betty added. "We haven't had a good fight in a long time. We're ready for one."

"Your movement is doomed," Ignatius slobbered after the girls, who were pushing one another down the carriageway. "Do you hear me? D-o-o-m-e-d. You know nothing about politics and voter persuasion. You will not carry a single ward in the nation. You won't even carry the Quarter!"

The door slammed and the girls were back in the party, which seemed to have regained its momentum. The music had started again, and Ignatius heard the squealing and shrieking growing louder than before. He knocked on the black shutters with his cutlass, screaming, "You will lose!" The tap and slide of many dancing feet answered his cry.

A man wearing a silk suit and a homburg came out of the shadow of an adjoining doorway for a moment to see whether the girls had gone. Then the man slipped back into the darkness, watching Ignatius, who was waddling back and forth before the building furiously.

Ignatius' valve responded to his emotions by plopping closed. His hands sympathized by sprouting a rich growth of tiny white bumps that itched maddeningly. What could he tell Myrna about the movement for peace now? Now, like the abortive Crusade for Moorish Dignity, he had another debacle on his itching hands. Fortuna, that vicious slut. The evening had hardly begun; he couldn't return to Constantinople Street and a variety of assaults from his mother, not now that his emotions had been stimulated toward a climax that had been snatched from his grasp. For almost a week he had been preoccupied with the kickoff rally, and now, ejected from the political arena by three dubious girls, he stood frustrated and furious on the damp flagstones of St. Peter Street.

Looking at his Mickey Mouse wristwatch which was, as usual, moribund, he wondered what time it was. Perhaps it was still early enough to see the first show at the Night of Joy. Perhaps Miss O'Hara had opened. If he and Myrna were not destined to joust on the field of political action, then it would have to be the field of sex. What a lance Miss O'Hara could be to hurl right between Myrna's offensive eyes. Ignatius looked at the photograph once more, salivating slightly. What kind of pet? The evening could still be wrenched from the jaws of failure.

Scratching one paw with the other, he decided that safety at least dictated his moving along. Those three savage girls might make good their threat. He billowed off down St. Peter toward Bourbon. The man in the silk suit and homburg came out of the shadow of the doorway and followed him. At Bourbon, Ignatius turned and began walking up toward Canal through the night's parade of tourists and Quarterites, among whom he did not look particularly strange. He shoved through the crowd on the narrow sidewalk, his hips swinging each way free and slamming people aside. When Myrna read of Miss O'Hara, she would spew espresso all over the letter in consternation.

As he crossed onto the Night of Joy's block, he heard the doped Negro calling, "Whoa! Come in, see Miss Harla O'Horror dancin with her pet. Guarantee one hunner percent real plantation dancin. Ever motherfuckin drink got a guarantee knockout drop. Whoa! Everybody guarantee to catch them some clap off they glass. Hey! Nobody never see nothin like Miss Harla O'Horror Old South pet dancin. Opening night tonight, maybe this be your one and only chance to catch this act. Ooo-wee."

Ignatius saw him through the crowd that was hurrying past the Night of Joy. Apparently no one was heeding the barker's plea. The barker himself had paused in his calling to emit a nimbus formation of smoke. He was wearing tails and a stovepipe hat that rested at an angle above his dark glasses, smiling through the smoke at the people who resisted his appeals.

"Hey! All you peoples draggin along here. Stop and come stick your ass on a Night of Joy stool," he started again. "Night of Joy got genuine color peoples workin below the minimal wage. Whoa! Guarantee plantation atmosphere, got cotton growin right on the stage right in front your eyeball, got a civil right worker gettin his ass beat up between show. Hey!"

"Is Miss O'Hara on yet?" Ignatius slobbered at the barker's elbow.

"Oo-wee!" The fat mother had arrived. In person. "Hey, man, how come you still warin that earrin and scarve? What you suppose to be anyway?"

"Please." Ignatius rattled his cutlass a bit. "I haven't time to chat. I have no success pointers for you tonight, I'm afraid. Has Miss O'Hara begun?"

"She be startin in a few minute. You better get your ass in there and get you a ringside seat. I talk to the head waiter, he say he have a table all reserve for you."

"Is that true?" Ignatius asked eagerly. "The Nazi proprietress is gone, I hope."

"She jet away to Califonia this afternoon, say Harla O'Horror so good she gonna go dip her ass in the ocean a while and stop worryin about her club."

"Wonderful, wonderful."

"Come on, man, get inside before the show start. Whoa! You don wanna miss one minute. Shit. Harla comin on in a few seconds, go get yourself right down by that motherfuckin stage, see ever goosebump on Miss O'Horror bum."

Jones propelled Ignatius rapidly through the padded door.

Ignatius stumbled into the Night of Joy with such momentum that his smock swirled around his ankles. Even in the darkness he noticed that the Night of Joy was somewhat dirtier than it had been on his previous visit. There was certainly enough dirt on the floor to permit a very limited cotton crop; but he saw no cotton. That must have been one of the Night of Joy's vicious come-ons. He looked about for the headwaiter and saw none, so he lumbered through the few old men scattered about at tables in the gloom and seated himself at a small table directly beneath the stage. His cap looked like a solitary green footlight. At this close range he could perhaps make some gesture to Miss O'Hara or whisper something about Boethius that would attract her attention. She would be overwhelmed when she realized that there was a kindred spirit in the audience. Ignatius glanced about at the handful of empty-eyed men seated in the place. Miss O'Hara certainly had to cast her pearls before a dismal lot of swine, who looked like the type of vague, drawn old men who molested children at matinees.

A three-piece band in the wings of the tiny stage was beginning to thump through *You Are My Lucky Star*. At the moment the stage, which itself looked a bit dirty, was empty of orgiasts. Ignatius looked over at the bar to try to attract some sort of service and caught the eye of the bartender who had served his mother and him. The bartender pretended not to see him. Then Ignatius winked wildly at a woman leaning on the bar, a fortyish Latin who leered a terrifying response with a gold tooth or two. She pried herself loose from the bar before the bartender could stop her and came over to Ignatius, who was huddled against the stage as if it were a warm stove.

"You wanna dreenk, chico?"

Some halitosis filtered through his moustache. He ripped the scarf from his cap and shielded his nostrils with it.

"Thank you, yes," he said in a muffled voice. "A Dr. Nut, if you please. And be certain that it's frosty cold."

"I see what we have," the woman said enigmatically and clopped back to the bar in her straw sandals.

Ignatius watched her speak to the bartender in pantomime. They made a variety of gestures, most of which were directed at Ignatius. At least, Ignatius thought, he would be safe in this den if the sinewy girls were out prowling the Quarter. The bartender and the woman made some more signs; then she clopped back to Ignatius with two bottles of champagne and two glasses.

"We no have Dr. Nut," she said and slammed the tray on the table. "*Mira*, you are owe twenty-four dollar for these champagne."

"This is an outrage!" He directed a few swipes of the cutlass at the woman. "Bring me a coke."

"No coke. No nawtheen. Only champagne." The woman took a seat at the table. "Come on, hawny. Open the champagne. I am very thirsty."

Again the breath wafted toward Ignatius, who pressed the

scarf to his nose so tightly that he felt he would suffocate. He would catch some germ from this woman that would speed to his brain and transform him into a mongoloid. Misused Miss O'Hara. Trapped with subhuman women as co-workers. Of necessity, Miss O'Hara's Boethian detachment must be rather lofty. The Latin woman dropped the check in Ignatius' lap.

"Don't you dare touch me!" he bellowed through the scarf.

"*Ave Maria! Que pato!*" the woman said to herself. Then she said, "*Mira*, you are pay now, *maricon*. We throw you out on your big *culo*."

"Such grace," Ignatius mumbled. "Well, I did not come here to drink with you. Now get away from my table." He breathed deeply through the mouth. "And take your champagne with you."

"*Oye, loco*, you are . . ."

The woman's threat was submerged by the band, which emitted a debilitated fanfare of sorts. Lana Lee appeared on the stage in what looked like gold lamé overalls.

"Oh, my God!" Ignatius spluttered. The doped Negro had tricked him. He wanted to bolt from the club, but realized that it would be wiser to wait until the woman had finished and left the stage. In a moment, he was crouched down against the side of the stage. Over his head, the Nazi proprietress was saying, "Welcome, ladies and genitals." It was so dreadful a beginning that Ignatius almost knocked over the table.

"You are pay me now," the woman was demanding, sticking her head under the table to find the face of her customer.

"Shut up, you slut," Ignatius hissed.

The band stumbled into a four-count version of *Sophisticated Lady*. The Nazi woman was screaming, "And now that pure Virgin-ny Belle, Miss Harlett O'Hara." An old man at one of the tables clapped feebly, and Ignatius peered over the rim of the stage and saw that the proprietress was gone. In her place stood a stand decorated with rings. What was Miss O'Hara up to?

Then Darlene swept onstage in a ball gown that trailed yards of nylon net. On her head was a monstrous picture hat and on her arm a monstrous bird. Someone else clapped.

"*Mira*, you are pay me now or else, *cabron*."

"There sure was plenty balls at that ball, but I still got my honor," Darlene said carefully to the bird.

"Oh, my God!" Ignatius bellowed, unable to remain silent any longer. "Is this cretin Harlett O'Hara?"

The cockatoo noticed him before Darlene did, for its beads of eyes had been focusing on Ignatius' hoop of a novelty earring ever since it had come onstage. When Ignatius bellowed, it flapped from Darlene's arm to the stage and squawking, hopping, dashed for Ignatius' head.

"Hey," Darlene cried. "It's the crazyman."

As Ignatius was about to dash from the club, the bird hopped from the stage to his shoulder. It sank its claws into his smock and snagged his earring with its beak.

"Good heavens!" Ignatius leaped up and beat at the bird with his itching paws. What avian menace had depraved Fortuna spun his way? The champagne bottles and the glasses shattered on the floor as he sprang and began staggering to the door.

"Come back here with my cockatoo," Darlene cried.

Lana Lee was on the stage now, screaming. The band had stopped. The few old male patrons moved out of the way of Ignatius, who was floundering around among the little tables making moose calls and beating at the mass of rose feathers welded to his ear and shoulder.

"How in the hell did that character get in here?" Lana Lee asked the confused septuagenarians in the audience. "Where's Jones? Somebody get me that Jones."

362

"Come here, you big crazyman," Darlene hollered. "On opening night. Why you hadda come here on opening night?"

"Good grief," Ignatius gasped, feeling for the door. In his wake he had left a trail of overturned tables. "How dare you fiends inflict a rabid bird upon your unsuspecting customers? You may expect to be sued in the morning."

"*Come!* You are owe twenty-four dollar to me. You are pay right now."

Ignatius knocked over another table as he and the cockatoo lurched forward. Then he felt the earring loosening, and the cockatoo, the earring firmly in its beak, fell from his shoulder. Terrorized, Ignatius bounced out of the door just ahead of the Latin woman, who was waving the check with great determination.

"Whoa! Hey!"

Ignatius stumbled past Jones, who had never expected the sabotage to assume such dramatic proportions. Gasping, clutching his cemented valve, Ignatius continued forward onto the street and into the path of an oncoming Desire bus. He first heard the people on the sidewalk screaming. Then he heard the pounding tires and the crying brakes, and when he glanced up he was blinded by headlights a few feet from his eyes. The headlights swam and faded from his sight as he fainted.

He would have fallen directly before the bus if Jones hadn't leaped into the street and pulled at the white smock with his two large hands. Ignatius instead fell backward, and the bus, exhaling diesel exhaust, rumbled past an inch or two from his desert boots.

"Is he dead?" Lana Lee asked hopefully, studying the mound of white material lying in the street.

"I am hope not. He is owe twenty-four dollar, the *maricon*."

"Hey, wake up, man," Jones said, blowing some smoke over the inert figure.

The man in the silk suit and homburg stepped from an alleyway, where he had hidden himself when he saw Ignatius enter the Night of Joy. Ignatius' departure from the club had been so violent and rapid that the man had been too startled to act until now.

"Let me take a look at him," the man in the homburg said, bending over and listening to Ignatius' heart. A kettledrum of a thump told him that life still breathed within the yards of white smock. He held Ignatius' wrist. The Mickey Mouse watch was smashed. "He's okay. He just passed out." The man cleared his throat and ordered weakly, "Everybody back. Give him air."

The street was filled with people and the bus had stopped a few yards down the street, blocking traffic. Suddenly it looked like Bourbon Street at Mardi Gras.

Through the darkness of his glasses Jones looked at the stranger. He looked familiar, like a well-dressed version of someone Jones had seen before. The weak eyes were most familiar. Jones remembered the same weak eyes on top of a red beard. Then he remembered the same eyes under a blue cap in the precinct on the day of the cashew nut incident. He said nothing. A policeman was a policeman. It was always best to ignore them unless they bothered you.

"Where he came from?" Darlene was asking the crowd. The rose cockatoo rested once again on her arm, the earring dangling from its beak like a golden worm. "What a opening night. What we gonna do, Lana?"

"Nothing," Lana said angrily. "Let that character lay there till the street sweeper comes around. Then let me get my hands on Jones."

"Whoa! Hey! That cat force his way in. We was fightin and grapplin, but that mother seem determine to get in the Night of Joy. I was ascare I be rippin this costume you rentin, you be havin to pay for it, Night of Joy be goin broke. Whoa!"

"Shut your smart mouth. I think I'm gonna have to call up all my pals at the precinct. You're fired. Darlene, too. I knew I shouldna let you get on my stage. Get that goddam bird off my sidewalk." Lana turned to the crowd. "Well, folks, now that you're all here, how's about coming into the Night of Joy? We got a class show."

"*Mira*, Lee." The Latin woman inflicted a little halitosis on Lana Lee. "Who is pay the twenty-four dollar for champagne?"

"You're fired, too, you dumb spic." Lana smiled. "Come on in folks, and enjoy a good drink made by our expert mixologists to your exact specifications."

The crowd, however, was craning at the white mound, which was wheezing loudly, and declined the invitation to elegance.

Lana Lee was about to go over and kick the mound into consciousness and get it out of her gutter when the man in the homburg said politely, "I'd like to use your telephone. Maybe I'd better call a ambulance."

Lana looked at the silk suit, the hat, the weak, insecure eyes. She could spot a safe one, a soft touch all right. A rich doctor? A lawyer? She might be able to turn this little fiasco into a profit.

"Sure," she whispered. "Look, you don't wanna waste your evening messing with that character laying in the street. He's some kinda bum. You look like you could use you some fun." She stepped around the white mountain of smock, which was wheezing and snorting volcanically. Somewhere in fantasyland Ignatius was dreaming of a terrified Myrna Minkoff being tried by a court of Taste and Decency and found wanting. A dreadful sentence was about to be pronounced, something guaranteeing physical injury to her person as penance for innumerable offences. Lana Lee got close to the man and reached into her gold lamé overalls. She squatted next to him and surreptitiously flashed the Boethian photograph cupped in her hand. "Take a look at this, baby. How'd you like to spend the evening with that?"

The man in the homburg turned his eyes from Ignatius' whitened face and looked at the woman, the book, the globe, the chalk. He cleared his throat once more and said, "I'm Patrolman Mancuso. Undercover agent. You're under arrest for soliciting and for possession of pornography."

Just then the three members of the defunct ladies' auxiliary, Frieda, Betty, and Liz, stomped into the crowd surrounding Ignatius.

Thirteen

Ignatius opened his eyes and saw white floating above him. He had a headache and his ear was throbbing. Then his blue and yellow eyes focused slowly, and, through his headache, he realized that he was looking at a ceiling.

"So you finally woke up, boy," his mother's voice said near him. "Just take a look at this. Now we really ruined."

"Where am I?"

"Don't start acting smart with me, boy. Don't start with me, Ignatius. I'm warning you. I had enough. I mean it. How I'm gonna face people after this?"

Ignatius turned his head and looked about him. He was lying in a little cell formed by screens on either side. He saw a nurse pass by the foot of the bed.

"Good heavens! I'm in a hospital. Who is my doctor? I hope that you have been selfless enough to secure the services of a specialist. And a priest. Have one come. I'll see whether he's acceptable." Ignatius sprayed a little nervous saliva on the sheet that snowcapped the peak of his stomach. He touched his head and felt a bandage plastered over his headache. "Oh, my God! Don't be afraid to tell me, Mother. I can tell from the pain that it must be rather fatal."

"Shut up and take a look at this," Mrs. Reilly almost shouted, throwing a newspaper on Ignatius' bandage.

"Nurse!"

Mrs. Reilly tore the newspaper from his face and slapped her hand over his moustache.

"Now shut up, crazy, and take a look at this here paper." Her voice was cracking. "We ruined."

Under the headline that said, WILD INCIDENT ON BOURBON STREET, Ignatius saw three photographs lined up together. On the right Darlene with her ball gown was holding the cockatoo and smiling a starlet's smile. On the left Lana Lee covered her face with her hands as she climbed into the rear seat of a squad car already filled with the three cropped heads of the members of the ladies' auxiliary of the Peace Party. Patrolman Mancuso, in a torn suit and a hat with a bent rim, purposefully held open the door of the car. In the center the doped Negro was grinning at what looked like a dead cow lying in the street. Ignatius scrutinized the center photograph through slitted eyes.

"Just look at that," he thundered. "What sort of clods does that newspaper employ on its photographic staff? My features are barely distinguishable."

"Read what it says underneath the pictures, boy." Mrs. Reilly stuck a finger into the newspaper as if she meant to lance the photograph. "Just read it, Ignatius. What you think people are saying on Constantinople Street? Go on, read that out loud to me, boy. A big brawl out on the street, dirty pictures, ladies of the evening. It's all there. Read it, boy."

"I'd rather not. It's probably full of falsification and smear. The yellow journalists doubtlessly suggested all sorts of lipsmacking innuendoes." Nevertheless, Ignatius treated the story to a desultory reading.

"Do you mean to tell me that they claim that that wayward bus did not hit me?" he asked angrily. "The very first comment is a lie. Contact Public Service. We must sue."

"Shut up. Read the whole thing."

A stripper's bird had attacked a hot dog vendor wearing a costume. A. Mancuso, undercover, had arrested Lana Lee for soliciting and for possession of and posing for pornography. Burma Jones, porter, had led A. Mancuso to a cabinet under the bar where pornographic materials were discovered. A.

Mancuso told reporters that he had been working on the case for some time, that he had already contacted one of the Lee woman's agents. Police suspect that the arrest of the Lee woman broke a citywide high school pornography distribution syndicate. Police found a list of schools in the bar. A. Mancuso said that the agent would be sought. While A. Mancuso was performing the arrest, three women, Club, Steele, and Bumper, emerged from the large crowd before the club and assaulted him. They were also booked. Ignatius Jacques Reilly, thirty, was removed to a hospital to be treated for shock.

"It's our bad luck they had a photographer hanging around doing nothing they could send out to take a picture of you laying in the street like a drunk bum." Mrs. Reilly began to sniffle. "I shoulda known something like this was gonna happen with your dirty pictures and running off dressed up like a Mardi Gras."

"I ran off into the most dismal night of my life," Ignatius sighed. "Fortuna was really spinning drunkenly last night. I doubt whether I can go much farther down." He belched. "May I ask what that cretin nemesis of a policeman was doing on the scene?"

"Last night after you run off I rung up Santa and told her to get Angelo at the precinct and for him to go see what you was doing down on St. Peter Street. I heard you give a address to that taxi man."

"How clever."

"I thought you was going to a meeting with a buncha communiss. Was I wrong. Angelo says you was hanging around with some funny people."

"In other words, you were having me trailed," Ignatius screamed. "My own mother!"

"Attacked by a bird," Mrs. Reilly wept. "That hadda happen to you, Ignatius. Nobody never gets attacked by a bird."

"Where is that bus driver? He must be indicted immediately."

"You just fainted, stupid."

"Then why this bandage? I don't feel at all well. I must have damaged some vital part when I fell to the street."

"You just scraped your head a little. They's nothing wrong with you. They took Xrays."

"Have people been fooling with my body while I was unconscious? You might have had the good taste to stop them. Heaven knows where these salacious medical people have been probing." Ignatius now realized that in addition to the head and ear, an erection had been bothering him ever since he had awakened. It was demanding attention. "Would you mind leaving my booth for a moment while I inspect myself to see whether I've been mishandled? Five minutes should be sufficient."

"Look, Ignatius." Mrs. Reilly rose from the chair and grabbed Ignatius by the collar of the clownlike dotted pajamas that had been put on him. "Don't act smart with me or I'll slap your face off. Angelo told me all about it. A boy with your education bumming around with funny people down in the Quarter, going into a barroom to look for a lady of the evening." Mrs. Reilly cried anew. "We just lucky the whole thing's not in the paper. We'd have to move outta town."

"You're the one who introduced my innocent being to that den of a bar. Actually, it's all the fault of that dreadful girl, Myrna. She must be punished for her misdeeds."

"Myrna?" Mrs. Reilly sobbed. "She ain't even in town. I heard enough of your crazy stories already about how she got you fired outta Levy Pants. You can't do this to me no more. You're crazy, Ignatius. Even if I gotta say it, my own child's out his mind."

"You look rather haggard. Why don't you push someone aside and crawl into one of the beds around here and take a nap. Call again in about an hour."

"I been up all night. When Angelo rang me up and said you was in the hospital, I almost took a stroke. I almost fell down on the kitchen floor right on my head. I coulda split my skull wide open. Then I run into my room to get dressed and I sprain my ankle. I almost got in a wreck driving over here."

"Not another wreck," Ignatius gasped. "I would have to go to work in the salt mines this time."

"Here, stupid. Angelo says to give this to you."

Mrs. Reilly reached down next to her chair and picked from the floor the large volume of *The Consolation of Philosophy*. She aimed one of its corners at Ignatius' stomach.

"Awff," Ignatius gurgled.

"Angelo found it in that barroom last night," Mrs. Reilly said boldly. "Somebody stole it off him in the toilet."

"Oh, my God! This has all been arranged," Ignatius screamed, rattling the huge edition in his paws. "I see it all now. I told you long ago that that mongoloid Mancuso was our nemesis. Now he has struck his final blow. How innocent I was to lend him this book. How I've been duped." He closed his bloodshot eyes and slobbered incoherently for a moment. "Taken in by a Third Reich strumpet hiding her depraved face behind *my* very own book, the very basis of my worldview. Oh, Mother, if only you knew how cruelly I've been tricked by a conspiracy of subhumans. Ironically, the book of Fortuna is itself bad luck. Oh, Fortuna, you degenerate wanton!"

"Shut up," Mrs. Reilly shouted, her powdered face lined by anger. "You want the whole recovery ward coming in here? What you think Miss Annie's gonna say now? How I'm gonna face people, you stupid, crazy Ignatius? Now this hospital wants twenty dollars before I can take you outta here. The ambulance driver couldn't take you to the Charity like a nice man. No. He has to come dump you here in a pay hospital.

371

Where you think I got twenty dollars? I gotta meet a note on your trumpet tomorrow. I gotta pay that man for his building."

"That is outrageous. You will certainly not pay twenty dollars. It is highway robbery. Now run along home and leave me here. It's rather peaceful. I may recover eventually. It's exactly what my psyche needs at the moment. When you have a chance, bring me some pencils and the looseleaf folder you'll find on my desk. I must record this trauma while it's still fresh in my mind. You have my permission to enter my room. Now, if you'll pardon me, I must rest."

"Rest? And pay another twenty dollars for another day? Get up out that bed. I called up Claude. He's coming down here and pay your bill."

"Claude? Who in the world is Claude."

"A man I know."

"What has become of you?" Ignatius gasped. "Well, understand one thing right now. No strange man is going to pay my hospital bill. I shall stay here until honest money buys my freedom."

"Get up out that bed," Mrs. Reilly hollered. She snatched at the pajamas, but the body was sunken into the mattress like a meteor. "Get up before I smack your fat face off."

When he saw his mother's purse rising over his head, he sat up.

"Oh, my God! You're wearing your bowling shoes." Ignatius cast a pink and blue and yellow eye over the side of the bed down past his mother's hanging slip and drooping cotton stockings. "Only you would wear bowling shoes to your child's sickbed."

But his mother did not rise to the challenge. She had the determination, the superiority that comes with intense anger. Her eyes were steely, her lips thin and firm.

Everything was going wrong.

II

Mr. Clyde looked at the morning paper and fired Reilly. The big ape's career as a vendor was finished. Why was that baboon wearing his outfit when he was off duty? One ape like Reilly could demolish ten years of trying to build up a decent commercial name. Hot dog vendors had an image problem already without one of them passing out in the street by a whorehouse.

Mr. Clyde and the cauldron bubbled and boiled. If Reilly tried to show up at Paradise Vendors, Incorporated, again, he would really get it in the throat with the fork. But there were those smocks and that pirate gear. Reilly must have smuggled the pirate gimmicks out of the garage the afternoon before. He would have to contact the big ape after all, if only to tell him not to come around. You really couldn't expect to get your uniforms back from an animal like Reilly.

Mr. Clyde telephoned the number on Constantinople Street several times and got no answer. Maybe they had put him away somewhere. The big ape's mother must be dead drunk on the floor somewhere. Christ only knew what she was like. It must be quite a family.

III

Dr. Talc had been having a miserable week. Somehow the students had found one of those threats that that psychotic graduate student had flooded him with a few years before. How it got into their hands he didn't know. The results were already awful. An underground of rumors about the note was slowly spreading; he was becoming the butt of the campus. At a cocktail party one of his colleagues had finally explained to him the reason for the laughter and whispering that were distrupting his previously respectful classes.

That business in the note about "misleading and perverting the young" had been badly misunderstood and misinterpreted. He wondered if he might have to explain to the administration eventually. And that phrase "underdeveloped testicles." Dr. Talc cringed. Bringing the whole matter into the open might be the best plan, but that would mean trying to find that former student, who was the sort who would deny all responsibility anyway. Perhaps he should simply try to describe what Mr. Reilly had been like. Dr. Talc saw again Mr. Reilly with his massive muffler and that awful girl anarchist with the valise who traveled around with Mr. Reilly and littered the campus with leaflets. Fortunately she hadn't stayed at the college too long, although that Reilly seemed as if he were planning to make himself a fixture on the campus like the palm trees and the benches.

Dr. Talc had had them both in separate classes one grim semester, during which they had disrupted his lectures with strange noises and impertinent, venemous questions that no one, aside from God, could possibly have answered. He shuddered. In spite of everything, he must reach Reilly and extract an explanation and confession. One look at Mr. Reilly and the students would understand that the note was the meaningless fantasy of a sick mind. He could even let the administration look at Mr. Reilly. The solution was, after all, really a physical one: producing Mr. Reilly in the abundant flesh.

Dr. Talc sipped the vodka and V-8 juice that he always had after a night of heavy social drinking and looked at his newspaper. At least the people in the Quarter were having rowdy fun. He sipped his drink and remembered the incident of Mr. Reilly's dumping all of those examination papers on the heads of that freshman demonstration beneath the windows of the faculty office building. The administration would remember it, too. He smiled complacently and looked at the paper again. The three photographs were hilarious. Common, bawdy people—at a distance—had always amused him. He read the article and choked, spitting liquid onto his smoking jacket.

How had Reilly ever sunk so low? He had been eccentric as a student, but now . . . How much worse the rumors would be if it were discovered that the note had been written by a hot dog vendor. Reilly was the sort who would come to the campus with his wagon and try to sell hot dogs right before the Social Studies Building. He would deliberately turn the affair into a three-ring circus. It would be a disgraceful farce in which he, Talc, would become the clown.

Dr. Talc put down his paper and his glass and covered his face with his hands. He would have to live with that note. He would deny everything.

IV

Miss Annie looked at her morning newspaper and turned red. She had been wondering why it was so quiet over at the Reilly household this morning. Well, this was the last straw. Now the neighborhood was getting a bad name. She couldn't take it anymore. Those people had to move. She'd get the neighbors to sign a petition.

V

Patrolman Mancuso looked at the newspaper again. Then he held it to his chest and the flashbulb bopped. He had brought his own Brownie Holiday camera to the precinct and asked the sergeant to photograph him against certain official backdrops: the sergeant's desk, the steps of the precinct, a squad car, a traffic patrolwoman whose specialty was school zone speeders.

When there was only one exposure left, Patrolman Mancuso decided to combine two of the props for a dramatic finale. While the traffic patrolwoman, pretending to be Lana Lee, climbed into the rear of the squad car grimacing and shaking a vengeful fist, Patrolman Mancuso faced the camera with his newspaper and frowned sternly.

"Okay, Angelo, is that all?" the patrolwoman asked, eager to get to a nearby school before the morning speed zone hours ended.

"Thank you very much, Gladys," Patrolman Mancuso said. "My kids wanted to get some more pictures to show to they little friends."

"Well, sure," Gladys called, hurrying out of the precinct yard, her shoulder bag bursting with black speeding tickets. "I guess they got a right to be proud of they poppa. I'm glad I could help you out, honey. Anytime you want to take you some more pictures, just gimme the word."

The sergeant tossed the last flashbulb into a trash can and clamped his hand on Patrolman Mancuso's vertical shoulder.

"Single-handed you break up the city's most active high school pornography racket." He slapped his hand on the incline of Patrolman Mancuso's shoulder blade. "Mancuso, of all people, brings in a woman even our best plainclothesmen couldn't fool. Mancuso, I find out, has been working on this case on the q.t. Mancuso can identify one of her agents. Who's the person really been going out on his own all the time looking for characters like those three girls and trying to bring them in? Mancuso, that's who."

Patrolman Mancuso's olive skin flushed slightly, except in limited areas scratched by the Peace Party auxiliary. There it was simply red.

"Just luck," Patrolman Mancuso offered, clearing his throat

of some invisible phlegm. "Somebody gimme a lead to the place. Then that Burma Jones told me to look in that cabinet under the bar."

"You staged a one-man raid, Angelo."

Angelo? He turned a spectrum of shades between orange and violet.

"I wouldn't be surprised if you was to get a promotion for this," the sergeant said. "You been a patrolman a pretty long time. And just a couple days ago I was thinking you was a horse's ass. How's about that? What do you say to that, Mancuso?"

Patrolman Mancuso cleared his throat very violently.

"Can I have my camera back?" he asked almost incoherently when his larynx was at last clear.

VI

Santa Battaglia held the newspaper up to her mother's picture and said, "How you like that, babe? How you like the way your grandson Angelo made good? You like that, darling?" She pointed to another photograph. "How you like poor Irene's crazy boy laying there in the gutter like a washed-up whale? Ain't that sad? That girl's gotta get that boy put away this time. You think any man's gonna marry Irene with that big bum laying around the house? Of course not."

Santa snatched at her mother's picture and gave it a moist smack. "Take it easy, babe. I'm praying for you."

VII

Claude Robichaux looked at the newspaper with a heavy heart as he rode the streetcar to the hospital. How could that big boy disgrace a fine, sweet woman like Irene? Already she was pale and tired from worrying about her son. Santa was right: that son of Irene's had to be treated before he brought any more disgrace to his wonderful mother.

This time it was only twenty dollars. Next time it might be much more. Even with a nice pension and some properties, a person couldn't afford a stepson like that.

But worst of all was the disgrace.

VIII

George was pasting the article in the Junior Achievement scrapbook that was one of his mementos from his last semester at school. He pasted it on an empty page between his biology drawing of the aorta of a duck and his civics project on the history of the Constitution. He had to give it to that Mancuso guy: he was really on the ball. George wondered if his name was on that list the cops had found in the cabinet. If it was, it might be a good idea to go visit his uncle who lived on the coast. Even then, they'd have his name. He really didn't have enough money to go anywhere. The best thing was to stay at home for a while. That Mancuso might spot him if he went downtown.

George's mother, vacuuming on the other side of the living room, hopefully watched her son work on his school scrapbook. Maybe he was getting interested in school again. She and his father didn't seem to be able to do anything with him. What chance did a boy without a high school education have nowadays? What could he do?

She turned off the vacuum cleaner and answered the doorbell. George was studying the photographs and wondering what that vendor had been doing at the Night of Joy. He couldn't have been some kind of police agent. Anyway, George hadn't told him where the pictures came from. There was something funny about the whole business.

"The police?" George heard his mother asking at the door. "You must have the wrong apartment."

George started for the kitchen before he realized that there was nowhere to go. The apartments in the housing project had only one door.

IX

Lana Lee tore the newspaper into shreds and then tore the shreds into smaller shreds. When the matron stopped by the cell to tell her to clean it up, one of the members of the ladies' auxiliary, all three of whom were sharing the cell, said to the matron, "Beat it. We're the ones living in this place. We like paper on the floor."

"Shove off," Liz added.

"Get lost," Betty said.

"I'll take care of this cell all right," the matron answered. "You four have been making noise ever since you come in last night."

"Get me out this goddam hole," Lana Lee screamed at the matron. "I can't take another minute with these three bats."

"Hey," Frieda said to her two apartment mates. "Doll doesn't like us."

"It's people like you been ruining the Quarter," Lana told Frieda.

"Shut up," Liz said to her.

"Can it, sweets," Betty said.

"Get me outta here," Lana screamed through the bars. "I just been through one fucking hell of a night with these three creeps. I got my rights. You can't stick me in here."

The matron smiled at her and walked away.

"Hey!" Lana screamed down the corridor. "Come back here."

"Take it easy, dearie," Frieda advised. "Quit rocking the boat. Now come on and show us those pictures of yourself you got hidden in your bra."

"Yeah," Liz said.

"Get out the snapshots, doll," Betty ordered. "We're tired of looking at these frigging walls."

The three girls lunged for Lana at the same time.

X

Dorian Green turned one of his severe calling cards over and printed on the reverse side: "Stunning apartment for rent. Apply at 1A." He stepped out onto the flagstone sidewalk and tacked the card to the bottom of one of the black patent leather shutters. The girls would be gone for quite a while this time. Police were always so adamant about second offenses. It was unfortunate that the girls had never been very sociable with their fellow residents in the Quarter; someone would certainly have pointed out that marvelous patrolman to them, and they would not have made the fatal mistake of attacking a member of the police force.

But the girls were so impulsive and aggressive. Without them, Dorian felt that he and his building were completely unprotected. He took special care to lock his wrought iron gate securely. Then he returned to his apartment to finish the job of cleaning up the litter left from the kickoff rally. It had been the most fabulous party of his career: at the height of it Timmy had fallen from a chandelier and sprained his ankle.

Dorian picked up a cowboy boot from which a heel had been broken and dropped it into a wastebasket, wondering whether that impossible Ignatius J. Reilly were all right. Some people were simply too much to bear. Gypsy Queen's sweet mother must have been heartbroken over the dreadful newspaper publicity.

XI

Darlene cut her picture out of the paper and put it on the kitchen table. What an opening night. At least she had received a little publicity from it.

She picked up her Harlett O'Hara gown from the sofa and hung it in the closet while the cockatoo watched her and squawked a bit from its perch. Jones had certainly taken over when he found out that man was a cop, leading him right over to the cabinet under the bar. Now she and Jones were both out of a job. The Night of Joy was out of business. Lana Lee was out of circulation. That Lana. Posing for French pictures. Anything for a buck.

Darlene looked at the golden earring that the cockatoo had brought home. Lana had been right all along. That big crazyman was really the kiss of death. He sure treated his poor momma cruel. That poor lady.

Darlene sat down to ponder job possibilities. The cockatoo flapped and squawked until she stuck the novelty earring, its favorite toy, in its beak. Then the phone rang, and when she answered it, a man said, "Listen, you got some great publicity. Now I run a club in the five hundred block of Bourbon, and . . ."

XII

Jones spread the newspaper on the bar of Mattie's Ramble Inn and blew some smoke at it.

"Whoa!" he said to Mr. Watson. "You sure gimme a good

idea with all this sabotage crap. Now I sabotage myself right back to bein a vagran. Hey!"

"It look like this sabotage go off like a nucular bum."

"That fat freak a guarantee one hunner percen nucular bum. Shit. Drop him on somebody, everybody gettin caught in the fallout, gettin their ass blowed up. Ooo-wee. Night of Joy really turn into a zoo las night. Firs we get a bird, then the fat mother come draggin along, then three cats look like they jus excape from gym. Shit. Everbody fightin and scratchin and screamin and that big fat freak layin in the gutter like he daid, peoples fightin and cussin and rollin all aroun that big cat pass out in the street. Look like a barroom fight in a westren movie, look like a gang rumble. We got us a big crowd on Bourbon Street look like we could have us a foot-ball game. Po-lice drivin up draggin off that Lee bastar. Hey! It turn out she don have no pal at the precinc anyways. Maybe they be haulin in some of them orphan she been sponsorin. Whoa! That paper sure sending out plenny mothers takin pictures and axin me all about wha happen. Who say a color cat cain get his picture on the front page? Ooo-wee! Whoa! I gonna be the mos famous vagran in the city. I tell that Patrolman Mancusa, I say, 'Hey, now this cathouse shut down, how's about tellin your frien on the force I help you out so maybe they don star draggin my ass off for vagran?' Who wanna get stuck in Angola with Lana Lee? She was bad enough on the outside. Shit."

"You got any plan for gettin you a job, Jones?"

Jones blew a dark cloud, a storm warning, and said, "After the kinda job I jus had workin below the minimal wage, I really deserve a pay vacation. Ooo-wee. Where I gonna fin me another job? Too many color mothers draggin they ass aroun the street already. Whoa! Gettin your ass gainfully employ ain exactly the easies thing in the worl. I ain the only cat got him a problem. That Darlene gal ain gonna have no easy time gettin herself and that ball eagle gainfully employ. Peoples see wha happen the firs time she stick her ass on a stage, they be throwin water in her face if she be comin aroun lookin for work. See wha I mean? You drop somebody like that fat mother for sabotage, plenny innocent peoples like Darlene gettin theyselves screwed. Like Miss Lee all the time sayin, that fat freak ruin *everybody* inves'men. Darlene and her ball eagle probly starin at one another right now sayin, 'Whoa! We really boffo smash for openin night. Hey! We real openin *big.*' I plenny sorry that sabotage goin off in Darlene face, but when I see that big mother, I couldn resis. I knowed he make some kinda esplosion in that Night of Joy. Ooo-wee. He really go off. Hey!"

"You pretty lucky them po-lice didn't take you in, too, workin in that bar."

"That Patrolman Mancusa say he appreciate showin him that cabinet. He say, 'Us mothers on the force need peoples like you, help us out.' He say, 'Peoples like you be helpin me get ahead.' I say, 'Whoa! Be sure and tell that to your frien at the precinc, they don star snatchin my ass for vagran.' He say, 'I sure will. Everbody at the precinc be appreciatin wha you done, man.' Now them po-lice mothers *appreciate* me. Hey! Maybe I be gettin some kinda awar. Whoa!" Jones aimed some smoke over Mr. Watson's tan head. "That Lee bastar really got her some snapshot of herself in that cabinet. Patrolman Mancusa starin at them pictures, his eyeballs about to fall out on the floor. He sayin, 'Whoa! Hey! Wow!' He sayin, 'Boy, I really be gettin ahead now.' I say to myself, 'Maybe some peoples be gettin ahead. Some other peoples be turnin vagran again. Some peoples ain gonna be gainfully employ below the minimal wage after tonight. Some peoples be draggin they ass all aroun town somewheres, be buyin me air condition, color TV.' Shit. Firs I'm a glorify broom expert, now I'm vagran."

"Things can always be worse off."

"Yeah. You can say that, man. You got you a little business, got you a son teachin school probly got him a bobby-cue set, Buick, air condition, TV. Whoa! I ain even got me a transmitter radio. Night of Joy salary keepin peoples below the air-condition level." Jones formed a philosophical cloud. "But you right in a way there, Watson. Things maybe be worse off. Maybe I be that fat mother. Whoa! Whatever gonna happen to somebody like that? Hey!"

XIII

Mr. Levy settled into the yellow nylon couch and unfolded his paper, which was delivered to the coast every morning at a higher subscription rate. Having the couch all to himself was wonderful, but the disappearance of Miss Trixie was not enough to brighten his spirits. He had spent a sleepless night. Mrs. Levy was on her exercising board treating her plumpness to some early morning bouncing. She was silent, occupied with some plans for the Foundation which she was writing on a sheet of paper held against the undulating front section of the board. Putting her pencil down for a moment, she reached down to select a cookie from the box on the floor. And the cookies were why Mr. Levy had spent a wakeful night. He and Mrs. Levy had driven out through the pines to see Mr. Reilly at Mandeville and had not only found he was not there but had also been treated very rudely by an authority of the place who had taken them for pranksters. Mrs. Levy had looked something like a prankster with her golden-white hair, her sunglasses with the blue lenses, the aquamarine mascara that made a ring around the blue lenses like a halo. Sitting there in the sports car before the main building at Mandeville with the huge box of Dutch cookies on her lap, she must have made the authority a little suspicious, Mr. Levy thought. But she had taken it all very calmly. Finding Mr. Reilly did not seem to bother Mrs. Levy particularly, it seemed. Her husband was beginning to sense that she did not especially want him to find Reilly, that somewhere in some corner of her mind she was hoping that Abelman would win the libel suit so that she could flaunt their resulting poverty in the face of Susan and Sandra as their father's ultimate failure. That woman had a devious mind that was only predictable when she scented an opportunity to vanquish her husband. Now he was beginning to wonder which side she was on, his or Abelman's.

He had asked Gonzalez to cancel his spring practice reservations. This Abelman case had to be cleared up. Mr. Levy straightened his newspaper and realized again that, were his digestive system able to take it, he should have given his time to supervising Levy Pants. Things like this would not happen; life could be peaceful. But just the name, just the three syllables of "Levy Pants," caused acid complications in his chest. Perhaps he should have changed the name. Perhaps he should have changed Gonzalez. The office manager was so loyal, though. He loved his thankless, low-salaried job. You couldn't just kick him out. Where would he find another job? Even more important, who would want to replace him? One good reason for keeping Levy Pants open was keeping Gonzalez employed. Mr. Levy tried, but he could think of no other reason for keeping the place open. Gonzalez might commit suicide if the factory were shut down. There was a human life to consider. Too, no one apparently wanted to buy the place.

Leon Levy could have named his monument "Levy Trousers." That wasn't too bad. Throughout his life, but especially when he was a child, Gus Levy had said, "Levy Pants," and had always received a standard reply, "He does?" When he was about twenty, he had mentioned to his father that a change of title might help their business, and his father had moaned, "'Levy Pants' all of a sudden isn't good enough for you? The food you're eating is 'Levy Pants.' The car you're driving is 'Levy Pants.' *I* am 'Levy Pants.' This is gratitude? This is a child's devotion? Next I should change *my* name. Shut up, bum. Go play with the autos and the flappers. Already I got a Depression on my hands, I don't need smart advice from you. Better you should give with the advice to Hoover. You should go tell him to change his name to *Schlemiel.* Out of my office! Shut up!"

Gus Levy looked at the pictures and the article on the front page and whistled through his teeth, "Oh, boy."

"What is it, Gus? A problem? Are you having a problem? All night you were awake. I could hear the whirlpool bath going all night. You're going to have a crackup. Please go to Lenny's doctor before you become violent."

"I just found Mr. Reilly."

"I guess you're happy."

"Aren't you? Look, he's in the papers."

"Really? Bring it over here. I've always wondered about that young idealist. I guess he's received some civic award."

"Just the other day you were saying he was a psycho."

"If he was clever enough to send us over to Mandeville like two stooges, he's not that psycho. Even somebody like the idealist can play a joke on you."

Mrs. Levy looked at the two women, the bird, the grinning door-man.

"Where is he? I don't see any idealist." Mr. Levy indicated the stricken cow in the street. "That's him? In the gutter? This is tragic. Carousing, drunken, hopeless, already a bloated derelict. Mark him down in your book next to Miss Trixie and me as another life you've wrecked."

"A bird bit him on the ear or something crazy. Here, look

386

at the bunch of police characters in these picture. I told you he had a police record. Those people are his buddies. Strippers and pimps and pornographers."

"Once he was dedicated to idealistic causes. Now look at him. Don't worry. You'll pay for all of this someday. In a few months, when Abelman has finished with you, you'll be out on the streets again with a wagon like your father. You'll learn what happens when you play games with somebody like Abelman, when you operate a business like a playboy. Susan and Sandra will go into shock when they find out they don't have a penny to their name. Will they give you the big go-by. Gus Levy, ex-father."

"Well, I'm going into town right now to speak with this Reilly. I'll get this crazy letter business straightened out."

"Ho ho. Gus Levy, detective. Don't make me laugh. You probably wrote that letter one day after you won at the track and felt good. I knew it would end like this."

"You know, I think you're actually looking forward to Abelman's libel suit. You actually want to see me ruined, even if you go down with me."

Mrs. Levy yawned and said, "Can I fight what you've been leading up to all your life? This really proves to the girls that what I've said about you all along was right. The more I think about Abelman's suit, the more I realize that the whole thing is inevitable, Gus. Thank goodness my mother has some money. I always knew I'd have to go back to her someday. She'll probably have to give up San Juan, though. You can't keep Susan and Sandra alive for peanuts."

"Oh, shut up."

"You're telling me to shut up?" Mrs. Levy bounced up and down, up and down. "I'm supposed to watch your smashup in silence? I have to make plans for myself and my daughters. I mean, life goes on, Gus. I can't end up on skid row with you. We can only be grateful that your father has left

387

us. If he had lived to see Levy Pants lost because of some practical joke, you'd really pay. Believe me. Leon Levy would have you run out of the country. That man had courage, determination. And whatever happens, the Leon Levy Foundation goes through. Even if Mother and I have to do without, I'm making those awards. I'm going to honor and reward people who have the kind of courage and bravery that I saw in your father. I won't let you drag his name down with you on your journey to skid row. After Abelman's finished, you'll be lucky to get hired as a water boy on one of those teams you love so much. Boy, will you have to work then, running around with a bucket and a sponge like a bum. But don't feel sorry for yourself. You had it coming."

Now Mr. Levy knew that his wife's strange logic made it necessary for him to be ruined. She wanted to see Abelman victorious; she would see in the victory some peculiar justification. Since his wife had read the letter from Abelman, her mind must have been working over the matter from every angle. Every minute that she was pedaling the exercycle or bouncing on the board, her system of logic was probably telling her more and more convincingly that Abelman must win the suit. It would be not only Abelman's victory, but hers, also. Every conversational and epistolary roadsign and guidepost that she had held up before the girls pointed to their father's final, terrible failure. Mrs. Levy couldn't afford to be disproved. She *needed* the $500 thousand libel suit. She wasn't even interested in his speaking with Reilly. The Abelman case had passed from a purely material and physical plane to an ideological and spiritual one where universal and cosmic forces decreed that Gus Levy must lose, that a childless and desolate Gus Levy must wander endlessly with bucket and sponge.

"Well, I'm going after Reilly," Mr. Levy said finally.

"Such determination. I can hardly believe it. Don't worry, you won't be able to pin anything on the young idealist. He's too clever. He'll play another joke on you. Just watch. Another wild-goose chase. Back to Mandeville. This time they'll keep you there, a middle-aged man driving a little toy of a collegian's sports car."

"I'm going right to his house."

Mrs. Levy folded her Foundation notes and turned off her board, saying, "Well, if you're going to town, take me with you. I'm worried about Miss Trixie since Gonzalez reported that she bit that gangster's hand. I must see her. Her old hostility toward Levy Pants is out in the open again."

"Do you still want to play around with that senile bag? Haven't you tormented her enough already?"

"Even a little good deed you don't want me to do. Your type isn't even in the psychology books. You should at least go to Lenny's doctor for *his* sake. Once your case was in the psychiatric journals, they'd be inviting him to Vienna to speak. You'd make him a famous man just like that crippled girl or whoever it was put Freud on the map."

While Mrs. Levy was blinding herself with layers of aquamarine eyeshadow in preparation for her errand of mercy, he got the sports car out of the monumental three-car garage, built like a substantial rustic carriage house, and sat looking over the calm, rippling bay. Little darts of heartburn pricked about in his chest. Reilly had to make some kind of confession. Abelman's shysters could wipe him out; he couldn't give his wife the satisfaction of seeing that happen. If Reilly would confess to writing the letter, if somehow he could come out of this all right, he would change. He would vow to become a new person. He might even give the company a little supervision. It was only sensible and practical to supervise that place. A neglected Levy Pants was like a neglected child: it could turn out to be a delinquent, something that created all sorts of problems that a little nurture, a little care and feeding could prevent. The more you stayed away from Levy Pants, the more it plagued you. Levy Pants was like a congenital defect, an inherited curse.

"Everyone I know has a fine big sedan," Mrs. Levy said as she got into the little car. "Not you. No. You have to own a kid's car that costs more than a Cadillac and blows my hair all around."

To prove her point, a lacquered strand flew stiffly out in the breeze as they roared out onto the coast highway. Both were silent during the journey through the marshes. Mr. Levy nervously considered his future. Mrs. Levy contentedly considered hers, her aquamarine lashes flapping calmly in the wind. At last they roared into the city, Mr. Levy's speed increasing as he felt himself getting closer to the Reilly kook. Hanging around with that crowd in the Quarter. Goodness only knew what Reilly's personal life was like. One crazy incident after another, insanity upon insanity.

"I think I've finally analyzed your problem," Mrs. Levy said when they slowed down in the city traffic. "This wild driving was the clue. A light has dawned. Now I know why you've drifted, why you don't have any ambition, why you've thrown a business down the drain." Mrs. Levy paused for effect. "You have the death wish."

"For the last time today, shut up."

"Fighting, hostility, resentment," Mrs. Levy said happily. "It will all end very badly, Gus."

Because it was Saturday, Levy Pants had ceased its assaults upon the concept of free enterprise for the weekend. The Levys drove past the factory, which, open or closed, looked equally moribund from the street. Weak smoke of the type produced by burning leaves rose from one of the antennae of smokestacks. Mr. Levy pondered the smoke. Some worker must have left one of the cutting tables sticking in a furnace on Friday evening. Someone might even be in there burning leaves. Stranger things had happened. Mrs. Levy herself, during a ceramics phase, had once commandeered one of the furnaces for a kiln.

When they had passed the factory and Mrs. Levy had gazed at it and said, "Sad, sad," they turned along the river and stopped before a dazed-looking wooden apartment building across from the Desire Street wharf. A trail of scraps beckoned the passerby to climb the unpainted front steps toward some goal within the building.

"Don't take too long," Mrs. Levy said while she was going through the heaving and lifting process that was necessary to remove one's body from the sports car. She took with her the sampled box of Dutch cookies that had originally been intended for the patient at Mandeville. "I've just about had it with this project. Maybe she'll keep busy with the cookies and I won't have to try to make much conversation." She smiled at her husband. "Good luck with the idealist. Don't let him play another trick on you."

Mr. Levy sped off uptown. At a stoplight he looked at Reilly's address in the morning newspaper folded and stored in the well between the bucket seats. He followed the river on Tchoupitoulas and turned at Constantinople, bouncing along in Constantinople's potholes until he found the miniature house. Could the huge kook live in such a doll-house? How did he get in and out of the front door?

Mr. Levy climbed the steps and read the "Peace at Any Price" sign tacked to one of the porch posts and the "Peace to Men of Good Will" sign tacked to the front of the house. This was the place all right. Inside a telephone was ringing.

"They not home!" a woman screamed from behind a shutter next door. "They telephone's been ringing all morning."

The front shutters of the adjoining house opened and a harried-looking woman came out on the porch and rested her red elbows on her porch rail.

"Do you know where Mr. Reilly is?" Mr. Levy asked her.

"All I know is he's all over this morning's paper. Where he oughta be is in a asylum. My nerves is shot to hell. When I moved next door to them people, I was signing my death warrant."

"Does he live here alone? A woman answered the phone once when I called."

"That musta been his momma. Her nerves is shot, too. She musta went to get him out the hospital or wherever they got him."

"Do you know Mr. Reilly well?"

"Ever since he was a kid. His momma was sure proud of him. All the sisters at school loved him he was so precious. Look how he ended up, laying in a gutter. Well, they better start thinking about moving off my block. I can't take it no more. They'll really be arguing now."

"Let me ask you something. You know Mr. Reilly well. Do you think he's very irresponsible or maybe even dangerous?"

"What you want with him?" Miss Annie's bleary eyes narrowed. "He's in some other kinda trouble?"

"I'm Gus Levy. He used to work for me."

"Yeah? You don't say. That crazy Idnatius was sure proud of that job he had at that place. I useta hear him telling his momma how he was really making good. Yeah, he made good. A few weeks and he was fired. Well, if he worked for you, you really know him good."

Had that poor Reilly kook really been proud of Levy Pants? He had always said that he was. That was one good sign of his insanity.

"Tell me. Hasn't he been in trouble with the police. Doesn't he have some kind of police record?"

"His momma had a policeman coming around her. A regular undercover agent. But not that Idnatius. For one thing his momma likes her little nip. I don't see her drunk much

392

lately, but for a while there she was really going good. One day I look out in the backyard and she had herself all tangled up in a wet sheet hanging off the line. Mister, it's already took ten years off my life living next to them people. Noise! Banjos and trumpets and screaming and hollering and the TV. Them Reillys oughta go move out in the country somewheres on a farm. Every day I gotta take six, seven aspirin." Miss Annie reached inside the neckline of her housedress to find some strap that had slipped from her shoulder. "Lemme tell you something. I gotta be fair. That Idnatius was okay until that big dog of his died. He had this big dog useta bark right under my window. That's when my nerves first started to go. Then the dog dies. Well, I think, now maybe I'll get me some peace and quiet. But no. Idnatius is got the dog laid out in his momma's front parlor with some flowers stuck in its paw. That's when him and his momma first started all that fighting. To tell you the truth, I think that's when she started drinking. So Idnatius goes over to the priest and ax him to come say something over the dog. Idnatius was planning on some kinda funeral. You know? The priest says no, of course, and I think that's when Idnatius left the Church. So big Idnatius puts on his own funeral. A big fat high school boy oughta know better. You see that cross?" Mr. Levy looked hopelessly at the rotting Celtic cross in the frontyard. "That where it all happened. He had about two dozen little kids standing around in that yard watching him. And Idnatius had on a big cape like Superman and they was candles burning all over. The whole time his momma was screaming out the front door for him to throw the dog in the garbage can and get in the house. Well, that's when things started going bad around here. Then Idnatius was at college for about ten years. His momma almost went broke. She even hadda sell the piana they had. Well, I didn't mind that. You oughta seen this girl he picks up at college. I says to myself, 'Well, good. Maybe that Idnatius is gonna get married and move out.' Was I wrong. All they done is sit in his room. It seem like every night she and him was putting on a regular hootenanny. The things I useta hear through my window! 'Put down that skirt.' and 'Get off my bed.' And 'How dare you? I'm a virgin.' It was awful. I went on aspirins twenty-four hours a day. Well, that girl done left. I can't blame her. She musta been funny to hang around with him anyways." Miss Annie reached in the opposite direction for another strap. "Of all the houses in the city, how come I hadda move in here? Tell me that."

Mr. Levy could think of no reason for her having moved to this particular location. But the Ignatius Reilly story had made him depressed, and he wished he were away from Constantinople Street.

"Well," the woman rushed on, eager for the audience to hear her tale of suffering, "this stuff in the paper's the last straw. Look at the bad publicity the block's got now. If they start anything now, I'm gonna call up the police and get him put under a peace bond. I can't take it no more. My nerves is shot to hell. Even when that Idnatius takes a bath, it sounds like a flood's coming in my own house. I think all my pipes is busted. I'm too old. I had enough with them people." Miss Annie glanced over Mr. Levy's shoulder. "It's been nice talking to you, mister. So long."

She raced back into her house and slammed her shutters. Her sudden disappearance confused Mr. Levy as much as her strange biography of Mr. Reilly had. What a neighborhood. Levy's Lodge had always been a barrier against knowing people like this. Then Mr. Levy saw the old Plymouth trying to dock at the curb, scraping its hubcaps against its moorings before finally coming to rest. In the rear seat he saw the silhou-ette of the big kook. A woman with maroon hair climbed down from the driver's seat and called, "Okay, boy, get out that car!"

"Not until you clarify your relationship with that drooling old man," the silhouette answered. "I thought that we had escaped from that degenerate old fascist. Apparently I was wrong. All along you've been carrying on an affair with him behind my back. You probably planted him there in front of D. H. Holmes. Now that I think of it you probably planted that mongoloid Mancuso there, too, to start this vicious cycle whirling. How unsuspecting, how ingenuous I've been. For weeks now I've been the dupe of a conspiracy. It's all a plot!"

"Get down from that car!"

"You see?" Miss Annie said through her shutters. "They're at it again."

The rear car door swung rustily open and a bursting desert boot stepped down onto the running board. The kook's head was bandaged. He looked tired and pale.

"I will not stay under the same roof with a loose woman. I'm shocked and hurt. My own mother. No wonder you've turned on me so savagely. I suspect that you are using me as a scapegoat for your own feelings of guilt."

What a family, Mr. Levy thought. The mother did look like something of a floozie. He wondered why the undercover agent had wanted her.

"Shut up your dirty mouth," the woman was screaming. "All this over a fine, decent man like Claude."

"Fine man," Ignatius snorted. "I knew you'd end like this when you started traveling around with those degenerates."

Along the block a few people had come out on their steps. What a day this was going to be. Mr. Levy ran the risk of getting into a public scene with these wild people. His heartburn was spreading out to the limits of his chest.

The woman with the maroon hair had fallen to her knees and was asking the sky, "What I done wrong, God? Tell me, Lord. I been good."

"You're kneeling on Rex's grave!" Ignatius shouted. "Now

tell me what you and that debauched McCarthyite have been doing? You probably belong to some secret political cell. No wonder I've been bombarded with those witchhunt pamphlets. No wonder I was trailed last night. Where is that Battaglia matchmaker. Where is she? She must be lashed. This whole thing is a coup against me, a vicious scheme to get me out of the way. My God! That bird was doubtlessly trained by a band of fascists. They'll try anything."

"Claude's been courting me," Mrs. Reilly said defiantly.

"What?" Ignatius thundered. "Do you mean to tell me that you have been permitting some old man to paw all over you?"

"Claude's a nice man. All he done is hold my hand a few times."

The blue and yellow eyes crossed in anger. The paws closed over the ears so that he would not have to listen to more.

"Goodness only knows what unmentionable desires that man has. Please don't tell me the whole truth. I would have a total breakdown."

"Shut up!" Miss Annie screamed from behind her shutters. "You people are living on borrowed time in this block."

"Claude ain't smart, but he's a nice man. He's good to his family and that's what counts. Santa says he likes the communiss because he's lonely. He ain't got nothing else to do. If he was to ax me to marry him this very minute, I'd say, 'Okay, Claude.' I would, Ignatius. I wouldn't haveta think twice about it. I got a right to have somebody treat me nice before I die. I got a right not to haveta worry about where my next dollar's coming from. When Claude and me went to get your clothes from that head nurse and she hands us over your wallet with almost thirty dollars in it, that was the last straw. All your craziness was bad enough, but keeping that money from your poor momma . . ."

"I needed the money for a purpose."

"For what? To hang around with dirty women?" Mrs. Reilly

lifted herself laboriously from Rex's grave. "You ain't only crazy, Ignatius. You mean, too."

"Do you seriously think that Claude roué wants marriage?" Ignatius slobbered, changing the subject. "You'll be dragged from one reeking motel to another. You'll end up a suicide."

"I'll get married if I want to, boy. You can't stop me. Not now."

"That man is a dangerous radical," Ignatius said darkly. "Goodness knows what political and ideological horrors lurk in his mind. He'll torture you or worse."

"Just who the hell are *you* to try to tell me what to do, Ignatius?" Mrs. Reilly stared at her huffing son. She was disgusted and tired, disinterested in anything that Ignatius might have to say. "Claude is dumb. Okay. I'll grant you that. Claude is all the time worrying me about them communiss. Okay. Maybe he don't know nothing about politics. But I ain't worried about politics. I'm worried about dying half-way decent. Claude can be kind to a person, and that's more than you can do with all your politics and all your graduating smart. For everything nice I ever done for you, I just get kicked around. I want to be treated nice by somebody before I die. You learnt everything, Ignatius, except how to be a human being."

"It's not your fate to be well treated," Ignatius cried. "You're an overt masochist. Nice treatment will confuse and destroy you."

"Go to hell, Ignatius. You broke my heart so many times I can't count them up no more."

"That man shall never enter this house while I am here. After he had grown tired of you, he would probably turn his warped attentions on *me*."

"What's that, crazy? Shut up your silly mouth. I'm fed up. I'll take care of you. You say you wanna take a rest? I can fix you up with a nice rest."

"When I think of my dear departed father barely cold in his grave," Ignatius murmured, pretending to wipe some moisture from his eyes.

"Mr. Reilly died twenty years ago."

"Twenty-*one*," Ignatius gloated. "So. You've forgotten your beloved husband."

"Pardon me," Mr. Levy said weakly. "May I speak with you, Mr. Reilly?"

"What?" Ignatius asked, noticing for the first time the man standing up on the porch.

"What you want with Ignatius?" Mrs. Reilly asked the man. Mr. Levy introduced himself. "Well, this is him in person. I hope you didn't believe that funny story he give you over the phone the other day. I was too tired to grab the phone out his hands."

"Can we all go in the house?" Mr. Levy asked. "I'd like to speak with him privately."

"It don't matter to me," Mrs. Reilly said disinterestedly. She looked down the block and saw her neighbors watching them. "The whole neighborhood knows everything now."

But she opened the front door and the three of them stepped into the tiny entrance hall. Mrs. Reilly put down the paper bag she was carrying that contained her son's scarf and cutlass, and asked, "What you want, Mr. Levy? Ignatius! Come back here and talk to this man."

"Mother, I must attend to my bowels. They are revolting against the trauma of the last twenty-four hours."

"Get out that bathroom, boy, and come back here. Now what you want with crazy, Mr. Levy?"

"Mr. Reilly, do you know anything about this?"

Ignatius looked at the two letters that Mr. Levy produced from his jacket and said, "Of course not. That is your signature. Leave this house immediately. Mother, this is the fiend who fired me so brutally."

"You didn't write this?"

"Mr. Gonzalez was extremely dictatorial. He would never permit me near a typewriter. Actually, he cuffed me once rather viciously when my eyes chanced to stray across some correspondence which he was composing in rather dreadful prose. If I was permitted to shine his cheap shoes, I was grateful. You know how possessive he is about that cesspool company of yours."

"I know. But he says he didn't write this."

"An obvious untruth. His every word is false. He speaks with a forked tongue!"

"This man wants to sue us for a lot of money."

"Ignatius done it," Mrs. Reilly interrupted a little rudely. "Whatever went wrong, Ignatius done it. He makes trouble everyplace he goes. Go on, Ignatius. Tell the man the truth. Go on, boy, before I knock you in the head."

"Mother, make this man leave," Ignatius cried, trying to push his mother against Mr. Levy.

"Mr. Reilly, this man wants to sue for $500 thousand. That could ruin me."

"Ain't that awful!" Mrs. Reilly exclaimed. "Ignatius, what you done this poor man?"

As Ignatius was about to discuss the circumspection of his behavior at Levy Pants, the telephone rang.

"Hello?" Mrs. Reilly said. "I'm his mother. Of course I'm sober." She glared at Ignatius. "He is? He did? What? Aw, no." She stared at her son, who was beginning to rasp one paw against the other. "Okay, mister, you'll get your stuff, all except the earring. The bird got that. Okay. Of course I can remember what you telling me. I ain't drunk!" Mrs. Reilly slammed down the telephone and turned on her son with, "That was the weenie man. You're fired."

"Thank God," Ignatius sighed. "I couldn't stand that cart again, I'm afraid."

"What you told him about me, boy? You told him I was a drunk?"

"Of course not. How ludicrous. I don't discuss you with people. No doubt he's spoken with you previously when you were under the influence. You've probably had a date with him for all I know, a drunken spree in several hot dog *boites*."

"You can't even peddle hot dogs in the streets. Was that man angry. He says you gave him more trouble than any vendor he ever had."

"He resented my worldview rather actively."

"Oh, shut up before I slap you again," Mrs. Reilly screamed. "Now tell Mr. Levy here the truth."

What a squalid homelife, Mr. Levy thought. This woman certainly treated her son dictatorially.

"Why, I am telling the truth," Ignatius said.

"Lemme see that letter, Mr. Levy."

"Don't show it to her. She reads rather dreadfully. She'll be confused for days."

Mrs. Reilly knocked Ignatius in the side of the head with her purse.

"Not again!" Ignatius cried.

"Don't hit him," Mr. Levy said. The kook's head was already bandaged. Outside of the prizefighting ring, violence made Mr. Levy ill. This Reilly kook was really pitiful. The mother ran around with some old man, drank, wanted the son out of the way. She was already on the police blotter. That dog was probably the only thing that the kook had ever really had in his life. Sometimes you have to see a person in his real environment to understand him. In his own way Reilly had been very interested in Levy Pants. Now Mr. Levy was sorry that he had fired Reilly. The kook had been proud of his job at the company. "Just let him alone, Mrs. Reilly. We'll get to the bottom of this."

"Help me, sir," Ignatius slobbered, grabbing histrionically at the lapels of Mr. Levy's sports jacket. "Fortuna only knows what she will do to me. I know too much of her sordid activities. I must be eliminated. Have you thought of speaking to that Trixie woman? She knows far more than you suspect."

"That's what my wife says, but I never believed her. After all, Miss Trixie is so old. I wouldn't think she could write a grocery list."

"Old?" Mrs. Reilly asked. "Ignatius! You told me Trixie was the name of some cute girl worked at Levy Pants. You told me you two liked each other. Now I find out she's a grammaw can't hardly write. Ignatius!"

It was sadder than Mr. Levy had thought at first. The poor kook had tried to make his mother think he had a girlfriend.

"Please," Ignatius whispered to Mr. Levy. "Come into my room. I must show you something."

"Don't believe a word Ignatius says," Mrs. Reilly called after them as her son dragged Mr. Levy through the door into the musty chamber.

"Just let him alone," Mr. Levy said to Mrs. Reilly somewhat firmly. This Reilly woman wouldn't even give her own child a chance. She was as bad as his wife. No wonder Reilly was such a wreck.

Then the door closed behind them and Mr. Levy suddenly began to feel nauseated. There was a scent of old tea leaves in the bedroom that reminded him of the teapot that Leon Levy had always had near his elbow, the delicately cracked china pot in whose bottom there was always a residue of boiled leaves. He went to the window and opened the shutter, but as he looked out his eyes met those of Miss Annie, who was staring back at him from between the blinds of her shutters. He turned from the window and watched Reilly thumbing through a loose-leaf folder.

"Here it is," Ignatius said. "These are some notes that I

jotted while working for your company. They will prove that I loved Levy Pants even more than life itself, that my every waking hour was spent in contemplating means of helping your organization. And often at night I had visions. Phantoms of Levy Pants flitted gloriously across my slumbering psyche. I would never write a letter like that. I *loved* Levy Pants. Here. Read this, sir."

Mr. Levy took the loose-leaf folder and, where Reilly's fat forefinger indicated a line, he read, "Today our office was at last graced by the presence of our lord and master, Mr. G. Levy. To be quite honest, I found him rather casual and unconcerned." The forefinger skipped a line or two. "In time he will learn of my devotion to his firm, of my dedication. My example, in turn, may lead him to once again believe in Levy Pants." The guidepost of a forefinger indicated the next paragraph. "La Trixie still keeps her own counsel, thereby proving herself even wiser than I had thought. I suspect that this woman knows a great deal, that her apathy is a façade for her seeming resentment against Levy Pants. She grows most coherent when she speaks of retirement."

"There is your evidence, sir," Ignatius said, snatching the folder from Mr. Levy's hands. "Interrogate the Trixie jade. The senility is a guise. It is part of her defense against her work and the company. Actually, she hates Levy Pants for not retiring her. And who can blame her? Many times when we were alone, she would babble for hours about plans to 'get' Levy Pants. Her resentment surfaced in the form of vitriolic attacks upon your corporate structure."

Mr. Levy tried to assess the evidence. He knew that Reilly had really liked the company; he had seen it at the company, the woman next door had told him, he had just read it. Trixie, on the other hand, hated the company. Even though his wife and the kook claimed that the senility routine was a front, he doubted that she would be able to write a letter like that.

But now he had to get out of the claustrophobic bedroom before he possibly got ill all over the tablets that covered the floor. When Mr. Reilly had been standing next to him pointing out the passages in the notebook, the scent had grown over-powering. He felt for the doorknob, but the Reilly kook threw himself against the door.

"You must believe me," he sighed. "The Trixie trollop had a fixation about a turkey or a ham. Or was it a roast? It was all rather fierce and confusing at times. She swore vengeance in connection with not being retired at the proper age. She was filled with hostility."

Mr. Levy eased him aside and got out into the hall, where the maroon-haired mother was waiting like a doorman.

"Thank you, Mr. Reilly," Mr. Levy said. He had to get out of that claustrophobic miniature of a heartbreak house. "If I need you again, I'll call you."

"You'll need him again," Mrs. Reilly called as he passed her and ran down the front steps. "Whatever it is, Ignatius done it."

She called out something else, but Mr. Levy's roar drowned out her voice. Blue smoke settled over the stricken Plymouth, and he was gone.

"Now you done it," Mrs. Reilly was saying to Ignatius, her hands grasping the white smock. "Now we in trouble for real, boy. You know what they can do you for forgery? They can throw you in a federal prison. That poor man's got a $500 thousand case on his hands. Now you done it, Ignatius. Now you really in trouble."

"Please," Ignatius said weakly. His pale skin was turning an off-white that shaded into gray. He felt really ill now. His valve was executing several maneuvers that exceeded in origi-nality and violence anything it had done before. "I told you it would be like this when I went out to work."

Mr. Levy picked the shortest route back to the Desire Street wharf. He sped out Napoleon to the Broad overpass and got onto the expressway, fired by an emotion that was a distant but recognizable version of determination. If resentment had really driven Miss Trixie to writing that letter, then Mrs. Levy was the person responsible for the Abelman suit. Could Miss Trixie write something as intelligible as that letter? Mr. Levy hoped that she could. He drove through Miss Trixie's neighborhood quickly, flashing past the bars and the BOILED CRAW-FISH and OYSTERS ON THE HALF SHELL signs that stuck out everywhere. At the apartment house he followed the trail of scraps up the stairs to a brown door. He knocked and Mrs. Levy opened it with, "Look who's back. The idealist's menace. Have you solved your case?"

"Maybe."

"Now you're talking like Gary Cooper. One word I get for an answer. Sheriff Gary Levy." She plucked at an offending aquamarine lash with her fingers. "Well, let's go. Trixie's gorging on the cookies. I'm getting nauseous."

Mr. Levy pushed past his wife into a scene he could never have imagined. Levy's Lodge had not prepared him for interiors like the one he had just seen on Constantinople Street—and for this one. Miss Trixie's apartment was decorated with scraps, with junk, with bits of metal, with cardboard boxes. Somewhere beneath it all there was furniture. The surface, however, the visible terrain, was a landscape of old clothes and crates and newspapers. There was a pass through the center of the mountain, a clearing among the litter, a narrow aisle of clear floor that led to a window where Miss Trixie was seated in a chair sampling the Dutch cookies. Mr. Levy walked down the aisle past the black wig that hung from atop a crate, the high pumps tossed on a pile of newspapers. The only aspect of the rejuvenation that Miss Trixie had apparently retained was the teeth; they gleamed between her thin lips as they knifed into the cookies.

"Suddenly you're very silent," Mrs. Levy observed. "What is it, Gus? Another mission ended in failure?"

"Miss Trixie," Mr. Levy screamed into her ears. "Did you write a letter to Abelman's Dry Goods?"

"Now you're scraping rock bottom," Mrs. Levy said. "The idealist fooled you again, I guess. You really fall for that Reilly's line."

"Miss Trixie!"

"What?" Miss Trixie snarled. "I must say you people know how to retire a person."

Mr. Levy handed her the letter. She picked a magnifying glass from the floor and studied the letters. The green visor cast a deadly color upon her face, upon the Dutch cookie crumbs that rimmed her thin lips. When she put down the magnifying glass, she wheezed happily, "You people in trouble now."

"But did you write that to Abelman? Mr. Reilly said you did."

"Who?"

"Mr. Reilly. The big man with the green cap who used to work at Levy Pants." Mr. Levy showed Miss Trixie the photographs in the morning paper. "That one there."

Miss Trixie applied her magnifying glass to the newspaper and said, "Oh, my goodness. So that's what happened to him." Poor Gloria. He seemed to be injured. "That's Mr. Reilly, is it?"

"Yes. You remember him, I guess. He says you wrote that letter."

"He did?" Gloria Reilly wouldn't lie. Not Gloria. True blue. Gloria had always been her friend. Miss Trixie tried hazily to recall. Perhaps she had written the letter. All sorts of things happened that she couldn't remember anymore. "Well, I guess I did. Yes. Now that you mention it, I guess I did write that. You people deserve it, too. You've driven me crazy these last few years. No retirement. No ham. Nothing. I must say I hope you lose everything you own."

"You wrote that?" Mrs. Levy asked. "After all I've done for you, you wrote something like that? A viper in our own bosom! You can kiss Levy Pants goodbye, traitor. Discarded? You'll get discarded!"

Miss Trixie smiled. That annoying woman was really getting excited. Gloria always had been her friend. Now the annoying woman would go to the poorhouse. Perhaps. But right now she was coming toward her, those aquamarine fingernails poised like talons. Miss Trixie started to scream.

"Let her alone," Mr. Levy said to his wife. "Well, well. Won't Susan and Sandra like to hear about this. Their mother tortures an old lady so much that the girls are in danger of losing all of their cardigans and culottes."

"So. Blame me," Mrs. Levy said wildly. "I stuck the paper in the typewriter. I helped her peck it out."

"Didn't you write that letter to get even with Levy Pants because you weren't retired?"

"Yes, yes," Miss Trixie said vaguely.

"To think I trusted you," Mrs. Levy spat at Miss Trixie. "Give me back those teeth."

Her husband blocked her grab for Miss Trixie's mouth.

"Quiet!" Miss Trixie snarled, all of her white fangs gleaming. "I can't even have a little peace in my own apartment."

"If it wasn't for your stupid, harebrained 'project' this woman would have been retired long ago," Mr. Levy said to his wife. "After all those years of predicting things, *you* turn out to be the one who almost threw Levy Pants down the drain."

"I see. You don't blame her. You blame a woman of standards and ideals. If a thief broke into Levy Pants, *I*'d be to blame. You need help, Gus. Badly."

"Yes, I do. And from Lenny's doctor, of all people."

"Wonderful, Gus."

"Quiet!"

"But you're the one who's going to call Lenny's doctor," Mr. Levy said to his wife. "I want you to get him to declare Miss Trixie senile and incompetent and to explain the motivation for writing the letter."

"This is your problem," Mrs. Levy answered angrily. "You call him."

"Susan and Sandra won't like to hear about their mother's little mistake."

"And blackmail, too."

"I've learned a few things from you. After all, we've been married for some time." Mr. Levy watched anger and anxiety play upon his wife's face. For once she had nothing to say. "The girls won't want to know that their dear mother was such a fool. Now plan to get Trixie over to Lenny's doctor. With her admission and any doctor's testimony, Abelman doesn't have an outside chance on this case. All you'd have to do is drag her into a courtroom and let a judge look at her."

"I'm a very attractive woman," Miss Trixie said automatically.

"Of course you are," Mr. Levy said, bending down next to her. "We're going to retire you, Miss Trixie. With a raise. You've had a lousy deal."

"Retirement?" Miss Trixie wheezed. "I must say this is unexpected. Thank goodness."

"You'll sign a statement that you wrote that letter, won't you?"

"Of course I will!" Miss Trixie cried. What a friend Gloria was. Gloria knew how to help her out. Gloria was smart. Thank goodness Gloria had remembered this magic letter. "I'll say anything you want me to."

"Everything is suddenly clear to me," Mrs. Levy's bitter voice said behind a pile of newspapers. "I'm blackmailed with my two darling girls. I'm pushed out of the way so that you can be a bigger playboy than ever. Now Levy Pants will be really down the drain. You think you have something on me."

"Oh, I do. And Levy Pants will be down the drain. But not because one of your games wrecked it." Mr. Levy looked over the two letters. "This Abelman business has made me think about a lot of things. How come nobody buys our pants. Because they stink. Because they're made from the same patterns my father used twenty years ago, the same fabrics. Because that old tyrant wouldn't change a thing in that plant. Because he destroyed whatever initiative I had."

"Your father was a brilliant man. Not another word of disrespect from you."

"Shut up. Trixie's oddball letter gave me an idea. From now on we make bermuda shorts only. Less trouble, higher profits on lower expenditures. I want a whole new line of wash and wear swatches from the mills. Levy Pants becomes Levy Shorts."

"'Levy Shorts.' That's rich. Don't make me laugh. You'll go broke in a year. Anything to obliterate the memory of your father. You can't run a business. You're a failure, a playboy, a racetrack tout."

"Quiet! I must say you people are a nuisance. If this is retirement, I'd rather be back at that Levy Pants." Miss Trixie raked at them with her cookie box. "Now get out of my house and mail me my check."

"I couldn't run Levy Pants. That's true. I think I can run Levy Shorts."

"Suddenly you're very smug," Mrs. Levy said in a voice that bordered on hysteria. Gus Levy operating a company? Gus Levy dominant? What could she say to Susan and Sandra? What could she say to Gus Levy? What would happen to her? "The Foundation goes down the drain, too, I guess."

"Of course not," Mr. Levy smiled inwardly. At last his wife

was rudderless, trying to steer some sort of course on a sea of confusion, asking him for directions. "We'll make an award. What were they supposed to be for, meritorious service and bravery?"

"Yes," Mrs. Levy said humbly.

"Here. This is brave." He picked up the newspaper and pointed to the Negro who stood over the fallen idealist. "He gets the first award."

"What? A criminal with dark glasses? A Bourbon Street character? Please, Gus. Not this. Leon Levy is dead only a few years. Let him rest in peace."

"It's very practical, the kind of maneuver old Leon would have made himself. Most of our workers are Negroes. Good public relations. And I'll probably need more and better workers before long. This will make for a good employment climate."

"But not to *that*." Mrs. Levy sounded as if she were retching. "The awards are for *nice* people."

"Where's the idealism you're always coming on so strong for? I thought you had an interest in minority groups. At least you've always said so. Anyway, Reilly was worth saving. He led me to the real culprit."

"You can't live the rest of your life on spite."

"Who's living on spite? I'm doing some constructive things at last. Miss Trixie, where's your telephone?"

"Who?" Miss Trixie was watching a freighter from Monrovia depart with a dockful of International Harvester tractors. "I don't have one. There's one at the grocery on the corner."

"Okay, Mrs. Levy. Go down to the grocery. Call Lenny's doctor and call the newspaper to find out if they know how we can reach Jones, but those people usually don't have telephones. Try the police, too. They might know. Give me the number. I'll call him personally."

Mrs. Levy stood staring at her husband, her colored lashes motionless.

"If you're going to the store, you can just get me that Easter ham," Miss Trixie rasped. "I want to see that ham right here in my home! I don't want any double talk this time. If you people want a confession from me, you'd better start paying off."

She snarled once at Mrs. Levy, flashing her teeth as if they were a symbol of something, a gesture of defiance.

"There," Mr. Levy said to his wife. "You have three reasons for going to the grocery now." He handed her a ten-dollar bill. "I'll wait for you here."

Mrs. Levy took the money and said to her husband, "I guess you're happy now. Now I'll be your maid. You'll hold this over my head like a sword. One little misjudgment and I suffer all this."

"One little misjudgment? A libel suit for half a million? What are you suffering? You're just going to the corner grocery."

Mrs. Levy turned and found her way along the aisle. The door slammed and, as if a weighty problem had been lifted from her, Miss Trixie fell into a juvenile slumber. Mr. Levy listened to her snoring and watched the Monrovian freighter moving out into the harbor and turning downstream toward the Gulf.

His mind grew calm for the first time in several days, and some of the events surrounding the letter began passing in review through his consciousness. He thought of the letter to Abelman, and then his mind was recalling another place where he had heard similar language. It was in the Reilly kook's yard just an hour ago. "She must be lashed." "Mongoloid Mancuso." So he had written it after all. Mr. Levy looked tenderly down at the little accused party snoring over her box of Dutch cookies. For everyone's sake, he thought, you will have to be declared incompetent and confess, Miss

Trixie. You are being framed. Mr. Levy laughed out loud. Why had Miss Trixie confessed so sincerely?

"Silence!" Miss Trixie snarled, snapping awake.

That Reilly kook had really been worth saving after all. He had saved himself, Miss Trixie, and Mr. Levy, too, in his own kook way. Whoever Burma Jones was, he deserved a generous award . . . or reward. Offering him a job at the new Levy Shorts would be even better for public relations. An award and a job. With some good newspaper publicity to tie in with the opening of Levy Shorts. Was that a gimmick or wasn't it?

Mr. Levy watched the freighter cross the mouth of the Industrial Canal. Mrs. Levy would be on a ship soon, destination San Juan. She could visit her mother on the beach, laughing and singing and dancing. Mrs. Levy wouldn't really fit into the Levy Shorts plan.

Fourteen

Ignatius spent the day in his room napping fitfully and attacking his rubber glove during his frequent, anxious moments of consciousness. Throughout the afternoon the telephone in the hall had been ringing, each new ring making him more nervous and anxious. He lunged at the glove, deflowering it, stabbing it, conquering it. Like any celebrity, Ignatius had attracted his fans: his mother's jinxed relatives, neighbors, people Mrs. Reilly had not seen for years. They had all telephoned. At every ring Ignatius imagined that it was Mr. Levy calling back, but he always heard his mother say to the caller the lines that were becoming tearfully standard, "Ain't this awful? What I'm gonna do? Now our name is really ruint." When Ignatius could stand it no longer, he would billow out of his room in search of a Dr. Nut. If he chanced to meet his mother in the hall, she would not look at him but rather study the fleecy spheres of lint that drifted along the floor in her son's wake. There seemed to be nothing that he could say to her.

What would Mr. Levy do? Abelman, unfortunately, was apparently a rather petty person, a man too small to accept a little criticism, a hypersensitive molecule of a human. He had written to the wrong person; the militant and courageous broadside had been delivered before the wrong audience. At this point his nervous system could not manage a court trial. He would break down completely before the judge. He wondered how long it would be before Mr. Levy descended upon him again. What senile conundrums was Miss Trixie babbling to Mr. Levy? An infuriated and confused Mr. Levy would return, this time determined to have him incarcerated at once. Now waiting for this return was like waiting for an execution. The dull headache persisted. The Dr. Nuts tasted like gall. Abelman certainly wanted a great deal of money; that sensitive plant of an Abelman must have been greatly offended. When the true author of the letter was discovered, what would Abelman demand in lieu of $500 thousand? A life?

The Dr. Nuts seemed only as an acid gurgling down into his intestine. He filled with gas, the sealed valve trapping it just as one pinches the mouth of a balloon. Great eructations rose from his throat and bounced upward toward the refuse-laden bowl of the milk glass chandelier. Once a person was asked to step into this brutal century, anything could happen. Everywhere there lurked pitfalls like Abelman, the insipid Crusaders for Moorish Dignity, the Mancuso cretin, Dorian Greene, newspaper reporters, stripteasers, birds, photography, juvenile delinquents, Nazi pornographers. And especially Myrna Minkoff. The consumer products. And especially Myrna Minkoff. The musky minx must be dealt with. Somehow. Someday. She must pay. Whatever happened, he must attend to her even if the revenge took years and he had to stalk her through decades from one coffee shop to another, from one folk singing orgy to another, from subway train to pad to cotton field to demonstration. Ignatius invoked an elaborate Elizabethan curse upon Myrna and, rolling over, frantically abused the glove once more.

How dare his mother contemplate a marriage. Only someone as simpleminded as she could be so disloyal. The aged fascist would conduct witchhunt after witchhunt until the formerly intact Ignatius J. Reilly was reduced to a fragmented and mumbling vegetable. The aged fascist would testify for Mr. Levy so that his future stepson would be locked away and he would be free to satisfy his warped and archaic desires upon the unsuspecting Irene Reilly, to perform his conservative practices upon Irene Reilly with free enterprise. Prostitutes were not protected by the Social Security and unemployment compensation systems. No doubt the Robichaux roué was thus attracted to them. Only Fortuna knew what he had learned at their hands.

Mrs. Reilly listened to the squeaking and belching emanating from her son's room and wondered whether, on top of everything else, he were having a fit. But she didn't want to look at Ignatius. Whenever she heard his door opening, she tried to run to her room to avoid him. Five hundred thousand dollars was a sum she could not even imagine. She could hardly imagine the punishment given someone who had done something bad enough to be worth five hundred thousand. If there were any cause for suspicion on Mr. Levy's part, there was none on hers. Ignatius had written whatever it was. Wouldn't this be fine? Ignatius in jail. There was only one way to save him. She carried the telephone as far down the hall as she could, and for the fourth time that day, she dialed Santa Battaglia's number.

"Lord, honey, you really worried," Santa said. "What happened now?"

"I'm afraid Ignatius is in worst trouble than just a picture in the paper," Mrs. Reilly whispered. "I can't talk over the phone. Santa, you was right all along. Ignatius gotta go to the Charity."

"Well, at last. I been talking myself hoarse telling you that. Claude just rang up a little while ago. He says Ignatius made a big scene at the hospital when they met. Claude says he's ascared of Ignatius, he's so big."

"Ain't that awful. It was terrible in the hospital. I already told you how Ignatius started screaming. All them nurses and sick people. I coulda died. Claude ain't too angry, huh?"

"He ain't angry, but he don't like you being alone in that

house. He ax me if maybe him and me shouldn't come over there and stay with you."

"Don't do that, babe," Mrs. Reilly said quickly.

"What kinda trouble Ignatius is in now?"

"I'll tell you later. Right now I can only say I been thinking about this Charity business all day, and I finally made up my mind. Now is the time. He's my own child, but we gotta get him treated for his own sake." Mrs. Reilly tried to think of the phrase that was always used in courtroom dramas on TV. "We gotta get him declared temporary insane."

"*Temporary?*" Santa scoffed.

"We gotta help out Ignatius before they come drag him off."

"Who's gonna drag him off."

"It seem like he pulled a boo-boo when he was working at Levy Pants."

"Oh, Lord! Not something else. Irene! Hang up and call them people at the Charity right now, honey."

"No, listen. I don't wanna be here when they come. I mean, Ignatius is big. He might make trouble. I couldn't stand that. My nerves is bad enough now."

"Big is right. It'll be like capturing a wild elephant. Them people better have them a great big net," Santa said eagerly. "Irene, this is the best decision you ever made. I tell you what. I'll call up the Charity right now. You come over here. I'll get Claude to come over, too. He'll sure be glad to hear this. Whoo! You'll be sending out wedding invitations in about a week. You gonna have you some little properties before the year's out, sweetheart. You gonna have you a railroad pension."

It all sounded good to Mrs. Reilly, but she asked a little hesitantly, "What about them communiss?"

"Don't worry about them, darling. We'll get rid of them communiss. Claude's gonna be too busy fixing up that house

415

of yours. He's gonna have his hands full turning Ignatius's room into a den."

Santa broke into some baritone peals of laughter.

"Miss Annie's gonna turn green when she sees this place fixed up."

"Then tell that woman, say, 'You go out and shake yourself a little. You'll get your house fixed up, too,'" Santa guffawed. "Now get off the line, babe, and get over here. I'm calling the Charity right now. Get out that house fast!"

Santa slammed the telephone down in Mrs. Reilly's ear.

Mrs. Reilly looked out the front shutters. It was very dark now, which was good. The neighbors would not see too much if they took Ignatius away during the night. She ran into the bathroom and powdered her face and the front of her dress, drew a surrealistic version of a mouth beneath her nose, and dashed into her bedroom to find a coat. When she got to the front door, she stopped. She couldn't say goodbye to Ignatius like this. He was her child.

She went up to his bedroom door and listened to the wildly twanging bedsprings as they reached a crescendo, as they built toward a finale worthy of Grieg's *In the Hall of the Mountain King*. She knocked, but there was no answer.

"Ignatius," she called sadly.

"What do you want?" a breathless voice asked at last.

"I'm going out, Ignatius. I wanted to say goodbye."

Ignatius did not answer.

"Ignatius, open up," Mrs. Reilly pleaded. "Come kiss me goodbye, honey."

"I don't feel at all well. I can hardly move."

"Come on, son."

The door opened slowly. Ignatius stuck his fat gray face into the hall. His mother's eyes watered when she saw the bandage.

"Now kiss me, honey. I'm sorry it all had to end like this."

"What do all of these lachrymose clichés mean?" Ignatius asked suspiciously. "Why are you suddenly pleasant? Don't you have some old man to meet somewhere?"

"You was right, Ignatius. You can't go to work. I shoulda known that. I shoulda tried to get that debt paid off some other way." A tear slid from Mrs. Reilly's eyes and washed a little trail of clean skin through the powder. "If that Mr. Levy calls, don't answer the phone. I'm gonna take care of you."

"Oh, my God!" Ignatius bellowed. "Now I'm really in trouble. Goodness knows what you're planning. Where are you going?"

"Stay inside and don't answer the phone."

"Why? What is this?" The bloodshot eyes flashed with fright. "Who was that you were whispering to on the phone?"

"You won't have to worry about Mr. Levy, son. I'm gonna fix you up. Just remember your poor momma's got your welfare at heart."

"That's what I'm afraid of."

"Don't never be mad at me, honey," Mrs. Reilly said and, jumping up in her bowling shoes that she had not taken off since Angelo had telephoned her the night before, she embraced Ignatius and kissed him on his moustache.

She released him and ran to the front door, where she turned and called, "I'm sorry I run into that building, Ignatius. I love you."

The shutters slammed and she was gone.

"Come back," Ignatius thundered. He ripped at the shutters, but the old Plymouth, one of its front tires fenderless and exposed as if it were a stock car, was rumbling to life. "Come back, please. Mother!"

"Aw, shut up," Miss Annie hollered from somewhere in the darkness.

His mother had something up her sleeve, some clumsy plan, some scheme that would ruin him forever. Why had she insisted that he stay inside? She knew that he would not be going anywhere in his present condition. He found Santa Battaglia's number and dialed it. He must speak with his mother.

"This is Ignatius Reilly," he said when Santa had answered. "Is my mother coming down there tonight?"

"No, she ain't," Santa replied coldly. "I ain't spoke with your momma all day."

Ignatius hung up. Something was going on. He had heard his mother saying "Santa" over the telephone at least two or three times during the day. And that last telephone call, that whispered communication just before his mother had left. His mother only whispered to the Battaglia bawd and then it was only when they were exchanging secrets. At once Ignatius suspected the reason for his mother's emotional farewell, for its finality. She had already told him that the Battaglia match-maker had advised a vacation for him in the psychiatric ward at Charity. Everything made sense. In a psychiatric ward he would not be liable to prosecution by Abelman and Levy, or whoever it was who would push the case. Perhaps both of them would sue him, Abelman for character defamation and Levy for forgery. To his mother's limited mind the psychiatric ward would seem an attractive alternative. It was just like her, with the very best of intentions, to have her child harnessed by a straitjacket and electrocuted by shock treatments. Of course, his mother might not be considering this at all. However, whenever dealing with her, it was always best to prepare for the worst. Wife of Bath Battaglia's lie was itself not very reassuring.

In the United States you are innocent until they prove you guilty. Perhaps Miss Trixie had confessed. Why hadn't Mr. Levy telephoned back? Ignatius would not be tossed into a mental clinic while, legally, he was still innocent of having written the letter. His mother, typically, had responded to Mr.

Levy's visit in the most irrational and emotional manner possible. "I'm gonna take care of you." "I'm gonna fix you up." Yes, she would fix him up all right. A hose would be turned on him. Some cretin psychoanalyst would attempt to comprehend the singularity of his worldview. In frustration, the psychoanalyst would have him crammed into a cell three feet square. No. That was out of the question. Jail was preferable. There they only limited you physically. In a mental ward they tampered with your soul and worldview and mind. He would never tolerate that. And his mother had been so apologetic about this mysterious protection she was going to give him. All signs pointed to Charity Hospital.

Oh, Fortuna, you wretch!

Now he was waddling around in the little house like a sitting duck. Whatever strong-arm men the hospital employed had their sights aimed directly at him. Ignatius Reilly, clay pigeon. His mother might only have gone to one of her bowling Bacchanalia. On the other hand, a barred truck might be speeding to Constantinople Street right now.

Escape. Escape.

Ignatius looked in his wallet. The thirty dollars was gone, apparently confiscated by his mother at the hospital. He looked at the clock. It was almost eight o'clock. Between napping and assaulting the glove, the afternoon and evening passed rather quickly. Ignatius searched his room, flinging Big Chief tablets around, mashing them underfoot, dragging them from beneath his bed. He came up with some scattered coins and went to work on the desk, where he found a few more. The total was sixty cents, a sum that limited and blocked escape routes. He could at least find a safe haven for the rest of the evening: the Prytania. After the theater had closed, he could pass along Constantinople Street to see whether his mother had come home.

There was a slipshod frenzy of dressing. The red flannel

nightshirt sailed up and hung on the chandelier. He jammed his toes into the desert boots and leaped as well as he could into the tweed trousers, which he could hardly button at the waist. Shirt, cap, overcoat, Ignatius put them on blindly and ran into the hall, careening against the narrow walls. He was just reaching for the front door when three loud knocks cracked against the shutters.

Mr. Levy returned? His valve sent out a distress signal that established communication with his hands. He scratched the bumps on his paws and peered through the shutters, expecting to see several hirsute brutes from the hospital.

There on the porch stood Myrna in a shapeless olive drab corduroy car coat. Her black hair was braided into a pigtail that twisted under one ear and fell on her breast. A guitar was slung over her shoulders.

Ignatius was about to burst through the shutters, splintering slats and latches, and wrap that one hemplike pigtail around her throat until she turned blue. But reason won. He was not looking at Myrna; he was looking at an escape route. Fortuna had relented. She was not depraved enough to end this vicious cycle by throttling him in a straitjacket, by sealing him up in a cement block tomb lighted by florescent tubes. Fortuna wished to make amends. Somehow she had summoned and flushed Myrna minx from a subway tube, from some picket line, from the pungent bed of some Eurasian existentialist, from the hands of some epileptic Negro Buddhist, from the verbose midst of a group therapy session.

"Ignatius, are you in that dump?" Myrna demanded in her flat, direct, slightly hostile voice. She beat on the shutters again, squinting through her black-rimmed glasses. Myrna was not astigmatic; the lenses were clear glass; she wore the glasses to prove her dedication and intensity of purpose. Her dangling earring reflected the rays of the streetlight like tinkling glass Chinese ornaments. "Listen, I can tell there's somebody in there. I heard you stomping around in that hall. Open up these crummy shutters."

"Yes, yes, I'm here," Ignatius cried. He tore at the shutters and pushed them open. "Thank Fortuna you've come."

"Jesus. You look terrible. Like you're having a nervous breakdown or something. Why the bandage? Ignatius, what's the matter? Look how much weight you've gained. I've just been reading these pitiful signs out here on the porch. Boy, have you had it."

"I've gone through hell," Ignatius slobbered, pulling Myrna into the hall by the sleeve of her coat. "Why did you step out of my life, you minx? Your new hair-do is fascinating and cosmopolitan." He snatched at her pigtail and pressed it to his wet moustache, kissing it vigorously. "The scent of soot and carbon in your hair excites me with suggestions of glamorous Gotham. We must leave immediately. I must go flower in Manhattan."

"I knew something was wrong. But *this*. You are really in bad shape, Ig."

"Quickly. To a motel. My natural impulses are screaming for release. Do you have any money on you?"

"Don't put me on," Myrna said angrily. She grabbed the soggy pigtail from Ignatius' paws and threw it over her shoulder onto the guitar where it landed with a twang. "Look. Ignatius. I'm beat. I've been on the road since nine o'clock yesterday morning. As soon as I mailed you that letter about the Peace Party routine, I said to myself, 'Myrna. Listen. This guy needs more than just a letter. He needs your help. He's sinking fast. Are you dedicated enough to save a mind rotting right before your eyes? Are you committed enough to salvage the wreckage of that mentality?' I came out of the post office and got in my car and just started driving. All night. Straight. I mean, the more I thought about that wild Peace Party telegram, the more upset I got."

Apparently Myrna was very hard up for causes in Manhattan.

"I don't blame you," Ignatius cried. "Wasn't that telegram horrible? A deranged fantasy. I've been in the depths of depression for weeks. After all these years that I've stuck by my mother's side, she has decided to get married and wants me out of the way. We must leave. I can't stand this house another moment."

"What? Who'd marry *her*?"

"Thank God you understand. You can see how ludicrous and impossible everything has become."

"Where is she? I'd like to outline for that woman what she's done to you."

"She's out somewhere failing her blood test at the moment. I don't want to see her again."

"I guess not. You poor kid. What have you been doing, Ignatius? Just lying around in your room doping off?"

"Yes. For weeks. I've been immobilized by the neurotic apathy. Do you remember the fantasy letter about the arrest and the accident? I wrote that when my mother first met this debauched old man. It was then that my equilibrium started to fail. Since then, it's been a continuously downward movement culminating in the schizophrenia of the Peace Party. Those signs outside were just one physical manifestation of my inward torment. My psychotic desire for peace was no doubt a wishful attempt to end the hostilities which have been existing in this little house. I can only be grateful that you were perceptive enough to analyze my fantasy life as embodied in my letters. Thank goodness they were distress signals written in a code which you could understand."

"I can tell how inactive you've been from your weight."

"I've gained pounds lying continuously in bed, seeking surcease and sublimation in food. Now we must run. I must leave this house. It has terrible associations."

"I told you to get out of this place a long time ago. Come

on, let's get you packed." Myrna's monotonous voice was growing enthusiastic. "This is fantastic. I knew you'd have to break away sooner or later to preserve your mental health."

"If only I had listened to you earlier, I wouldn't have had to go through this horror." Ignatius embraced Myrna and pressed her and her guitar flatly against the wall. He could see that she was beside herself with joy over finding a legitimate cause, a bona fide case history, a new movement. "There will be a place for you in heaven, my minx. Now we must dash."

He tried to drag her out the front door, but she said, "Don't you want to pack anything?"

"Oh, of course. There are all of my notes and jottings. We must never let them fall into the hands of my mother. She may make a fortune from them. It would be too ironic." They went into his room. "By the way, you should know that my mother is enjoying the questionable attentions of a fascist."

"Oh, no!"

"Yes. Look at this. You can imagine how they've been torturing me."

He handed Myrna one of the pamphlets that his mother had slipped under the door of his room, *Is Your Neighbor Really an American*? Myrna read a note written in the margin of the cover: "Read this Irene. It is good. There is some questions at the end you can ask your boy."

"Oh, Ignatius!" Myrna moaned. "What has it been like?"

"Traumatic and dreadful. At the moment I think they're out somewhere lashing some moderate whom my mother overheard speaking in favor of the United Nations in the grocery this morning. She's been mumbling about the incident all day." Ignatius belched. "I've been though weeks of terror."

"It's so strange to find your mother gone. She used to be around here all the time." Myrna hung her guitar on a bedpost and stretched across the bed. "This room. We used to have a ball in here, exposing our minds and souls, composing anti-Talc manifestos. I guess that fraud is still hanging around that school."

"I would imagine so," Ignatius said absently. He wished that Myrna would get off the bed. Soon her mind would turn to exposing other things. Anyway, they had to get out of the house. He was in the closet, where he was looking for the overnight bag that his mother had bought for him for a disastrous one-day stay at a boys' camp when he was eleven. He pawed through a pile of yellowed drawers like a dog digging for a bone, throwing the drawers up behind him in an arc. "Perhaps you'd better rouse yourself, my little lily. There are tablets to be collected, notes to be gathered. You might look under the bed."

Myrna swung herself off the damp sheets, saying, "I've tried to describe you to my friends in the group therapy group, working away in this room, sealed off from society. This strange medieval mind in its cloister."

"No doubt they were intrigued," Ignatius murmured. Having found the bag, he was filling it with some socks he found lying on the floor. "Soon they'll be able to see me in the flesh."

"Just wait till they hear all that originality pouring out of your head."

"Ho hum," Ignatius yawned. "Perhaps my mother has done me a great favor by planning to remarry. Those Oedipal bonds were beginning to overwhelm me." He threw his yo-yo into the bag. "Apparently you had safe passage through the South."

"I didn't have a moment to really stop along the way. Almost thirty-six hours of drive, drive, drive." Myrna was making piles of the Big Chief tablets. "I did stop at a Negro diner last night, but they wouldn't serve me. I think the guitar threw them off."

"That must have been it. They took you for some red-neck hillbilly singer. I've had some experience with those people. They're rather limited."

"I can't believe that I am *actually* taking you out of this dungeon, this hole."

"It is unbelievable, isn't it? To think that I fought your wisdom for years."

"We are going to have the most fantastic time in New York. Honestly."

"I can't wait," Ignatius said, packing his scarf and cutlass. "The Statue of Liberty, the Empire State Building, the thrill of opening night on Broadway with my favorite musicomedy stars. Gab sessions in the Village over espresso with challenging, contemporary minds."

"You're coming to grips with yourself at last. Really. I can hardly believe what I've heard in this shack tonight. We'll work on your problems. You're going into a whole new and vital phase. Your inactivity is over. I can tell. I can hear it. Just think of the great thought that is going to come streaming out of that head when we've finally cleared away all the cobwebs and taboos and crippling attachments."

"Goodness knows what will happen," Ignatius said disinterestedly. "We must leave. Now. I should warn you that my mother may return momentarily. If I see her again, I'll regress horribly. We must dash."

"Ignatius, you're jumping all over the place. Relax. The worst is over."

"No, it isn't," Ignatius said quickly. "My mother may return with her mob. You should see them. White supremacists, Protestants, or worse. Let me get my lute and trumpet. Are the tablets gathered together?"

"This stuff in here is fascinating," Myrna said, indicating the tablet through which she was flipping. "Gems of nihilism."

"That is merely a fragment of the whole."

"Aren't you even going to leave your mother some very bitter note, some articulate protest or something?"

"It would hardly be worthwhile. She'd be weeks in comprehending it." Ignatius cradled the lute and trumpet in one arm and the overnight bag in the other. "Please don't drop that looseleaf folder. It contains the Journal, a sociological fantasy on which I've been working. It is my most commercial effort. Wonderful film possibilities at the hands of a Walt Disney or a George Pal."

"Ignatius." Myrna stopped in the doorway, her arms laden with tablets, and moved her colorless lips for a moment before she spoke, as if she were formulating an address. Her tired, highway-drugged eyes searched Ignatius' face through the sparkling lenses. "This is a very meaningful moment. I feel as if I'm *saving* someone."

"You are, you are. Now we must flee. Please. We'll chat later." Ignatius pushed past her and lumbered down to the car, opening the rear door of the little Renault and climbing in among the placards and piles of pamphlets that covered the seat. The car smelled like a newsstand. "Hurry up! We don't have time to stage a *tableau-vivant* here before the house."

"I mean, are you really going to sit back there?" Myrna asked as she dropped her load of tablets through the rear door.

"Of course I am," Ignatius bellowed. "I am certainly not going to sit up in that deathtrap of a front seat for highway travel. Now get in this go-cart and get us out of here."

"Hold on. I left a lot of tablets behind," Myrna said and ran into the house, her guitar thumping against her side. She came down the steps with another load and stopped on the brick sidewalk, turning to look at the house. Ignatius could tell that she was attempting to *record* the scene: Eliza crossing the ice with a particularly large genius in her arms. Like Harriet Beecher Stowe, Myrna was still around to offend. At last, in response to Ignatius' cries, she came down to the car and threw the second load of tablets onto Ignatius' lap. "There are still some left under the bed, I think."

"Never mind about those!" Ignatius screamed. "Get in and start this thing. Oh, my God. Don't stick that guitar in my face like that. Why can't you just carry a purse like a decent young lady?"

"Go fall in a hole," Myrna said angrily. She slid into the front seat and started the car. "Where do you want to spend the night?"

"Spend the night?" Ignatius thundered. "We're not spending the night anywhere. We must drive straight."

"Ignatius, I'm about to drop dead. I've been in this car since yesterday morning."

"Well, get across Lake Pontchartrain at least."

"Okay. We can take the causeway and stop in Mandeville."

"No!" Myrna would drive him right into the alerted arms of some psychiatrist. "We can't stop there. The water's polluted. They're having an epidemic."

"Yeah? Then I'll take the old bridge to Slidell."

"Yes. It's far safer anyway. Barges are always hurtling into that causeway. We'll plunge into the lake and drown." The Renault was dragging very low in the rear and accelerated slowly. "This car is rather small for my frame. Are you sure that you know how to get to New York? I seriously doubt whether I can survive more than a day or two in this fetal position."

"Hey, where are you two beatniks going?" Miss Annie's voice called faintly from behind her shutters. The Renault moved into the center of the street.

"Does that old bitch still live there?" Myrna asked.

"Shut up and get us out of here!"

"Are you going to bug me like this?" Myrna glared at the green cap in the rear-view mirror. "I mean, I'd like to know."

"Oh, my valve!" Ignatius gasped. "Please don't make a scene. My psyche will crumble entirely after the assaults it has recently received."

"I'm sorry. For a while it sounded like old times with me playing chauffeur and you bugging me from the back seat."

"I certainly hope it isn't snowing up north. My system simply will not function under those conditions. And please watch out for Greyhound Scenicruisers along the way. They'll demolish a toy like this."

"Ignatius, all at once you're your old horrible self. All at once I think I'm making a very big mistake."

"A mistake? Of course not," Ignatius said sweetly. "But watch out for that ambulance. We don't want to begin our pilgrimage with an accident."

As the ambulance passed, Ignatius hunched over and saw "Charity Hospital" printed on its door. The rotating red light atop the ambulance splashed over the Renault for a brief moment as the vehicles passed each other. Ignatius felt insulted. He had expected a massive barred truck. They had underestimated him in sending out an old, well-used Cadillac ambulance. He would easily have been able to smash all of those windows. Then the glowing Cadillac fins were two blocks behind them and Myrna was turning onto St. Charles Avenue.

Now that Fortuna had saved him from one cycle, where would she spin him now? The new cycle would be so different from anything he had ever known.

Myrna prodded and shifted the Renault through the city traffic masterfully, weaving in and out of impossibly narrow lanes until they were clear of the last twinkling streetlight of the last swampy suburb. Then they were in darkness in the center of the salt marshes. Ignatius looked out at the highway marker that reflected their headlights. U.S. 11. The marker flew past. He rolled down the window an inch or two and breathed the salt air blowing in over the marshes from the Gulf.

As if the air were a purgative, his valve opened. He breathed again, this time more deeply. The dull headache was lifting.

He stared gratefully at the back of Myrna's head, at the pigtail that swung innocently at his knee. Gratefully. How ironic, Ignatius thought. Taking the pigtail in one of his paws, he pressed it warmly to his wet moustache.

PENGUIN RED CLASSICS

ALICE'S ADVENTURES IN WONDERLAND LEWIS CARROLL

'Precise, dream-like, subversive' Quentin Blake,
Independent on Sunday

'A book of wonder and nonsense laced with lethal wit' *Guardian*

Bored on a hot afternoon, Alice follows a White Rabbit down a rabbit-hole – without giving a thought about how she might get out. And so she tumbles into Wonderland: where animals answer back, a baby turns into a pig, time stands still at a disorderly tea party, croquet is played with hedgehogs and flamingos, and the Mock Turtle and Gryphon dance the Lobster Quadrille. In a land in which nothing is as it seems and cakes, potions and mushrooms can make her shrink to ten inches or grow to the size of a house, will Alice be able to find her way home again?

'A marvellous confidence in the primacy of the imagination' Will Self

'Most precious Alice' Zadie Smith

For classic fiction, read Red

www.penguinclassics.com/reds

Little Witches

in a Hotchpotch

Valerie Wilding

Illustrated by Lesley Harker

Hodder
Children's
Books

a division of Hodder Headline plc

CONTENTS

For my niece,
Catherine Watkinson,
with love.

CHAPTER ONE

WITCH ON A RUBBISH BIN

Skusting rolled over. "Ouch!"

Last night's syrup sandwich crust
was jammed beneath her lumpy pillow.
Her hair had stuck to it. She felt inside
the pillow case and pulled out one of
the largest lumps - a coconut macaroon.

"Brekky," she murmured. "Yum."

"Are you out of that revolting bed yet?" her sister, Skwizit, called in her tinkly voice. "We've got to put out the rubbish bin, and then I want to polish my nails."

Skusting got up, grumbling.

She licked a finger, rubbed a patch on the mirror and peered at her face.

"Clean enough."

Her skirt was under the bed but yesterday's jumper had vanished - pesky rats - so she tucked her nightie into the skirt.

"Are you coming?" Skwizit nagged. "I can hear the dustcart."

"On me way."

Skusting padded across the room, collecting a splinter through a hole in her sock.

"Drat!"

She hopped to the bathroom and rummaged through Skwizit's half of the cabinet. Neat rows of make-up and perfume tumbled and spilled as she searched for the box labelled Tuggo Eyebrow Tweezers.

"Got em!"

Skusting yanked out the splinter and headed for the staircase.

7

"Watch out below," she yelled.

WHEEee

She slid down the banisters and landed, grinning, at her sister's feet.

Skwizit wore the flowery plastic coveralls which she used for housework. She patted her glossy curls and shuddered.

The only thing she and Skusting had in common, apart from the fact that they were sisters, was that they were both witches.

And not very good witches, it must be said.

Skwizit pulled on pink rubber gloves.

"*You* take the bin," she said. "I'll open the gate."

"OK." Skusting thundered ahead while Skwizit plink-plonked along the path in high heels.

The dustcart stopped outside.

A burly bin man leapt down and picked up Skusting.

"Let go!" she shrieked.

The man dropped her and stepped back.

"A talking bin!" he said in wonder.

"Har! Har!" said Skusting. "Same joke, every week."

Suddenly, she put her head on one side. "Wait - lift me up again, bin man. I saw something."

He stood her on the bin. She stretched up and looked across the village green.

"It's holiday time, isn't it? So why is everyone going into the school?"

"The new term starts tomorrow," said Skwizit.

"Tomorrow's tomorrow," said Skusting. "Today's today."

"Can't argue there," said the man, "but I've work to do."

He set her down and opened the bin.

10

Skusting snatched a squashed half of lemon from the top of the rubbish and sucked it noisily.

You are disgusting Skusting. I used that to clean my elbows.

"Then it'll clean my tum." Skusting smacked her lips. "Skwizit, something's going on at the school. We could help."

"Help?" Her sister's eyes brightened. The little witches liked helping. "Let's go and see. I'll just change my clothes."

"No time now," said Skusting.

She seized Skwizit's rubber-gloved hand and tucked it firmly under her arm. "You come along with me. I reckon those school people will be very glad to see us. Very glad indeed."

11

CHAPTER TWO

ROSEMARY CROW SAYS, "NO!"

The school playground was busy.

People in work clothes
bustled about with paint
tins, ladders and tool
boxes.

Skusting leaned over the gate.

"Yoo-hoo! What's going on?"

Mrs Rosemary Crow spun round.
She threw down her clipboard and
flung both arms in the air.

"Oh no!" she cried. "It's Skusting!"

Rosemary Crow was Leader of the
Parish Council, and she didn't like
witches.

She turned and whispered to her
nephew, Joe, from Class 3. She talked,
he nodded, and when she'd finished he
ambled towards Skusting.

"Hurry!" bellowed Rosemary Crow.

Joe jumped in fright and shot off like a missile. He skidded to a stop by the gate.

He took off his glasses and pushed hair out of his eyes.

"Hi, Skusting. Aunt Rosemary says we're busy, so . . ."

He stopped. "Why is there a rubber glove by your foot?"

Skusting looked down.

"Botheration!" she said. "Skwizit's escaped."

"Escaped?" said Joe.

"I wouldn't let her get dressed up before. Now she's gone to put on one of her frilly froo-froo frocky things."

Skusting climbed the gate and sat on top. "What's happening here?"

"Aunt Rosemary said not to tell you, but . . . It's a working party. School starts tomorrow," Joe explained, "and there still isn't enough money for everything we need, so all the parents are doing odd jobs . . ."

"Odd jobs?"

"Yes, like putting up extra shelves and cupboards, and a new computer trolley and—"

Rosemary Crow's crystal clear voice shrieked,

Come away Joe.

"You'd better go," said Skusting, "before she blows her top."

"Dead right." Joe made a face. "See you, Skusting."

He ran off but stopped suddenly, turning to say, "Sorry about Aunt-"

"Joe!" yelled Rosemary Crow.

A whiff of sugary scent wafted over Skusting. Skwizit was back, freshly dressed and powdered. She was thrilled to hear about the working party.

"We *must* help." She clapped her hands. "I'll go and change into coveralls."

15

"Hold it!" Skusting pointed out Rosemary Crow. "*She* doesn't want our help - as usual."

"Oh, *her*." Skwizit flung open the gate, tumbling Skusting to the ground.

She marched straight over to the Leader of the Parish Council.

"Good morning, Rosemary," she said loudly. "My sister and I would like to help. What shall we do?"

The children chanted, "Skusting's going to help us! Skusting's going to help us!"

The parents said, "How kind," and, "Lovely when everyone pulls together."

Rosemary Crow forced a sickly smile.

"Well . . . since you put it like that. I suppose there must be some little job you can't bungle."

She glanced round. "Where's my list?"

Joe spread a sheet of paper on a bench.

Rosemary Crow bent over it.

Skusting bent over Rosemary Crow, who sprang back, pressing a hanky to her nose.

"What a long list," said Skwizit. "You'll be glad of our help."

"Hey!" Joe cried. "You're witches! You could help with magic!"

Skusting fidgeted. "We haven't exactly *got* any magic."

Joe looked puzzled. "But I've seen you use magic. Everybody has."

"We haven't got any, honest." Skusting scratched her roly-poly tummy. "Not magic of our own. We have to sort of - apply for it."

"We failed the witchery exams," Skwizit explained, red-faced.

"*She*," said Skusting, "went to the hairdressers and forgot all about the exam."

"And *she*," said Skwizit, "smeared peanut butter and tomato pips all over her paper. They wouldn't mark it."

Skusting, anxious to change the subject, quickly ran her finger down the list, leaving a grimy trail.

"Playground," she read. "What's wrong with the playground?"

"It's boring," said Joe. He showed them. "The hopscotch has faded, the middle's worn out of the target and the snakes and ladders game, well . . ."

Skwizit tapped her pointed toe on the remains of a snake's eye. "It needs painting again."

"Specially as new kids start tomorrow," said Joe. "Teachers want it nice for them. And for us old ones," he added. "It's boring playing here."

Skwizit took a silver pencil from her satin handbag, crossed Playground off the list and said, "That's our job."

Rosemary Crow snatched the list back.

Just don't get in anyone's way and don't make a mess!

"We can hardly make a mess with two paint brushes," Skusting snapped. "As for getting in anyone's way - we'll do it after tea."

Rosemary Crow smirked. "Before dark, I trust?"

Skwizit fumed. "Of *course* before dark. We're not silly."

Skusting laughed her hearty laugh. "We'll do it when you people have gone. Then no one can tread in our paintwork and make one of those messes you're so worried about."

On the way home, Skwizit said, "That was good thinking."

Skusting winked. "I'm not just a pretty face, sister dear. I've got brains. A lot goes on up here." She tapped her head. "Hello," she muttered, as her finger came away with a piece of cheese stuck to it. "I wondered where that had got to."

CHAPTER THREE

TOO LATE

That afternoon, Skwizit sunbathed on a lacy white rug, wearing a star-studded bikini.

Skusting watched a video and emptied the biscuit tin.

And a bag of toffees.

And a bag of ketchup crisps.

The film had just finished when Skwizit appeared to check her tan in the mirror.

"Lovely and golden..."

"Now I'm going upstairs to crimp my hair," she said.

Skusting followed her, and began rooting through cupboards and drawers for her swimming costume.

"Skwizit, have you been wearing my cossy?" she demanded.

Skwizit gave a small squeal.

"As if I would! I'd *never* wear your clothes - ever! I feel woozy even thinking about it."

Skusting snorted and continued the search. She found her swimsuit behind the radiator, where she'd stuffed it to dry last summer. It was dotted with mould, but Skusting quite liked the blue speckles.

Outside, she flopped on the rug and pasted herself all over with Skwizit's Grillo Sun Cream. She polished off a bag of popcorn and fell asleep, snoring like a camel with a cold.

Much later, Skusting woke with a
snort and a shiver to find Skwizit
twirling in something floaty.

"What do you think of my dress?"
she asked.

"It's red," mumbled Skusting.

Skwizit stamped. "I've spent hours
sewing daisies on it. Hours! And all you
can say . . ."

"Hours?" Skusting sat up, her greasy
body plastered with ants and popcorn.
"The sun's gone down. Must be supper
time."

"Supper time?" Skwizit laughed her tinkly laugh and fluffed her newly-crimped hair. "Goodness, I was so busy I forgot to wake you for tea!"

Tea? That rang a bell with Skusting.

"Weren't we doing something after tea?"

They frowned in thought.

Brrrinng

"Front doorbell," said Skwizit. "You go."

Skusting got up and lumbered indoors. Skwizit took one look at her beautiful white rug and screeched with rage. Right in the middle was a huge grubby mark - exactly the same shape as Skusting.

She stopped screeching when she saw who the visitor was.

"It's Joe," said Skusting. "And guess what . . ."

Skwizit caught her breath. "Oh, no! We forgot the playground!"

They leapt into action. Skwizit grabbed her make-up bag, and Skusting headed for the door.

"Hurry!" she bellowed.

"But it's nearly dark," Joe wailed. "It's too late."

Skwizit stopped, near to tears. "I can just imagine Rosemary Crow's face," she whispered to Skusting. "She'll go on about how we can't be trusted and she warned them and wasn't she right all–"

"Never mind Rosemary Crowface," said Skusting. "What about Joe? And the kids? They're expecting a fun, bright playground. And all they'll get is a washed-out one, dusty from that working party. Well . . ." She straightened her back. "We can't disappoint them."

"But it's dark."

Skusting put her hands on her hips, and stuck out her chin and tummy.

"We'll get help."

Skwizit stared, aghast. "You don't mean–"

"I do mean. There's no choice, Skwizit, none at all. We need–"

Her sister swallowed nervously. "Wiziwych?"

Skusting nodded. "Wiziwych!"

She turned to Joe. "You'd better go home. This is something we have to do," she gulped, "on our own."

Joe took one look at their serious faces and backed away. He bumped into the door, spun round and raced off home.

The witches plodded upstairs and paused outside the spare room door.

"Deep breaths," said Skusting.

Skwizit straightened her collar. "I hate this," she whispered. "Wiziwych makes me feel - silly, and useless."

"Makes *me* feel like a brainless lump." Skusting popped a boiled sweet into her mouth. "Here goes." She twanged the legs of her swimsuit and, ever so slowly, opened the door.

CHAPTER FOUR

Wiziwych

The gleaming gold computer that was
Wiziwych crackled into life. The screen
lit up.

"Oh, per-lease," said a thin metallic
voice. "Not you two again."

"Yes, dear Wiziwych," Skusting simpered, "it is we."

The screen flashed. "Somebody hasn't washed lately."

Skusting went red. "Tuesday I did."

Skwizit clasped her hands, dipping and bobbing as if trying to curtsy.

"Dear Wiziwych," she began.

"Stop grovelling. Remove that lipstick. It disturbs my sensors."

Skwizit pressed a hanky to her lips, spluttering apologies.

Skusting looked smug.

"Well, O grubby one? What is it?" snapped Wiziwych.

Skusting explained about the playground.

So you see dear Wiziwych, time just flew.

"You mean you forgot!" came the sharp response. "And when you remembered, it was too late. And why?"

Wiziwych gave her no chance to reply.

"Because you wasted time," it rapped. "You with your food and television and sleep and more food, and Skwizit with her mirrors and make-up. You WASTED time."

Skusting flinched. "Maybe a bit," she agreed. "The point is, dear, wise Wiziwych, it's too dark to paint the playground now. Could you help? Please?"

"I don't intend to make the sun rise at night."

Skusting gave a hearty false laugh.

"Har, har, jolly funny. But, dear Wiziwych, you don't quite understand . . ."

"WHAT?"

The computer screen flashed angrily and so brightly that the witches had to cover their eyes.

"*I* don't understand?" the metallic voice shrilled. **"I? I who have spent an ETERNITY with you - you**

LAZY, GREEDY, SCRUFFY, SMELLY . . ."

Skwizit nudged Skusting. "That's you."

"And YOU! Vain, conceited, prissy . . ."

Wiziwych's voice rose like an angry wasp until, with a final snap of, "I understand EVERYTHING!" The screen went dead.

Seconds passed.

Skusting blinked.

Skwizit was pale with shock.

"That's that, then," Skwizit said. "Tomorrow, *you* can explain to Rosemary Crow."

But Skusting edged closer to the computer.

"Please, Wiziwych," she said in a small voice. "It's not for us. It's for the children. Imagine their faces when they turn up at school tomorrow - especially the littlest ones . . ." She warmed up. "Oooh, dear, I expect they'll sit right down on that grey old playground and sob their little hearts out for sheer fed-upness."

Wiziwych's keyboard rattled.

"It's sulking," said Skwizit. "I never sulk. It gives you wrinkles."

The screen lightened.

"And sneering witches overload my circuits, so, Skwizit, be warned. I'll help - for the children's sake. You may draw what you want."

"Wiziwych," said Skusting, "you're wonderful."

"I know," said the computer. "Clear screen. Design mode."

Blocks of bright colour appeared across the bottom of the screen.

"Proceed."

The witches struggled for first go. Skwizit almost won, but Skusting had a secret weapon. She pulled out a half-chewed Chocco Bar and jammed it on Skwizit's nose.

Skwizit screamed and struggled to remove it.

"Har, har!" said Skusting. "Looks like
I get first turn!"

CHAPTER FIVE

LETTERPILLAR

Skusting sat on Skwizit to keep her still, then reached a finger towards the screen.

"Don't touch me with that filthy digit!" screamed Wiziwych.

Skusting examined her hands. She hooked a clump of dust and dirt from beneath a thumb nail and picked a squashed sultana from between two fingers.

"Wash!" Wiziwych yelled.

Skusting stomped off to the bathroom. She dampened her hands and rubbed them on Skwizit's flannel until it looked like an old floor cloth. "I'll teach her," she muttered and returned to the computer.

Skwizit was drawing on the screen with a finger.

The outline of a blue hopscotch grid grew beneath her crimson nail. She touched the red block at the bottom of the screen and wrote numbers in each square.

"There!" she said. "Perfect."

"My turn." Skusting shoved her sister aside, touched green and set to work.

Skwizit watched. "You've drawn a string of sausages!"

"Sausages aren't green, stupid," said Skusting. "It's a caterpillar."

Changing to orange, she wrote a letter of the alphabet in each segment. "It's to help the littlest kiddies learn to read. I'll call it a Letterpillar!" she added brightly. "Now, a target."

"No, you don't," Skwizit snapped. "I'm next."

She dug Skusting's ribs with stiff fingers.

"Yowch!"

Skwizit concentrated on the screen. Her tongue stuck out, following the drawing finger.

"That's the target done," she said. "You can draw a number line across the playground if you wish."

"I don't wish." Skusting picked a piece of popcorn off her swimsuit.

"Not while you're touching me!"
Wiziwych's keyboard rattled.

"OK, OK. Don't get your floppies in
a flap," said Skusting. "I'll keep it for
later." She tucked the popcorn behind
her ear. It stuck.

"I'll draw the number line," Skwizit
declared.

Skusting wasn't having that. She
reached out and ruffled her sister's hair.
Skwizit yelled. She'd used a whole can
of Sticko Hair Spray that afternoon, and
ruffling really hurt.

43

Touching purple, Skusting drew rapidly on the screen.

"If that's meant to be a straight line," Skwizit scoffed, "it's bent."

"It's bent because it's a snail," said Skusting. "The eyeball's the start."

"Then what?"

Skusting typed rapidly. "Then," she explained, "you hop down its neck where it says hop, then you run round its bottom where it says run, then you jump round and round where it says jump, then you skip into the middle where it says-"

"-pisk."

"Beg pardon?"

"It says pisk."

Skusting examined the screen. "Should be skip. Wiziwych made a mistake."

44

Instantly, an ear-splitting, electronic whine blasted both witches backwards.

The keyboard rattled and jerked, the screen flashed, and jagged lightning zig-zagged from the computer.

The witches huddled together in terror.

"Skusting!" Skwizit whimpered. "What have you done?"

CHAPTER SIX

HOTCHPOTCH!

"No, no, dear Wiziwych!" Skusting shrieked. "It is I, the dopey one, who made the mistake."

"A slip of the tongue, dear Wiziwych," Skwizit burst out.

"Oh, get up and get on with it. I've had enough of your squabbling. Do you want my help, or . . ."

"We do, we do!" said Skwizit. She nudged Skusting. "Let's get a move on. I'll start the snakes and ladders."

She touched grey, but screamed as Skusting grabbed her in a bear hug and rolled her to the floor.

"It's not your turn!" said Skusting as she tapped yellow, but Skwizit staggered upright and grabbed the crossed straps at the back of her sister's swimsuit.

She pulled hard and let go.

Twa-a-a-ang!

"Yeeowch!" Skusting yelped in
shock. "Look what you've done!"

Her yellow line trailed down the
computer screen like melted butter.

"You've ruined my drawing, Skwizit!
Now I'll ruin yours!"

Skusting scribbled yellow zig-zags over the target. She jammed her free hand in Skwizit's hairdo, then pulled it out. Clumps of hair stuck to it.

Skwizit curled one arm round her head and used her free hand to criss-cross all over the snail. "That's fixed you!" she cried.

Skusting reached for the screen, but Skwizit gripped her arm and held her

back. "Me next!" she snapped.

"You are so shellfish!" Skusting bawled.

Skwizit jeered, "You mean selfish."

"I know what I mean, you old crab!" Skusting shrieked.

They flew at each other, pinching and pushing. Whenever one got an arm free, she scrawled across the screen.

Only when both collapsed, exhausted, did the witches notice the steady tap-tap-tapping coming from Wiziwych's keyboard.

Skwizit peered closer. "It's the X key," she said. "Why X?"

"It's cross?" Skusting wondered.

The keyboard rattled faster, as if the computer was gathering speed.

Wiziwych spoke. "Design ready," it said. "Execute."

The witches' eyes flew to the screen. To the rainbow-coloured, chaotic jumble, the mess of lines and squiggles and blobs. Where were the snail trail and the letterpillar? Where was the target? The hopscotch?

Hopscotch?

It was a hotchpotch. A horrible haphazard hotchpotch.

Together, they screamed.

"NO!"

Wiziwych went dark, and still.

Skusting dived for the keyboard and typed

DESINE NOT REDDY DONT EGGS ACUTE

The keys rippled up and down, back and forth.

"What's it doing?" Skusting whispered.

"It's laughing," Skwizit said hopelessly. "Wiziwych is laughing at us."

51

CHAPTER SEVEN

WHO DID IT?

Skusting only managed half her supper of fried potatoes and sausage rolls that night. Both witches slept badly.

Next morning, Skwizit whispered, "I'm so upset I can't eat."

"Same here," said Skusting. "Fry me a slice of bread."

"You ate all the loaves yesterday," said Skwizit. "Skusting, everyone will be talking about us. Rosemary Crow will see to that. She'll be overjoyed to be proved right."

Skusting stood up. "I'm going to school before the kids arrive. I've written a sorry note."

"I'll come, too," said Skwizit, adding her own name to the note.

The witches put on green cloaks and hurried to the school. They stopped at the gate and stared, speechless.

It was worse than they'd imagined. The scrawls and scribbles didn't cover just the playground - they went up the walls, too. There was even a wavy blue line snaking over the gym block.

Suddenly they heard a knife-like voice.

Rosemary Crow! And the rest of the Parish Council was with her!

The witches sank down, making themselves as small as possible beneath their green cloaks.

They heard choking sounds, then the clear voice shrilled out. "Just as I thought!"

There was no mistaking her pleased tone.

The witches kept absolutely still but, seconds later, Rosemary Crow hissed in their ears, "Do you imagine I can't see you?"

"We're not us, we're bushes," said Skusting in what she hoped was a leafy sort of voice.

"Ridiculous.
Stand up at once."
Slowly, the
witches rose, heads
hanging in shame.

"Skusting!" It
was Joe, with four
other children.
He wiped his
glasses with a
finger and stared
through them, flabbergasted.

"Did you do
this?" he asked.

The witches'
heads drooped
lower.

The children
jumped on the
gate.

Rosemary
nodded. "You see?"

56

". . .that's mega, that's what that is!" said Joe.

Rosemary was confused. "Eh?"

The witches peeked at Joe. His eyes shone.

"Skusting! Skwizit!" he cried. "You did it!" He swung the gate open. "Let's try it out!"

"Mmmyeeowwwww!" A girl ran her toy aeroplane over the blue line on the wall.

Two boys played Dinosaurs-and-Dead-Men on the zig-zag lines.

Rosemary Crow clapped. "Stop, children! You can't play on a muddle."

Other children arrived.

"You won't be able to play properly," Rosemary shrieked. "You won't know what to do!"

More children poured through the gate to investigate their new playground.

Rosemary jumped up and down in fury.

Skusting grinned. "They don't! They'll use their imagi– imaginam– imagimin–"

Skwizit helped out. "They'll make up all the games they want."

Rosemary Crow seethed.

However, her face changed as, from behind the witches, a deep voice said, "What on earth. . . ?"

It was the head teacher.

"I've never seen anything like this in my life!" he said.

Rosemary Crow bent to hiss in Skusting's ear. "Now you're for it."

The head teacher goggled at the playground, his mouth open in astonishment. "This isn't what I expected at all. Who did it? I demand to know."

Skusting and Skwizit turned scarlet as Rosemary Crow pointed triumphantly. "They did!"

The head teacher gasped. "You - you two - are responsible for this - this. . . ?"

He waved a hand, unable to find the right word.

They nodded miserably.

61

A smirk spread over Rosemary Crow's smug face.

"Then I've only one thing to say," said the head teacher.

63

The little witches hugged each other in delight.

Skwizit strutted about proudly in front of the furious Rosemary Crow, but Skusting tugged her sleeve.

"Let's go home," she begged. "I'm starving."

Skwizit nodded. "We could both do with a little breakfast."

"Breakfast be blowed!" Skusting rubbed her tummy and grinned. "There's last night's supper to finish yet - then I'll have me brekky!"